Focus on Computer Graphics

Tutorials and Perspectives in Computer Graphics

Edited by W.T. Hewitt, R. Gnatz, and W. Hansmann

S. Coquillart W. Straßer P. Stucki (Eds.)

From Object Modelling to Advanced Visual Communication

With 128 Figures, 38 in Colour

Springer-Verlag
Berlin Heidelberg New York
London Paris Tokyo
Hong Kong Barcelona
Budapest

Focus on Computer Graphics

Edited by W. T. Hewitt, R. Gnatz, and W. Hansmann
for EUROGRAPHICS –
The European Association for Computer Graphics
P. O. Box 16, CH-1288 Aire-la-Ville, Switzerland

Volume Editors

Sabine Coquillart
Institut National de Recherche
en Informatique et en Automatique (INRIA)
Domaine de Voluceau, Rocquencourt
B. P. 105, F-78153 Le Chesnay Cedex, France

Wolfgang Straßer
Universität Tübingen
Wilhelm-Schickard-Institut für Informatik
Graphisch-Interaktive Systeme
Auf der Morgenstelle 10, C9, D-72076 Tübingen, Germany

Peter Stucki
Institut für Informatik der Universität Zürich
Winterthurerstr. 190, CH-8057 Zürich, Switzerland

ISBN-13: 978-3-642-78293-0 e-ISBN-13: 978-3-642-78291-6
DOI: 10.1007/978-3-642-78291-6

Library of Congress Cataloging-in-Publication Data
From object modelling to advanced visual communication/S. Coquillart, W. Strasser, P. Stucki, eds.
p. cm. — (Focus on computer graphics) Papers presented at the EUROGRAPHICS '91 in Vienna.
ISBN 3-540-56822-0 (Berlin: acid-free paper).
ISBN 0-387-56822-0 (New York: acid-free paper)
1. Computer graphics-Congresses. I. Coquillart, S. (Sabine), 1958- . II. Strasser, Wolfgang, 1941- . III. Stucki, P. (Peter) IV. EUROGRAPHICS '91 (1991: Vienna, Austria) V. Series.
T385.F74 1994 006.6 — dc20 93-49419 CIP

Softcover reprint of the hardcover 1st edition 1994

Cover: Konzept & Design Ilvesheim, FRG
Typesetting: Camera ready copy by authors/editors
45/3140 – 5 4 3 2 1 0 – Printed on acid-free paper

Preface

This book is a collection of the best papers originally presented as state-of-the-art reports or tutorials at the EUROGRAPHICS'91 conference in Vienna. A choice has been made giving priority to information of lasting value. Another goal was to cover all aspects of computer graphics - except hardware - as completely as possible from modelling to advanced visualization and communication. The editors consider that the ten contributions by internationally renowned experts fulfil this goal perfectly. Some important problem areas are treated from different viewpoints thus enhancing and deepening the reader's perspective.

Sabine Coquillart
Wolfgang Straßer
Peter Stucki

Table of Contents

Through the Cracks of the Solid Modeling Milestone

Jarek R. Rossignac

ABSTRACT
Solid modeling provides designers with tools for creating, archiving, and inspecting computerized models of mechanical parts and manufacturing processes. Recent advances have fostered the hope for a shortened design cycle and for the reliable automation of an extended domain of important applications. Nevertheless, solid modelers still suffer from a limited geometric coverage, from insufficient reliability and performance, and from inefficient design tools. The coverage pertains to the topologies, geometries, and structures that can be captured in the modeler's representations and to the operations available for creating or processing such representations. The efficiency of algorithms for constructing, merging, rendering, or interrogating such representations requires maintaining and exploiting complex auxiliary data structures. The reliability of a solid modeler is based on the correctness of its algorithms and on the accuracy with which properties of the represented solids may be computed. It is hindered by round-off errors and geometric approximations and is often jeopardized by inconsistent logical decisions derived from numeric calculations. The ergonomy, or ease of use, is proportional to the level of automation with which the modelers derive users' intent from simple and intuitive input. It may be further increased by raising the level of abstraction available for manipulating auxiliary views or aggregates of functionally related geometric elements, such as features. This report presents the key components of the solid modeling technology and discusses how they impact the overall coverage, efficiency, and ergonomy limitations. It also discusses the recent research advances aimed at improving the modelers topological coverage by extending the concepts of CSG and Boundary representations to their non-regularized (sometimes also called "non-manifold") counterparts.

1 Introduction

The term "Solid Modeling" refers to a rapidly growing body of techniques that deal with the representation, design, visualization, and analysis of three-dimensional computer-models of real objects.

Solid modeling emerged from early computerized 3D wireframe-based drafting systems and from surface modelers used for NC machining. A historical perspective may be found in [150], and descriptions of a few pioneering systems in [35, 36, 34, 134, 205, 78]. The techniques supporting these early systems were deeply rooted in the mathematics of projective geometry and in early manual drafting practices. They were sufficient for producing wireframe drawings, but inadequate for representing and modeling solids.

By incorporating concepts from a large variety of disciplines in both mathematics and computer sciences, pioneers of contemporary solid modeling technology have developed techniques for unambiguously representing formally defined entities called "solids". These representations are well suited for automating a variety of design tasks and thus for improving the design process and the resulting products. Early investments of the automotive and aeronautic industry in the solid modeling technology have started to pay off. Indeed, solid modelers are commonly used for inspecting large mechanical assemblies reducing the need for expensive clay mock-up models and leading to the early detection and correction of numerous design errors.

Solid modelers provide the designer with tools for rapidly exploring design alternative and for automatically analyzing design solutions in terms of physical properties and of manufacturing cost. Probably the most important function provided by solid modelers is the detection of interferences in mechanical assemblies. Since this task requires fairly intensive computations, a considerable number of algorithms have been developed to improve its performance for boundary models [33, 186, 136, 46, 27] and for CSG models [198, 45, 218, 157]. Other notable applications of solid modeling include the automatic computation of integral properties: [107, 108]; the planning of collision-free motions for robotics and assembly tasks: [56, 64, 44, 14, 170] and [43, 48, 114]; and the design and simulation of mechanisms: [197].

Solid modeling has also considerably facilitated the ongoing research on the automatic generation of finite element meshes: [16, 171, 173, 57]; on the allocation and analysis of dimension and tolerance information: [146, 149, 79, 17, 102]; and on the generation of manufacturing process plans: [206].

Although the usage of solid modelers is widespread throughout the manufacturing industry, the support that solid modelers provide is limited by deficiencies in their internal representations, by the lack of reliable techniques for performing the necessary calculations, by the poor performance and insufficient reliability of known algorithms, and by the inadequacy of the design tools they offer.

More than a decade ago, several research issues emerged as fundamental to solid modeling [151]. Unfortunately, one must admit that many of these issues still remain practically unsolved, at least, as far as users and developers of solid modelers are concerned. The main issues addressed in this report are briefly summarized below.

The geometric coverage of a solid modeler determines its suitability for a particular application. Voxel-based or polyhedral modelers, for example, may not be adequate for turbine blades design and analysis. Thus, developers are faced with difficult compromises between the generality and representational compactness of higher degree curved surfaces and the algorithmic simplicity of their lower degree approximations. Increasing the precision of polyhedral approximations to curved objects results in excessively large models and intractable numeric problems. Supporting higher degree surfaces requires the use of inefficient and even less reliable surface-intersection procedures.

The algorithmic reliability of a modeler is based on the correct implementation of well defined operations and on the inference of non-contradicting logical decisions from error-prone numerical calculations. The correct implementation of mathematically defined operations often requires an exhaustive treatment of all singular or degenerate cases, which considerably complicate the data structure and the algorithms. However, round-off errors in numerical calculations make the consistent detections of these special cases practically impossible. As a result, solid modeling algorithms often produce slightly inconsistent representations, such as non-coplanar vertices of a planar face, and sometimes even completely wrong answers.

Topological and structural limitations of a solid modeler are more subtle to assess. The solid modeling technology is based on a precise definition of solids leading to a complete and unambiguous representation that permits to distinguish between the interior, the boundary, and the exterior of the represented solid [144]. Although this definition played an essential role in the development of correct algorithms for Boolean operations on solids [152], it has confined solid modeling to a limited domain of applications. Indeed, most "classic" solid modelers did not support internal structures nor lower-dimensional entities. Although assemblies of solids, curves, and surfaces can be grouped (overlayed) in the same model and moved or displayed together as a single entity, Boolean and other operations on such groupings have not been implemented, nor even formally defined. This state of the art report discusses some of these "topological" restrictions and presents some attempts to overcome them in contemporary extensions of the domain of solid modelers to more general geometric objects that may have internal structures, cracks, or even "dangling" lower-dimensional entities. Specifically, GROGS (Generative Representations Of Geometric Structures), that extend CSG representations, and DROGS (Descriptive Representations Of Geometric Structures), that extend the traditional boundary representations used for solids, are presented.

Although interactive shaded graphics and flashy, menu-driven graphic user interfaces have made solid modeling more attractive to the novice user–and even to the experienced designer–the available design tools remain limited. Shapes are still designed in terms of extrusions and Boolean operations, although sometimes disguised as "functional features". A whole spectrum of high-level operations for manipulating and creating complex models are needed.

The reminder of this State of The Art Report is organized as follows. Section 2 discusses issues related to the geometric coverage and introduces the primitive geometric entities commonly used in solid modeling. It also discusses what type of functions must be available for processing these entities by higher-level algorithms. Section 3 provides an original categorization of the different ways in which these primitive entities may be combined (or composed) to produce representations of more complex geometric objects, such as faces, solids or more general geometric structures.

Section 4 proposes a topological characterization of the pointsets and geometric structures representable in a given modeler. It provides intuitive definitions of terms used to describe the topological coverage of a modeler. (In fact, some of these terms are used in previous sections, but were grouped here for consistency. We hope that the reader will not mind these implicit forward references.) Section 5 compares several fundamental representation techniques. Algorithms that create and process these representations are reviewed in Section 6. Some techniques for improving their performance and reliability are reviewed in Section 7. Finally, Section 8 overviews research aimed at improving the design process.

Despites its length, this report is not an attempt at providing a complete picture of the state-of-the-art in solid modeling. It should rather be viewed as a superficial introduction to some of the issues that must be addressed when developing a solid modeler or when simply evaluating one. Although some apparently original views or concepts are included, they are loosely formulated and will require further discussions. The numerous references randomly scattered throughout the paper are intended to provide a starting point to non-practitioners eager to understand the details regarding a particular issues and willing to conduct their own bibliographic search. The references were selected among the ones available to the author and their choice does not reflect any selection or opinion as to the best or earliest publications on a particular subject.

2 Geometric Coverage

The geometric coverage of a solid modeler is characterized by the nature of the geometric entities (such as points, curves, surfaces) it supports and by the ways in which these entities may be created, combined, and manipulated. In this section, we attempt to summarize the difficulties that must be overcome in order to enlarge this coverage.

It would be inconceivable to provide a data structure and the associated procedures for each geometric entity that could be represented in a modeler, especially when procedures for combining entities of all supported types are needed. Therefore, only a small number of classes, or types, of parameterized primitive geometric entities are typically supported. Adding a new type implies not only the design of a representation format, but also the provision for new algorithms for operating on entities of the new type. A reasonable geometric coverage for solid modelers is typically achieved by supporting several techniques for assembling or combining instances of primitives that belong to a restricted set of types. For example, boundary representations are constructed by "sewing" faces along their common edges. One only needs a representation for an arbitrary face and the support of objects constructed by gluing faces together. Faces of polyhedral models may be represented through lists of vertices.

Questions such as "What is a primitive geometric entity and what is a derived structure?" are of a rather philosophical nature. For example, vertices may be considered as grouping of coordinates, which in turn are groupings of bits. To each derived entity is associated an implied semantics upon which the algorithms that process the derived entity are based. By "primitive geometric entity" we mean data-structures, which, in the programmer's mind, are associated with mathematically well defined geometric objects, such as points, curves, surfaces, or simple volumes, which are not expressed in terms of other primitives using some general composition scheme. It is important to separate such entities from more complex structures, such as faces or solids, in order to identify the geometric support they imply and to provide a clean interface between geometry and derived structures.

The same geometric support could be used in different modelers to form and process different geometric structures. Furthermore, a separation of the geometric utilities from the rest of the modeling algorithms and data structures would enable the development of modeling techniques that are independent of the geometric coverage and that could be combined with different geometric libraries.

This section overviews the most common primitive geometric entities used for solid modeling and the usual operations performed on them. Most commercially available solid modelers provide a limited support for a useful set of these entities and associated operations.

2.1 Primitive geometric entities

Primitive geometric entities used in solid modeling are points, curve segments, surfaces, faces, and volumes. We discuss in this sections various representation techniques and their limitations.

Points

Points may be represented explicitly by their coordinates in some coordinate system or *indirectly* as intersections of higher-dimensional entities (such as three surfaces used to construct an intersection point). The latter solution preserves logical information about the origin of the point, which may be later used to avoid errors or unnecessary numeric calculations. In fact, in many modelers, several representations are available for the points that define the locations of the vertices of solids. Due to numerical inaccuracies, these different representations are often inconsistent. For example, a point computed as the intersection of three planes may be represented by the references to these planes and also by its (x, y, z) coordinates computed during the intersection calculation. Unfortunately, the point (x, y, z) often does not lie on any of the three planes! This discrepancy may considerably complicate algorithms that process both representations. It is hence desirable to associate with the evaluated coordinates (x, y, z) of a point a measure of the maximum error that may have been committed in computing the coordinates. For example, one could provide the radius of a sphere centered around (x, y, z) that is guaranteed to contain the true intersection. Unfortunately, the positions of the planes from which the point was computed may not be known exactly, since they may have been derived from other planes by linear transformations. The error bound, or sphere radius, must take into account all these uncertainties. Straightforward error propagation techniques [125] yield results that are too pessimistic for practical use. More precise techniques are needed.

The indirect representation (i.e. as the intersection of higher-dimensional entities) is simple for vertices that are computed as intersections of three planes in general position, i.e. three planes that intersect in a single point. Indirect representation for vertices as intersections of three curved surfaces or of a curve and a surface may be ambiguous, since there usually is more that one intersection point between these entities. Bounds (in 3D or in some parametric space) that separate the point from other intersections must also be computed and stored. Computing valid bounds that guarantee separability is difficult and may require symbolic manipulation and expensive iterative procedures.

Another important representation of points, often called "point-in-curve", is provided by a vector valued function C and a parameter "t". In solid modeling, the vector valued function often corresponds to a curve and the point $C(t)$ is a point on that curve. Values for the parameter "t" are often computed during curve/surface intersection calculations and are approximate. To permit the detection of ambiguities that may arise from numerical approximations, parameters of points on curves should in fact be replaced by parameter intervals that are guaranteed to contain the exact parameter for the point. Similarly, so called, "surface-points" are defined using pairs of parameter values in the parametric representation of a surface (or patch)[1]. Such a parametric representation is often used for representing the vertices of faces in the parametric space of the underlying surface and for representing points of intersection between a curve and the surface.

In order to preserve the integrity of a geometric representation when transferring it from one model to another or from a modeler to a database, it is important to support these multiple representations and the associated bounds and error measures. Thus they should be included in all future data exchange standards. Of course, one also needs to define operations on such complex representations. For example, when are two points equal? This question is trivially answered if points are represented by their coordinates. Michael O'Connor and the author have spent long rainy days at IBM Research developing complex

[1] See the following sub-sections.

algorithms to answer this question without possible error when points are represented as the only intersection of several surfaces within some bounding volume or the only intersection of a curve and a surface within an interval of the curve parameterization.

Curves

The geometry of a line, or a line segment, may be *derived* from two points or from a point and a vector and can thus be represented by these entities. Such a representation scheme was used in early polyhedral modelers, whose geometric coverage was limited to points and entities that may be recursively derived from them using a delimitation approach discussed in the next section. Representation based on points may be extended to simple conics (for example a circular arc may be represented by three points) and even to non-planar curves.

Curves and curve segments may be represented in several ways. For predefined types, they may be simply represented intrinsically by their type, parameters, and location in space. For example, a circular arc may be represented by its radius, the angle it spans, and a rigid body transformation that brings it to its final position from a default predefined location. Conic sections are usually represented in this manner, because in "natural position" they may be completely defined by a type and a small number of parameters. More complex planar curves can in principle be represented by the coefficients of an implicit equation, $f(x, y) = 0$, in the coordinate system of the plane [208], but are rarely represented that way in solid modeling because subsets of implicitly defined curves must be represented indirectly by their bounding vertices or by volumes that delimit the extent of the curve segment.

A popular representation for a curve segment is a vector-valued function and a parameter interval. Polynomial (or rational polynomial) functions have often been used. Clever choices of the polynomial bases express the shape of the curve in terms of control points. Pieces of such curves may be combined in a smooth manner to form piecewise-polynomial curves. The most popular representations are cubic B-spline curves, Bézier curves, and Cardinal-splines. Trigonometric parametric representations have been used successfully [42] for representing "exactly" (i.e. within the precision provided by floating point operations) the intersections of simple quadric surfaces. These parametric representations offer, over the implicit representations, facilities for marching along the curve. These facilities are important for graphics and for some numerical intersection methods. They also permit the reduction of curve/surface intersection calculations to finding the zeros of a function. A subset of a parametric curve may be conveniently represented by a parameter interval.

Curve segments are often assumed connected and for many algorithms should be free of cusps and self-intersections. Computing such cusps and self-intersections is difficult, especially when these computations are performed in floating point.

Since curves are often computed by intersecting surfaces, they also have an implicit representation in terms of the surfaces they lie on. However, implicit representations fail to distinguish between the various connected components of the curve and do not identify its singularities. For example, the intersection curve between two cylindrical surfaces in tangential contact may be formed of two branches that share a common point. References to the two surfaces are insufficient for distinguishing between the two branches. Nevertheless, as it is the case for points, indirect representations for curves complement, in important ways, other more explicit representations.

A popular representation for curves that are intersections of surfaces is based on a parametric representation of the surfaces. If a surface may be defined as a bi-parametric, vector-valued mapping, $S(u,v)$, then a curve on the surface may be represented as a two-dimensional curve in the u-v parameter space. This representation may be implicit or parametric. For example, a parametric curve defined by $C_x = X(t), C_y = Y(t)$ in the parameter space of the surface S corresponds to the 3D curve $S(X(t),Y(t))$. The advantage of this representation over 3D parametric curves is not only the lower dimensionality, but also the fact that the curve is guaranteed to lie on the surface. This fact becomes important when parametric curves are used to approximate intersections of surfaces.

In general, intersections of curved surfaces do not have a simple parametric representation, and must thus be approximated. Often, parametric curves are used for such approximations. A 3D approximation of the intersection of two surfaces generally does not lie on any of the two surfaces. An approximation in the parametric space of one of the surfaces does at least lie on that surface. Thus, intersection curves are sometimes represented in three ways: as a 3D parametric curve and as two curves in the parametric space of the intersecting surfaces. Discrepancies between these representations yield an ambiguous representation of the faces, and thus of the solid and may lead to algorithmic problems.

Surfaces

Surfaces are sometimes represented implicitly as real algebraic varieties, in which case they are composed of points whose coordinates satisfy a particular polynomial equation. For example, $x^2 + y^2 = 1$ defines a cylinder of radius 1 centered along the z-axis. Implicit equations are useful for testing point-in-surface inclusions and for computing line/surface intersections. However, since such equations fail to distinguish the connected components or the singularities of the pointsets they represent, implicit equations are often restricted to low degree polynomials and are used in conjunction with other representation schemes.

Surfaces may also, as curves do, be represented explicitly by a type and the associated parameters. For example, the infinite cylindrical surface centered around the z-axis may be completely represented by its radius. However, in order to reduce the number of surface-types supported by a modeler, explicit representations are limited to a small number of surfaces, such as the natural quadrics (plane, cylinder, cone, and sphere).

Despite their limited geometric coverage, the natural quadric surfaces have been popular because, among many other useful properties, they have (1) a simple parametric form, (2) a low degree implicit equation, and (3) an explicit representation characterized by a single parameter (when the surface is in its default position and orientation). Furthermore, explicit forms for the intersection curves between pairs of such surfaces have been developed and can be efficiently computed.

Faces and patches

The term "face" is commonly used to refer to a connected subset of a single surface. Simple faces, such as a planar rectangle or disc or half of a spherical surface, may be represented explicitly by their type and dimensions. Often, these implicit faces also correspond to the image of a rectangle, $[u_0, u_1] * [v_0, v_1]$, by a vector-valued bi-parametric function. In such cases, the term "patch" is used often instead of "face". In practice, the use of such explicit models is limited to mapping that produce subsets of natural quadrics or of the torus and are bounded by straight line-segments or circular arcs.

Since the special cases of surfaces listed above may not provide a sufficiently general geometric domain for some applications, bi-variate vector-valued functions that map a rectangle in parametric space into a surface patch in three dimensions have been used.

Piecewise bi-cubic (rational) polynomial mappings formulated as rational B-splines or Bézier surfaces are the most popular techniques for representing subsets of curved surfaces [28] and support exact (within the floating point approximation) representations of quadrics. Parametric formulations are important for deriving surface tesselations, i.e. for efficiently producing grids of points and associated normals on the surface. Many attempts were made to incorporate these surfaces in solid modeling: [101, 91, 193, 154, 50, 54, 51]. The major impediment to the advent of these surfaces is the lack of reliable and efficient algorithms for computing their intersections.

Volumes

The simplest volumes primitives are 3D regions defined as all the points that satisfy a single inequality: $H(x, y, z) \leq 0$. Such volumes are called half-spaces. Care must be taken to ensure that the inequality does not define lower-dimensional "dangling" singularities. Most popular half-spaces are those bounded by natural quadric surfaces. For example, $x^2 + y^2 - R^2 < 0$ defines a cylinder around the z-axis with radius R. They form the primitive three-dimensional entities used in Constructive Solid Geometry.

Volume primitives may also be defined explicitly by a type and a few parameters. For example, standard shapes, such as blocks, truncated cylinders, truncated cones, and spheres in default positions may be represented by their dimensions. They must be associated with procedures for testing point/primitive inclusion and for producing their bounding faces, so as to support the fundamental solid modeling algorithms. Surfaces are used for graphics and for partitioning pointsets (for example curves) into subsets that lie in, on, or out of the volume. Point/primitive inclusion tests may be used for classifying the subsets that result from the partitioning.

Alternatively, a large class of volumes may be defined by trivariate vector-valued rational polynomial functions of low degree that map the unit cube onto a subset of $\mathbb{R}^3$. The coefficient of these functions may be automatically computed from the coordinates of a three-dimensional array of control points. Although, such parametric mappings may be used to exactly represent the standard solid primitives mentioned above, they require a considerably more expensive processing. On the other hand, they are well suited for the interactive design of curved shapes that approximate real objects. The term "approximating" is used here to emphasize the difficulty of producing an exact trivariate representation of an given shape. Furthermore, trivariate mappings may "self-intersect" and produce inversions of space. For example, a mapping $V(u, v, w)$ that maps the unit cube into a volume of $\mathbb{R}^3$, may map several (u, v, w) points into the same space point, i.e. $V(u_1, v_1, w_1) = V(u_2, v_2, w_2)$. Such self-intersections are very difficult to detect (visually or automatically) and may lead to evaluation errors. (For example, when computing the mass or other integral properties of the volume, care must be taken to avoid counting twice the same portion of space.)

2.2 Operations on primitive entities

In order to support the above primitive geometric entities in a solid modeling environment, a set of functions must be provided.

Point Membership Classification

To each primitive geometric entities must correspond a procedure for testing point inclusion. Such a procedure is simple for entities that have a semi-algebraic expression, i.e.

that are intersections (or even complex Boolean combinations) of algebraic equalities and inequalities. For example, to test if a point (x, y, z) lies inside a truncated cylinder of radius R around the z-axis clipped by the planes $z = 0$ and $z = H$, it suffices to verify if the three inequalities $x^2 + y^2 \leq R^2$, $z \geq 0$, and $z \leq H$ are satisfied.

When testing points against volumes, it may be necessary to distinguish between points in the interior of the volume and points on the boundary. Procedures for point-primitive classification may be written independently for each primitive entity. Sometimes, these procedures take advantage of a particular property of the primitive volume. For instance, to test if the point lies on the infinite cylindrical surface, it suffices to verify that $x^2+y^2 = R^2$. To test if the point lies on the cylindrical boundary of the truncated cylinder primitive, one can test $x^2+y^2 = R^2$ $z \geq 0$, and $z \leq H$, thus, excluding the edges where the cylindrical surface touches the top and the bottom disks. In the presence of numerical errors, these equality tests must be replaced with toleranced tests, for example: instead of $x^2+y^2 = R^2$, one would test $|x^2 + y^2 - R^2| < \epsilon$, where ϵ is a small tolerance value.

For some parameter domains, portions of the volume primitive may degenerate into lower-dimensional elements, which cannot be considered as part of the volume's boundary if the volume is regularized. These special cases further complicate the tests. For example, if R or H are zero, the above cylinder degenerates into a line or a disk.

Testing the inclusion of a point in a volume represented in trivariate parametric form requires a numerical inversion procedure (used for example in [55]). If the volume is a mapping V from the $[0,1] \times [0,1] \times [0,1]$ unit cube in the (u, v, w) parametric space into $\mathbb{R}^3$, then for a given point (x, y, z), one needs to establish if a triplet (u, v, w) exists with $0 \leq u \leq 1$, $0 \leq v \leq 1$, and $0 \leq w \leq 1$, such that $(x, y, z) = V(u, v, w)$. Typically, such queries are performed by recursively subdividing the $[0,1] \times [0,1] \times [0,1]$ cube using convex hull properties to establish whether the point lies in a particular portion of the cube or not, but other (less robust) techniques, based on sampling and numerical convergence are also used in practice.

Testing a point for inclusion in a parametric curve segment may require a similar inversion procedure to compute the parameter of the point and then compare it with the parameter interval that defines the segment. For implicit curves segments, it must be first established whether the point lies on the entire curve or not. If the curve is the intersection of two simple surfaces, such as cones or cylinders, and if the curve parameterization is inherited from a natural parameterization of one of the surfaces (as explained below), point-in-curve inclusion tests and the inversion procedure may be carried out using the surfaces directly. For example, if a curve C on a cylinder is parameterized using the angle of the cylindrical coordinates along the cylinder's axis, the parameters of a 3D point on C may be found from their cylindrical coordinates.

Curve tracing

Curve sampling produces a sequence of points spaced along a connected curve segment in some prescribed manner. These points are often used to derive geometric approximations of the curve segment. For example, in graphics, consecutive points are joined by straight line segments. Curve sampling is relatively simple when a parametric form of the curve is available. Derivatives of the parametric functions may then be used to estimate the parameter increment corresponding to optimal stepping.

Curve sampling is also important for computing parametric approximations to intersection curves [203, 15]. For example, given two surfaces and a common intersection point P, an intersection curve may be traced from P as follows. First, compute the normals at P to both surfaces. If both normals are defined and non-collinear, their cross-product defines a tangent of the intersection curve at P. (The tangent computed using the normal in the same order is consistently oriented along connected curve segments free of the curve's cusps and self-intersection[2].) Moving away from P in the direction of the tangents by a sufficiently small amount produces another point Q that lies close to both surfaces. Starting from Q, iterative projection methods may then be used to find a new position for point P lying on both surfaces. Curve segments are often traced in this manner.

Two difficulties are encountered during such a marching process. First, the displacement of P along the tangent must be small enough so as to ensure that the next position of P stays on the segment being traced and does not jump to a portion of that same segment or of another segment that happens to pass in the vicinity of P. Second, in the vicinity of tangential contacts between both surfaces, the two normals become collinear and the above method for computing the tangent may not be used. To overcome these difficulties, the maximal curvature of the intersection curve may have to be estimated from the surface data.

Surface sampling

Surface sampling is a requirement imposed on surface and volume primitives. Two sampling techniques are important for graphics: tesselation and ray-casting.

A portion of a surface or of a patch may be approximated to an arbitrary precision by a triangulation or tesselation [153]. The tesselation is defined by a grid of points on the face and sometimes by normals associated with these points. Note that normals may not be uniquely defined when the tesselation points fall on singularities. Tesselation is often used for graphics or as an alternate approximate representation for further processing.

It is often difficult to generate minimal tesselations that guarantee a good approximation. Therefore, it may be necessary to obtain a measure of the maximum deviation between the approximating elements and the approximated surface [143]. Such measures may be very expensive to estimate accurately, leading to grossly sub-optimal tesselations.

When parametric representations of the surfaces are available, adaptive tesselation may be achieved by subdivisions in the parametric space. On the other hand, when the surfaces are given in implicit form, tesselation is more difficult to achieve, and is often addressed by ray-casting.

Ray-casting has been extensively used for displaying solids and surfaces [92]. Typically an array of (evenly spaced) rays are cast from the viewpoint through pixels on a model of the screen. The first intersection of a ray with a primitive must be reported. The normal to the intersected surface may be important for graphics, and thus may also be required.

Ray-casting on volumes bounded by implicit surfaces may be performed by first finding the intersections of the ray with the bounding surfaces, and then by using the point-inclusion test against the volume.

Ray-casting on trivariate parametric models requires computing the intersections between a line and the bi-parametric faces of the volume, which in general is an expensive procedure. Furthermore, care must be taken to ensure that the volume is confined to the area bounded by the faces, which is not always the case if the internal control points lie outside. Convex-hull properties may be used to guide the intersection procedure in these cases.

[2]The tangent changes directions only at singular points where the normals are collinear.

Surfaces may also be sampled by one or two families of curves. Such curves may correspond to constant values of one of the parameters of the surface, to the surface intersection with a family of evenly offset planes, or to plots that follow lines prescribed by some property of the surface's geometry.

Intersections of surfaces

The most delicate utility in solid modeling is the calculation of the intersection between primitive elements. By "calculation" I mean the derivation of a more explicit representation of the intersection. Methods for computing the curves of intersection between pairs of surfaces largely depend on the nature of the surfaces. A short survey of the various approaches may be found in [29].

Intersections between surfaces that are either planar or spherical are limited to circles and lines and may be directly obtained from the geometric parameters describing the positions (and orientations) of the surfaces.

Closed form solutions exist also for the intersections of pairs of natural quadric surfaces which, besides the sphere and the plane, include the cylinder and the cone. The latter two may be formulated as parametric families of straight lines. Since the intersection of each line with a quadric may be computed in closed form using a square root, the parameterization of the family of lines provides a parameterization of the intersection curve [76]. Special cases, when the intersection curve degenerates, must often be identified a priori [122, 132, 140].

The above domain of natural quadrics represents the state of the art for closed form solutions to surface/surface intersections. The availability of closed-form solutions is essential for achieving performance and reliability.

Several extensions beyond the domain of natural quadrics have been developed and are listed below:

General quadrics

General quadrics may in principle be integrated in solid modelers based on natural quadrics using a closed form parametric solution for the intersection curves of arbitrary quadric surfaces, as developed in [109]. The resulting curve is parameterized using a parameterization of one of the surfaces. This parameterization is derived from a ruled quadric surface in a linear combination of that surface with another quadric.

Tori

Tori are quartic surfaces, nevertheless, the intersection curves of a torus with another torus or with a natural quadric surface may be expressed in parametric closed form [155] in terms of roots of fourth degree polynomials in one variable. Consequently, intersection curves of tori are often approximated. An approximation in terms of piecewise circular curves instead of cubic parametric splines considerably reduces the cost of further processing [164].

Canal surfaces

Canal surfaces are envelopes of families of spheres that move along a curve. They have been extensively studied by Monge in the 19th century. When the radius of the spheres is constant and their trajectory is the intersection of offset surfaces, canal surfaces correspond to constant radius blending surfaces. The author has proposed a scheme for approximating them with smoothly connected sections of tori [155]. Other blending surfaces have also been proposed (see [218]), but their full support in solid modeling has not been provided.

General implicit surfaces

Implicit surfaces yield, under certain conditions [65], exact parametric forms for their intersection curves. In the general case however, these intersections must be approximated.

Parametric surfaces

Parametric surfaces are intersected using numerical methods [123, 18] that involve variations of the curve tracing procedure outlined above. Typically a loop detection phase [176, 60] is necessary to ensure that at least one starting point on all connected intersection loops is found. A procedure that exploits the characteristics of the field defined by the distance to one of the surfaces as measured from points on the other surface has been suggested for guiding such loop detection algorithms [53]. The results are approximated by smooth curves, typically in the parametric space of both surfaces. These approximations in general do not agree and produce gaps or over-shootings when used to trim the surfaces.

Combinations of parametric and implicit surfaces

Two surfaces, one of which is in implicit form and the other one in parametric form may be intersected through implicitization [175]. Robust methods have been developed for intersecting algebraic surfaces with polynomial patches [103].

Curve/surface intersections

Algorithms that compute the boundaries of solids obtain through Boolean operations require the computation of vertices, i.e. of the intersections of a curve with another surface.

Given an implicit representation of a surface $S(x, y, z) = 0$ and a parametric representation of a curve $(C_x = X(t), C_y = Y(t), C_z = Z(t))$, the intersection points may be computed numerically from the values of t for which the function $S(X(t), Y(t), Z(t))$ is zero.

When C is a closed form representation of a curve of intersection of natural quadrics and when S is a quadric, the root t-values may be computed by evaluating the roots of a polynomial.

Intersections between a parametric surface and a parametric curve are computed through iterative methods and hence imply a considerable loss of performance and reliability. The intersection may also be performed in two dimensions as the intersection of two intersection curves in the parametric space of one of the surfaces. It may also be important to detect singularities, such as cusps, and self-intersections that could be missed by numerical iterative methods. This problem typically requires a considerably more complicated procedure.

Self-intersections of surfaces

Self-intersections of algebraic surfaces are singularities where the normal to the surface is not defined. Therefore they must be detected in a manner similar to the detection of cusps. The problem of computing self-intersections may be formulated in terms of a system of two equations and amounts to finding the intersections of two algebraic surfaces.

The situation is even more complicated when dealing with parametric surfaces. Self-intersections may occur within a single surface patch. Most commercial systems rely on the user to ensure that designed patches are free from self-intersections. Even if such practices are acceptable during interactive design, they lead to considerable problems for automatically generated surfaces, such as fillets and blends. In addition to the self intersecting problem in 3D, the parameterization of a surface may fold onto itself, even when the geometric set of points does not exhibit a self-intersection. For example, when all the control points of a Bézier surface are coplanar, the patch is a portion of a plane, say the $z = 0$ plane. The parameterization folds on itself when the same point $(x, y, 0)$ is the image of two different points in the parametric space. The borders of such folds are loci of points where tangents to isoparametric curves vanish. These borders correspond to projections of silhouette edges of non-planar surfaces.

Ordering

Algorithms that evaluate the boundaries of solids constructed through Boolean operations often rely on geometric utilities that order geometric entities along or around other geometric entities.

Vertices must often be ordered along edges so as to establish connected edge-segments that are free of intersections with the faces under consideration. If the edge is parameterized, and if the parameters corresponding to each vertex are known, the ordering operation amounts to ordering the parameter values. Unfortunately, curve parameterization considerably complicates the code for processing curves. For instance, closed curves must be artificially "opened" by introducing a vertex where the parameterization starts and ends and connected curve segments containing that point may have to be split. Furthermore, when two curves, each containing a number of vertices, are identified as coincident, it may be necessary to express the vertices of both curves in the same parameterization scheme. Thus, it may be preferable, when possible, not to use any curve parameterization for representing and storing vertices.

Suppose that each curve is decomposed into connected components that are free of self-intersections and consistently oriented. Then relative ordering is unambiguously defined and parameterization is unnecessary. The term "relative" ordering must be clarified: two points may be ordered on an oriented open curve, but not on a closed curve. On the other hand, the three points A, B, and C, on a closed curve are either encountered in this order while traveling along the curve in the direction of its orientation or along the opposite direction. Therefore, ordering questions are best phrased in terms of interval separation. The geometric routines provided for each type of curve should be able to determine whether a point on that curve splits a given curve segment or not.

A curve segment on an open curve without singularities is defined by a single point and by a Boolean flag specifying whether the segment behind that point or the segment in front of that point are implied. The terms, "behind" and "in front" are defined by the curve orientation. We refer to this flag as the *neighborhood* of the point with respect to the curve segment. If the curve is bounded, one could use one of its end-points instead of the neighborhood flag.

A curve segment on a closed curve is defined by an ordered pair of points (A,C) on that curve. The segment contains all points B that are encountered in the order A-B-C while traveling along the curve in the direction of its parameterization.

For simple curves, geometric procedures often exist for answering the above queries without using any parameterization. For example, using the sign of a simple expression, one may easily establish whether or not three points on a circle occur in clockwise order, with respect to a chosen orientation of the plane that contain the circle.

For closed curve segments that have V as their only end-point, the two different branches must be distinguished. The orientation, or neighborhood-flag may be used.

A different type of ordering is used for computing vertex-neighborhoods and edge-neighborhoods [152] from local information of the entities that intersect at that vertex of edge. Given a surface S and a vertex V on that surface and a set of curve segments C_i lying on S and having V as only one of their end-vertices, the curve segments may be ordered "around" V. A positive ordering direction may be defined as a clockwise traversal around a selected normal direction to S at V. In general, the ordering may be established by considering the directions of the tangents to C_i at V oriented towards the interior of the curve segments. However, it is possible that several curve segment have the same tangent direction. The curvature of the C_i at V, and even higher derivatives may be necessary to establish the ordering. For example, two *different* conic sections, such as a circle and an ellipse, may be tangent at a point V and may have identical curvatures at V and even identical curvature variation. Closed-form solutions for ordering curves in these singular situation have been developed for conic sections and are used in PADL-2. The ordering of more complex curves must be derived from other geometric calculations.

When several surfaces S_i pass through the same curve C, it may be necessary to establish their ordering "around" C. This can be done by first splitting C at points where the ordering changes (for example where surfaces become tangent), and then (1) by picking a point in each one of the curve segments, (2) by generating the plane through that point orthogonally to the curve tangent at that point, (3) by computing the intersections of all the surfaces S_i with that plane, and (4) by ordering the intersections curves as discussed above. This approach was used in the PADL-2 solid modeller to deal with curve-neighborhoods for intersections of natural quadrics.

This very expensive procedure may require computing higher derivatives of arbitrarily complicated intersection curves. In the absence of closed form representations for these curves, such computation may be impossible to perform with sufficient accuracy to be of use for solid modeling. Global methods may be needed which infer local neighborhood around points of edges from classification of higher-dimensional elements, such as edges and faces with respect to faces and volumes. For example, to order four edges, E_1, E_2, E_3, and E_4, that have a point V as common endpoint (see Figure 1), one can construct, using additional edges, two loops, say $(E_1, E'_i, ..., E'_j, E_2)$ and $(E_3, E'_m, ..., E'_n, E_4)$, then compute all the intersection points between these loops, and finally test each intersection-free connected loop segment adjacent to V of each loop for inclusion against the other loop. From these results, the ordering of the edges around V may be inferred logically. Note that in algorithms for solid modeling the loops are often available and their intersections must be computed anyway.

Testing a loop segment for inclusion against another loop may be done by generating a point inside the loop segment and classifying it against the other loop. The classification process itself is complex and may require ordering information of edge segments around vertices on a curved surface, or in the parametric space of that surface. For example, consider the problem of testing a point V for inclusion in a spherical face F defined by a closed curve C on the sphere. Suppose for simplicity that V is not on C. The sphere's outward pointing normal orientation and the curve's orientation define consistently the left and right side of the curve on the sphere, and thus may be used to distinguish F from its complement on the sphere. The standard technique for classifying V against F is to

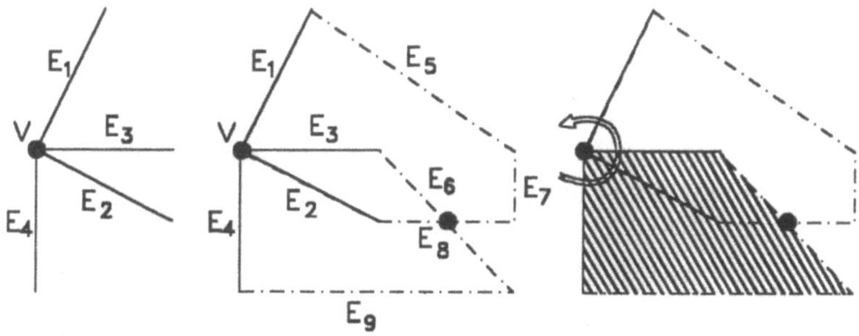

Figure 1. **Global information for local ordering:** Two loops of edges that intersect at a vertex V are used to establish the local ordering of four edges around V.

throw a ray L (curve segment on the sphere or line segment in the parametric space of the sphere) from V to a point Q on C. Then compute all the intersections of L and C and extract the first intersection point P encountered while moving on L away from V towards Q. The interior of the segment (V,P) of L is free of intersections with C and is thus either entirely inside F or outside of it. Deciding which of these two is the case would provide the classification for V. This decision must be performed using local information at P and involves ordering three edge segments around P. However, one can argue that it is in practice always possible to select points P where this ordering may be established reliably by considering only the tangents at P to the three curve segments.

Volume intersections

Intersections of primitive volumes will be addressed later in this report as part of the methods for performing Boolean operations. However, it may be noted that if two primitive volumes A and B correspond to intersections of half-spaces, and if a similar representation is acceptable for the result of their intersection, it suffices to include the half-spaces of both primitives. Note that it may be important to remove redundant half-spaces in order to improve the performance of algorithms that will further process the resulting entity. On the other hand, more explicit representations of the result may be required in order to evaluate the topological properties of the result.

2.3 Examples of geometric domains

Polyhedra

Polyhedra have clearly been the most popular geometric domain for solid modeling because of the simplicity of the surface/surface intersection calculations. The planarity restriction imposed on the surfaces, implies that curves are line segments, and hence, curve/surface intersections may also be easily computed.

It should be pointed out that most common data-structures for representing planes through a few floating point coefficients are inadequate for representing all possible planes. (For example, a plane with equation $z = z_0 + e/2$ may not be represented through vertex coordinates if "e" is the maximum resolution of the floating point representation of the vertex coordinates.) A similar problem occurs for edges and vertices [187]. Consequently, an arbitrary polyhedron may not be representable in the chosen format and will usually be approximated. The approximation may itself be invalid because points and lines, as represented in floating point format, may not lie on the surfaces they originally came from.

Unfortunately, good polyhedral approximations of curved objects often imply models with a prohibitive number of small facets, which not only reduces performance, but also creates considerable numerical problems. Consequently, curved surfaces are needed in order to support approximations of general shapes at a lesser expense.

Natural quadrics

The "natural" quadrics (i.e. planes, spheres, cylinders, and cones) provide a powerful geometric domain. As pointed out earlier, their intersections may be efficiently and accurately computed using closed from solutions for parameterizing intersection-curves.

Nevertheless, the support of these curves and of the intersection of each type of curves with each type of surfaces requires a formidable amount of code that can be avoided if the edges are restricted to be line segments or circular arcs. Such a domain suffices for modeling orthogonal extrusions and rotational sweeps of 2D contours bounded by lines segments. However, it does not support results of Boolean combinations of such solids.

Natural quadrics and tori

Rotational extrusions of 2D areas bounded by circles may generate spherical and toroidal surfaces. Tori are needed in solid modeling for constructing, among many other things, elbows in pipes and constant radius fillets and blends in pockets.

Adding the torus surface in solid modelers that already support natural quadrics requires not only providing routines for computing the intersection of a torus with another torus and with each one of the four types of natural quadric surfaces, but also providing a representation for each type of the intersection curves and routines for intersecting these curves with all the five types of surfaces. To avoid this explosion of cases, the author has used [155] smooth piecewise-circular approximations to all curves (for simplicity a line segment is considered as a special case of a curve segment). Only five curve/surface intersection routines are necessary: circle/plane, circle/cylinder, circle/sphere, circle/cone, and circle/torus. All five have been implemented in closed form [164] using a geometric approach to reduce them to roots of second or fourth degree polynomial equations. However, the vertices computed using these approximations may not exactly lie on the surfaces they logically belong to.

Parametric surfaces

By considering a parametric formulations as the only type of surfaces and the only type of curves, one can considerably reduce the number of special cases that must be implemented. Since bi-quadratic rational B-spline surfaces may be used to model exactly the popular natural quadrics and to reasonably approximate most shapes, they are good candidates for solid modeling. In fact, if intersection (and ordering) geometric queries are formulated in terms of surface and curve parameterization, curves and surfaces of different types may be combined in the same modeller, as long as they provide the same interface. That is, as long as the same basic operations are supported consistently for all the instances of these different types.

This generality and flexibility comes at a high price in terms of speed and reliability.

Performance may be addressed by relaxing the precision requirements or by detecting simple situations and treating them directly. For example, it would be very inefficient to compute the intersection of two planes by treating them as parametric surfaces. Such simple situations may be detected and treated as special cases. Similar situations involving spheres and planes and even all natural quadrics may also benefit from specialized treatments. The inclusion of all these special cases in addition to the code for processing arbitrary parametric forms may increase the code size beyond the limit of what can be maintained. The rapidly growing speed of personal workstations could alleviate soon the performance problem and make the special case treatment unnecessary. On the other hand, the applications of solid modeling have so far been limited to models with a few hundreds or thousands of primitives, because no user was willing to wait hours for a result that might never come. As the reliability and performance of solid modelers increase, so will the size of the problems.

The reliability problem can be diminished by performing calculations with more precision and by generating more precise approximations, but this increased accuracy considerably hinders performance and, by itself, will never guarantee correctness of the result. The solution may require a new approach to solid modeling, where no logical decision is made using unreliable geometric information.

2.4 State of the art summary on the geometric coverage

Representations of solid models are constructed from simple geometric primitives such as points, curves, and surfaces. Real curved objects must be approximated using the geometric primitives available in a solid modeller. Operations on linear geometries are simple to support, but good linear approximations of curved objects require prohibitive numbers of primitive elements. Domains based on curved surfaces offer more parsimonious approximations, but require more complex and more expensive surface/surface intersection calculations. These calculations may be computed in closed form for natural quadrics, but require less reliable and slower numerical procedures for the more general parametric surfaces that slowly find their way into contemporary solid modellers. In order to fully support solid modeling algorithms, the geometric utilities must include, in addition to geometric intersection calculations, topological and ordering queries, and must offer a general programming interface to the developers of higher-level algorithms.

3 Composing Geometric Primitives

In this section, we discuss how the simple geometric primitives described in Section 2 may be combined to represent more complex geometric structures, such as solids or even faces. We first visit *discretization* schemes, which use a distribution of lower-dimensional geometric elements to "mark" the space occupied by continuous 3D volumes. Then, we discuss *instantiation, superposition, and subdivision* techniques, which lead to the *selective subdivision*–the basis for CSG modeling. We then move on to the *delimitation* technique–the basis of the boundary representation. Finally, we conclude by *constructive* techniques, which include skinning, Minkowski sums, sweeps, and various extrusions.

3.1 Discretizations

The space occupied by a 3D solid model may be conveniently marked by lower-dimensional entities such as a cloud of points or an array of line segments. Such approximations discretize the volume with respect to one, two, or even three dimensions. Although the simplicity of discretization schemes makes them attractive at first sight, a heavy penalty is often payed by application algorithms that try to derive from discrete data the smooth boundary of a continuous 3D model.

Zero-dimensional discretizations

Clouds of points provide a zero-dimensional approximation for solids. They may be simply represented by enumerating all the points in the cloud. However, realistic shaded graphics and other applications may require that these clouds be interpreted as solids. Besides convex hulls, which are inappropriate for non convex objects, unambiguous and efficient interpretations of clouds are not available. They would require an efficient procedure for establishing whether a given point is in the represented solid or not. (The use of these points as vertices for mesh elements or as centers to voxels falls outside of this subsection.)

Clouds of unevenly spaced points may be transformed by rigid body motions or other space mappings, but Boolean operations are impossible without a clear interpretation of the associated solid. On the other hand, for points distributed on a 3D grid, Boolean operations may be performed in a discrete manner for each grid point, but the application of a rigid body motion to all grid points requires marking grid points hit by the image of the original point. This process is expensive and accompanied with a loss of precision that makes them non-invertible, i.e. applying a rotation and its inverse will not produce exactly the same object.

Hierarchical structures that, for example, group points into octrees provide a more storage-efficient representation scheme for zero-dimensional discretizations of points on regular grids [169, 119].

One-dimensional discretizations

Families of line segments provide a one-dimensional discretization of solids [1, 2]. They can be computed through ray-casting in software or even in hardware directly from CSG models [63].

One-dimensional discretizations, such as the intersection of a solid with an evenly spaced family of parallel rays, provide approximations of solids that have floating-point precision in one direction and is only a course approximation in the two other directions. It may be interesting to consider three families of rays, one in each direction of some orthonormal coordinate system.

Ray-discretizations have similar advantages and drawbacks to point-discretizations. Booleans between two objects represented on the same set of rays are simple, i.e. they amount to perform a large number of Booleans on 1D intervals. Rotations of a ray-discretized representation, however, are more expensive and in general not invertible.

Two-dimensional discretizations

Cross-sections stacking may be used as a two dimensional discretization of 3D solids. Such techniques have been used in medical imaging, where cross-section contours are obtained (often by manual segmentation) from MRI or CT scanners. They have also been used in computer vision where cross-section contours are obtained from range finders.

Cross-sections do not explicitly define a solid. Many attempts were made to automatically infer a complete volumetric description of the solid from 2D cross-sections. The task is difficult when consecutive cross-sections have grossly different shapes and even topology. An excellent survey may be found in [174].

Note that cross-sections are two-dimensional regions and cannot in general be represented by primitive geometric entities. Similarly to faces of solids, cross-sections are usually defined by their bounding edges as discussed below.

3.2 Quasi-disjoint enumeration

Quasi-disjoint enumeration combine mutually disjoint solids that may be represented by simple enumeration. Instances of parametrized primitives or simply voxels (see papers in [97]) possibly grouped in octrees for compactness [169] may be used.

Often, to prevent gaps between neighboring elements, the elements are only *quasi-disjoint*, i.e., they are glued at common boundaries.

Finite element meshes found in analysis packages or simplicial complexes found in mathematics are very good examples. Some solid modeling schemes are based on enumerations of convex polyhedra.

Quasi-disjoint enumeration may be viewed as the most explicit representation scheme and is usually combined with other techniques discussed in this section. It offers a simple divide-and-conquer approach to most algorithms, since most calculations on compound objects represented through enumeration may be performed by distributing it onto the primitive elements. Combining the results is usually simple. For example, a point is inside a compound object if and only if it lies in one of its constituent primitive elements. Two objects A and B represented through enumerations are disjoint if each primitive constituent of A is disjoint from all primitive constituents of B.

More subtle examples of the enumeration technique are found in boundary representation schemes discussed in the Delimitation section below. For example, the boundary of a face is represented through an enumeration of its quasi-disjoint bounding edges. The boundary of a solid is often represented by enumerating its quasi-disjoint faces.

3.3 Superposition

When an element is defined as the union of the pointsets of primitive elements, it may not always be necessary to require that the primitive elements be quasi-disjoint.

For example, the boundary of a solid could be represented as the union of a set of overlapping faces, without explicit representation of how and where they overlap. Although some graphic applications can easily accommodate such representations, many algorithms assume quasi-disjointedness and would not work on such models.

A solid, S, can be represented as the union of simpler primitive volumes P_i, that are not necessarily quasi-disjoint. Unless additional information is provided, the boundary, *vardeltaS*, of S is unknown. However, the properties of the union imply the following:

- The boundary of S is a subset of the union of the boundaries of P_i,
- Boundaries of P_i are either on the boundary of S or in the interior of S.

These two properties are used to improve the efficiency of depth-buffer rendering algorithms for solids represented as unions of simple shapes [158].

Point-containment may also be performed by testing the point against all primitives and combining the results through a logical OR operation.

If non-disjoint primitives are used, one may also allow primitives that have self-intersecting boundaries, i.e., that have a representation of only a superset of their boundary that lies inside the closure of the primitive volume. For example, consider a torus with a cross-section radius larger than the spine radius. Points may be tested against the torus using the same equation, whether the torus is self-intersecting or not, but a point on the toroidal surface does not necessarily lie on the torus.

Unions of overlapping primitives have not been sufficiently exploited in solid modeling, because early drafting-style graphics made the elimination of internal boundary parts expensive and because other operations on such intersections may lead to an explosion of entities. For example, to compute the intersection of two solids each represented by 10 disjoint primitives one would need to compute and maybe represent 100 intersections of primitives. Nevertheless, superpositions of overlapping primitives have been used to produce convex decompositions of 2D regions.

Superposition also plays an important role for zero-dimensional and one-dimensional entities. For example, the intersection of two orthogonal cylindrical surfaces of the same radius and with intersecting axes is composed of two ellipses that intersect at two points. For graphic purposes, the intersection may be represented as two non-disjoint ellipses. When the intersection curves are used to define the boundary cylindrical faces, it is important to separate the ellipses into two arcs each and to identify the intersection points. Such a separation yields a subdivision as discussed in the next section.

3.4 Subdivision

Given a collection of primitive elements, it may be important to compute and store a description of how they intersect with each other. For example, the subdivision, $C = A\#B$, of the two primitives A and B is an enumeration of three disjoint sets: $A - B$, $B - A$, and $A \cap B$, called the *regions* of the subdivision. Note that some of the regions may be empty.

Subdivisions of subdivisions, or subdivisions of more than two regions may be defined recursively by distributing the subdivision operation over all pairs of regions. Note that $(A\#B)\#C = A\#(B\#C)$.

Subdivision may also be carried on a pointset to isolate, as separate regions, singular subsets. For example, a technique for performing subdivisions of algebraic varieties that isolates intersections, cusps, and self intersections may be found in [9, 10].

Subdivision criteria may also take into account the topological properties of the original pointsets. For example, it may be important to distinguish the boundary of a solid from its interior. It may also be important to separate the connected components of regions.

Subdivision is at the heart of many solid modeling algorithms. It raises two issues, discussed throughout the remainder of this paper: "What properties do the regions resulting from the subdivision have?" and "How are these regions and their topological relations represented?".

For example, given a set of lines in the plane, points of intersection of the lines define entities which can be represented by the mere fact that they lie on specific lines. However, two segments of the same line separated by these intersection points have the same semi-algebraic expression, i.e. they belong to one line and are disjoint from all other lines. If we want to be able to distinguish these line segments, we must impose on the regions of a subdivision that they be connected. Additional data-structures must be used to distinguish these line segments.

Criteria for subdividing a pointset often include the identification of geometric singularities (such as cusps and self-intersections of curves and surfaces), the identification of topologically different entities (such as boundaries or non-manifold points), and the identification of connected components,

3.5 Selective subdivision

For some applications, it may be important to select only a subset of the elements resulting from the above described subdivision. Set theoretic Boolean operations provide a blatant example. For example, the subtraction operation between A and B would select only the region $A - B$ of the subdivision $A \# B$.

Regions of a subdivision can be selected by simply tagging them as "active" or "inactive". Of course, tagging is only possible if individual regions may be identified and processed independently. For example, to compute the boundary of a Boolean combination of two objects, each defined by a single-region boundary, one must construct the subdivision of both boundaries and select subsets of the resulting regions according to their relation to both objects.

Furthermore, selection may be performed according to predefined rules which guarantee specific properties of the resulting pointset, such as closure or dimensional homogeneity. For example, in the Boolean combination mentioned above, the one-dimensional subsets of the region that belong to both boundaries, i.e. the intersection curves, should be included in the result.

When the result of a selective subdivision is specified through a Boolean expression, two regions that have identical classifications with respect to all the initial (primitive) sets must be either both active or both inactive. This restriction is, for example, enforced in standard CSG modelers, where two disconnected parts of the same region or two regions that have the same classification with respect to all primitives cannot be distinguished. Typically boundary modelers provide a subdivision that captures these differences.

3.6 Delimitation (or boundary representation)

As discussed in the previous section, primitive geometric entities are in practice limited and may only provide support for simple faces or solids. More complex faces or solids may be expressed in semi-analytic form (as selective subdivisions that correspond to a Boolean combination of primitive pointsets) or implicitly as subsets of some primitive manifold (a surface or the entire three-dimensional space) delimited by its boundary.

Delimitation uses lower-dimensional entities to delimit the extent of a manifold by representing its boundary for instance in its enumerated form. Each element of the boundary may in turn be represented through delimitation as a subset of a lower-dimensional manifold delimited by its lower-dimensional boundary, and so on.

To be valid, a delimitation must satisfy a set of properties, that can be summarized by the following requirement: one must be able to unambiguously distinguish interior points from exterior points, relative to the delimited set. For practical purposes, this theoretic capability must permit the derivation of efficient methods for classifying points against sets defined through delimitation.

Specifically, a delimitation must separate the underlying space ($\mathbb{R}^3$ or a surface) into two regions, one of which corresponds to the desired subset. Thus delimitation may be viewed as a subdivision of the underlying space with the delimiting boundary, followed by a selection of some of the regions. The validity of a pointset as a delimiting boundary may be difficult to assess. For example, taking into account the different symmetries, there are three ways to place a circle on a torus, none of which is a valid delimitation. Typically, delimitations are required to be non-self intersecting, but this requirement raises the issue of "non-manifold" boundaries addressed in the next section.

If the region represented through a valid delimitation is bounded, the enumeration of the elements of the delimitation suffices to distinguish the region from its complement in the supporting manifold. For unbounded regions, more information may be required. For example, a circle on a sphere defines two faces but is insufficient to distinguish which one is of interest. The additional information may be provided in terms of relative orientation. For example, edges are often oriented counter-clockwise around a face with respect to a consistent choice of outside normal direction throughout the surface. A consistent choice of outside normal and its representation is simple for planes or spheres. The situation is more complicated when the surface contains singular points, such as the apex of a cone and topological non-manifold self-intersection cusps where several branches of the surface abut. Some orientation problems are discussed in [83].

3.7 Construction

The above techniques restrict the boundary of the represented solid to be defined as a subset of the boundaries of its primitive constituents. The constructive techniques discussed here use operators that create new geometries which are not subsets of primitive shapes. *transformations* that move or deform objects by mapping $\mathbb{R}^3$ onto itself (such as rigid-body motions, scaling, or bending) are not included here.

Extrusions and sweeps

Extrusions take a lower-dimensional element A (such as a face) and extrude it to produce a higher-dimensional element B (such as a solid) by defining the region swept by A as it moves according to a prescribed law. The law may restrict the motion to be a pure translation, a pure rotation, a screw combination, the motion of a Frenet trihedron along a space curve, or any other motion, linear transformation, or deformation.

Translational extrusions may be formulated as the Minkowski sums [179, 155] of a set with a curve segment. Note that the set need not be planar and that the curve segment need not be linear, but the extruded set remains parallel to itself.

The result of the extrusion of a 2D region need not be homogeneously three-dimensional. For example, extruding a planar region along a direction parallel to the plane containing the region will generate another 2D region. Although these degeneracies may be easily detected for translational extrusions of a planar region along a straight line segment, their detection may require intensive computations or subtle techniques of differential geometry for more arbitrary extrusions, such as those used in [182]. Nevertheless, it is important to guarantee dimensional homogeneity of volumes generated through extrusions.

Since 2D regions are often represented through delimitation by the supporting surface and their bounding edges, the result of an extrusion is often computed by extruding the boundary of the 2D region and by using it to delimit the resulting volume (in conjunction with the two instances of the 2D region in its initial and final positions).

For non-trivial extrusions the boundary generated by the above technique may self-intersect. For example, the rotational extrusion of a circle around an axis that intersects the circle in two points generates a self-intersecting toroidal surface. If the delimitation scheme assumes boundaries that do not self-intersect, the boundary must be subdivided and portions that do not bound the resulting volume de-activated.

Furthermore, the boundary generation as described above may not provide a superset of the boundary of the 3D region swept by the extruded 2D region. For example, consider a translational extrusion of a semi-spherical 2D region along a direction parallel to the plane of the circle that bounds the 2D region. The boundary of the region swept by the semi-sphere will contain a cylindrical surface that is not swept by any of the edges bounding the 2D region.

Extracting the correct boundary from a self-intersecting two-cycle superset is difficult because the superset does not always uniquely define the desired region, and thus its boundary. Variations of the winding-number rules which treat the entire superset as boundary do not account for regions of space traversed more than once (see Figure 2).

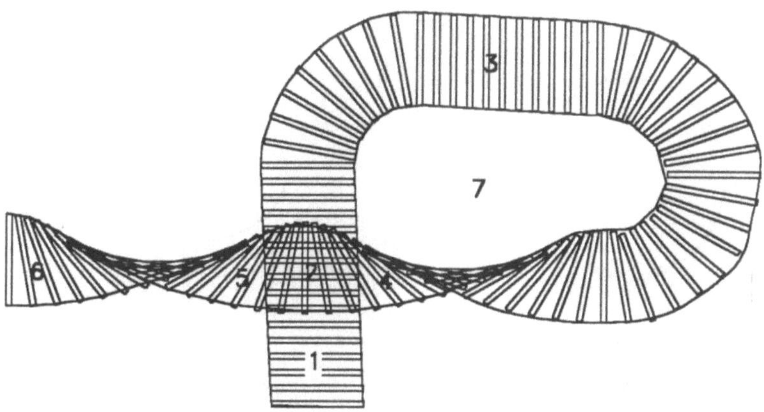

Figure 2. Where is the object?: The oriented self-intersecting curve B was generated by the trajectory of the two endpoints of a moving line segment. It is used to compute subsets of the boundary of the area A swept by the line segment. B defines 7 bounded regions. Only regions 1 through 6 are inside A. Winding numbers, parity-based techniques, and in/out counting would all misclassify region 2.

Instead of extruding a 2D region, one can also sweep a 3D pointset (solid) along 3D curves with or without rotations and other transformations. The region swept by the moving (and possibly deforming) solid defines another solid. The bounding faces of the swept region solid may be far more complex than the faces of the initial solid. Techniques for generating the boundary of the swept region may be based on unions of regions obtained by sweeping separately the faces of the original solid. (It can be shown that the result of a sweep is the union of the solid in its initial position with all the regions swept by its faces.) Here again, self-intersection and geometric singularities of the boundaries of the individual sweeps must be addressed.

The case of sweeps of polyhedral objects as they move along a piecewise screw motion has been recently studied at IBM Research by J. Kim and the author. Such cases offer important simplifications that lead to efficient algorithms for approximating the resulting boundary.

Interpolations

Discretized models, such as stacks of contours, may be interpolated to form surfaces that delimit volumes. Interpolation methods that work on a general domain are complex [174].

Interpolating surfaces defined by pairs of parameterized closed curves and occasionally some other "guiding" curves are available in many commercial systems and are heavily used for creating "skins" that may be later used to delimit volumes. It is however the user's responsibility to provide the adequate parameterization and guiding curves. Attempts to interpolate the two planar curves shown in Figure 3 by a smooth surface free of self-intersections proved more difficult than expected on several commercial systems.

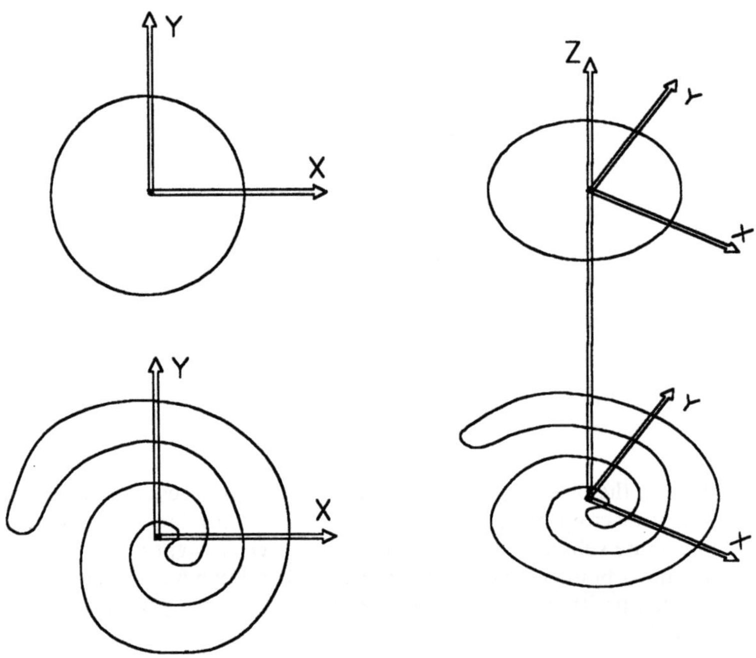

Figure 3. Interpolating two curves: The two smooth planar closed curves, a circle and a spiral, are positioned one above the other. They are used as constraints for building a smooth connected surface that interpolates both curves and does not self-intersect. Non-automatic tools for building such a surface are available. Manual tools require carefully parameterizing the two curves and producing intermediate cross-sections.

A technique for interpolating between two or more solids has recently been implemented [98] for polyhedral objects. The technique is based on a weighted Minkowski sum, $(1-t)A \oplus tB$ of two objects A and B, where $X \oplus Y = \{x + y : x \in X, y \in Y\}$. By changing the parameter t the designer can animate the metamorphosis that takes A into B and select the desired compromise between the shapes of A and B. By choosing B to be a line segment, a sphere, or a half-cone, one can obtain versions of A that are elongated, rounded, or chamfered to a desired degree. When A and B are convex polyhedra, efficient algorithms for computing the exact boundary of $(1-t)A \oplus tB$ exist. For non-convex polyhedra, one can easily generate a parameterized description of the superset of the boundary of $(1-t)A \oplus tB$ that is adequate for realtime animation, but insufficient for performing Boolean operations or even for efficiently detecting whether a point is inside the resulting solid or not. Extensions of these techniques to curved objects have only been addressed for the limited case where one of the objects is a ball [155].

Blending

CAD systems support an increasing amount of automation in the analysis of the geometric and topological properties of solids models. This analysis is only possible when precise and unambiguous representations of the solids are available. Thus the fillets and blends commonly found in most mechanical parts must be represented explicitly in the model.

Annotations on engineering blue prints are insufficient for unambiguously specifying the shape of blending surfaces that connect several curved surfaces, even for constant radius blends and fillets [162]. Techniques for generating blending surfaces are reviewed in [218], but must be complemented by reliable techniques for incorporating them into boundary representations while guaranteeing validity.

Precise representations of the constant radius blending surfaces are based on canal surfaces [124]. Unambiguous representations of blended solids have been defined in terms of combination of offsetting operations [163], i.e. Minkowski additions and subtractions with a ball. An integration of these operations in the solid modeling environment was developed in [155] using smooth piecewise toroidal approximations of canal surfaces [164] to eliminate the need for supporting canal surfaces and their intersections. However, offsetting approximations are very expensive and the resulting approximations produce gaps in the boundary representation between the blend and the surfaces it interpolates. These gaps may lead to algorithmic errors.

Other techniques (see [82] and also the survey in [218]), provide a semi-algebraic formulation of low degree for the blended unions and intersections of two half-spaces, but the resulting blends are not constant-radius and their shape is difficult to control.

3.8 State of the art conclusion on compositions

Aggregations or superimpositions of simple primitive geometric elements are insufficient for modeling an acceptable class of solids. Selective subdivision may be used to trim geometric primitives by primitives of the same dimension as in the case of CSG. Delimitation is used to trim geometric primitives with primitives of lower dimensions by enumerating their boundaries. Although selective subdivision and delimitation are the most commonly used solid modeling techniques, they are incapable of producing geometries that are not included in the boundaries of the original geometric primitives. Constructive techniques, such as extrusions, sweeps, interpolations, and blending have already been used with success for modeling surfaces. However, techniques for ensuring or even verifying that the surfaces generated by these operations are valid boundaries of solids have not yet been fully mastered. Thus the full integration of general extrusion and interpolation operations in solid modelers has not yet been achieved.

4 Topological and Structural Domain

After discussing terms useful for describing the topological domain and limitations of solid modellers, we review several modeling schemes.

4.1 Topological concepts

In this subsection, the topological concepts pertinent to solid modeling and its extensions are introduced at a very intuitive level. For more precise definitions, the reader should consult standard textbooks on geometry and topology [120].

Throughout this paper it is assumed that we work in $\mathbb{R}^3$, the three-dimensional space, endowed with the usual Euclidean topology. For simplification, all the geometric entities considered here are well behaved. For example, surfaces or curves do not fill space.

Topological closure, interior, and boundary

A set O is open in the relative topology of a sub-manifold M of $\mathbb{R}^3$ if around each point of O there exists an open ball of M with a strictly positive radius that is included in O.

As far as solid modeling is concerned, a 3D set is open if it includes none of its bounding faces, edges, or vertices. When a face F lies on a surface M, we say that M is a supporting surface. Relative to a supporting surface, a face is open if it does not include its bounding edges. Similarly, an edge is open, relative to a supporting curve, if it does not include its bounding vertices. Note that a closed edge (i.e. an edge that forms a closed loop) is open. For simplicity, we will assume that the term open, when used for faces or edges, always refers to open relative to the supporting surface or curve.

The *interior* O of a set S relatively to a supporting manifold M is the largest open subset of S relative to M. Thus the interior of a solid is the solid excluding its bounding faces, edges, and vertices. The interior of a face (relative to its supporting surface) is the face minus its bounding edges and vertices. A face is closed relative to $\mathbb{R}^3$ and thus its interior relative to $\mathbb{R}^3$ is empty. But, for simplicity, when speaking about faces, we will use the word "interior" to mean interior relative to the supporting surface. Similarly, the interior of a curve is the curve without its vertices.

The *closure* of a set S is the union of S with all the points P such that a ball of any strictly positive radius centered at P will intersect S and its complement (relatively to the supporting manifold). For example, the closure of an open face is the face plus its bounding edges and vertices.

The *boundary* of a set S is the difference between its closure and its interior. Again, the term boundary is used as relative to the supporting manifold. In case of ambiguity, we shall clearly specify the manifold. For example, if an object is composed of faces and dangling edges in 3D, its interior with respect to $\mathbb{R}^3$ is empty. Yet, the interior of each face or edge independently is not empty when considered relative to the supporting surface or curve.

Dimensional homogeneity

A subset of $\mathbb{R}^3$ is full-dimensional if it contains a three-dimensional part, i.e. a part that contains a 3D ball of positive radius. A subset of a surface is full-dimensional, relatively to the surface, if it contains a disc of positive radius. Note that non-empty open subsets are always full-dimensional.

A subset of $\mathbb{R}^3$ is dimensionally-homogeneous if it does not contain any dangling edges or vertices. More precisely, if a set S is dimensionally-homogeneous, then all its points are either in the interior of S or in the closure of the interior of S. A pointset is inhomogeneous if it is not dimensionally-homogeneous.

Semi-analytic sets

A set is semi-analytic if it can be represented through a Boolean combination of analytic inequalities or equalities on the x, y, z variables. Similarly, semi-algebraic sets may be expressed as Boolean combinations of algebraic equalities and inequalities.

Regularization

Regularization is defined [144, 199] as an operation that takes a pointset and returns a regularized pointset that is closed and dimensionally homogeneous. More precisely, regularization is computing the closure of the interior of the solid. Note that a regularized solid is equal to the closure of its interior and thus regularization leaves regularized solids unchanged.

Regularization not only removes dangling faces, edges, and isolated vertices, it also fills cracks and puts a "tight skin" around the object. A crack is defined as the part of the boundary of the solid that is not in the boundary of the closure of the solid.

It has been argued that mechanical parts are best represented by r-sets [144] (compact, and thus bounded, regularized sets that have a semi-analytic expression). Since, the term "solid" in the context of solid modeling has been associated with r-sets or with convenient subsets of r-sets. Since regularized sets, and thus r-sets do not form a closed[3] set under the set-theoretic Boolean operations (union, intersection, complement, difference), a regularized version of these operators was introduced [199]. A regularized Boolean operator performs the corresponding set-theoretic operation followed by a regularization. Thus, the result is always a valid solid, even though it may be the empty set. Note that the result of a Boolean expression involving several regularized Boolean operations may also be obtained by evaluating all the operations in their set-theoretic form (i.e. without the regularization part) and then performing the regularization of the result.

Also note that, when applied to regularized pointsets, the set-theoretic union operation always returns regularized sets. This does not imply that the boundary of the union is simpler to compute than the boundary of the intersection or difference. Consider again two cubes glued to each other through a common face. The set-theoretic intersection returns the common face which is discarded by the regularization operation, since its interior is empty. When computing the boundary of the intersection, one can compute the intersection of the boundary of each object with the other object and then apply the regularization process to remove portions of the resulting boundary that are not bounding the intersection of the solids. Now consider the set-theoretic union of these two cubes. The interior of the common face is part of the interior of the result and thus is not on the boundary. It is removed, even if we do not apply regularization. The distinction between these two boundary "cleaning" operations will be clarified further when we consider the selection and the simplification processes defined in [161].

A different regularization was proposed in [7], where first the closure operation is applied and then the interior. The result is an open set that has no cracks.

---

[3]Topological closure should not be confused with the closure of the set of solids under Boolean operations.

Connectedness

A pointset S is *connected* if a curve segment that connects any two points of S exists in S. Inversely, two sets are *disjoint* if their intersection is empty. Note that a solid, i.e. an r-set, needs not be connected.

A pointset is *interior-connected* if its interior is connected. For example, the union of two cubes touching at a vertex is not interior connected.

Two sets are *quasi-disjoint* if they are not disjoint, but if their regularized intersection is empty. For example, two cubes glued together at a common face are not disjoint but are quasi-disjoint. Note that two open sets may not be quasi-disjoint.

A set is *simply-connected* if it does not have any handles, that is if any closed curve inside the set may be contracted into a single point by performing a smooth deformation that maintains the curve inside the pointset. For example, a sphere is simply-connected, but a torus is not. Similarly, a face is simply-connected if it does not have a hole. Note that a volume with an interior hole, such as a sphere with a spherical hole at its center, is simply-connected, on the other hand, an infinite cylinder with a cylindrical coaxial cylindrical hole is not simply connected.

Non-Manifold conditions

A solid X is said to be a closed *manifold* if around each point of the solid one can construct an open ball of positive radius whose intersection with X is homeomorphic to an open ball or to a half-space, for manifolds with boundary. For example, a solid defined as the union of two cubes touching at a vertex is not a manifold solid.

The boundary B of a manifold solid forms a two-manifold, where around each point of B one can construct an open ball of positive radius whose intersection with B is homeomorphic to an open disk. We say that a two-manifold, or manifold boundary, does not *self-intersect*.

Note that Boolean operations on manifold solids may very well create non-manifold solids.

Similarly, a face F of a surface S is a manifold face if around each point of F one can construct an open ball of positive radius whose intersection with F is homeomorphic to an open disk. The boundary of a manifold face is a set of curves that do not self-intersect.

4.2 Specific domains and their limitations

Solid modelers may be differentiated in terms of their topological domain, independently of their geometric coverage. We review below several such topological domains. In addition to topological properties of the represented pointset, we consider its internal decomposition into regions that may be of significance to solid modeling applications.

Bounded manifold solids

Some algorithms march from face to face along a solid's boundary and benefit from additional face-adjacency information. A convenient way of storing this information is to represent explicitly edges of an object and associate with them pointers to the surfaces that they bound. For data-structure simplicity some developers have restricted to two the number of faces intersecting at an edge. This restriction limits the scope of the modeler to shapes that are bounded by a set of faces that form a two-manifold boundary, i.e. to manifold solids.

Note that a manifold solid need not be connected.

Typically, a face of a solid is defined as the maximal closed connected pointset of the boundary of the solid that lies on a given surface, although see [183] for alternate definitions of faces.

Note that the faces of a manifold solid are quasi-disjoint. On the other hand, a manifold solid may have non-manifold faces (see Figure 4).

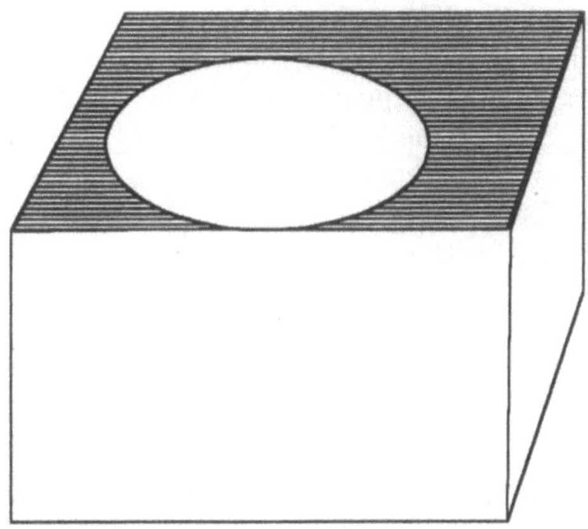

Figure 4. Non-manifold face: The subtraction of a sphere from the top face of a block creates a non-manifold face, even though the solid is manifold.

An interesting restriction is to require that all faces be simply connected (which does not imply that the solids are simply-connected). With this restriction, each face may be represented by a simple bounding loop. For polyhedral objects, a simply connected face is thus unambiguously represented by an ordered list of vertices. When the face is bounded, the choice in the order of the vertices may be used to indicate the direction of the outward pointing normal of the face with respect to the solid it bounds. Such simplified models for faces are still popular graphic. In order to represent, in such a simplified scheme, a face with one or several holes, one must decompose it into several simply connected faces, which do not satisfy the definition of maximal faces suggested above. An even more problematic solution introduces double edges, or bridges, inside the face to connect holes with the external loop of the face's boundary. The resulting list of edges forms a single loop, that intersects itself along one-dimensional portions. If we consider closed faces, this loop may not be called the boundary of the face, because its interior points are included in the interior of the face.

The drawback of manifold models is that they cannot accommodate a designer's intent to create non-manifold objects and are insufficient to model the result of regularized Boolean operations, even when these operations are applied to manifold objects.

R-sets

The term r-sets has been used to formally define the class of pointsets that are supported by solid modellers that are not restricted to manifold models. As mentioned before, an r-set is a closed and bounded set that is equal to the closure of its interior and whose boundary is composed of algebraic, or at least analytic, surface-elements. R-sets are semi-algebraic or semi-analytic, i.e. representable by a Boolean combination of algebraic or analytic functions. In fact, most modellers are restricted to semi-algebraic r-sets, i.e. Boolean combinations of half-spaces defined by polynomial functions in three variables.

This precise definition of what is a valid solid helped develop theoretically correct algorithms for Boolean operations. (The main problem was to ensure that these algorithms always returned valid solids when applied to valid solids.) Nevertheless, this definition appears too restrictive for some new applications of solid modeling. In particular, three-dimensional r-sets cannot capture the internal structure of a solid, cannot represent unbounded solids nor solids with lower-dimensional cracks or exterior elements, and cannot be used to model the interference of touching solids. Models for Non-Regularized Geometry (NRG) are needed to deal with such general cases.

Open regular sets

Closed pointsets are inappropriate for capturing cracks or the separation of a connected solid into distinguishable components. Such separation is important for modeling assemblies. The s-sets of [7] may be used for such purposes, however, it must be noted that the domain of s-sets is not closed under set-theoretic Boolean operations. On the other hand, open-regularized Boolean operations always produce s-sets, but the cracks used for example to separate the various components of an assembly are "filled-in" by the closure part of the open-regularization. Consequently, Boolean operation cannot be performed on assemblies of quasi-disjoint sets modelled by an s-set without loosing the internal separations and the cracks.

It may be preferable to represent assemblies through quasi-disjoint enumeration of r-sets [42].

Non-manifold boundaries

The radial-edge data-structure [211, 212] was introduced to provide an extension of the earlier manifold boundary representations to support non-manifold solids. It was however extended to represent non-manifold pointsets that combine faces and edges and that do not necessarily form valid boundaries of any solid.

In the solid modeling community, the term non-manifold boundaries traditional referred to valid boundaries of solids. In [211, 210] however, the term "non-manifold geometric boundary" refers to a more general scheme that includes dimensionally inhomogeneous pointsets.

The pointsets defined in this manner are restricted to be quasi-disjoint enumerations of closed bounded pointsets of dimension one and two.

When these pointsets contain "shells", i.e. face cycles that enclose a connected region of space, one can use them to represent 3D solids by delimitation. However, a set of faces that contains, in addition of the shell, faces that lie inside the enclosed region cannot be considered to be the boundary of a 3D solid, because the solid is closed and the faces inside the enclosed region are in the interior of the solid and thus are not part of its boundary. When representing such objects, i.e. solids with internal faces, by schemes such as those proposed in [211], one in fact uses the faces of the outside shell to define a 3D region. The interior faces are not part of the boundary, but are modeled together with the solid through superposition.

CNRGs

Objects composed of mutually disjoint non-regularized regions that need not be connected, bounded, nor dimensionally-homogeneous, may be specified by CNRG (Constructive Non-Regularized Geometry) graphs [165], which combine primitive regions through operators that include set-theoretic Boolean operators and topological operators (such as closure and interior). These operators preserve the subdivision of their arguments into distinguishable regions. They produce pointsets that correspond to the usual interpretation of the Boolean and topological operators plus a subdivision of these pointsets that capture explicitly all the geometric interactions between the primitive regions. A simplification operation is available for removing the undesirable subdivision and thus for merging regions into bigger ones.

CNRGs are an example of GROGS (Generative Representations of Geometric Structures). They do not have any of the previously discussed limitations and are convenient for representing assemblies and solids with internal structures and cracks. They also provide a clear semantics for Boolean operations on such objects.

GROGS, such as CSG and CNRG, are convenient for specifying or interactively editing pointsets or objects with structures. However, because they are generative, i.e. not evaluated, the existence and other topological properties of the resulting pointsets or structures cannot be directly evaluated. Therefore, for many applications, GROGS should be converted into DROGS (Descriptive Representations of Geometric Structures), such as the boundary representations and SGCs described below.

SGCs

An SGC is a non-regularized inhomogeneous pointset represented through enumeration as the union of mutually disjoint connected open cells [161]. Note that because cells are open, they are dimensionally-homogeneous. Furthermore, cells are required to be connected and are singularity-free sub-manifold of algebraic varieties.

SGCs are formed as subdivisions of primitive geometric entities. They differ from CNRGs in that they represent the connected components of disconnected regions as separate cells or unions of cells. (A connected component of a region may be further subdivided so as to isolate singularities and split it into primitive entities representable in the modeler.) SGC cells may be grouped into CNRG regions through book-keeping techniques.

SGC cells are represented through delimitation. Therefore, cells that constitute the boundary of a cell are also part of the SGC. For example, an SGC solid-cell in 3D is represented by an SGC decomposition of its boundary; an SGC face-cell is represented by a supporting surface and its bounding edge-cells and vertex-cells; and so on. Treated as a disjoint enumeration of all its cells, the SGC would always represent a closed pointset. However, in addition to their capabilities for modeling inhomogeneous pointsets with internal structures, SGCs can also be used to represent non-closed pointsets with cracks. This generalization is achieved through the SGC mechanism for selective subdivision: cells in the enumeration are marked as active or inactive; the pointset represented by an SGC is the union of the pointsets represented by its active cells. Using inactive cells, SGCs may also define a subdivision of the complement of the pointset they represent.

A simplification mechanism which removes unnecessary subdivisions or unnecessary inactive cells while maintaining the validity of the SGC representation exists. Its results are unique.

SGCs provide support for representing explicitly the subdivision of primitive geometric entities. This subdivision may be used to improve the efficiency of the evaluation of boundaries of CSG models during interactive editing of CSG. They are also important for verifying the topological and geometric properties of geometric surface and volume features [158].

4.3 State of the art conclusion on topologies

Although manifold objects are simpler to represent than non-manifold ones, restricting the topological domain of a solid modeler to manifold solids imposes considerable constraints on the designers by preventing them from creating non-manifold situations and from performing Boolean operations on manifold solids in arbitrary relative positions.

The domain of r-sets includes non-manifold solids, but is insufficient for modeling the internal structure of the solids, except through quasi-disjoint enumeration or superposition. S-sets, which can represent internal separations of the solids into disjoint regularized-open sets, are not closed under standard Boolean operations and loose their internal structure information under open-regularized Booleans.

Non-manifold boundary data structures developed for representing non-regularized objects with internal structures are finding their way into the solid modeling technology, but precise mathematical definitions of what these data structures represent are only beginning to emerge. The semantics of Boolean and topological operations on non-regularized objects with internal structures has been provided through Constructive Non-Regularized Geometry. The result of such constructive specifications may be represented in boundary form through Selective Geometric Complexes.

5 Representation of Geometric Structures

In this section we focus on *delimitative representations,* where solids, more general pointsets, and their internal structure are represented by enumerating their boundary elements; and on *constructive representations,* where pointsets are represented in a non-evaluated form that defines a recipe for computing a selective subdivision of primitive entities. These two representation schemes are illustrated by the traditional Boundary representations and CSG graphs considered as the two fundamental solid modeling techniques. Other representation schemes are used either for model construction [38, 61, 115] or as auxiliary representations [13, 49] produced for performance improvement or for specific applications. Conversions between representations will be briefly discussed in the next section.

5.1 Boundary graphs

We discuss here the various adjacency-graph representations for boundary models. After an introductory section, we define a notation for presenting the adjacency relations explicitly stored in a boundary graph, discuss validity criteria of boundary representations, and review several approaches and their limitations.

The adjacency graphs capture an implicit definition of the objects' faces and sometimes of their connectivity [6]. For disconnected objects, for objects with internal holes, or for objects with internal structures and several 3D regions, the concept of *shells* is used to group faces into boundaries of different 3D sub-solids. Since a face is represented, through delimitation, by its edges, edges are often organized into *loops,* so as to support faces with holes [37, 38]. Loops and shells are redundant when representing a single pointset, but are useful to speed-up many graphic and solid modeling algorithms. They also play an important role when modeling the internal structures of pointsets.

For polyhedral objects, edges are often represented by their end-points (vertices) and faces may be represented by their edges. When curved surfaces are used, the vertices are insufficient for defining edges and the bounding edges of a face are insufficient for defining the shape of the face. Edges may be represented, as discussed in Section 2, through coordinates and in parametric form. General faces must be represented by the supporting surface and the bounding edges. Additional neighborhood information (or interior indicators) is necessary, as mentioned in Section 2, for specifying which portion of a surface is represented by a loop of edges. Instead of neighborhood information associated to edges, ordering information has been used to disambiguate the model.

In summary, the boundary B of a solid A is typically represented by an *adjacency graph* whose nodes correspond to vertices, edges, faces, connected 3D regions or combination of these, and whose links capture information related to delimitation, adjacency, orientation, and ordering.

Delimitation information is necessary to unambiguously specify the extent of the faces. *Adjacency* information indicates when two faces of the same shell are connected, i.e share a common edge or vertex. *Orientation* information is especially important when modeling multiple regions for solids with internal structures, but is also used for defining locally how (i.e. on which side) an edge or face is bounding a face or solid region. *Ordering* information is stored to facilitate specific traversals of the boundary. For example, graphic applications often require that the vertices of a face or loop be given in counter-clockwise order around the outward normal of the face.

Notation

We use the symbols V, E, F, and R to denote respectively the *basic types:* vertex, edge, face, and solid region. The additional *grouping types* for loops and shells are denoted L and S. *Auxiliary types* correspond to the association of two or more elements of the basic types. They will be written using the concatenation of the letters of the basic types in lower case. These auxiliary types are restricted to combinations of basic types of different dimensions and such that an element of dimension k is bounding any other element in the combination that has dimension greater then k. The basic elements concatenated in a auxiliary type are listed in decreasing order of dimension. For example, the type fv denotes all the associations between faces and their bounding vertices.

We use auxiliary types only when the associated entities correspond to non-trivial nodes in the graph representation. For example, the representation of a face in a boundary graph may include a variable number of references to all the edges that bound the face. Such references may be captured in a list of auxiliary elements, called for example edge-references. The face would point to the first edge-reference entry in the list and each edge-reference record would point to an actual edge node and also to the next edge-reference in that list. These implementation details are not of interest here and data-structure elements such as the edge-reference records will not be taken into account. We simply say that the face points to a variable number of edges and indicate this by $F \rightarrow E$. Using the notation of [3], a superscript over the arrow indicates the number of these references when it is constant. For example, $E \xrightarrow{2} V$ indicates that each edge points to exactly two vertices.

Sometimes, to each edge-reference is associated a single vertex-reference. (To the edge is associated a list of pairs of pointers; one to a vertex and one to another edge.) We indicate it by $F \rightarrow (E, V)$, extending the notation of [3].

Many data structures associate to each node of a particular type one or several pointers to other neighboring nodes of the same type. For example, consider pointers from an edge E to a subset of its neighboring edges. The number of such pointers is in general not constant, but could be a function of the number of faces bounded by E. Suppose that we need only one such pointer per face. We could use the auxiliary type fe and write: $E \rightarrow fe \xrightarrow{1} E$, thus indicating that each edge points to a variable number of auxiliary fe-nodes and that each fe-node points to an edge. Instead, we use the more explicit notation: $E \xrightarrow{F} E$, which indicates that from each edge E there are pointers to other edges, one per face bounded by E. Note that if the edges had also references to abutting faces, we could write: $E \rightarrow (F, E)$. Extending the superscript notation even further, $E \xrightarrow{F \times V} E$, indicates that from each edge E there are pointers to other edges, one for each face-vertex pair such that the vertex is bounding E and the face is bounded by E.

When the multiple arcs emanating from a node are ordered (possibly in cyclic fashion), we use a double arrow "$\Rightarrow$" instead of "$\rightarrow$". For example, $F \Rightarrow V$ indicates that to each face is associated a list of links to vertices that are ordered in a circular fashion around the face. (This ordering is often used for simply-connected faces.) For a face with several loops, we write: $F \rightarrow L \Rightarrow V$, ignoring, for simplicity, the fact that nested loops may also be partially ordered.

A entire graph will be described by a syntax that first lists all the node-types used in the graph and then all the types of arcs between these nodes. It is illustrated by the following example:

$$\{R, F, L, V : R \rightarrow F \rightarrow L \Rightarrow (V, F)\},$$

which indicates that the graph has nodes of type R, F, L, and V, and has a variable number of links from R to F and from F to L. It also has a variable number of link-pairs from L to V and to F that are ordered. (Regions are defined by a variable number of faces; each face is defined by a variable number of loops; each entry in the loop is a double reference to a vertex and to another face.)

Validity of delimitative representation

A bounded pointset, A, in $\mathbb{R}^3$ may be unambiguously represented by its boundary, B, which must form a closed shell separating the interior pointset from its unbounded complement. In fact, the boundary may be composed of several nested shells that define a permutation of solids and holes.

The extent of A may be precisely specified in terms of B by the *alternating classification* rule (also called parity rule), which states that a point that can be moved to infinity without crossing or hitting the boundary is classified as outside of A. A is assumed bounded. If we now move the point so as to visit all the connected open regions of the complement of B in $\mathbb{R}^3$, the classification changes each time we cross the interior of a 2D face of B. Care must be taken here to avoid crossing at lower-dimensional, singular elements of B, such as cusps or edges or vertices where several faces of B meet. The term crossing is to be taken in its intuitive meaning of traversing a face from one side to the other.

This definition, when used for unambiguously specifying solids, imposes strong constraints on B: ***the classification of any point must be unique!*** For example, the union, B, of the boundaries of two quasi-disjoint cubes that share a common face defines three shells (the two boundaries of the original cubes and a new shell that bounds the union). B divides its complement in $\mathbb{R}^3$ into three open sets: the interiors of the two cubes and the complement of the union. The alternating classification rule would produce an ambiguous classification for the two bounded regions, because each can be reached from infinity by traversing an even number of faces and also by traversing an odd number of faces of B. To avoid such ambiguities, shells used for defining the boundary of a solid must be properly nested.

The validity requirements for B may be formulated more precisely as combinatorial conditions and geometric conditions. The combinatorial conditions require that B be a compact homogeneously 2D polyhedron and that each edge of B be adjacent to a positive, even number of faces. The geometric conditions impose that all vertices be mutually disjoint, that edges be pairwise quasi-disjoint, and that faces be pairwise quasi-disjoint.

When B is a valid boundary, A may be represented by simply enumerating the faces of B. No ordering or shell-grouping is necessary!

On the other hand, for polyhedral domains, one can avoid representing edges explicitly by introducing ordering information. A simply-connected manifold planar polygonal face may be represented by an ordered list of its vertices, i.e. a loop. Faces with holes require lists of nested loops. Thus, a simple data-structure for polyhedral objects would be a list of vertices, which provides the coordinates of each vertex, and a list of faces, each face being defined by a list of loops. A loop is an ordered list of references to vertices in the vertex-list. Note that this data structure does not contain any edges and that there is no information at vertices to indicate what faces they are bounding. If needed, such additional information must be computed by traversing the face-list and by matching vertex indices or pointers.

Euler formula

The Euler formula is often wrongly associated with the topological validity of a boundary graph. In fact, it is only one among many other conditions for validity and provides a very weak constraint.

The Euler formula may be used to establish the number of handles, N_H, in a region bounded by a single shell as follows:

$$2N_H = 2 - N_V + N_E - N_F,$$

where N_V, N_E, N_F are respectively the numbers of vertices, edges, and faces in the boundary. Intuitively, handles are through-holes in the object. A solid homeomorphic to a ball has no handles; a solid homeomorphic to a torus has one handle, and so on. The above formula has been extended to objects with many shells and even to non-regularized objects. Such extensions have no other purpose than to define one among many constraints that must be satisfied by a boundary representation.

Delimitation graphs

Under the above validity conditions, delimitation information, and possibly orientation information, are sufficient for unambiguously defining a solid [161, 190]. This type of information may be captured in a *delimitation graph* where each 3D region points to an unordered list of faces, each face points to an unordered list of edges, and each edge points to its vertices. Of course, with faces and edges are associated descriptions of the surfaces and curves that support them, as discussed in Section 2. Orientation/neighborhood information may be associated with the pointers (i.e. with the arcs of the graph). Some geometric ambiguities related to orientation are raised in [82].

Thus, in our notation, delimitation graphs correspond to:

$$\{R, F, E, V : R \rightarrow F \rightarrow E \rightarrow V\}.$$

Note that delimitation graphs have only nodes of the basic types and that the arcs are not bi-directional (inverse pointers are not stored) and only go towards entities of lower dimension. Furthermore, no ordering information is explicitly stored in delimitation graphs. Ordering information may be valuable for efficient boundary traversal, but may be expensive (or impossible) to compute.

Selective Geometric Complexes

By storing the redundant inverse pointers, i.e. from lower dimensional entities to higher-dimensional ones, one can avoid expensive searching problems when computing connectivity relations.

For example, in the above delimitation graphs, finding the faces connected to a particular edge requires traversing all the faces and for each face checking whether it contains a reference to that particular edge. Thus, it may be suitable to store redundant back-pointers that would facilitate the recovery of adjacency information. The result yields:

$$\{R, F, E, V : R \rightarrow F \rightarrow E \rightarrow V, V \rightarrow E \rightarrow F \rightarrow R\}.$$

Variations on this simple representation were discussed in [216] and also used in [67].

Such a graph is the basis of the Selective Geometric Complexes (SGC) representation [161]. However, SGC's also support links between elements whose dimensions differ by more than one. These links are necessary for supporting isolated lower-dimensional boundary elements, such as a vertex at the center of a ball. For simplicity, SGC graphs are presented as also containing the transitive closure of all these links, i.e., $R \rightarrow E, R \rightarrow V, F \rightarrow V$ and their inverses.

SGCs do not require that each lower-dimensional element be in the boundary of a volume element of highest dimension. Thus, not all faces, edges, and vertices are accessible through volumes and a list of SGC nodes organized by dimension is also stored for ease of traversal.

To each arc between elements of an SGC graph that have consecutive dimensions is associated a neighborhood (LEFT, RIGHT, or BOTH) which defines the relative position of the higher-dimensional element with respect to lower dimensional elements. For example, a single vertex V on a circle C defines the boundary of an edge E on C in 1D. The neighborhood of V with respect to E is BOTH.

Since all basic-type nodes are explicitly stored in the graph, these nodes may be tagged with an active/inactive flag, which is used to select nodes whose pointset should be included in the object.

The SGC graph extends this recursive delimitation scheme to higher dimensions: regions bound hyper-regions and so on.

Ordering information in SGCs

In their basic form SGCs do not store any ordering information. This was a deliberate choice motivated by algorithmic simplicity and by the concern that ordering information may not always be available, especially in higher dimensions and for non-linear entities.

References from each node to its bounding and star nodes are organized by dimension. (The star of an entity B is the set of entities bounded by B.) These lists may be easily partitioned to indicate groupings of edges into loops or of faces into shells.

Further ordering information captured in most other representations, including the schemes of [40, 110] may easily be added to SGC graphs for arbitrary dimensions as follows.

With each node C of dimension k in the graph, we associate a two-dimensional table of pointers to nodes of the same dimension. The table is indexed in one direction by elements of dimension $k-1$ that bound C and in the other by elements of dimension k+1 bounded by C. (Remember that nodes of SGCs are of basic types only and always correspond to cells whose boundary is composed of other cells of the SGC.) Each entry in the table defines the *next* cell of dimension k around a cell of dimension k-1 in the boundary of a cell of dimension k+1. We use the term NAIL for these references. (NAIL stands for Next-element-Around-some-other-element-In-the-boundary-of-some-third-element Link).

For example, an edge E may be bounded by two vertices V_1 and V_2 and by four faces, F_1, F_2, F_3, and F_4. The NAIL table for E has two rows (one for each vertex) and four columns (one for each face). Each entry in the table refers to an edge that shares a vertex and a face with E. (When E has the same vertex at each one of its ends, it may refer to itself in the NAIL table.) Such tables associated with the edges of a solid permit to traverse the face-loops in an ordered fashion by following NAIL pointers for the same face and swapping vertices. Similarly, NAILs associated with faces provide a way for going from one face to the next face bounding the same volume around an edge.

NAIL tables capture exactly the information provided by the SWITCH operator on Brisson's cell-tuples [40] and by Lienhardt's v-maps generalization of [110]. However, NAILs are much smaller tables than Brisson's cell-tuples or Lienhardt's maps. (Independently of the author's work, Brisson has also proposed to eliminate some redundancy from his cell-tuples and reduce it to the information we capture in NAILs.)

In 3D, NAIL tables need only be associated with edges and faces and thus have at most two rows or two columns (each edge is bounded by at most two vertices and each face is bounding at most two regions).

Other adjacency structures

Recent surveys of previously published techniques may be found in [215, 3, 110]. Representation schemes may be divided according to their domain into two categories: graphs for oriented manifold shells and graphs for non-manifold objects. Both have been studied in the 3D case and in a more general n-D setting.

Edge-Less Adjacency Graph

We present here a very simple representation scheme for non-manifold polyhedral r-sets that does not require edge-nodes. The schemes provides insight for studying more elaborate schemes. It also provides a convenient and simple representation scheme for polyhedra.

For polyhedral models with simply connected faces, the edges are defined implicitly in terms of vertices and are not necessary if vertices are ordered. Thus, for faces without holes we may use a graph based on face-vertex adjacency:

$$\{R, F, V : R \rightarrow F \Rightarrow V\},$$

and for multiply connected faces:

$$\{R, F, L, V : R \rightarrow F \rightarrow L \Rightarrow V\}.$$

Delimitation graphs are not suited for "walking" from one face to the next face through their common edges. A simple extension to the above face-vertex graph may be used to capture not only face/face adjacency, but also the ordering of faces around edges. For future reference, we shall call this extension: ELAG (for Edge-Less Adjacency Graph).

In a ELAG, each pair of consecutive vertices in a loop defines an edge. (The loop implies a circular ordering and thus the last vertex is followed by the first one. If the loop is non-manifold, several entries in the loop may refer to the same vertex.) We can arbitrarily associate this edge with the first one of the two vertex-entries, in the order of their appearance in the loop. Thus each vertex in a loop implicitly defines a face-edge pair, i.e. an element of type fe. Given a face F and an edge E in the boundary of a solid region R, the pair fe unambiguously defines at most two faces F_1 and F_2, that have E in their boundary and that are adjacent to F in the circular ordering around E of all the faces of R bounded by E. Thus, one can associate two face-pointers with each vertex-entry in each loop. We obtain the following specification:

$$\text{ELAG} = \{R, F, L, V : R \rightarrow F \rightarrow L \Rightarrow (V, 2F)\},$$

where the notation "$L \Rightarrow (V, 2F)$" indicates that each loop has a variable number of entries, each pointing to one vertex and two faces.

Given the orientations of the faces and of the edges and their neighborhood information with respect to R, we can add to the loop-face links neighborhood information that will enable us to traverse the boundary of a region R by walking from one face to the next in such a manner that the sector specified by these two faces in the vicinity of the edge is inside R and is not intersected by any other face adjacent to E.

Note that for manifold boundaries $F_1 = F_2$, and only one pointer is necessary:

$$\text{Manifold ELAG} = \{R, F, L, V : R \rightarrow F \rightarrow L \Rightarrow (V, F)\}.$$

When, in addition, faces are simply connected, we can merge the face-nodes with the loop-nodes altogether:

$$\text{Manifold ELAG with simply connected faces} = \{R, F, L, V : R \rightarrow F \Rightarrow (V, F)\}.$$

Delta

An interesting variation of this face-vertex delimitation structure is proposed by Ala in [3], where in addition to face-vertex links, are stored vertex-edge and edge-face back pointers, yielding the Δ data-structure:

$$\Delta = \{R, V, E, F : R \rightarrow F \rightarrow V \rightarrow E \xrightarrow{2} F\}.$$

The reverse Δ data structure is given by:

$$\text{reverse-}\Delta = \{V, E, F : F \rightarrow E \xrightarrow{2} V \rightarrow F\}.$$

Ala argues that these data-structures offer an optimal compromise between the data-structure efficiency and cost of adjacency queries.

Triangulations

When restricted to manifolds shells, the ELAG concept was used in [137] for representing 2D triangulations by associating with each triangular face three pointer-pairs:

$$\text{Triangulation} = \{F, E : F \overset{3}{\Rightarrow} (V, F)\}.$$

The concept was further extended in [52, 66] to higher dimensional triangulations.

Ala also extends his reverse Δ structure to represent 3D triangulations by using region-nodes that correspond to tetrahedra [3]:

$$\text{3D-Delta} = \{V, E, F, R : R \overset{4}{\rightarrow} F \overset{3}{\rightarrow} E \overset{2}{\rightarrow} V \rightarrow R\}.$$

Winged-edge representation

The pioneering winged-edge representation developed by Baumgart [20, 19] is a bi-directional delimitation graph to which ordering information is added as links between edges. The graph can only represent orientable manifold shells. Each edge-node points to four other edge-nodes that share with it a vertex and a face. These edge-references correspond exactly to the content of the NAIL information in the extended SGC structure applied to 2D manifold boundaries in $\mathbb{R}^3$. Indeed there are two vertices and two faces for each edge in a manifold shell and there is one "next" edge (in the NAIL sense) associated with each combination.

However, these "next-edge" pointers are not stored in a table indexed by the identities of the faces and vertices, but are "hard-coded" in an order that captures the relative orientation information, which in SGCs is provided through neighborhoods.

In our notation, the winged-edge data structure yields:

$$\text{winged-edge} = \{F, E, V : F \rightarrow E \overset{2}{\Rightarrow} (V, E), V \rightarrow E \overset{2}{\Rightarrow} (F, E)\}.$$

The winged-edge data structure was extended in several ways (see [216] for example). A comparative analysis of different data structures of these extensions may be found in [3, 215].

Half-edge

Since, in manifold shells, an edge is bounding two faces, it may be convenient to use two fe-nodes to represent each edge. To each fe-node corresponds a different orientation of the edge and is associated one of the two vertices that bound the edge. These fe-nodes have been used in many data structures and have been called "split-edges", "half-edges", "edge-uses", and so on. These half-edges are usually linked to each other, either directly or through an edge-node so as to capture face-face adjacency [117, 94].

As shown in [3] half-edge data structures may be symbolized by:
Half-edge =

$$\{R, F, L, fe, E, V : R \rightarrow F \rightarrow L \rightarrow fe \overset{1}{\rightarrow} (V, E), E \overset{2}{\rightarrow} fe, V \overset{1}{\rightarrow} fe \overset{1}{\rightarrow} L \overset{1}{\rightarrow} F \overset{1}{\rightarrow} R\},$$

plus redundant pointers from R to all the L, V, E, and S nodes.

Quad-edges

The winged-edge representation was extended by Guibas and Stolfi to subdivisions of orientable surfaces using a quad-edge data structure in [73]. Simple primitive operators were provided to move from edge to edge around face loops and around vertices. Each edge refers to four of its neighbors.

Cell-tuples and V-maps

Brisson [39, 40] uses cell-tuples to extend the face-edge data structure [59, 106] and the quad-edge data structures [73] to higher dimensions. A cell-tuple is a combination of cells of all the dimensions, such that each cell (except the full-dimensional one) is in the boundary of the cell of the next dimension in the cell-tuple. For example, in 3D a cell tuple is defined by selecting a region, one of its faces, one of the edges bounding the face, and a vertex bounding that edge. The SWITCH(k) operator parameterized by the dimension k produces the other tuple that has the same elements, except for the element of dimension k, which is uniquely defined. For example, SWITCH(0) exchanges the two vertices of the edge and SWITCH(1) exchanges the two edges that bound the face and share the vertex. SWITCH is its own inverse. A permutation of SWITCH operators for dimension k and k+1. may be used to order k-cells and (k+1)-cells around (k-1)-cells on a (k+2)-cells. For example, an alternation of SWITCH(1) and SWITCH(2) may be used to visit, the edges and faces of the cone of a shell formed around a vertex.

Independently, Lienhardt [111, 110] defines n-dimensional generalized maps. For manifold objects, both Lienhardt's and Brisson's representations are equivalent.

Extensions to non-manifold boundaries

A technique for extending boundary graphs to non-manifold cases, where the solids have internal structures is based on the use of 3D region nodes, R_i, in the delimitation graphs. Each 3D regions is associated with a well defined subset of the boundary that forms a valid shell, or set of shells. (Typically, for simplicity, the solids are restricted to be connected, although not necessarily simply connected. More than one shell may be needed when the solids have internal holes.)

Dobkin and Laszlo extend the approach of [73] to a subdivision of $\mathbb{R}^3$. They define a facet-edge data structure [59, 106] in which each face F points to other adjacent faces that bound the two regions bounded by F.

The two-cycle requirement for shells of regularized solids, does not allow the use of "non-manifold" boundaries in the larger sense of the word, i.e., boundaries that are not two-cycles, because they have dangling faces or edges or because they define a partitioning of the solid into several connected regions. As mentioned earlier, internal structures may be specified by superimposing on the solid the internal dangling faces and edges.

Mantyla's Half-Edge and Kalay's Hybrid-Edge [117, 94] data structures may be used to represent such dangling faces together with shells of 3D regions.

In the winged-edge representation, to each face-edge-vertex and each edge-vertex delimitation link is associated a link to a face. Thus, the winged-edge data structure has implicit $ev \xrightarrow{1} E$ and $fe \xrightarrow{1} E$ links. Using these auxiliary fe and ev entities as nodes in the graph, Weiler has defined the vertex-edge and the face-edge data structures [209], leading to the radial-edge data structure [210].

The radial-edge data structure explicitly captures how faces are ordered around an edge and how edges are ordered around a face. It does not however provide any information on the radial ordering of dangling face-loops around vertices (except by the indirect use of shells or neighborhood-loop nestings). This vertex-neighborhood ordering problem is important for a consistent traversal of the object's boundary at non-manifold vertices and is addressed in the NOODLES system by Gursoz, Choi, and Prinz [75, 74].

Extensions to higher dimensions

Besides the already mentioned n-dimensional data-structures of [52, 66, 161, 110, 40], approaches to the modeling of n-dimensional sets in delimitative form by adjacency graphs may also be found in [184, 24].

5.2 Constructive representations

We discuss in this subsection the traditional CSG graphs, some variations, and their recent extensions to non-regularized geometric structures.

A Constructive Solid Geometry (CSG) representation defines a recipe for constructing a solid through selective subdivision. The geometric entities used for that subdivision are half-spaces or volume primitives. The operations used are Boolean set-theoretic operations or more precisely their regularized counterparts [148, 145, 199].

Using this recipe as a fundamental representation instead of a boundary graph has many advantages. The non-evaluated representation is always valid and can be easily parameterized. (As discussed earlier, ensuring or even verifying the validity of boundary graphs is expensive.) Editing non-evaluated representation is simple and very efficient; it suffices to change the specification. Non-evaluated representations are less verbose than their evaluated counterparts and lead to considerable storage savings. Finally, many solid modeling algorithms work directly on CSG representations through divide-and-conquer and are numerically more reliable than their counterparts that work on evaluated boundary representations.

Constructive Solid Geometry

CSG solids correspond to set-valued Boolean expressions that combine solids through regularized union, difference, and intersection. Parsing a CSG expression yields a binary tree. Thus, all other non-binary forms have an equivalent binary-tree form.

CSG graphs

In addition to primitive and half-space instantiation and to regularized Boolean operations, solid modelers offer facilities for grouping CSG sub-solids and for moving them together so as to achieve the desired position and orientation. Motions correspond to rigid body transformations, and sometimes to scaling operations. They may be stored as individual nodes in the graph or as sequences of model-modifying operations attached to nodes [156].

When the same sub-solid component, S, is used in several places in a CSG solid, it suffices to represent its CSG tree only once and refer to it several time in the final expression. The position and orientation of each instance of S is computed by combining the effect of all the rigid-body motion transformations that apply to it. The CSG structure is thus a directed acyclic graph. The root node defines the solid. Its internal nodes define Boolean expressions and motion transformations. Its leaves carry the description of the primitives or half-spaces.

N-ary graph

In PADL-2 [42], a binary tree is used where each node corresponds to a Boolean operation between its two child-operands or to the application of its right-child motion to a left-child sub- solid. In GDP [213], n-ary nodes are used that define a simple Boolean expression combining the child-solids. The expression does not contain any parentheses and are simply evaluated from left to right.

Other operations

Given two bounded solids A and B, there are only five non-trivial bounded combinations (i.e. selective subdivisions) of A and B: $A \cup B$, $A \cap B$, $A - B$, $B - A$, and the symmetric difference $A \otimes B$, which is equivalent to $(A \cup B) - (A \cap B)$. The symmetric difference is rarely supported as a single operator, even though it is very convenient for expressing the difference between two sets. In fact, it is not even necessary to support all three (union, intersection, difference) operators. For example, if the universe ($\mathbb{R}^3$) is considered as a primitive, it is possible to express the intersection through the union and difference. However, for convenience, all three operations are usually available.

Positive form

Each CSG graph may be expressed in a positive form, precisely defined in [166].

Thinking in terms of the positive form permits a better understanding of most CSG algorithms, because it considerably reduces the number of cases that must be analyzed. (The positive form does not contain any difference operators, which have been pushed down to the primitives using de Morgan's laws.)

Positive forms have proven valuable for studying properties of CSG representations, for simplifying their proofs and for writing algorithms for CSG. Note that the positive forms never need to be computed explicitly. In [166], the author provides algorithms that use the original CSG graph to process its positive form. It is based on a recursive routine for graph traversal that passes to child-nodes their sign. (The sign of the root is positive and it changes as one goes down the graph each time the right child of a difference operator is reached.)

Positive Alternated N-Ary Graph

An even more systematic way of viewing a CSG graph is in the form of a positive alternated n-ary graph (PANAGraph), where, going from the root down to the leaves, one encounters a union-node that is the union of all its children, then an intersection-node that is the intersection of all its children, then a union node, and so on.

The PANAGraph form explicitly captures all the commutativity and associativity properties of Boolean operators and provides a canonical form–the order in which the binary Boolean operations are preformed at a given node is not important.

Furthermore, the depth of a PANAGraph indicates the depth of the stack necessary for a standard evaluation of the Boolean expression. This depth may be important when classifying points in parallel against the CSG object, or when computing the boundary through incremental boundary evaluation, as discussed in the next section.

Variations on CSG

Many variations of CSG graphs have been developed either because they are produced by some algorithm, because they simplify some computation, or because they provide a convenience to the user. These variations are in general a restriction of the CSG form. Some notable ones are reviewed here.

Disjunctive sum

A CSG expression may be converted into disjunctive sum, i.e. union of products of the original primitives or of their complements. The disjunctive form is a PANAGraph of depth two achieved by duplicating primitive instances (a primitive that appeared once in the original CSG graph may appear in many products).

Because the disjunctive form only requires a stack of depth 2, it has been used for evaluating CSG graphs in parallel in the context of rendering with two or three depth-buffers [72, 158].

Another advantage of the disjunctive form is that products are intersections of primitives or of their complements. Therefore, for linear half-space primitives, products are convex polyhedra, and thus the tree may be expressed as the union of possibly overlapping convex polyhedra.

Unfortunately, in the worst case, the size of the disjunctive form grows exponentially in the number of primitives of the original graph.

TIPS

An interesting variation of the two-stages PANAGraph was used in the TIPS system [134, 133]. It is based on a difference between two n-ary union nodes.

This formalism prevented users from "plugging" a hole, and thus was extended to more general forms in the subsequent versions of the TIPS system.

Repeated difference

Some techniques for Boundary-to-CSG conversions [214] generate a binary CSG tree that has only difference operators. The left child of each difference-operator-node is a convex hull that contains the solid represented by the node. Clipping the tree to a given depth by replacing some nodes by their left-child primitives (convex hulls) yields a simplification of the object where some details (cavities or bosses) have been removed. Unfortunately, this scheme does not always lead to a simplified boundary representation of the original object.

A generalization of this technique may be found in [142], where the bounds need not be convex hulls and may in fact be represented as unions of simpler shapes.

BSP-trees

A Binary Space Partitioning (BSP) tree [129, 128] is an interesting variation of the binary CSG trees where every primitive is a half-space. In CSG trees or graphs, the half-spaces are associated with the leaves. In BSP trees, half-spaces are associated with internal nodes.

Let H be a closed half-space associated with an internal node N that has two children L and R (for left and right respectively). The pointset pN associated with N may be defined in CSG terms as: $pN = (H \cap pL) \cup (pR - H)$, where pL and pR define the pointsets of L and R.

The half-spaces define a partitioning of the entire space into quasi-disjoint cells that are regularized products of half-spaces or of their complements. Each leaf (called cell) corresponds to such a product. (When linear half-spaces are used, leaves correspond to possibly empty convex polyhedra.) The solid is defined by selecting leaf-cells. The selection is indicated by marking some of the leaves as "active".

A CSG tree may be converted into BSP form by factoring its normal disjunctive form. The normal disjunctive form is the union of products that represent mutually disjoint regions and that are expressed as the intersection of *all* the primitive half-spaces, in their positive or complemented form. A much more complicated procedure for CSG-to-BSP conversion is provided in [128]. It removes redundant half-spaces and cells but does not produce an optimal BSP representation.

CSG extensions

CSG representations have been extended by adding new operators. A few examples are listed below.

CNRG

An extension of CSG graphs to n-dimensional objects composed of disjoint non-regularized regions is proposed in [165]. CNRGs are graphs that combine primitive objects using a modified version of the set theoretic Boolean operations and topological operations, such as closure and interior. As for CSG, the leaves of CNRG graphs are primitive shapes (not restricted to be r-sets) and the nodes correspond to operators. The operators preserve the decomposition of their arguments into separate regions and thus return a collection of regions that may have been partitioned according to the regions of the arguments.

Sweeps

Primitives that are extrusions of 2D regions may be converted into pure CSG form by providing a CSG expression for the 2D regions and extruding it into 3D [207]. The extrusion process is simple, except where the 3D region swept by the 2D area during the extrusion self-intersects. (Extrusion distributes over union, but not over intersection or difference.)

It may be convenient to preserve, in the CSG graph, the original description in terms of extrusions. The classification algorithms that work directly off the CSG graph and are described in the next section can easily be adapted to such a representation.

Minkowski sums, offsetting, and blending

Other operations, such as Minkowski sums [69], offsetting [163] and blending [155, 218] have been suggested for inclusion in CSG. Their support however is considerably complicated by the lack of techniques for distributing the computation over their arguments.

The power of the CSG representation is its suitability for supporting divide-and-conquer techniques. For example, a point may be classified against a solid defined in CSG as a Boolean operation on two arguments by simply classifying the point against the two arguments and then combining the classification according to the nature of the Boolean operator. Classifying a point against the two arguments of a Minkowski sum does not help classify it against the sum.

Split

It may be convenient to use a small portion of a surface to separate a connected solid into two parts, only one of which is of interest and should be kept. Such a split operation, cannot in general be simply expressed in semi-analytic form. Furthermore, a split may be invalid if the face does not separate the solid. For example, the portion of the surface may not be large enough to split the solids. Nevertheless, this operation is of considerable convenience to the users and is available in some commercial modellers.

Unfortunately, the presence of split nodes in a CSG graph impedes the divide-and-conquer approach and complicates algorithms that operate directly on CSG by requiring that the boundary of objects resulting from split operations be precomputed.

5.3 State of the art conclusion on representations

Although a solid may be represented by simply enumerating its faces, a number of data structures have been developed for representing faces efficiently and for capturing their adjacency and some ordering information that is of use for visiting adjacent faces. Many of these data-structures are limited to manifold solids. Some provide a framework for representing the adjacency between faces in non-manifold shells. Some representations even support internal decomposition of n-dimensional solids.

Since ordering information may not always be available, especially when curved surfaces, or their higher-dimensional counterparts are used, it is preferable to separate the delimitation information from the ordering information. Delimitation information is conveniently captured by an SGC graph, where, in addition to the geometric description of the supporting sub-manifold, to each element or cell C (vertex, edge, face, 3D region,...) one associates references (arcs) to all the elements that bound C and that are bounded by C. Ordering information, when available, may be captured in a structure superimposed on SGCs as groupings and through NAIL tables.

Boundary representations are impractical for design, since it is difficult to parameterize them and to ensure their validity. Constructive formulations are preferable during design, even if boundary representations have to be evaluated ultimately.

Constructive representations have many forms, all based on a Boolean expression that combines primitive shapes or half-spaces through a selective subdivision. All these forms are equivalent to a binary CSG tree generated by parsing their Boolean expression. However, specific forms offer computational or other advantages for specific applications.

Extensions of CSG to support topological operations and Boolean operations that preserve internal structures have been proposed in the form of CNRGs.

Extensions to other operations have been proposed, but suffer from the lack of a formulation that can express a property of a CSG node in terms of properties of its operands. Therefore, these extensions are only useful for holding a recipe, and not for supporting calculations directly on CSG.

6 Fundamental Algorithms

Algorithms used in solid modeling may be grouped into: set membership classification, property evaluation, and representation conversion. We discuss some set membership classification and property evaluation algorithms for both CSG and Boundary representations. Then review some techniques for representation conversion.

6.1 Set Membership Classification

Given a solid S and a set C, a set membership classification of C against S partitions C into three subsets: C in the interior of S, C on the boundary of S, and C in the interior of the complement of S [195].

We consider the cases where C is a point, a line or curve-segment, and a face. Cases where C is a solid are treated in the subsection on representation conversion.

Point-membership classification

Algorithms that classify points against solids are the foundation of solid modeling because their existence guarantees the validity of the representation and because they are needed to support most applications.

Good examples of the applications of point membership classification (PMC) may be found in graphics [164] and in mass properties calculations [108, 107].

They are also used to classify higher-dimensional pointsets against solids when these pointsets do not intersect the boundary of the solid.

Classification with respect to boundary representations

The point-containment problem may be addressed in several ways. The two most popular techniques are **ray-casting** and *integration.*

The ray-casting approach works as follows. To test whether a point P lies inside the solid represented by its bounding faces, one typically constructs a semi-line L starting from P to infinity in an arbitrary direction and then counts the parity of the number of times the line crosses a face of the solid. When L hits an edge or when it is tangent to one of the supporting surfaces, a careful treatment of special cases may be necessary. On the other hand, it may be more appropriate to choose another line L that does not run into any singular situation. Even parity of the number of line/face intersections implies that the point lies outside of the solid. Odd parity implies that the point lies inside. (A point on a face is by definition on the solid.)

The question remains: "How does one find intersections of L with the faces of the solid?" For polyhedral models, many efficient approaches for point-in-face tests have been proposed (see for example [93, 105, 80, 84]), however, for curved faces, the problem is more complex.

A simplistic version of a commonly used solution proceeds as follows. For each face F, compute the intersections of L with the surface S supporting F. If the line is in general (singularity free) position, these intersections will be composed of isolated points. For each such intersection point Q, construct a curve segment C on S from Q to a point Q' whose classification (as "in" or "out") with respect to F is known. Then, compute all the intersections R of C with the edges bounding F and use the parity of the total number of intersections to decide whether Q is in F or not. For example, if we find two intersections and Q' is out of F, then Q is also out of F.

An alternate technique uses edge and face orientation and neighborhood information. It constructs a curve segment C on S that joins Q with any point on the bounding edges of F. Then one computes the first intersections of C with all the edges of F and finds H, the closest one to Q along C. From the neighborhood of the edge intersected by C at H and from the orientation of both C and the curve containing H, one deduces the classification of Q. For example, if at H the curve C starting at Q leaves the F, then Q is inside F.

We must still determine how to compute the intersections of C with the edges of F. Again, one first computes the intersections of the supporting curves of both C and F. Then, for each intersection, one compares its parameter values (with respect to both curves) to the corresponding parameter intervals defining C and the edge of F. If both parameter values are inside the corresponding intervals, the point is a valid intersection.

In some cases, a diminishing convex-hull property may be used to numerically compute the intersection of two curve segments directly, without first intersecting the entire curves.

Although many subtleties were left out, this long description should convince the reader of the complexity of the most basic function that must be provided by a solid modeler, namely a test that establishes whether a point is inside the solid or not. Many algorithms that perform cross-sections or Boolean operations use such tests extensively.

The integration approaches are based on the evaluation of a function F that yields one value for points inside the object and a different value for points outside.

In 2D, such formulae are variations of the winding number formula. For example, one can count how many times one circles the point while traversing a loop in the appropriate direction.

In 3D, an interesting formula was developed by Franklin at RPI (see [127]). F is simply computed by summing expressions derived from the local geometry of all the face-edge-vertex triplets for which the vertex bounds the edge and the edge bounds the face. The interest of this formula is that it does not require any topological information.

The order in which points are tested for inclusion against the boundary elements of various dimensions is important.

The classification of a point against a solid or against a cell of a non-regularized structure may involve the classification of that point against the boundary elements of the solid or of the cell. For example, to classify a point against an SGC, one first classifies if against all the vertices, then against all the edges, then against all the faces, and so on. Point/cell classification is simplified, because, by this bottom-up approach, the point cannot lie in the boundary of a cell, otherwise it would have been classified as belonging to a lower-dimensional cell. Thus, point/cell classification always returns a binary answer. Point/cell classification for faces and higher-dimensional cells is performed as discussed above. The same approach may be used when classifying a point against a solid.

Since in this process points have to be tested against points, curves, and surfaces, it may be advantageous to organize the geometric tests in an order that does not follow the bottom-up approach. For example, to classify a point P against a face F, the bottom-up approach would first compare P to the vertices of F, then to the curves supporting the edges of F, and finally to the surface S supporting F. If a match is found at an early stage, comparisons of P with curves and the surface S may be avoided. On the other hand, if the point does not lie on S, the early tests could be avoided by first testing P against S, which has greater discriminatory power than the vertices. Thus, it is preferable to perform the geometric tests against the supporting entities top-down, that is, before testing whether P lies on vertex, we test whether it lies on the surface and the curves that contain the vertex.

Classification with respect to CSG representations

PMC algorithms for CSG graphs are usually written in recursive divide-and-conquer form. Before anything is computed, the recursion reaches the primitives and tests the point to be classified against them.

Point/primitive classification is accomplished easily, because commonly used primitives, in their "natural" positions are defined in a way that simplifies this test, as discussed in Section 2. When a primitive is transformed through a rigid body transformation, classifying the point against the transformed primitive is done by applying the inverse of the transformation to the point and classifying the result against the primitive in its natural position.

Once point/primitive classification results are known, they are combined through the original Boolean expression that defines the CSG graph. Special processing based on neighborhood combinations may be necessary for points that lie on boundaries of several primitives [152].

In fact not all primitives need to be tested. For example, if the point is out of primitive A, it is also out of the composed subsolid $A \cap B$. Therefore, the recursive algorithms would first test the point against A. If the result is out, then the recursive call can return OUT without visiting the subtree B. If the result is IN, then B must be visited and its result returned.

Ray-casting

Ray-casting methods have been extensively used for graphics. They are a special case of curve/solid set membership classification.

Ray-casting on Boundary representations

Part of the line/face classification was already discussed in the previous subsection. However, it was assumed that the line did not meet any vertex. A more complete treatment of the singular situations where a ray meets a vertex is offered in [194] for the case of line/polygon classification.

Many papers have since appeared on the same topic. The main problem is to correctly interpret situations where the line intersects a vertex and establish whether the line changes classification by traversing the boundary at the vertex or whether the line simply touches the boundary. Since the vertex may be adjacent to more than two edges, the case-by-case analyses available throughout the literature yield somewhat over complicated algorithms.

A simpler approach was developed by P. Borrel and the author (and probably independently by a large number of practitioners too busy to publish such details). It splits all the edges adjacent to the vertex into three sets: the edges on the left of the ray, the edges on the right, and the edges parallel to the ray. Odd parities of the number of entries in the first two sets imply changes in the classification of the left and right neighborhoods of the ray. In turn these neighborhoods imply he classification of each ray-segment.

Techniques for ray classification against 3D polyhedra may be mapped into a series of ray/plane intersections followed by point-in-polygon or ray/polygon classifications (see for example [95]).

Their extension to curved objects requires line/surface intersection capabilities and point/face classification on curved surfaces, which may sometimes be performed in parametric 2D space, if the parameters of a 3D point on the face can be computed (see Section 2).

Ray-casting on CSG representations

Ray-casting against CSG is performed as follows [168]. The ray is intersected with primitive boundaries and the parameter intervals along the ray that correspond to segments of the ray inside the primitives are combined through one-dimensional regularized Boolean operations. The resulting intervals represent the intersection of the ray with the solid.

Specific improvements to these techniques for graphic applications where many rays are to be classified are discussed in [41, 126, 86, 87, 90].

Surface trimming

The intersection of a surface with a solid is important for computing cross-sections. It also is used in some algorithms for performing Boolean operations between solids.

Surface trimming by a Boundary representations

The intersection of a surface S with a 3D solid R may be computed in its delimitative form by computing the intersections of S with each faces F of R. Face/surface intersection may be computed by intersecting S with the surface supporting F, and then by classifying the resulting curve against F, as described above.

To trim a face F' subset of S using a solid R, one can compute the intersection F" of with S with R and then perform the appropriate Boolean operation between F' and F" in 2D.

Surface trimming by a CSG representations

A trimmed portion of a surface may be represented in an extended CSG form, simply as a CSG node that has the surface and the CSG representation of the solid as children [172].

An evaluated, delimitative representation may be obtained by distributing the intersection with the surface over the Boolean operators, performing the intersections of the surface with all the primitive volumes, and then combining the results by performing a CSG-to-Boundary conversion in 2D.

A more efficient approach generates tentative edges, as the intersections of the surface with the primitives' boundaries, and classifies them against the solid.

6.2 Property evaluation

The properties computed from solid models may be categorized into numerical and topological.

Integral properties, such as volumetric calculations may be performed either on Boundary representations [127] or directly on CSG [108, 107].

Topological properties on the other hand are very difficult to compute directly from CSG. For example, to test if a bounded solid represented by its boundary is empty, it suffices to check whether the boundary is empty. If the solid is represented in CSG, the test require an expensive partial boundary evaluation [198, 166].

Other characteristics, such as connectedness and numbers of handles may be computed by graph traversals and by the use of Euler characteristic on boundary representations and even on CSG [23].

6.3 Representation conversion

The most important representation conversion process interprets Boolean specifications and computes a boundary representation. Thus, it converts from CSG to Boundary. Conversions in the other directions and into and from other representations are also briefly reviewed.

CSG-to-boundary conversion

Boundary evaluation algorithms are complex. They can be articulated around vertices [116], around edges [152], or faces [104, 166, 178]. In any case, they are based on the generate-and-classify paradigm, where candidate elements (points, edge-segments, or face-cells) are first generated through geometric intersection and subdivision, and then classified.

Boundary evaluation may be performed *incrementally* [80] or *directly,* i.e., in a non incremental manner [152].

The incremental method merges boundary models two-by-two, starting at the leaves of the tree and finishing at the root. The boundary evaluation of a node starts only when the boundaries of the two children are available. A recent overview of a few algorithms for performing Boolean operations between two solids represented in boundary form may be found in [204]. Details are available in [36, 152, 104, 117, 178, 80] and also in [95, 192].

The direct method produces one-by-one the candidate elements and then classifies them against the entire CSG graph. References to the origin of these entities are preserved throughout these calculations, so as to simplify the reconstruction of the final adjacency graph. For example, candidate edge-elements may be connected edge segments obtained by intersecting pairs of supporting surfaces and then segmenting the resulting curves at their intersections with all other surfaces. Keeping track of the surfaces that intervene in these intersections is crucial for reconstructing faces from the selected segments.

The direct method may require more calculations than the incremental method, because it may intersect two surfaces that bound two primitives A and B, generate their intersection curves, segment them, and classify the segments; even though these surfaces are not supporting any faces of the parent nodes of A and B. On the other hand, direct methods avoid a lot of data manipulation.

On the other hand, the incremental method may require a large amount of intermediate storage, even when the final result is an empty solid. For example, when the root node defines the empty intersection between two complex solids, the incremental method must first compute the boundary of both sub-solids, before starting the evaluation of the final result. Furthermore, before the boundary of the second sub-solid is computed, we must compute and store the boundary of the first sub-solid and also the boundaries of the two children of the second sub-solid, and so on. We may need to store a number of intermediate boundary representation equal to the height of the CSG tree minus one.

A solution based on Active Zones [166] combines the advantages of both methods. It does not require unnecessary storage, because it uses the generate-and-test paradigm. It avoids redundant calculations because it classifies the candidate sets against the active zone and can stop the classification process as soon as the candidate set is rejected.

Extensions of the Boolean operations to non-regularized solids or to r-sets with internal structures can be found in [85, 202, 221, 161, 74, 172] These algorithms may be best studied in terms of the three primitive operations: *subdivision, selection,* and *simplification* introduced in [161].

Subdivision takes two objects, each composed of one or several mutually disjoint regions (or cells), and subdivides each region of one object with respect to all the regions of the other object and vice versa. Subdividing a region A with respect to another region B amounts to splitting A into two disjoint parts: $A \cap B$ and $A - B$. If the primitives geometric entities are required to be connected, regions may be further subdivided into connected homogeneously-dimensional cells.

Selection simply selects regions of interest using Boolean formulae or topological filters. For example, to represent $A - B$ the subdivision of A may have produced a number of cells that represent the full dimensional regions of $A - B$ and $A \cap B$ as well as their lower-dimensional boundaries. For a regularized difference, higher-dimensional cells of $A - B$ and their boundaries will be selected.

Simplification removes internal structures by deleting non selected regions or cells, and by joining or merging cells, whenever possible.

Booleans in higher dimensions

Techniques for performing Boolean operations on boundary representations in higher dimensions are beginning to emerge [141, 66, 24, 161]. They are based on a recursive formulation that reduces the problem to lower dimensions.

These publications either assume a linear domain or ignore the problem of the geometric computation of the intersections and ordering of hyper-surfaces.

Boundary to CSG

The inverse process of computing semi-algebraic expressions for solids represented by their boundary is also very important, because it may provide more efficient algorithms. Research is flourishing, at least in the 2D case [11, 207, 139, 181]. In 3D, variations of the BSP tree have been used [58, 100, 142].

Fleshing out lower-dimensional boundaries

In order to support user-friendly input techniques several methods for generating solid 3D models from drawings [25] and from 3D wireframes [118] have been proposed. All of them have to deal with a lack of information that implies ambiguity.

The approaches must either generate all possible interpretations and let the user select the desired one, or use heuristics (sometimes called AI techniques or expert systems) to guess a preferred interpretation. The first (systematic) approach overwhelms the user with thousands of choices. The second often annoys the user by guessing wrong. Clearly, a compromise that offers to the users a formal scheme for disambiguating the interpretation is needed.

CSG or Boundary to octree

Procedures that convert from boundary or from CSG to octree representations are based on a fundamental step that classifies a cube (octree cell) against the solid.

When the solid is represented in boundary form, the classification is performed by detecting the intersections of the object's faces with the cube.

When the solid is represented in CSG, one can use a ball B that encloses the cube and check whether the ball intersects the boundary of the cube or if it is inside or outside of the solid. From the classification of the ball one can decide whether to stop the octree subdivision, and if so, whether the cube is inside the solid or outside.

To classify the ball B against the CSG solid S [108, 107], one can classify its center against a version of the original CSG tree in which primitives have been grown or shrunk. If all the half-spaces that appear in positive form in the tree are grown by a Minkowski sum with B and the half-spaces that appear in negative form are shrunk, one obtains a solid that contains the Minkowski sum of S and B [155]. If the center of B is outside of this grown solid, then B does not intersect the boundary [114] and lies outside of S. The inverse (shrinking) operation is used to test if the ball lies inside S. If both tests fail, then B and thus the cube may intersect the boundary of S and the cube will be further subdivided until the appropriate resolution is reached. Inner and outer bounds may be used [108, 107] instead of shrunk or grown primitives. Such bounds may easily be obtained for simple primitives by changing their dimension-parameters. For example, given a cylinder C=CYL(R,L) of radius R and length L, an outer bound containing the grown version of C by a distance D is obtained by CYL(R+d,L+2D) translated by D along its axis. Similar expressions are available for blocks, cones, and tori [155].

6.4 Programming interfaces to geometric libraries

The interaction between the domain-dependent geometric utilities and the higher-level algorithms that compose the geometric primitives should be implemented through a well defined programming interface, so that extensions to the geometric domain may be carried out without affecting the higher-level algorithms.

Clearly, the interface should support commands for generating geometric primitive entities, for computing their intersections, and for testing points-inclusions. It is however not clear how the intersection should be reported. Suppose that the geometric library is invoked to compute the intersection of two cylinders. The result could be the empty set, a single connected closed curve, two disjoint closed curves, one or two infinite lines, or a more complicated structure involving arcs and points (for example the four elliptic arcs and the two vertices). More combinations are possible with more complex surfaces. Often the intersection routine returns the address of a buffer containing the data and a type variable indicating what is the nature of the intersection and thus implicitly what the buffer contains. Such an approach requires that the buffer processing code be part of the high-level application algorithms.

To avoid such specialization, a uniform scheme must be used. The Selective Geometric Complexes [161] provide a solution. Intersections are returned as adjacency graphs linking entities such as points and curves.

In order to construct a representation of the subdivision of space that identifies the connected elements it may be necessary to establish the relative position and ordering of curves and surfaces, as discussed in Section 2.

6.5 Conclusions on state of the art algorithms

Numerous algorithms for CSG and boundary representations have been developed. The most ambitious ones address the problem of converting from CSG to boundary. The most popular techniques perform this conversion incrementally by merging boundary representations two at a time. Direct techniques based on active zones reduce the storage requirement of the incremental method without adding redundant calculations. The incremental method has been recently extended to non-regularized objects.

Besides the limitations of some of these algorithms to a particular geometric domain and their sensitivity to numerical errors, the major problem is performance. Most of these algorithms perform an incredible amount of computation when compared to the size of their output. Most of them are based on the "generate-and-test" paradigm, and simply spend their time generating, testing, and rejecting. Performance enhancement methods briefly discussed in the next section play a crucial role in eliminating a large fraction of these unnecessary tests.

7 Reliability and Performance

Despite a high level of functionality and attractive front-end, a solid modeller may fail on the market place if its performance is insufficient or if it does not behave as expected and produces wrong results.

7.1 Reliability and numerical inaccuracy

Solid representations are most of the time invalid (due to numerical inaccuracies) and algorithms that operate on them must take decisions based on approximate calculations.

The solid modeling process may be viewed as a succession of *approximations,* which lead to inaccurate numerical results.

Real shape (for example an egg) is first *idealized* into perfect form (for example a perfectly symmetrical egg with a smooth surface).

No mathematical *formulation* may be available for the perfect form model. Thus, an approximate model is used for which a mathematical formulation exists. (For example, the surface of the egg may be approximated by a revolute extrusion of a cubic curve segment.)

The mathematical formulation may not be exactly representable in a particular solid modeller and thus will be approximated by a *simplified* form. (For example, the revolute surface will be replaced with a sphere!)

The simplified form is *represented* in the computer using coefficients whose approximate values are computed and stored in floating point format. For example, the radius and the three coordinates of the sphere's center will be stored as floating points numbers.

Integral properties of the represented solid will be *evaluated* on the approximated data using approximate numeric methods.

Inconsistency between geometry and structure

The topological relations captured in a boundary representation may not reflect the geometry and relative position of the primitive elements they refer to. We have already mentioned the cases of non-coplanar vertices of a planar face and the cases of multiple representations of edges. We have also discussed the problems of detecting self intersecting boundaries. When the topological and the geometric representations disagree, a decision must often be made to resolve the conflict. Since the geometry is approximate, it is reasonable to assume that some geometry not too different from the one represented in the modeler exists and agrees with the topology represented in the boundary graph [121]. However, very often this geometry may not be available within the geometric domain of the modeler. It is not even clear whether such a geometry always exists in a particular case.

Simulation of simplicity [62] avoids processing singular geometric configurations by consistently ordering expressions that are numerically equal. This considerably simplifies the code by alleviating the need to special cases. However, when used with floating point calculations, the approach suffers from possible logical inconsistencies. Furthermore, it systematically destroys singular topological configuration, which may be important for the user.

Logical decisions on numerical tests

Most solid modeling systems use a floating point representation of geometric entities. For example, a parametric curve may be represented in terms of coefficients by a set of floating point numbers. The coordinates of a point on the curve are obtained by evaluating analytical expressions and are thus approximate. The situation is even worse for points of intersection between three surfaces or between a curve and a surface, because the approximations of these points, computed in floating point arithmetic, do not lie on the starting surfaces or curves. Epsilon-based comparisons are often used to force equalities of approximated expressions. For example, if a point lies less than epsilon from a surface, it will be classified as "on" the surface. Unfortunately, no technique has yet been reported for using epsilon-based tests consistently within a solid modeler. Consequently, decisions taken in one place in the algorithm may logically contradict decisions taken elsewhere. This inconsistency is probably the most difficult and recurring problem in solid modeling [30].

Some commercial systems rely on the user for avoiding, or correcting, errors emanating from floating point round-offs. The possibility of fixing the system's errors implies the capability of detecting an error without loosing the data or crashing the system. Avoiding such errors may be impossible, since they occur during geometric calculations on internal representations that may be unknown to the user. For example, the top faces of two different cubes may be clearly disjoint, but their supporting surfaces, although differentiated by an epsilon-based test, may have a common intersection line so far away that attempting to represent it will cause an overflow. Of course, such simple errors are easily fixed, and indeed have been fixed in most systems (see [204] for a detailed discussion of the 2D problem). Nevertheless, many other, more complex situations have not been predicted and may jeopardize the reliability of the system at the most inopportune moments.

Techniques for coping with numerical inaccuracies

Several attempts have recently been made to resolve the numerical issue:

Logical inference

Organize the algorithms so that decisions that can be easily derived by logic from other results are not computed numerically. For example, when three points of a rectangular face lie on a plane, the fourth point needs not be tested; it must also lie on that plane. Unfortunately, the logical dependency between decisions taken during standard solid modeling operations, such as performing Boolean operations on boundary representations, are too complex and no technique is known to eliminate the redundant numerical calculations [81].

Error bounds

Use interval arithmetic to derive a bound on the error made during numerical calculations [4]. If a decision can be made using the error bounds, logical errors may be avoided [178]. Unfortunately, straightforward interval arithmetic techniques lead to very pessimistic bounds and are often useless for logical decisions [177].

Extended precision

Use extended precision rational number representation to perform all calculations exactly [131, 26, 96]. Language of the LISP family automatically support calculations on extended precision rationals, but their automatic invocation of a simplification procedure after each operation makes things unnecessarily slow. Even without this penalty, the precision required for 3D geometric modeling operations reaches levels that make the exact approach impractical in terms of space and speed. Furthermore, rational numbers are insufficient for representing exact rotations and for computing intersections of non-planar surfaces.

Symbol manipulations

Symbol manipulation techniques have been used for computing intersections of simple quadric surfaces [132], but they are far too slow for use in an interactive environment.

7.2 Performance enhancements

Techniques for improving the performance of solid modeling algorithms are based on a priori elimination of a large number of candidate elements without having to generate and test them.

They can use bounds on the geometric elements [21, 47], spatial localization [68, 219, 70, 191, 220], or structural localization [196, 200, 166, 77].

Hardware assist for interactive graphics

Parallel machines and dedicated architectures provide additional support for graphics [89, 71, 72, 119, 99, 63] and for solid modeling calculations [222, 63]. Algorithms that exploit these new possibilities are beginning to emerge [88, 12, 164, 135, 167, 185].

Concluding remarks on accuracy and performance

Despite much progress, the problem of numerical accuracy remains largely unsolved and several research groups are currently working on it. Approaches that avoid singularities lead to a simplification of the code at the expense of the user's convenience. Approaches that force singularities are preferable, but require more complex algorithms. Both approaches are unreliable, unless extended precision or symbol manipulation techniques are used. These are both computationally expensive and limited to simple domains.

The performance issues are being addressed extensively through localization techniques (space-grids, boxing) and through improved hardware support (parallelism, dedicated graphic hardware). As the performance improves, the demand for the increased capability to generate and process huge models will emphasize the importance of reducing the asymptotic worst case complexity of the fundamental algorithms. But for the time being, even a 50is an achievement, at least as far as users are concerned.

8 Construction and Editing Facilities

The interaction between a user and a solid modeling system typically involves incremental editing. The user can invoke operations, select entities, and specify parameters. The system updates the model and provides visual feedback.

Solid modelers offer an impressive set of facilities for constructing and editing points, curves, and even surfaces. Unfortunately, these low-level utilities are often too primitive for editing solids. Higher-level operations are more difficult to integrate in solid modeling, because they must preserve the validity of the representation and yet offer sufficient flexibility.

Finally, editing commands to fix one problem may result in shape modifications that create again a previously fixed problem. Constraint-based modeling and procedural descriptions may offer a partial solution.

8.1 Extending CSG operators

It is impractical for humans to specify boundary representations by enumerating the faces that bound the solid. One would have to provide a description of all the surfaces supporting the faces and of their bounding edges. Therefore, solid models are often specified through higher level operations that combine predefined parametric volume primitives.

A particularly useful set of operations are the Boolean union, intersection, and difference, which are not only powerful for defining solids, but also for modeling the effect of several manufacturing operations and for testing the correctness of the design or of a manufacturing process. For example, subtraction is commonly used to design features, such as pockets, but is also used to simulate material removal through a machining process. Intersection is important for testing interference (if the intersection of two solids is empty, they are disjoint).

The primitive solids typically used for solid modeling are simple parametric shapes such as blocks, spheres, cylinders, and so on. They may be arbitrarily positioned and oriented in space and are combined by Boolean expressions to form sub-solids, which in turn may be recursively combined to form the desired solid.

The main advantage of the CSG representation is that it can be easily edited and that it is parameterized, and hence corresponds to a family of shapes that are always valid.

However, Boolean operations on a limited set of primitive solids are insufficient for modeling many parts. As mentioned in Section 3, other operations, (such as Minkowski sums, general sweeps, offsetting and blending) should also be supported.

For solid modeling, these operations must be guaranteed to transform a valid solid into another valid solid and must offer a clear semantics and convenient parameterization, so that the user may predict their effect and specify the correct parameter values.

The difficulty of specifying the shape of fillets and blends near their ends or when more than two surfaces are involved is a good example of the limitation of a low-level interface. The user should be able to specify smoothness and maximal curvature constraints and the system should provide an acceptable solution or guide the user through an interactive exploration of the solution space. Unfortunately, today's technology is still only focused on the generation of the individual geometric entities needed for these operations, and it is the users' responsibility to ensure that the geometric elements provide a topologically and geometrically acceptable solution.

8.2 Interactive editing

Besides the trivial motion and scaling operations, and the less trivial deformations of space [32], a boundary model may be edited by changing its adjacency graph or the parameters in the representation of its geometric entities. Low-level editing operations that change the adjacency graph while maintaining its validity are provided through Euler operations [61, 115]. However, the use of these operations does not guarantee compatibility between the geometry and the topology; nor even the geometric validity of the boundary representation. Therefore, boundary operations should be edited only through operations that transform valid solids into valid solids. Some techniques for developing localized version of such operations that edit features are proposed in [158].

An alternate approach for supporting safe editing operations is the use of a procedural model. CSG graphs are procedural models, because they specify the nature, order, and parameters of operations that should be executed in order to create the model. However, CSG graphs may only be edited by changing their structure or the values of their parameters (dimensions of primitive solids or coefficients of the motions applied to them). These parameters may fail to provide natural "handles" through which the users could define how the model should be altered. Techniques based on dimensional constraints may be used to offer users a considerable flexibility in the choice of parameters for a model [113, 112, 138]. However, these systems must face the delicate problem of solving systems of simultaneous constraints and of providing guidance to users in correcting incompatible or under-specified systems.

Instead of formulating the parameters of the model as variables in a system of constraints [188, 189, 31, 130, 8], a system can offer techniques for editing sequences of *modifying procedures* [156, 159, 160].

In the MAMOUR system [159], sequences of operations (steps) are used without distinction between steps that instantiate primitive solid; steps that specify Boolean and other operations; and steps that define or modify the parameters used by subsequent operations. During incremental editing, users have the choice between (1) inserting a new step in the middle or at the end of the sequence and (2) editing the parameters and types of previously defined operations.

In [156], modifying operations were distinguished from the usual shape-creating CSG operation as follows. To each node N of a CSG graph was associated a list of modifying operations. These operations would change the location of any grouping of instances of primitives or sub-solids spanned by the CSG graph of N. The evaluation of the graph is performed bottom up, as usual, in a recursive form. The initial position of each primitive instance is first computed for the two children of the node. Then, for motion-nodes the new positions and orientations of the primitives in the expression of N are computed. Finally the list of modifying operations is traversed and each operation executed. Each operation refers to a group of instances of primitive or sub-solids. Executing an operation moves all these instances by a rigid body transformation. The instances moved together need not be grouped at any particular node of the CSG. The incremental motions are specified using geometric measures and constraints on distances and angles that achieve specific configurations between the curved surfaces that bound the primitives.

8.3 High-level vocabulary

The use of geometric features [180] provides a high level vocabulary for specifying incremental modifications. For example, details such as slots, pockets, or bosses, may be created by invoking a feature-making procedure and by providing the appropriate parameters. Modifications of the model and the verification of its validity may also be easily expressed in terms of features. For example, one may wish to change the depth of a pocket, or test whether the hole is a "through-hole" or not.

Features provide a domain dependent abstract description–or view–of a model. For example, a list of machining features with their types and parameters is a suitable part description for planning a manufacturing process. However, manufacturing features need not correspond to design features and may have to be identified a posteriori, either by the user (manufacturing engineer) or automatically.

Operations that create additive or subtractive volume features, such as bosses or slots, simplify the computer-aided design of mechanical parts. Surface features, whether extracted automatically or selected interactively, group functionally related boundary elements, and thus provide an expedient interface between CAD systems and analysis or manufacturing applications. Both types of features must be supported in a solid modeller. Unfortunately, surface features are defined in terms of a particular boundary representation and their definition may not be of any use when the parameters of a model have been altered and a new boundary representation has been derived. Since it is impractical to ask the user to select the faces that define each surface feature each time a parameter is changed, and since AI techniques for automatically extracting surface features from their functional description are not yet reliable, *persistent representations* of surface features in parametric models are necessary. A semi-algebraic expression for face of CSG models is used in [147] to define features used for specifying dimensions.

8.4 Graphic input

Graphic input is commonly used for selecting boundary elements or even primitives in a CSG model. Graphic input has also been used for specifying singular relative positions and orientations between geometric entities [5, 22, 201] and even for specifying Boolean expressions of CSG objects [217, 201].

Graphics provides the most efficient user interface, however purely graphic techniques for constructing parameterized models are still in their infancy and a graphic language is needed for expressing general relations and constraints.

8.5 Concluding remarks on user-interfaces

Since design is based on incremental editing, it is best supported through the editing of constructive and procedural models. Surface and volume features as well as geometric constraints provide a convenient high-level vocabulary for such editing. However, in order to guarantee validity, high-level statements should be mapped into valid solid modeling operations that may be stored in a parametric or implicit form that will evolve correctly as the parameters of the model are varied. A graphic support of such high-level statements offers considerable challenges.

9 Concluding Remarks

Solid modeling has gone a long way and a substantial body of knowledge has evolved from early attempts. Industrial applications have opened new challenges. To make progress, system developers must be able to share their results and build on top of other people's work. The schemes for representing solid models are limited and must be extended and generalized. New operations for designing solids and for modeling the effect of manufacturing operations must be supported. Finally, intelligent front-ends must be developed to relieve the designers from tedious and repetitive tasks.

9.1 Geometric support

Efficient and relatively reliable techniques for processing geometric entities in the context of solid modeling exist, but are limited to simple geometric entities such as the natural quadric surfaces and their intersections. Enlarging this domain is necessary for many applications, but is accompanied with a considerable loss of precision and performance. It is not sufficient to provide algorithmic solutions to the computation of intersections between surfaces; geometric tools for answering topological questions that may be phrased as in terms of geometric ordering are also necessary.

9.2 Geometric Tool Kits

The lack of flexibility and the difficulty of integration are the two primary factors that impede the integration of solid modeling solutions into large CAD systems. Indeed, the cores of most solid modelers, i.e. the algorithms that perform the geometric calculations and the datastructure manipulations necessary to support graphics or Boolean operations, are large programs built around frozen data structures optimized for a narrow range of applications. Consequently, enhancing these systems to support a wider geometric domain or customizing then to serve a broader spectrum of applications requires to re-engineer much of the code, and thus involves a considerable investments of time and may require the collaboration of the original developers.

As mathematical or graphic libraries offer to system developers a well integrated set of powerful, yet simple to use, functions, geometric modeling cores should be available for application builders. The developer of a new operations, for example a Minkowski sum, should be able to use primitive functions that another developer has engineered for Boolean operations. Mathematical or graphic libraries use relatively simple data models. Solid modelers, however, use complicated graphs structures and a variety of ways for representing even the simplest geometric entity. For example, a face has a complex representation in terms of its supporting surface, its bounding edges, and their orientation and neighborhood information. Passing all this data to a geometric library, in order to obtain the intersection of the face with a curve segment would be too complicated. Therefore, primitive geometric routines must either be very low-level, or must access the data structure representing their arguments. Should the data-structure be modified for a particular application, a portion of the geometric routine may have to be changed. Which in turn may create problems in another portion of the software system

Object oriented programming technology, through its data encapsulation facilities, is a suitable vehicle for attacking this problem and object-oriented geometric tool-kits are under development.

9.3 Generalized topological structures

Geometric modeling is central to many CAD/CAM applications. Different applications require different representations: solids are used for mechanical parts design; lower dimensional sets for tolerances, or contact and friction analysis; higher dimensional objects for path planning in configuration space or for modeling scalar or vector fields; solids composed of different materials for the 3D modeling of silicon devises; solids and faces with separations for finite element mesh analysis; non-closed objects or objects with internal structures for crack analysis. Data structures and set operations that are available in popular solid modelers are not designed to represent and process such objects. The SGC extensions of the representation and algorithms developed for solids accommodate new *geometric objects* which are collections of disjoint *cells* in an n-dimensional manifold. In 3D, for instance, these cells are connected open subsets of the three-dimensional space, of two dimensional surfaces, or of one dimensional curves, or simply points. The connectivity of such objects is captured in a graph whose links indicate "boundary" relations between cells. By choosing various cells of an object to be *active* one can associate various point sets with an object. Boolean and other set-theoretic operations, as well as other special purpose operations that may be defined by the user, can be decomposed into three fundamental steps: a *subdivision* step, which makes two objects "compatible" by subdividing their cells, a *selection* step, which defines active cells, and a *simplification* step, which, by deleting or merging certain cells, reduces the complexity of an object without changing the represented point set and is useful for extracting topological information.

Since SGCs are constructed by applying Boolean, topological, and other operations to primitive objects, it is necessary to provide a representation that would capture such a specification and support editing, parameterization, and interrogation. The CSG graphs played that important role in solid modeling. The concept to CNRG was developed to extend the domain of CSG to objects that can be represented by SGCs. The cells of an SGC produced by evaluating a CNRG representation may be grouped into regions that may be conveniently identified by a CNRG signature. This signature is independent of parameterization and is thus well suited for storing identifiers to selected elements or features in such a way that these identifiers will not be invalidated when the dimensions or positions of the primitive elements are altered by a change of parameters.

9.4 Advanced operations

Operations for constructing solids in currently available commercial CAD systems are limited to instantiations of simple parameterized primitive solids, translational and rotational sweeps of two dimensional cross sections, rigid motions, and Boolean combinations. Such facilities are insufficient to accommodate many CAD/CAM applications.

In addition to the automatic generation of engineering drawings and realistic pictures, and to the analysis of volumetric properties of solid models, the use of CAD systems for planning and simulating manufacturing operations is an essential part of design automation. Experimental systems providing restricted types of bending, twisting, growing, shrinking, rounding, and filleting operations have been publicized. Much more must be done to develop efficient and robust algorithms for these and other operations.

9.5 Intelligent front-ends

The interactive design of computer representations of manufactured parts is a trial-and-error process involving incremental modifications and repetitive inspection of geometric models. Geometric features provide an abstraction mechanism for capturing functionally important characteristics of a part and a syntax for expressing conditions for the compliance of the model with the designer's intent. Many validity conditions that cannot be evaluated using conventional solid models may be derived from a SGC representation, by simply inquiring about the existence and the adjacency of geometric elements of specific dimensions associated with specific features. Intentional features, originally identified by the designer, should not be confused with their geometric embodiments which may vary as the model is edited. This distinction is essential for representing and interrogating invalid features and helps tracing features evolution through the life-cycle of a design model.

9.6 Acknowledgements

The author is solely responsible for the opinions and (mis)interpretations stated in this report. However, the author would like to acknowledge the direct or indirect contributions of his collaborators and colleagues to this report. Specifically, the advances in the topological domain discussed here stemmed from the author's collaborative work on SGC's with M. O'Connor and on CNRG's with A. Requicha. The author's understanding of data structures for geometric modeling and their limitations has clearly benefited from his involvement in the KORS task forces on advanced modeling that included M. Karasick, M. O'Connor, and V. Srinivasan. Many topological concepts pertinent to geometric modeling have been clarified during a meeting of an ongoing collaboration, also involving N. Stewart, T. Takala, and M. O'Connor, aimed at defining all the mathematical concepts necessary for analyzing the limitations of geometric modeling schemes. The author's ideas about high-level design techniques have evolved through a long-lasting collaboration with P. Borrel.

Special thanks go to C. Casparian for building and maintaining the bibliographical database used in printing this report and the associated library and also to A. Requicha for contributing his bibliography list to this data base. Finally the author's thanks go to C. Milon, P. Borrel, A. Rappoport, and especially A. Requicha for having the courage to proof-read this report.

10 References

[1] V. Akman and Wm. Randolph Franklin. Ray Representation for K-Trees. *Pattern Recognition Letters*, 10:315–320, 1989.

[2] V. Akman and Wm. Randolph Franklin. Representing Objects as Rays, or How to Pile up an Octree? *Computer and Graphics*, 13(3):373–379, 1989.

[3] S. Ala. Universal Data Structure: A tool for the Design of Optimal Boundary Data Structures. In *ACM/SIGGRAPH Sym. on Solid Modeling Foundations and CAD/CAM Applications*, Austin, Texas, June 1991.

[4] Jarmo Alander. On Interval Arithmetic Range Approximation Methods of Polynomials and Rational Functions. *Computer and Graphics*, 9(4):365–372, 1985.

[5] David C. Anderson. Closing the Gap: A Workstation Mainframe Connection. *Computers in Mechanical Engineering*, May 1986.

[6] S. Ansaldi, F. De Floriani, and B. Falcidieno. Geometric Modelling of Solid Objects by Using a Face Adjacency Graph Representation. *ACM Computer Graphics*, 19(3):131–139, 1985.

[7] F. Arbab. Set Models and Boolean Operations for Solids and Assemblies. Technical Report Tech. Report CS-88-52: bimon, Univ. of S. Calif., Computer Science Dept., Univ. of S. Calif., Los Angeles, CA, July 1988.

[8] Farhad Arbab. A Paradigm for Intelligent CAD. Technical Report TR CRI 87-27, May 1987.

[9] D. Arnon, G.E. Collin, and S. McCallum. Cylindrical Algebraic Decomposition I: The Basic Algorithm. *SIAM Journal on Computing*, 13(4):856–877, November 1984.

[10] D. Arnon, G.E. Collins, and S. McCallum. Cylindrical Algebraic Decomposition II: An Adjacency Algorithm for the Plane. *SIAM Journal on Computing*, 13(4):878–889, November 1984.

[11] Tetsuo Asano and Takao Asano. Minimum Parition of Polygonal Regions into Trapezoids. In *IEEE 24th Annual Symposium on Foundations of Computer Science*, volume IEEE 83CH1938-0, pages 233–241, 1983.

[12] Mikhail J. Atallah, Richard Cole, and Michael T. Goodrich. Cascading Divide-and-Conquer: A Technique for Designing Parallel Algorithms. In *28th Annual Symposium on Foundations of Computer Science*, volume IEEE 87CH2471-1, pages 151–160, 1987.

[13] D. Ayala, P. Brunet, R. Juan, and I. Navazo. Object Representation by Means of Nonminimal Division Quadtrees and Octrees. *ACM Trans. on Graphics*, 4(1):41–59, January 1985.

[14] Chanderjit Bajaj and Myung Soo Kim. Compliant Motion Planning with Geometric Models. In *Proceeding of the Third Annual Symposium on Computational*, pages 171–180, 1987.

[15] C.L. Bajaj, C.M. Hoffmann, J.E.H. Hopcroft, and R.E. Lynch. Tracing Surface Intersections. *Computer Aided Geometric Design*, 5:285–307, 1988.

[16] Timothy J. Baker. Developments and Trends in Three-Dimensional Mesh Generation. *Applied Numerical Mathematics*, 5:275–304, 1989.

[17] Richard J. Balling, Joseph C. Free, and Alan R. Parkinson. Consideration of Worst-Case Manufacturing Tolerances in Design Optimization. *Transactions of the ASME - Journal of Mechanisms, Transmissions*, 86-DET-30:1–4, 1986.

[18] R.E. Barnhill, G. Farin, M. Jordan, and B.R. Piper. Surface/surface Intersection. *Computer Aided Geometric Design*, 4:3–16, 1987.

[19] B. Baumgart. A Polyhedron Representation for Computer Vision. In *AFIPS Nat. Conf. Proc.*, volume 44, pages 589–596, 1975.

[20] B.G. Baumgart. Winged Edge Polyhedron Representation. Technical Report AIM-79, STAN-CS-320, Stanford Univ., 1972.

[21] G.R. Beacon, J.R. Dodsworth, S.E. Howe, R.G. Oliver, and A. Saia. Boundary Evaluation Using Inner and Outer Sets: The ISOS Method. *IEEE Computer Graphics and Applications*, 9(2):39–51, March 1987. (ISSN 0272-1716).

[22] E.A. Skitters Bier and Jacks. Interactive 3D Positioning Tools. In F. Crow and S.M. Pizer, editors, *86 Workshop on Interactive 3D Graphics*, volume 44, pages 183–196. ACM Press, 1975.

[23] H. Bieri and W. Nef. A Sweep-Plane Algorithm for computing the Euler-Characteristic of Polyhedra Represented in Boolean Form. *Computing*, 34:287–302, 1985.

[24] H. Bieri and W. Nef. Elementary Set Operations with d-Dimensional Polyhedra. In *4th Workshop for Computational Ge-ometry*, Wuerzburg, Germany, March 1988.

[25] Ho. Bin. Inputting Constructive Solid Geometry Representations Directly from 2D Orthographic Engineering Drawings. *Computer-Aided Design*, 18(3):147–155, April 1986.

[26] Lenore Blum and Michael Shub. Evaluating Rational Functions: Infinite Precision is Finite Cost and Tractable on Average. In *25th Annual Symposium on Foundations of Computer Science, IEEE 84*, volume 44, pages 261–267. ACM Press, October 1975. CH2085-9.

[27] James E. Bobrow. A Direct Minimization Approach for Obtaining the Distance Between Convex Polyhedra. *The Inter-national Journal of Robotics Research*, 8(3):65–76, June 1989.

[28] W. Boehm, G. Farin, and J. Kahmann. A Survey of Curve and Surface Methods in CAGD. *Computer Aided Geometric Design*, 1(1):1–60, July 1984.

[29] E. Boender. A Survey of Intersection Algorithms for Curved Surfaces. *Computers and Graphics*, 15(1):109–115, 1991.

[30] A. Bogomolny. Digital Geometry May Not Be Discrete. *Computer Vision, Graphics, and Image Processing*, 43:205–220, 1988.

[31] A. Borning. The Programming Language Aspects of Thinglab, A Constraint-oriented Simulation Laboratory. *ACM Transactions of Programming Languages and Systems*, 3(4):353–387, October 1981.

[32] P. Borrel and D. Bechmann. Deformations of n-dimensional Objects. In *Proc. of ACM/SIGGRAPH Symp. on Solid Modeling Foundations*, pages 351–369, Austin, June 1991.

[33] J.W. Boyse. Interference Detection Among Solids and Surfaces. *Comm. ACM*, 22(1):3–9, January 1979.

[34] I.C. Braid. *Designing with Volumes.* PhD thesis, Univ. of Cambridge, U.K., 1973.

[35] I.C. Braid. Six Systems for Shape Design and Representation - A Review. In *Proceedings of CAM-I's International CAM Seminar*, pages 60–67, April 1975. Report No. P-75-MM-01.

[36] I.C. Braid. The Synthesis of Solids Bounded by Many Faces. *Comm. ACM*, 18(4):209–216, April 1975.

[37] I.C. Braid. Notes on a Geometric Modeler. Technical Report 101, Computer Lab, Univeristy of Cambridge, UK, CAD Group Doc., June 1979.

[38] I.C. Braid, R.C. Hillyard, and I.A. Stroud. Stepwise Construction of Polyhedra in Geometric Modelling. In K.W. Brodie, editor, *Mathematical Methods in Computer Graphics and Design*, pages 123–141, London, 1980. Academic Press.

[39] E. Brisson. Representing Geometric Structures in D-Dimensions: Topology and Order. In *Fifth ACM Symposium on Computational Geometry*, pages 218–227, Saarbruchen, June 1989.

[40] E. Brisson. *Representation of d-Dimensional Geometric Objects.* PhD thesis, Dept. of Compt. Sci. and Engr. University of Washington, Seattle, WA, 1990.

[41] W.F. Bronsvoort, J.J. Van Wijk, and F.W. Jansen. Two Methods for Improving the Efficiency of Ray Casting in Solid Modelling. *Computer-Aided Design*, 16(1):51–55, January 1984.

[42] C.M. Brown. PADL-2: A Technical Summary. *IEEE Computer Graphics and Applications*, 2(2):69–84, March 1982.

[43] S.A. Cameron. *Modelling Solids in Motion.* PhD thesis, Univ. of Edinburgh, 1984.

[44] S.A. Cameron. A Study of the Clash Detection Problem in Robotics. In *International Conference on Robotics and Automation*, pages 488–493, St Louis, 1985.

[45] S.A. Cameron. Efficient Intersection Tests for Objects Defined Constructively. *Iternational Journal of Robotics Research*, 1987.

[46] S.A. Cameron and R.K. Culley. Determining the Minimum Translational Distance Between Two Convex Polyhedra. In *Proc. 86 IEEE Int'l. Conf. on Robotics and Automation*, pages 591–596, 1986.

[47] S.A. Cameron and J.R. Rossignac. Relationship between S-bounds and Active Zones in Constructive Solid Geometry. In H. Seidel W. Strasser, editor, *Theory and Practice of Geometric Modeling*, pages 369–348. 1989.

[48] J. Canny. A New Algebraic Method for Robot Motion Planning and Real Geometry. *IEEE*, pages 39–48, 1987.

[49] I. Carlbom, I. Chakravarty, and D. A Vanderschel. Hierarchical Data Structure for Representing the Spatial De-composition of 3-D Objects. *IEEE Computer Graphics and Applications*, 5(4):24–31, April 1985.

[50] W.E. Carlson. An Algorithm and Data Structure for 3D Object Synthesis Using Surface Patch Intersection. In *Proc. ACM Siggraph '82*, pages 255–263, Boston, Ma., July 1982.

[51] M.S. Casale and J.E. Bobrow. A set operation algorithm for sculptured solid models with trimmed patches. *Computer-Aided Geometric Design*, 6:235–247, 1989.

[52] C. Cattani and A. Paoluzzi. Solid Modeling in Any Dimension. Technical report, Dip. di Mathematica, Univer. La Sapienza, Rome, Italy, 1989.

[53] K. Cheng. Using Plane Vector Fields to Obtain all the Intersection Curves of Two General Surfaces. In H. Seidel W. Strasser, editor, *Theory and Practice of Geometric Modeling*. Springer-Verlag, Berlin, 1988.

[54] H. Chiyokura and F. Kimura. Design of Solids with Free-Form Surfaces. In *Proc. ACM Siggraph '83*, pages 73–82, Detroit, MI., July 1983.

[55] Sabine Coquillart. Extended Free-Form Deformation: a Sculpturing Tool for 3D Geometric Modeling. *Proc. ACM Siggraph '90*, 24(4):187–196, August 1990.

[56] R.K. Culley and K.G. Kempf. A Collision Detection Algorithm Based on Velocity and Distance Bounds. In *Proc. 86 IEEE Int'l Conf. on Robotics and Automation*, pages 1064–1069, 1986.

[57] T. Dey. Decomposition and CSG representation of Polyhedra with Arbitrary Genus. 47907, 1991.

[58] T.K. Dey, C.L. Bajaj, and K. Sugihara. On Good Triangulations in Three Dimensions. In *ACM/SIGGRAPH Symposium on Solid Modeling Foundations and CAD/CAM Applications*, Austin, Texas, 1991.

[59] D.P. Dobkin and M.J. Laszlo. Primitives for the Manipulation of Three-Dimensional Subdivisions. In *Third ACM Symp. on Computational Geometry*, pages 86–99, Waterloo, Canada, June 1987.

[60] T. Dokken. Finding Intersections of B-Spline Represented Geometries Using Recursive Subdivision Techniques. *Computer-Aided Geometric Design*, 2(1):189–195, 1985.

[61] C.M. Eastman and K. Weiler. Geometric Modelling Using the Euler Operators. In *Proc. 1st Annual Conf. on Computer Graphics in CAD/CAM*, pages 248–259, 1979.

[62] H. Edelsbrunner and Mucke. P. Simulations of Simplicity: A Technique to Cope with Degenerate Cases in Geometric Algorithms. In *Proc. 4th ACM Sym. on Computational Geometry*, pages 118–133, 1988.

[63] J. Ellis, G. Kedem, R. Marisa, J. Menon, and H. Voelcker. Breaking Barriers in Solid Modeling. In *CIME*, pages 28–34, February 1991.

[64] D.M. Esterling and J. Van Rosendale. An Intersection Algorithm for Moving Parts. In *Proc. NASA Symposium on Computer-Aided Geometry Modeling*, number 2272, pages 129–133, 1983.

[65] R.T. Farouki, C.A. Neff, and M.A. O'Connor. Automatic Parsing of Degenerate Quadric-surface Intersection. *ACM Transactions on Graphics*, 8:174–203, August 1988.

[66] V. Ferrucci and A. Paoluzzi. Extrusion and Boundary Evaluation for Multidimensional Polyhedra. *Computer-Aided Design*, 23(1):40–50, January/February 1991.

[67] L. Floriani and B. Falcidieno. A Hierarchical Boundary Model for Solid Object Representation. *ACM Trans. Graphics*, 7(1):42–60, 1988.

[68] W.R. Franklin. Efficient Polyhedron Intersection and Union. In *Proc. Graphics Interface '82*, pages 73–80, May 1982.

[69] P.K. Ghosh and S.P. Mudur. Theoretical Framework for Shape Representation and Analysis. In R.A. Earnshaw, editor, *Fundamental Algorithms for Computer Graphics*, pages 949–993. Springer-Verlag, Berlin, 1985.

[70] A.S. Glassner. Space Subdivision for Fast Ray Tracing. *IEEE Computer Graphics and Applications*, 4(10):15–22, October 1984.

[71] J. Goldfeather, J.P.M. Hultquist, and H. Fuchs. Fast Constructibe Solid Geometry Display in the Pixel-Power Graphics System. *ACM SIGGRAPH '86 Proc., Computer Graphics*, 20(4), August 1986.

[72] J. Goldfeather, S. Molnar, G. Turk, and H. Fuchs. Near Real-Time CSG Rendering Using Tree Normalization and Geometric Pruning. *IEEE Computer Graphics and Applications*, 9(3):20–28, May 1989.

[73] L. Guibas and J. Stolfi. Primitives for the Manipulation of General Subdivisions and the Computation of Voronoi Diagrams. *ACM Trans. on Graphics*, 4(2):74–123, April 1985.

[74] E. Gursoz, Y. Choi, and Prinz. F. Boolean Set operations on Non-Manifold Boundary Representation Objects. *Computer-Aided Design*, 23(1):33–39, January/February 1991.

[75] E. Levent Gursoz and F.B. Prinz. Node-based Representation of Non-Manifold Surface Boundaries in Geometric Modeling. In J. Turner M. Wozny and K. Preiss, editors, *Geometric Modeling for Product Engineering*. North-Holland, 1989.

[76] D.G. Hakala, R.C. Hillyard, P.J. Malraison, and B.E. Nourse. Natural Quadrics in Mechanical Engineering. In *CAD/CAM VIII, Autofact West*, Anaheim, CA, November 1980.

[77] A.R. Halbert, S.J.P. Todd, and J.R. Woodward. Generalizing Active Zones for Set-Theoretic Solid Models. *Computer Journal*, 32(1):86–89, February 1989.

[78] R.C. Hillyard. The BUILD Group of Solid Modellers. *IEEE Computer Graphics and Applications*, 2(2):43–52, March 1982.

[79] R.C. Hillyard and I.C. Braid. Analysis of Dimensions and Tolerances in Computer-aided Mechanical Design. *Computer-Aided Design*, 10(3):161–166, May 1978.

[80] C. Hoffmann. *Geometric and Solid Modeling*. Morgan Kaufmann, San Mateo, CA, 1989.

[81] C. Hoffmann, J. Hopcraft, and M. Karasick. Towards Implementing Robust Geometric Computations. In *ACM Sym. Computational Geometry*, 1988.

[82] C. Hoffmann and J. Hopcroft. Quadric Blending Surfaces. *Computer Aided Design*, 18:301–307, 1986.

[83] C. Hoffmann and J. Hopcroft. Geometric Ambiguities in Boundary Representations. *Computer Aided Design*, 19:141–147, January 1987.

[84] W.P. Horn and D.L. Taylor. A theorem to determine the spatial containment of a point in a planar polyhedron. *Computer Vision, Graphics, and Image Processing*, 45:106–116, 1989.

[85] M. Hosaka, F. Kimura, and N. Kakishita. A Unified Method for Processing Polyhedra. In *Information Processing '74*, Amsterdam, 1974. North-Holland.

[86] F.W. Jansen. A CSG List Priority Hidden-Surface Algorithm. In *Proc. Eurographics '85 Conf.*, pages 51–62, Amsterdam, 1985. Elseviers Science Publishers.

[87] F.W. Jansen. Data Structures for Ray Tracing. In L.R.A. Kessener, F.J. Peters, and M.L.P. van Lierop, editors, *Data Structures for Raster Graphics*, pages 57–73. Srpinger Verlag, 1986.

[88] F.W. Jansen. A Pixel-parallel Hidden Surface Algorithm for Constructive Solid Geometry. In A.A.G. Requicha, editor, *Proc. Eurographics '86*, Amsterdam, 1986. North-Holland.

[89] F.W. Jansen. CSG Hidden-Surface Algorithms for VLSI Hardware Systems. In W. Strasser, editor, *Advances on Graphics Hardware I*. Springer Verlag, 1987.

[90] F.W. Jansen. *Solid Modelling with Faceted Primitives*. PhD thesis, Technische Universiteit Delft, The Netherlands, September 1987.

[91] G.E.M. Jared and T. Varady. Synthesis of Volume Modelling and Sculptured Surfaces in BUILD. In *Proc. CAD '84*, pages 481–495, Brighton. U.K., April 1984.

[92] J.T. Kajiya. Ray tracing parametric patches. *Computer Graphics*, 16(3):245–254, 1982.

[93] Y.E. Kalay. Determining the Spatial Containment of a Point in General Polyhedra. *Computer Graphics and Image Processing*, 19(4):303–334, August 1982.

[94] Y.E. Kalay. The Hybrid Edge: A Topological Data Structure for Vertically Integrated Geometric Modeling. *Computer -Aided Design*, 21(3):130–140, 1989.

[95] M. Karasick. *On the Representation and Manipulation of Rigid Solids.* PhD thesis, McGill University, Montreal, Quebec, 1988. available as Cornell University Deptartment of Computer Science 89-976.

[96] M. Karasick, D. Lieber, and L. Nackman. Efficient Delaunay Triangulation Using Rational Arithmetic. Technical report, IBM, Yorktown Heights, NY, 1989.

[97] A. Kaufman. *Volume Visualization.* IEEE Computer Society Press, Los Alamitos, CA, 1991.

[98] A. Kaul and J. Rossignac. Solid-Interpolating Deformations: Constructions and Animation of PIPs. In *Proc. Eurographics '91*, pages 493–505, Vienna, September 1986.

[99] G. Kedem. Computer Systems for Curve-Solid Classification and Solid Modeling. Technical report, The University of Rochester, Rochester, NY, March 1987.

[100] Y.S. Kim. *Convex decomposition and solid geometric modeling.* PhD thesis, Dept. of Mechanical Engineering, Stanford University, 1990.

[101] F. Kimura. Geomap - III: Designing Solids with Free-form Surfaces. *IEEE Computer Graphics and Applications*, 4(6):58–72, June 1984.

[102] F. Kimura, H. Suzuki, and L. Wingard. A Uniform Approach to Dimensioning and Tolerancing in Product Modelling. In *Computer Applications in Production on Engineering CAPE '86*, pages 165–178. North Holland, 1987.

[103] G.A. Kriezis, P.V. Pradash, and N.M. Patrikalakis. Method for Intersecting Algebraic Surfaces with Rational Polynomial Patches. *Computer Aided Geometric Design*, 3:217–229, 1986.

[104] D. Laidlaw and J. Hughes. Constructive Solid Geometry for Polyhedral Objects. *Computer Graphics*, 20(4):161–170, 1986.

[105] J. Lane, R. Magedson, and M. Rarick. An Efficient Point in Polyhedron Algorithm. *Computer Vision, Graphics, and Image Processing*, 26(10):118–125, April 1984.

[106] M.J. Laszlo. *A Data Structure for Manipulating ThreeDimensional Subdivisions.* PhD thesis, Princeton Univ., August 1987.

[107] Y.T. Lee and A.A.G. Requicha. Algorithms for computing the Volume and Other Integral Properties of Solids: I - Known Methods and Open Issues. *Comm. ACM*, 25(9), September 1982.

[108] Y.T. Lee and A.A.G. Requicha. Algorithms for computing the Volume and Other Integral Properties of Solids: II - A Family of Algorithms based on Representation Conversion and Cellular Approximation. *Comm. ACM*, 25(9):643–650, September 1982.

[109] J. Levin. Mathematical model for determining the intersection of quadric surfaces. *Computer Graphics and Image Processing*, 11:73–87, 1979.

[110] L. Lienhardt. Topological Models for Boundary Representation: A Comparison With N-dimensional Generalized Maps. *Computer-Aided Design*, 23(1):59–82, January/February 1991.

[111] P. Lienhardt. Subdivision of N-Dimensional Spaces and N-Dimensional Generalized Maps. In *ACM Sumposium on Computational Geometry*, pages 228–236, Saarbruecken, Germany, June 1989.

[112] R. Light and D.C. Gossard. Modification of Geometric Models Through Variational Geometry. *Computer-Aided Design*, 14(4):209–214, July 1982.

[113] V.C. Lin, D.C. Gossard, and R.A. Light. Variational Geometry in Computer-aided Design. *ACM Computer Graphics*, 15(3):171–177, August 1981.

[114] T. Lozano-Perez and M.A. Wesley. An Algorithm for Planning Collision-Free Paths Amongs Polyhedral Obstacles. *Comm. ACM*, 22(10):560–570, October 1979.

[115] M. Mäntylä. A Note on the Modeling Space of Euler Operators. *Computer Vision, Graphics, and Image Processing*, 26:45–60, April 1984.

[116] M. Mäntylä. Boolean Operations of 2-manifold Through Vertex Neighborhood Classification. *ACM Trans. On Graphics*, 5(1):1–29, 1986.

[117] M. Mäntylä. *An Introduction to Solid Modeling.* Computer Science Press, Rockville, Maryland, 1988.

[118] G. Markowsky and M.A. Wesley. Fleshing out Wireframes. *IBM J. Research and Development*, 24(5):582–597, September 1987.

[119] D. Meagher. Fourth-Generation Computer Graphics Hardware Using Octrees. In *NCGA '91*, 1991.

[120] B. Mendelson. *Introduction to Topology.* Allyyn and Bacon, Inc, Boston, MA, 1975. Volume 3rd ed.

[121] V. Milenkovic. *Verifiable Implementations of Geometric Algorithms Using Finite Precision Arithmetic.* PhD thesis, Carnegie Mellon University, Pittsburgh, PA, 1988.

[122] J. Miller. Geometric Approaches to Nonplanar Quadric Surface Intersection Curves. *ACM Transactions on Graphics*, 6(4):274–307, October 1987.

[123] C. B. Millham and J. L. Zheng. Linear pivoting heuristic procedure for computing the curve of intersection of two bicubic surface patches. *Comput. Graphics*, 13(1):25–38, 1989.

[124] G. Monge. *Applications de l'analyse a la geometrie.* Bachelier, Paris, 1849. 5th ed.

[125] R. Moore. *Interval Analysis.* Prentice Hall, Englewood Cliffs, NJ, 1966.

[126] D.T. Morris. An Algorithm for Direct Display of CSG Objects by Spatial Subdivision. In R.A. Earnshaw, editor, *Fundamental Algorithms for Computer Graphics*, pages 725–736, Berlin, 1985. Springer Verlag.

[127] C. Narayanaswami and R. Franklin. Determination of Mass Properties of Polyhedral Objects in Parallel. In *ACM/SIGGRAPH Symposium on Solid Modeling Foundations and CAD/CAM Applications*, Austin, Texas, 1991.

[128] B. Naylor, J. Amanatides, and W. Thibault. Merging BSP Trees Yields Polyhedral Set Operations. *ACM Computer Graphics SIGGRAPH '90*, 24(4):115–124, August 1986.

[129] B Naylor and W. Thibault. Application of B.S.P. Trees to Ray Tracing and C.S.G. Evaluation. Technical report, Sch. of Info. and Comp. Sci., Georgia Institute of Technology, Atlanta, GA, February 1986.

[130] G. Juno Nelson. A Constraint-based Graphics System. *Proc. ACM Siggraph '85*, 19(3):235–243, 1985.

[131] S. Ocken, J. Schwartz, and M. Sharir. Precise Implementation of CAD Primitives Using Rational Parametrizations of Standard Surfaces. In J. Boyse M. Pickett, editor, *Solid Modeling by Computers.* Plenum Press, New York, 1984.

[132] M.A. O'Connor. Projection of Natural Quadrics. Technical report, IBM Research Report, TJ Watson Center, Yorktown Heights, NY, June 1985. RC 11188.

[133] N. Okino. TIPS - 1. Technical report, Institute of Precision Engineering, Hokkaido Univeristy, 1978.

[134] N. Okino, Y. Kakazu, and H. Kubo. TIPS-1: Technical Information Processing System for Computer-Aided Design, Drawing and Manufacturing. In J. Hatvany, editor, *Computer Languages for Numerical Control*, pages 141–150. North-Holland, Amsterdam, 1973.

[135] N. Okino, Y. Kakazu, and M. Morimoto. Extended Depth-buffer Algorithms for Hidden-surface Visualization. *IEEE Computer Graphics and Applications*, 4(5):79–88, May 1984.

[136] Orlowski. The Computation of the Distance Between Polyhedra in 3-Space. In *SIAM Conference on Geometric Modeling and Robotics*, Albany, July 1985.

[137] A. Paoluzzi, M. Ramella, and A. Santarelli. Boolean Algebra Over Linear Polyhedra. *CAD*, 21(8):474–484, 1989.

[138] G. Parden and R.G. Newell. A Dimension Based Parametric Design System. In *Proc. CAD '84*, pages 252–259, Brighton, U.K., April 1984.

[139] D.P. Peterson. Boundary to Constructive Solid Geometry Mapping : A Focus on 2-D Issues. *Computer-Aided Design*, 18(1):3–14, January/February 1986.

[140] L. Piegl. Geometric methods for intersecting natural quadrics represented in trimmed surface form. *Computer-Aided Design*, 21:201–221, 1989.

[141] L.K. Putnam. Computation of the Union, Intersection and Difference of N-Dimensional Objects. Technical report, Dept of Computer Science, Univ. of Utah, 1982.

[142] A. Rappoport. The n-Dimensional Extended Convex Difference Tree (ECDT) for representing polyhedra. In *ACM/SIGGRAPH Symposium on Solid Modeling Foundations and CAD/CAM Applications*, Austin, Texas, 1991.

[143] A. Rappoport. Rendering curves and surfaces with Hybrid subdivision and forward differencing. *ACM Transactions on Graphics*, July 1991.

[144] A.A.G. Requicha. Mathematical Models of Rigid Solid Objects. Technical report, Univ. of Rochester, November 1977. Technical Memo, No.28.

[145] A.A.G. Requicha. Part and Assembly Description Languages I: Dimensioning and Tolerancing. Technical report, Production Automation Project, Univ. of Rochester, May 1977. Technical Memo, No.19.

[146] A.A.G. Requicha. Representation of Tolerances in Solid Modeling: Issues and Alternative Approaches. In M.S. Pickett and J.W. Boyse, editors, *Solid Modelling by Computers*, pages 3–22. Planum Press, New York, 1984.

[147] A.A.G. Requicha and S.C. Chan. Representation of Geometric Features, Tolerances and Attributes in Solid Modellers Based on Constructive Geometry. *IEEE Journal of Robotics and Automation*, 2(3), September 1986.

[148] A.A.G. Requicha and R.B. Tilove. Mathematical Foundations of Constructive Solid Geometry: General Topology of Regular Closed Sets. Technical report, Production Automation Project, Univ. of Rochester, June 1978. Technical Memo, No.27.

[149] A.A.G. Requicha and H.B. Voelcker. Constructive Solid Geometry. Technical report, Production Automation Project, Univ. of Rochester, November 1977. Technical Memo, No.25.

[150] A.A.G. Requicha and H.B. Voelcker. Solid Modelling: A Historical Summary and Contemporary Assessment. *IEEE Computer Graphics and Applications*, 2(2):9–24, March 1982.

[151] A.A.G. Requicha and H.B. Voelcker. Solid Modelling: Current status and Research Directions. *IEEE Computer Graphics and Applications*, 3(7):25–37, October 1983.

[152] A.A.G. Requicha and H.B. Voelcker. Boolean Operations in Solid Modelling: Boundary Evaluation and Merging Algorithms. *Proc. IEEE*, 73(1):30–44, January 1985.

[153] A. Rockwood, K. Heaton, and T. Davis. Real-time Rendering of Trimmed Surfaces. *Proc. ACM Siggraph '89, Computer Graphics*, 23(3):107–116, 1989.

[154] A.P. Rockwood. Introducing Sculptured Surfaces into a Geometric Modeler. In M.S. Pickett and J.W. Boyse, editors, *Solid Modelling by Computers*, pages 237–258. Planum Press, New York, 1984.

[155] J.R. Rossignac. *Blending and Offsetting Solid Models*. PhD thesis, Univ. of Rochester, July 1985.

[156] J.R. Rossignac. Constraints in Constructive Solid Geometry. In F. Crow and S.M. Pizer, editors, *Proc. 86 Workshop on Interactive 3D Graphics*, pages 93–110, Chapel Hill, October 1986. ACM Press.

[157] J.R. Rossignac. Considerations on the Interactive Rendering of Four-dimensional Volumes. In *Proc. of the Chapel Hill Wkshp on Volume Visualization*, pages 67–76, April 1989.

[158] J.R. Rossignac. Issues on Feature-based Editing and Interrogation of Solid Models. *Computers and Graphics*, 14(2):149–172, 1990.

[159] J.R. Rossignac, P. Borrel, and L.R. Nackman. Interactive Design with Sequences of Parameterized Transformations. In *Second Eurographics Workshop on Intelligent CAD Systems: Implementation Issues*, pages 95–127, Veldhoven, The Netherlands, April 1988.

[160] J.R. Rossignac, P. Borrel, and L.R. Nackman. Procedural Models for Design and Fabrications. In *Proc. of the MIT Sea Grant Symposium*, Cambridge, MA, October 1988.

[161] J.R. Rossignac and M.A. O'Connor. SCG: A Dimension-independent Model for Pointsets with Internal Structures and Incomplete Boundaries. In K. Preiss M. Wozny, J. Turner, editor, *Geometric Modeling for Product Engineering*, pages 145–180. North-Holland, Rensselaerville, NY, September 1989.

[162] J.R. Rossignac and A.A.G. Requicha. Constant-radius Blending in Solid Modeling. *ASME Computers in Mechanical Engineering (CIME)*, 3(1):65–73, July 1984.

[163] J.R. Rossignac and A.A.G. Requicha. Offsetting Operations in Solid Modelling. *Computerr-Aided Geometric Design*, 3(2):129–148, August 1986.

[164] J.R. Rossignac and A.A.G. Requicha. Piecewise Constant Curvature Approximations for Geometric Modelling. Technical report, IBM Research Report, T.J. Watson Research Center, Yorktown, October 1986. RC 12171.

[165] J.R. Rossignac and A.R. Requicha. Constructive Non-Regularized Geometry. *Computer-Aided Design*, 23(1):21–32, January/February 1991. Special Issue: Beyond Solid Modeling.

[166] J.R. Rossignac and H.B. Voelcker. Active Zones in CSG for Accelerating Boundary Evaluation, Redundancy Elimination, Interference Detection and Shading Algorithms. *ACM Transactions on Graphics*, 8(1):51–87, January 1989.

[167] J.R. Rossignac and J. Wu. Correct Shading of Regularized CSG Solids Using a Depth-Interval Buffer. In *Eurographics Workshop on Graphics Hardware*, Lausanne, Switzerland, September 1990.

[168] S.D. Roth. Ray Casting for Modelings Solids. *Computer Grahpics and Image Processing*, 18(2):109–144, February 1982.

[169] H. Samet. *Applications of Spatial Data Structures*. Addison-Wesley, 1990.

[170] H. Samet and M. Tamminen. Bintrees, CSG Trees, and Time. *ACM Computer Graphics*, 19(3):121–130, July 1985.

[171] N.S. Sapidis and R. Perucchio. Domain Delaunay Tetrahedralization of Arbitrary Shaped Curved Polyhedra Defined in a Solid Modeling System. In *ACM/SIGGRAPH Symposium on Solid Modeling Foundations and CAD/CAM Applications*, Austin, Texas, 1991.

[172] T. Satoh. Boolean Operations on Sets Using Surface Data. In *ACM/SIGGRAPH Symposium on Solid Modeling Foundations and CAD/CAM Applications*, Austin, Texas, 1991.

[173] W.J. Schroeder and M.S. Shephard. An O(N) Algorithm to Automatically Generate Geometric Triangulations Satisfying the Delaunay Circumsphere Criteria. *Engineering with Computers*, 5:177–193, 1989.

[174] L. Schumaker. Reconstructing 3D Objects from Cross-Sections. In W. Dahmen et al., editor, *Computation of Curves and Surfaces*, pages 275–309. Kluwer Academic Publishers, The Netherlands, 1990.

[175] T. Sederberg, D. Anderson, and R. Goldman. Implicit Interpretation of Parametric Curves and Surfaces. *Computer Vision, Graphics, and Image Processing*, 28:72–84, 1984.

[176] Thomas W. Sederberg and Ray J. Meyers. Loop detection in surface patch intersections. *Comput Aided Geom Des*, 5(2):161–171, July 1988.

[177] M. Segal. Using Tolerances to Guarantee Valid Polyhedral Modeling Results. *Computer Graphics, SIGGRAPH '90*, 24(4):105–114, August 1990.

[178] M. Segal and C. Sequin. Partitioning Polyhedral Objects into Nonintersecting Parts. *IEEE Computer Graphics and Applications*, pages 53–67, January 1988.

[179] J. Serra. *Image Analysis and Mathematical Morphology.* Academic Press, New York, 1982.

[180] J.J. Shah, P. Sreevalsan, M.T. Rogers, R. Billo, and A. Mathew. Current Status of Features Technology. Technical report, CAM-I Inc., Arlington, Texas, November 1988. Report R-88-GM-04.1.

[181] V. Shapiro and D. Vossler. Construction and Optimization of CSG Representations. *Computer-Aided Design*, 23(1):4–20, January/February 1991.

[182] Y. Shiroma, N. Okino, and Y. Kakazu. Research on 3-D Geometric Modeling by Sweep Primitives. In *Proc. CAD '82*, pages 671–680, Brighton, U.K., March/April 1982.

[183] C.E. Silva. Alternative Definitions of Faces in Boundary Representations of Solid Objects. Technical report, Production Automation Project, Univ. of Rochester, November 1981. Tech. Memo No. 36.

[184] C. Sobhanpanah. Extension of a boundary representation technique for the description of n-dimensional polytopes. *Computers and Graphics*, 13(1):17–23, 1989.

[185] H. Soto, M. Ishii, K. Sato, and M. Ikesaka. Fast Image Generation of Constructive Solid Geometry Using a Cellular Array Processor. *ACM Computer Graphics, Proc. Siggraph'85*, 19(3):95–102, July 1985.

[186] H.A. Steinberg. Overlap and Separation Calculations Using the SynthaVision Three Dimensional Solid Modeling System. In *Proc. Conf. on CAD/CAM Technology in Mechanical Engineering*, pages 13–19, 1982.

[187] K. Sugihara. On Finite-Precision Representation of Geometric Objects. Technical report, Dept. Math. Engr. and Info. Systems, University Tokyo, Tokyo, Japan, 1987.

[188] G.J. Sussman and G.L. Steele Jr. CONSTRAINTS - A Language for Expressing Almost-Hierarchical Descriptions. *Artificial Intelligence*, 14:1–39, 1980.

[189] I. Sutherland. *Sketchpad, A Man-Machine Graphical Communication System.* PhD thesis, MIT, USA, 1963.

[190] T. Takala. Geometric Boundary Modelling Without Topological Data Structures. In A.A.G. Requicha, editor, *Eurographics '86*, Amsterdam, 1986. North-Holland.

[191] M. Tamminen, O. Karonen, and M. Maentylae. Ray-casting and Block Model Conversion Using a Spatial Index. *Computer-Aided Design*, 16(4):203–208, July 1984.

[192] M. Tawfik. An Efficient Algorithm for CSG to B-Rep Conversion. In *ACM/SIGGRAPH Symposium on Solid Modeling Foundations and CAD/CAM Applications*, Austin, Texas, 1991.

[193] S.W. Thomas. *Modelling Volumes Bounded by B-spline Surfaces.* PhD thesis, Univ. of Utah, USA, June 1984.

[194] R.B. Tilove. A study of geometric set-memebership classification. Technical report, Production Automation Project, Univ. of. Rochester, 1977. TM-30.

[195] R.B. Tilove. Set Membership Classification: A Unified Approach to Geometric Intersection Problems. *IEEE Trans. on Computers*, 29(10):874–883, October 1980.

[196] R.B. Tilove. *Exploiting Spatial and Structural Locality in Geometric Modelling.* PhD thesis, Univ. of Rochester, USA, October 1981.

[197] R.B. Tilove. Extending Solid Modeling Systems for Mechanism Design and Kinematic Simulation. *IEEE Computer Graphics and Applications*, 3(3):9–19, May/June 1983.

[198] R.B. Tilove. A Null-object Detection Algorithm for Constructive Solid Geometry. *Comm. ACM*, 27(7):684–694, July 1984.

[199] R.B. Tilove and A.A.G. Requicha. Closure of Boolean Operations on Geometric Entities. *Computer-Aided Design*, 12(5):219–220, September 1980.

[200] R.B. Tilove, A.A.G. Requicha, and M.R. Hopkins. Efficient editing of Solid Models by Exploiting Structural and Spatial Locality. *Computer-Aided Geometric Design*, 1:227–239, 1984.

[201] M. van Emmerik. *Interactive Design of Parameterized 3D Models by Direct Manipulation.* PhD thesis, Delft University Press, The Netherlands, 1990.

[202] G. Vanecek and D. Nau. Non-Regular Decomposition: An Efficient Approach for Solving the Polygon Intersection Problem. In *Proc. Symposium on Integrated and Intelligent Manufacturing*, pages 271–279, 1987.

[203] T. Varady and M. Pratt. Design Techniques for the Definition of Solid Objects with Free-Form Geometry. *Computer-Aided Geometric Design*, 1:207–225, 1984.

[204] A. Verroust. *Etude de problemes liés a la définition, la visualisation et l'animation d'objects complexes en Informatique graphique.* PhD thesis, Université de ParisSud, Centre D'Orsay, 1990.

[205] H.B. Voelcker and et al. An Introduction to PADL: Characteristics, Status and Rationale. Technical report, Production Automation Project, Univ. of Rochester, December 1974. Tech. Memo No. 22.

[206] H.B. Voelcker and A.A.G. Requicha. Geometric Modelling of Mechanical Parts and Processes. *IEEE Computer*, 10(12):48–57, December 1977.

[207] D.L. Vossler. Sweep-to-CSG Conversion Using Pattern Recognition Techniques. *IEEE Computer Graphics and Applications*, 5(8):61–68, August 1985.

[208] R.J. Walker. *Algebraic Curves.* Princeton University Press, Princeton, New Jersey, 1950.

[209] K. Weiler. Edge-based Data structures for Solid Modeling in Curved-Surface Modeling Environments. *IEEE Computer Graphics and Applications*, 5(1):21–40, January 1985.

[210] K.J. Weiler. The Radial Edge Structure: A Topological Representation for Non-Manifold Geometric Modeling. In H. McLaughlin M. Wozny and J. Encarnacao, editors, *Geometric Modeling for CAD Applications.* Springer Verlag, May 1986.

[211] K.J. Weiler. *Topological Structures for Geometric Modeling.* PhD thesis, Rensselaer Polytechnic Institute, August 1986.

[212] K.J. Weiler. Non-Manifold Geometric Boundary Modeling. In *SIGGRAPH'87,Advanced Solid Modeling Tutorial*, Anaheim, CA, July 1987.

[213] M.A. Wesley, T. Lozano-Perez, and L.I. Lieberman. A Geometric Modelling System for Automated Mechanical Assem-bly. *IBM Journal of Research and Development*, 24(1):64–74, January 1980.

[214] T Woo and T. Thomasma. An Algorithm for Generating Solid Elements in Objects with Holes. *Computers and Structures*, 8:333–342, 1984.

[215] T.C. Woo. A Combinatorial Analysis of Boundary Data Structure Schemata. *IEEE Computer Graphics and Applications*, 5(3):19–27, March 1985.

[216] T.C. Woo and J.D. Wolter. A Constant Expected Time, Linear Storage Data Structure for Representing Three-Dimensional Objects. *IEEE Trans. Systems, Man and Cybernetics*, SMC-14(3):510–515, May/June 1984.

[217] J.R. Woodwark. Graphical Input to a Boolean Solid Modeller. In *Proc. CAD '82*, pages 681–688, Brighton, U.K., March/April 1982.

[218] J.R. Woodwark. Blends in Geometric Modelling. In R. Martin, editor, *The Mathematics of Surfaces II*, pages 255–298. Clarendon Press, Oxford, 1987.

[219] J.R. Woodwark and K.M. Quinlan. Reducing the Effect of complexity on Volume Model Evaluation. *Computer-Aided Design*, 14(2):89–95, March 1982.

[220] G. Wyvill, T.L. Kunii, and Y. Shirai. Space Division for Ray Tracing in CSG. *IEEE Computer Graphics and Applications*, 6(4):28–24, April 1986.

[221] F. Yamaguchi and T. Tokieda. A unified Algorithm for Boolean Shape Operations. *IEEE Computer Graphics and Applications*, 4(6):24–37, June 1984.

[222] F. Yamaguchi and T. Tokieda. A Solid Modeler with a 4x4 Determinant Processor. *IEEE Computer Graphics and Applications*, 5(4):51–59, April 1985.

Kinematics and Dynamics for Computer Animation

H. Ruder, T. Ertl, K. Gruber, M. Günther, F. Hospach,
M. Ruder, J. Subke, K. Widmayer

1 Introduction

In the first phase of computer animation the traditional techniques of animation were brought to the computer resulting in computer animated films where the keyframes were linked by image-based and parametric interpolation. Especially when trying to compute aesthetic human movement it soon became obvious that a more realistic computer animation has to take into account the basic physical properties of the objects and the fundamental physical principles that govern their movement. In algorithmic animation the evolution of the state of a system of objects is not determined by interpolation, but by physical laws given either as algebraic formulae in the simple case or more complicated as set of coupled nonlinear differential equations. In kinematic animation the objects are moved according to a set of given equations for the velocities or the accelerations at certain points of the objects. This procedure results in a realistic animation only if the prescribed velocities and accelerations were derived from a complete dynamic physical model. Therefore, the most general approach for generating physically correct animation sequences is to perform a full dynamical simulation of the given model taking into account all external and internal forces and torques.

However, a complete dynamical simulation of a synthetic human actor in realtime (which requires much more than just the correct movement of the skeleton) is far beyond the capabilities of modern computers and simulation software. Only rigid objects with a few degrees of freedom or very simple elastic models can be treated today and there are many unresolved questions of how to control the internal torques in order to get the desired motion. Thus, generating appealing animation today still requires a lot of heuristics, experimental data and a combination of keyframing, kinematic and dynamic algorithms. Nevertheless, the importance of dynamic modelling will continue to grow since it is the only method which guarantees the equivalence of modelling and animation, which means that the temporal behaviour of physical based objects is bound up in the model itself.

This tutorial will focus on the physical principles of kinematics and dynamics. After explaining the basic equations for point masses and rigid bodies a new approach for the dynamic simulation of multi-linked models with wobbling mass is presented, which has led to new insight in the field of biomechanics, but which has not been used in computer animation so far.

2 Kinematic fundamentals

We will briefly review the kinematics of point masses and extended rigid bodies, which is just the geometrical description of the motion. Those motions take place in a three-dimensional coordinate system, where points in space are denoted by the position vector pointing from the origin of the coordinate system to the respective end points (cf. Fig. 2.1). Whenever it is convenient, we leave the coordinate-free formulation and switch to cartesian, cylindrical or spherical coordinates. Besides the space coordinates $\boldsymbol{r}$ which we are completely free to choose, kinematics introduces a time coordinate t which can be looked at as the independent variable.

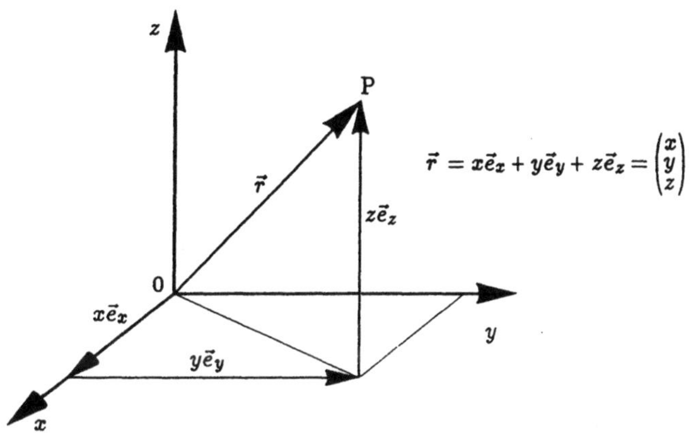

Fig. 2.1. The position vector $\boldsymbol{r}$ of a point P and its coordinates in a cartesian coordinate system.

2.1 Kinematics of a point mass

When describing the motion of an object where the size of the object is negligible compared to the distances covered and where rotations and deformations are of no interest, the object may be idealized by a mathematical point characterized by a mass. The motion of a point mass is completely described by its trajectory in space, e.g. its position vector $\boldsymbol{r}(t)$ and its velocity $\boldsymbol{v}(t)$ at the time t (cf. Fig. 2.2) The velocity is given by

$$\boldsymbol{v}(t) = \dot{\boldsymbol{r}}(t) \quad , \tag{2.1}$$

where the time derivative is defined as usual:

$$\dot{\boldsymbol{r}}(t) = \frac{\mathrm{d}\boldsymbol{r}}{\mathrm{d}t} = \lim_{\delta t \to 0} \frac{\boldsymbol{r}(t+\delta t) - \boldsymbol{r}(t)}{\delta t} \quad . \tag{2.2}$$

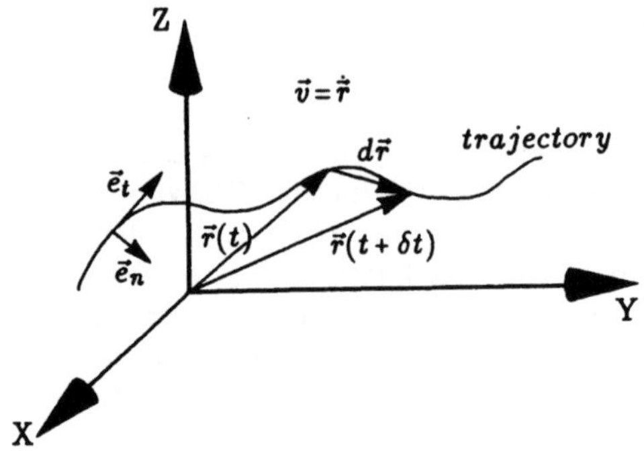

Fig. 2.2. Trajectory of a point mass in space. The unit vector e_t is tangential to the trajectory, whereas the unit vector e_n is perpendicular to the trajectory in the local osculating plane.

The component of the velocity tangential to the trajectory is the absolute value of the velocity v, the component normal to the trajectory is zero

$$\boldsymbol{v}_t = v\,\boldsymbol{e}_t \tag{2.3a}$$

$$\boldsymbol{v}_n = 0 \quad , \tag{2.3b}$$

where $\boldsymbol{e}_t$ denotes the unit vector tangential to the trajectory. Therefore, the length of the path s covered since t_0 is

$$s(t) = \int_{t_0}^{t} v\,\mathrm{d}t' \quad . \tag{2.4}$$

A further important quantity is the acceleration $\boldsymbol{a}(t)$ of the mass point, defined as:

$$\boldsymbol{a}(t) = \dot{\boldsymbol{v}}(t) = \ddot{\boldsymbol{r}}(t) \quad . \tag{2.5}$$

Its components tangential and normal to the trajectory are given by

$$\boldsymbol{a}_t = \dot{v}\,\boldsymbol{e}_t \tag{2.6a}$$

$$\boldsymbol{a}_n = \frac{v^2}{\rho}\boldsymbol{e}_n \quad . \tag{2.6b}$$

Here, $\boldsymbol{e}_n$ means the unit vector normal to the trajectory, which lies in the local osculating plane and ρ is the corresponding local curvature radius.

One elementary example is the parabola of a throw in a uniform gravitational field (cf. Fig. 2.3). Using appropriate initial conditions,

$$\boldsymbol{a} = \boldsymbol{g} = -g\boldsymbol{e}_z \tag{2.7a}$$

can be integrated to

$$\boldsymbol{v}(t) = \boldsymbol{v}_0 + \boldsymbol{g}\,t = v_0\cos\alpha\,\boldsymbol{e}_x + (v_0\sin\alpha - g\,t)\boldsymbol{e}_z \quad , \tag{2.7b}$$

which again can be integrated to

$$\boldsymbol{r}(t) = (v_0 t\cos\alpha + x_0)\boldsymbol{e}_x + (v_0 t\sin\alpha - \frac{1}{2}gt^2 + z_0)\boldsymbol{e}_z \quad . \tag{2.7c}$$

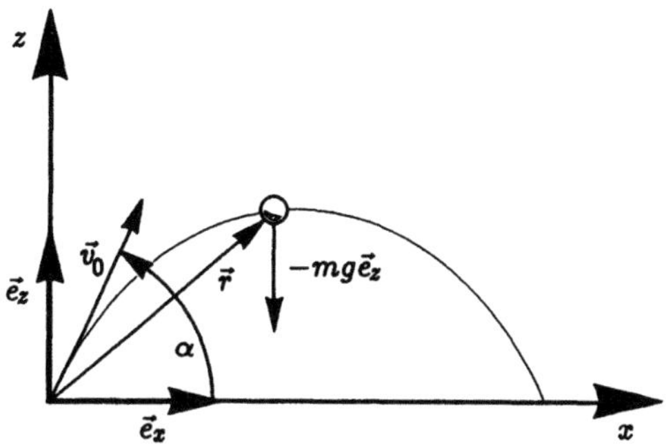

Fig. 2.3. The throw in a uniform gravitational field with initial velocity v_0 and inclination α.

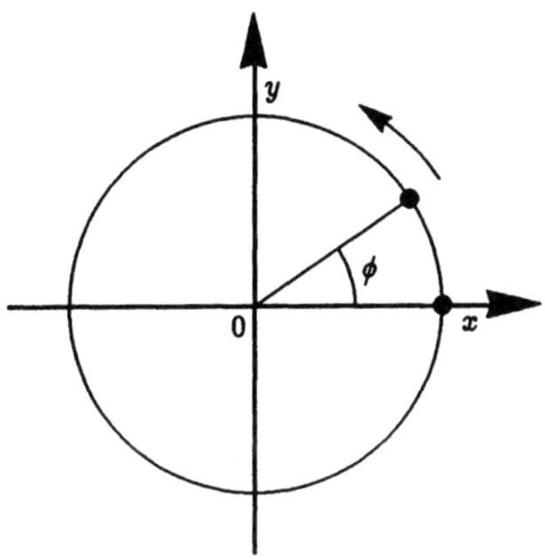

Fig. 2.4. The circular motion with constant angular velocity $\omega = \phi/t$.

This procedure, which derives the motion $\boldsymbol{r}(t)$ from a given acceleration $\boldsymbol{a}(t)$ is called *direct kinematics* and results in the well known parabolic path:

$$z = \tan\alpha\, x - \frac{g}{2v_0^2\cos^2\alpha}x^2 \quad \text{with} \quad x_0 = 0\,,\; z_0 = 0 \quad . \tag{2.8}$$

In *inverse kinematics* the acceleration $\boldsymbol{a}(t)$ is derived from the path $\boldsymbol{r}(t)$ by differentiation like in the example of the circular motion with constant angular velocity $\omega = \frac{\phi}{t}$ (cf. Fig. 2.4):

$$\boldsymbol{r}(t) = r\cos\omega t\,\boldsymbol{e}_x + r\sin\omega t\,\boldsymbol{e}_y \tag{2.9a}$$

$$\boldsymbol{v}(t) = \dot{\boldsymbol{r}}(t) = -\omega r\sin\omega t\,\boldsymbol{e}_x + \omega r\cos\omega t\,\boldsymbol{e}_y \tag{2.9b}$$

$$\boldsymbol{a}(t) = \dot{\boldsymbol{v}}(t) = \ddot{\boldsymbol{r}}(t) = -\omega^2\boldsymbol{r}(t) \quad . \tag{2.9c}$$

The velocity $\boldsymbol{v}$ is always perpendicular to the position vector $\boldsymbol{r}$ ($\boldsymbol{r}\cdot\boldsymbol{v} = 0$) and the vector of the angular velocity $\boldsymbol{\omega}$ can be introduced by $\boldsymbol{r}\times\boldsymbol{v}/r^2 = \omega\boldsymbol{e}_z = \boldsymbol{\omega}$.

More complicated than the circular motion is the motion of the planets around the sun. The three Kepler laws

1. The orbit of each planet is an ellipse with the sun at one focus.
2. The radius vector from the sun to a planet sweeps out equal areas in equal intervals of time.
3. The squares of the periods of revolution of any two planets are proportional to the cubes of the semimajor axes of the respective orbits.

are a purely kinematic description based on observations. They can be used to derive the structure of the gravitational force or vice versa Newton's law of gravitation can be used to derive Kepler's observations .

2.2 Kinematics of a rigid body

In order to uniquely describe the position and the orientation of a rigid body in space six independent coordinates are necessary. Of course, there exist a lot of different possibilities for realization. An appropriate way is to use the three cartesian coordinates of the center of mass x_c, y_c, z_c defined by

$$\boldsymbol{r}_c = (x_c, y_c, z_c) = \frac{\int_{\text{vol}} \boldsymbol{r}\rho(x,y,z)dxdydz}{\int_{\text{vol}} \rho(x,y,z)dxdydz}, \tag{2.10}$$

where $\rho(x,y,z)$ is the mass density, and α, β, γ are the three Eulerian angles for the orientation of a body-fixed coordinate system $\xi\eta\zeta$, whose origin coincides with the center of mass (cf. Fig. 2.5), with respect to the directions of the space-fixed axes $(X), (Y), (Z)$.

The most general motion of the rigid body is the superposition of the velocity of its center of mass $\dot{\boldsymbol{r}}_c(t) = \boldsymbol{v}_c$ and a rotation around the center of mass with an angular velocity $\boldsymbol{\omega}(t)$:

$$\dot{\boldsymbol{r}}(t) = \boldsymbol{v}_c(t) + \boldsymbol{\omega}(t) \times (\boldsymbol{r}(t) - \boldsymbol{r}_c(t)) \tag{2.11}$$

The vector $\boldsymbol{\omega}$ of the instantaneous angular velocity can be projected onto the space-fixed axes as well as onto the axes of the body-fixed coordinate system. These components can be expressed by the Eulerian angles and their time derivatives

$$\omega_x = -\dot{\beta}\sin\alpha + \dot{\gamma}\sin\beta\cos\alpha \tag{2.12a}$$

$$\omega_y = \dot{\beta}\cos\alpha + \dot{\gamma}\sin\beta\sin\alpha \tag{2.12b}$$

$$\omega_z = \dot{\alpha} + \dot{\gamma}\cos\beta \tag{2.12c}$$

$$\omega_\xi = -\dot{\alpha}\sin\beta\cos\gamma + \dot{\beta}\sin\gamma \tag{2.13a}$$

$$\omega_\eta = \dot{\alpha}\sin\beta\sin\gamma + \dot{\beta}\cos\gamma \tag{2.13b}$$

$$\omega_\zeta = \dot{\alpha}\cos\beta + \dot{\gamma} \tag{2.13c}$$

An example is the force-free motion of a symmetric top.

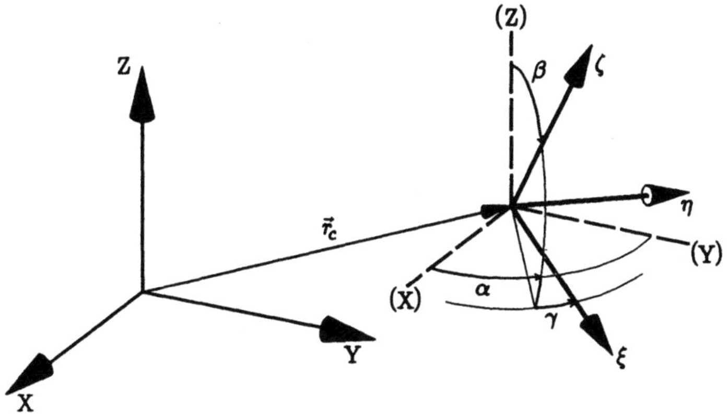

Fig. 2.5. Coordinates for the determination of position and orientation of a rigid body in space. The Euler angle β is the angle between the (Z)- and ζ-axis, the Euler angle α is defined as the angle between the line of intersection of the $(Z)\zeta$-plane with the $(X)(Y)$-plane and the (X)-axis, and the Euler angle γ is the angle between the line of intersection of the $(Z)\zeta$-plane with the $\xi\eta$-plane and the ξ-axis.

2.3 Kinematics of the special theory of relativity

When computing animation sequences which involve relative motions of the objects or of the observer, usually a Galilei transformation

$$\begin{aligned} x' &= x - Vt \\ y' &= y \\ z' &= z \\ t' &= t \end{aligned} \tag{2.14}$$

is applied to transform from a coordinate system XYZ to a system $X'Y'Z'$ moving relative to each other in X (and X') direction with the velocity V (cf. Fig. 2.6). This is a very good approximation for terrestrial scenarios with relative velocities much smaller than the velocity of light. The correct space-time structure of our physically real world, however, is much more complex and not imaginable for us. This very strange structure is revealed only at velocities, which approach the velocity of light. Therefore, the correct relativistic behaviour must be taken into account for the animation of extraterrestrial scenes in astrophysical simulations and, of course, in a correct modelling of science fiction.

As the essential step in the transition from non relativistic to relativistic kinematics the Galilei transformation (2.14) has to be replaced by the Lorentz transformation

$$\begin{aligned} x' &= \frac{x - Vt}{\sqrt{1 - \left(\frac{V}{c}\right)^2}} \\ y' &= y \\ z' &= z \\ t' &= \frac{t - \left(\frac{V}{c^2}\right)x}{\sqrt{1 - \left(\frac{V}{c}\right)^2}} \quad . \end{aligned} \tag{2.15}$$

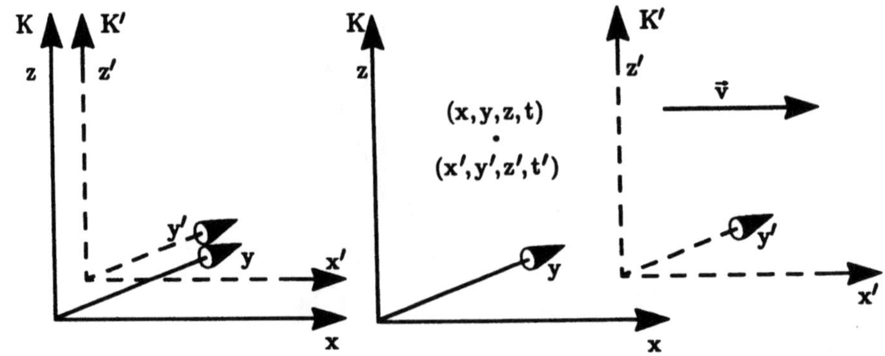

Fig. 2.6. Two coordinate systems K and K' moving relative to each other in X (and X') direction with the velocity V.

The main consequences are the Lorentz contraction of moving bodies, the time dilatation (better known as the famous twin paradoxon) and the strange properties of the relativistic theorem for adding velocities. For velocities in the range of human experience the relativistic effects are tiny. Even a racing car at a speed of 300 km/h is shortened by 1.5×10^{-13} m which is only 1/1000 of the diameter of an atom. But at velocities approaching the velocity of light $c = 300\,000$ km/s the effects become dramatic. However, it should be noted that the Lorentz transformation (2.15) tells us what we measure but not what we see.

2.4 Effects of signal propagation time

Especially in scientific visualisation, it might become necessary to distinguish between the kinematic behaviour which can already be quite complicated like in special relativity and the visual appearance of this behaviour for the observer. The only way we can experience the state of a distant object is by receiving physical signals from there. Those signals spread with a certain characteristic velocity which leads to the fact that a signal which was sent out from a part of the object which was further away is received at later time.

Therefore, a picture which we take of the object at a certain time contains information about the object at various time steps before. If, for example, one tries to animate what bats "see", one has to take into account the velocity of sound in air.

This effect is even more dramatic in special relativity where we have to deal with the finite velocity of light in order to gain a correct visual impression of the spacetime structure. The picture we would see of a relativistic moving object is produced by photons which arrive at the same time at the eye or at a detector, but which were emitted from the object when it was at various positions. Fig. 2.7 shows that a straight rod, which is moving towards us at a very high speed will appear bent, because the photons from the outer parts have to travel a longer way than the ones from the inner parts and have thus to be started, when the rod was further away.

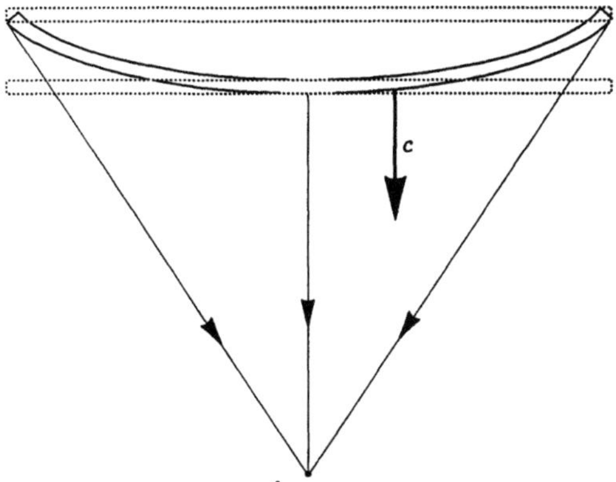

Fig. 2.7. A straight rod which is moving towards the observer with a velocity of almost the speed of light will appear bent, because the photons from the outer parts of the rod have to travel a longer way and therefore have to start earlier in order to arrive at the same time at the observer.

Combining the effects of the Lorentz-transformation (like contraction and aberration) and light travel time an even simple kinematic animation like flying with almost the velocity of light through Berlin's Brandenburg gate gives a visual impression one would naively have never expected (cf. Fig. 2.8) (Ertl et al., 1991).

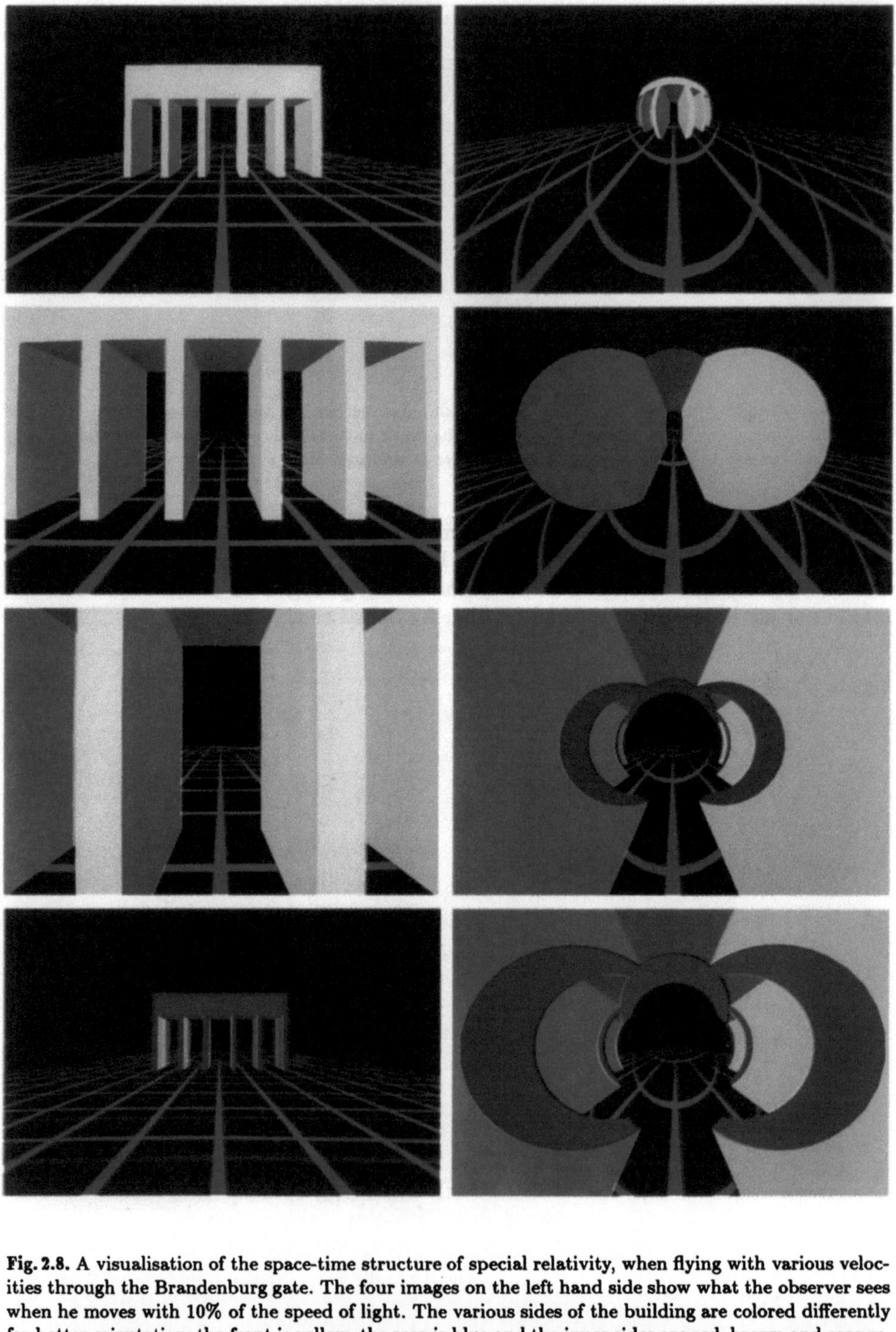

Fig. 2.8. A visualisation of the space-time structure of special relativity, when flying with various velocities through the Brandenburg gate. The four images on the left hand side show what the observer sees when he moves with 10% of the speed of light. The various sides of the building are colored differently for better orientation: the front is yellow, the rear is blue and the inner sides are red, brown and orange. In the bottom picture the observer has turned 180 degrees and looks back towards the rear side. The four images in the right column show what an observer would see, if he moved with 99% of the speed of light. The gate appears dramatically distorted and although the observer looks into the direction of the motion he is able to see the inner and the rear sides as well.

3 Basic principles of dynamics

In this chapter we will present a short review of the physical laws which are necessary to produce physically correct motion for computer animation. Dynamics describes the motion of point masses and rigid bodies under the influence of external forces.

3.1 Mechanics of point masses

In ordinary computer animation sequences the occuring velocities are much smaller than the velocity of light and the gravitational forces are small as well. Therefore, Newton's laws are the appropriate theory for correct description of the dynamical behaviour:

1. Without external forces, a body is at rest or moves with constant velocity on a straight line.
2. An external force $\boldsymbol{F}$ acting on a body of mass m results in an acceleration $\boldsymbol{a}$ with $\boldsymbol{F} = m\boldsymbol{a}$.
3. *actio* = *reactio* that means to every action corresponds a reaction in opposite direction and of equal size.

3.1.1 Newton's law for the motion of a point mass

The motion of a point mass m under the influence of an external force $\boldsymbol{F}$ is given in an inertial frame by Newton's second law:

$$m\ddot{\boldsymbol{r}} = \boldsymbol{F} \quad . \tag{3.1}$$

Forces with constant magnitude corresponding to the kinematic examples in the last chapter are the gravity $\boldsymbol{F} = m\boldsymbol{g}$ and the centrifugal force $\boldsymbol{F} = m\omega^2\boldsymbol{r}$.

Eq. 3.1 is a differential equation of second order for the position vector $\boldsymbol{r}$. With given initial values at $t = 0$ for position $\boldsymbol{r}_0$ and velocity $\boldsymbol{v}_0$ and known force $\boldsymbol{F}(\boldsymbol{r}, t)$, the motion can immediately be calculated by integration of (3.1). This procedure is called *direct dynamics* and the result is the position vector $\boldsymbol{r} = \boldsymbol{r}(t)$ as a function of time.

$$\boldsymbol{a}(t) = \frac{1}{m}\boldsymbol{F}(t) \tag{3.2a}$$

$$\boldsymbol{v}(t) = \frac{1}{m}\int_0^t \boldsymbol{F}(t')\,dt' + \boldsymbol{v}_0 \tag{3.2b}$$

$$\boldsymbol{r}(t) = \frac{1}{m}\int_0^t \left(\int_0^{t'} \boldsymbol{F}(t'')\,dt''\right) dt' + \boldsymbol{v}_0 t + \boldsymbol{r}_0 \quad . \tag{3.2c}$$

It is convenient to introduce the momentum $\boldsymbol{p}$:

$$\boldsymbol{p} = m\boldsymbol{v} \quad . \tag{3.3}$$

Newton's law then reads

$$\dot{\boldsymbol{p}} = \boldsymbol{F} \quad , \tag{3.4}$$

which leads to the consequence that without external forces momentum is conserved:

$$\boldsymbol{F} = 0 \quad \Longrightarrow \boldsymbol{p} = \text{constant} \quad . \tag{3.5}$$

The angular momentum of a point mass with momentum $\boldsymbol{p}$ with respect to the origin of the coordinate system is defined as

$$\boldsymbol{L} = \boldsymbol{r} \times \boldsymbol{p} \quad , \tag{3.6}$$

and the torque $\boldsymbol{T}$ produced by a force acting at $\boldsymbol{r}$ as

$$\boldsymbol{T} = \boldsymbol{r} \times \boldsymbol{F} \quad . \tag{3.7}$$

This quanitites are used in the dynamic equation for rotation:

$$\dot{\boldsymbol{L}} = \frac{d}{dt}(\boldsymbol{r} \times \boldsymbol{p}) = \boldsymbol{r} \times \dot{\boldsymbol{p}} + \dot{\boldsymbol{r}} \times \boldsymbol{p} = \boldsymbol{r} \times \dot{\boldsymbol{p}} = \boldsymbol{T} \quad . \tag{3.8}$$

In the absence of external torques the angular momentum is conserved:

$$\boldsymbol{T} = 0 \quad \Longrightarrow \boldsymbol{L} = \text{constant} \quad . \tag{3.9}$$

3.1.2 Relativistic dynamics of a point mass

For animation problems in our daily environment Newton's mechanics is the appropriate theory. For animation problems in astrophysics and above all in science fiction with velocities near the velocity of light, the special theory of relativity must be applied. Besides the different kinematics discussed in Sect. 2.3, there are also modifications in dynamics compared with Newton's theory.

For a point mass the relativistic equations of motion are formally quite similar to Newton's equations

$$\frac{d\boldsymbol{p}}{dt} = \boldsymbol{F} \tag{3.10a}$$

$$\frac{dE}{dt} = \boldsymbol{F} \cdot \boldsymbol{v} \quad . \tag{3.10b}$$

The essential difference is that the relativistic momentum $\boldsymbol{p}$ and the relativistic energy E for a mass point with rest mass m_0 has the form

$$\boldsymbol{p} = \frac{m_0 \boldsymbol{v}}{\sqrt{1 - \left(\frac{v}{c}\right)^2}} \tag{3.11a}$$

$$E = \frac{m_0 c^2}{\sqrt{1 - \left(\frac{v}{c}\right)^2}} \tag{3.11b}$$

with the consequence that for any object the velocity of light c is the limiting velocity.

The treatment of extended bodies in the frame of a relativistic theory is a highly complicated task and far beyond the scope of this tutorial. Even the terminus rigid body is not allowed, since in a rigid body the sound velocity is infinite and therefore larger than c.

3.1.3 Non-inertial coordinate systems

For some purposes it can be convenient to observe the motion from a moving, an accelerated or a rotating system. There are two ways to solve this problem. The first is to solve (3.1) in the inertial system and then to transform the solution into the desired system. The other possibility, which is completely equivalent to the first, is to transform (3.1) into the non-inertial system. When transforming into a rotating system we use the general law for the transformation of the time derivative

$$\frac{d}{dt} = \frac{d'}{dt} + \omega \times , \tag{3.12}$$

where $\frac{d'}{dt}$ denotes the time derivative in the rotating system. The resulting modified equation of motion contains additional terms. E.g., in the transition to a rotating system with the angular velocity $\boldsymbol{\Omega}(t)$ terms describing Coriolis forces, centrifugal forces and forces caused by the time dependence of $\boldsymbol{\Omega}$ arise:

$$m\frac{d'^2\boldsymbol{r}}{dt^2} = \boldsymbol{F} - 2m\boldsymbol{\Omega} \times \frac{d'\boldsymbol{r}}{dt} - m\boldsymbol{\Omega} \times (\boldsymbol{\Omega} \times \boldsymbol{r}) - m\dot{\boldsymbol{\Omega}} \times \boldsymbol{r} \quad . \tag{3.13}$$

Although (3.13) seems to be far more complicated there are many cases, where (3.13) is the better formulation. One example is the motion of particles in a binary system with two orbiting stars as presented in Fig. 3.1.

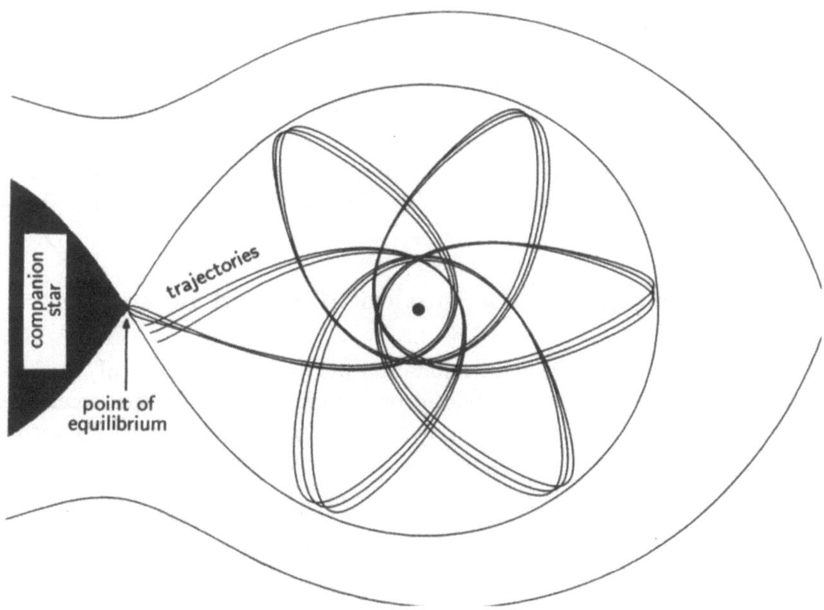

Fig. 3.1. The trajectories of particles in a rotating frame under influence of the gravitational forces of two orbiting stars

3.1.4 Computer animation by particle simulation

The method of particle simulation is a powerful tool to treat hydrodynamic problems. Furthermore, this approach automatically leads to animation sequences. The basic idea is to replace the $10^{25} - 10^{60}$ atoms or molecules of a macroscopic gaseous or fluid object by $10^4 - 10^5$ pseudo particles which interact in such a way that the macroscopic properties like pressure or viscosity are correctly simulated. The equations of motion of these pseudó particles including all external and internal forces are integrated and macroscopic physical quantities are derived form the positions and velocities of the particles. In order to obtain smooth simulation pictures the pseudo particles are smeared out to a continuous density.

A good example for this very general method is the formation of an accretion disk in a close binary system (Ruder et al., 1990). Such a system consists of a normal star and a degenerated object, e.g. a white dwarf star, a neutron star or a black hole. The normal star fills its Roche volume and matter flows from the equilibrium point between the two stars to the compact object and forms a disk caused by the angular momentum of the overflowing matter. In the corotating system of the two stars the dynamic equation which must be solved for each particle has the form

$$\frac{d'\boldsymbol{v}}{dt} = \nabla\left(\frac{Gm_1}{|\boldsymbol{r}_1 - \boldsymbol{r}|} + \frac{Gm_2}{|\boldsymbol{r}_2 - \boldsymbol{r}|}\right) - 2\boldsymbol{\Omega} \times \boldsymbol{v} - \boldsymbol{\Omega} \times (\boldsymbol{\Omega} \times \boldsymbol{r}) - \frac{1}{\rho}\nabla P + \nu\Delta\boldsymbol{v}\,, \tag{3.14}$$

where, on the right hand side, the terms represent the gravitational forces of the two stars, the Coriolis force, the centrifugal force, the pressure (ρ is the density) and the viscosity.

Due to viscous interaction the orbits around the compact object become circular, mass flows inwards and angular momentum flows outwards in the disk. In Fig. 3.2 some snapshots of the time evolution series are shown. In addition, the viscosity causes dissipation of energy, which leads to a local temperature. A realistic animation sequence is obtained by converting the corresponding spectral (Planck) distribution for these temperatures to colours on a graphic screen. For the simulation of a stationary disk, as shown in Fig. 3.3, 40 000 pseudo particles are necessary and the computation based on a well vectorized code requires more than a day of cpu time on a Cray 2 supercomputer.

3.2 Euler's equations for the motion of a rigid body

A point mass is a very special case for animation purposes. More general, the objects, which should be animated, are rigid bodies or systems of rigid bodies connected by joints. A rigid body is defined by its total mass M and its tensor of inertia $\underline{\underline{\boldsymbol{\Theta}}}$, which in a body-fixed $\xi\eta\zeta$-system with the origin in the center of mass has the following form

$$\underline{\underline{\boldsymbol{\Theta}}} = \begin{pmatrix} \int(\eta^2+\zeta^2)\rho d\tau' & -\int\xi\eta\rho d\tau' & -\int\xi\zeta\rho d\tau' \\ -\int\xi\eta\rho d\tau' & \int(\xi^2+\zeta^2)\rho d\tau' & -\int\eta\zeta\rho d\tau' \\ -\int\xi\zeta\rho d\tau' & -\int\eta\zeta\rho d\tau' & \int(\xi^2+\eta^2)\rho d\tau' \end{pmatrix} . \tag{3.15}$$

$\rho = \rho(\xi, \eta, \zeta)$ is the local density of matter and $d\tau' = d\xi d\eta d\zeta$ is the volume element.

Its position and orientation in space is defined by the three cartesian coordinates x_c, y_c, z_c for the position of the center of mass and by the three Euler angles α, β, γ for

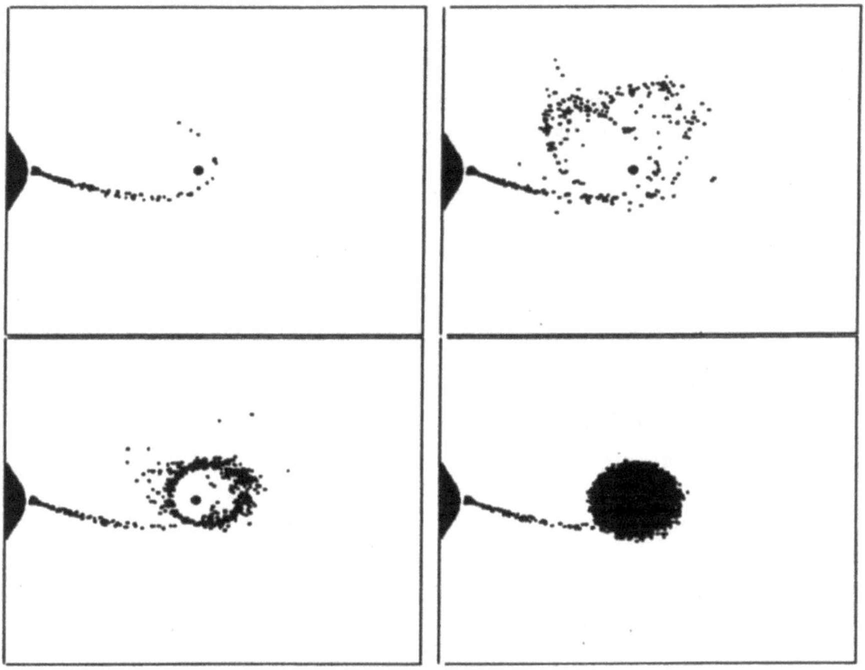

Fig. 3.2. A time series showing the formation of an accretion disk as a result of a dynamic computer simulation. Because of the gravitational pull of the compact object, matter is pulled away from the red star forming a thin disk around the white dwarf.

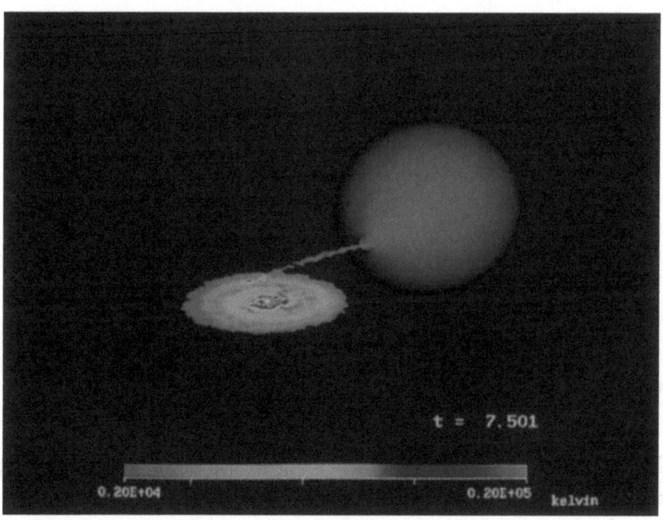

Fig. 3.3. An evolved stationary accretion disk where the color coding represents the local temperature produced by viscous interaction of the particles.

the orientation of a body-fixed coordinate system (cf. Fig. 2.5). The introduction of a body-fixed system is essential since in a space-fixed coordinate system the components of the tensor of inertia of a rigid body are not constant, but depend on the position and orientation of the body in space in a complicated way.

The definition of the body-fixed system is arbitrary, however, a special choice, namely the principal axes of inertia and the origin in the center of mass is very advantageous. In this system, the tensor of inertia takes a simple diagonal form

$$\underline{\underline{\Theta}} = \begin{pmatrix} A & 0 & 0 \\ 0 & B & 0 \\ 0 & 0 & C \end{pmatrix} \tag{3.16}$$

with

$$\begin{aligned} A &= \int (\eta^2 + \zeta^2)\rho(\xi,\eta,\zeta)d\xi d\eta d\zeta \\ B &= \int (\xi^2 + \zeta^2)\rho(\xi,\eta,\zeta)d\xi d\eta d\zeta \\ C &= \int (\xi^2 + \eta^2)\rho(\xi,\eta,\zeta)d\xi d\eta d\zeta \quad , \end{aligned} \tag{3.17}$$

where A, B, C are the principle moments of inertia.

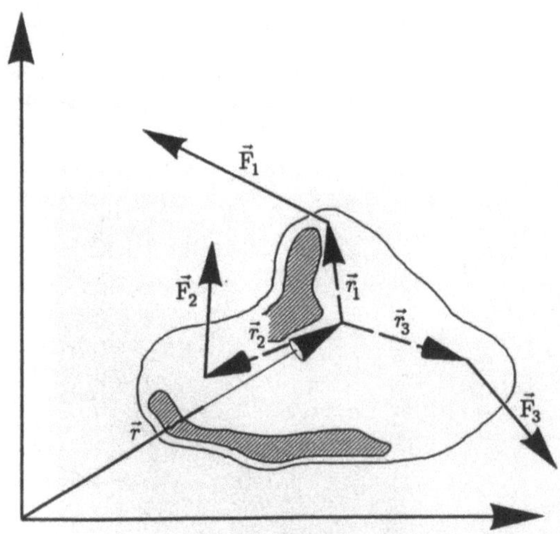

Fig. 3.4. Forces acting on a rigid body

In general, a number of forces act on the rigid body (cf. Fig. 3.4) and the problem is the resulting motion in space. Using center-of-mass coordinates x_c, y_c, z_c and fixing the origin of the body-fixed $\xi\eta\zeta$-system at the center of mass the equations of motion for the system decouple in an equation for the center of mass and one relative to it:

$$M\ddot{\boldsymbol{R}}_c = \dot{\boldsymbol{P}} = \sum_i \boldsymbol{F}_i \quad , \tag{3.18a}$$

$$\dot{\boldsymbol{L}} = \frac{d}{dt}(\underline{\underline{\Theta}}\,\omega) = \sum_i (\boldsymbol{r}'_i \times \boldsymbol{F}_i) + \sum_i \boldsymbol{T}_i \quad . \tag{3.18b}$$

Here $M = \int \rho \, d\xi d\eta d\zeta$ denotes the total mass of the rigid body, $\boldsymbol{F}_i$ the external forces, $\boldsymbol{L}$ the angular momentum and $\boldsymbol{T}_i$ the external torques relative to the center of mass. The motion of the center of mass can easily be calculated by integrating (3.18a). The integration of (3.18b) needs a further processing since with respect to space-fixed axes the components of the tensor of inertia are, in general, time-dependent. Therefore, the time derivative $\frac{d}{dt}$ in the space-fixed system must be expressed by the time derivative $\frac{d'}{dt}$ in the rotating body-fixed system with the help of the general relation (3.12). Using (3.12) and $\underline{\underline{\Theta}} = \text{const}$ in the body-fixed frame, the Eulerian equations of motion of a rigid body follow immediately from (3.18b)

$$\frac{dL_\xi}{dt} = A\dot{\omega}_\xi + \omega_\eta \omega_\zeta (C - B) = T_\xi \tag{3.19a}$$

$$\frac{dL_\eta}{dt} = B\dot{\omega}_\eta + \omega_\xi \omega_\zeta (A - C) = T_\eta \tag{3.19b}$$

$$\frac{dL_\zeta}{dt} = C\dot{\omega}_\zeta + \omega_\xi \omega_\eta (B - A) = T_\zeta \quad . \tag{3.19c}$$

Knowing the torques these equations can be integrated, yielding the components $\omega_\xi, \omega_\eta, \omega_\zeta$ of the angular velocity projected on the body-fixed axes as functions of time. To arrive finally at the motion of the body-fixed system a further integration is necessary, namely the integration of the first-order differential equation system connecting the components $\omega_\xi, \omega_\eta, \omega_\zeta$ with the Eulerian angles α, β, γ and their time derivatives, which can immediately be obtained from (2.13)

$$\dot{\alpha} = -\frac{1}{\sin\beta}(\omega_\xi \cos\gamma + \omega_\eta \sin\gamma) \tag{3.20a}$$

$$\dot{\beta} = \omega_\xi \sin\gamma + \omega_\eta \cos\gamma \tag{3.20b}$$

$$\dot{\gamma} = \omega_\xi \cot\beta \cos\gamma - \omega_\eta \cot\beta \sin\gamma + \omega_\zeta \quad . \tag{3.20c}$$

Eqs. (3.1), (3.18a) and (3.20) represent the basic equations of motion for a point mass and for a rigid body. With given initial conditions for position and velocity and known external forces and torques the position of the center of mass and the orientation of the body-fixed axes can be calculated by means of a standard integration routine.

3.3 A simple example: the falling rod

To warm up let us consider as a simple example a rod freely falling down from a certain height, hitting the bottom and jumping off again. The rod possesses the mass M and the length l. Its tensor of inertia $\underline{\underline{\Theta}}$ relative to the center of mass and in the body-fixed sytem of the principle axes of inertia is of the form

$$\underline{\underline{\Theta}} = \begin{pmatrix} A & 0 & 0 \\ 0 & A & 0 \\ 0 & 0 & 0 \end{pmatrix} \tag{3.21}$$

with $A = \frac{1}{12}Ml^2$.

The rod is described by the three Cartesian coordinates x_c, y_c, z_c of its center of mass lying in the middle of the rod and by the two Eulerian angles α, β for the orientation. The third Eulerian angle γ is without meaning since the principle moment of inertia around the axis is zero and, therefore, the rod is not able to rotate around this axis with the consequence that ω_ζ is zero. In free fall, the only external force is the gravity Mg which acts on the center of mass. This is also the reason why the external torques vanish.

Taking into account the above considerations the equations of motion (3.18a) and (3.19) simplify to

$$M\ddot{x}_c = 0 \tag{3.22a}$$
$$M\ddot{y}_c = 0 \tag{3.22b}$$
$$M\ddot{z}_c = -Mg \tag{3.22c}$$
$$\dot{\omega_\xi} = 0 \tag{3.22d}$$
$$\dot{\omega_\eta} = 0 \quad , \tag{3.22e}$$

which immediately can be solved analytically, yielding

$$x_c = v_{cx0}t + x_{c0} \tag{3.23a}$$
$$y_c = v_{cy0}t + y_{c0} \tag{3.23b}$$
$$z_c = -\frac{1}{2}gt^2 + v_{cz0}t + z_{c0} \tag{3.23c}$$
$$\omega_\xi = \omega_{\xi 0} \tag{3.23d}$$
$$\omega_\eta = \omega_{\eta 0} \quad , \tag{3.23e}$$

where the values of the position and velocity of the initial state are denoted by an index zero.

The motion of the rod is the superposition of the parabola of its center of mass and a rotation with constant angular velocity $\omega = \sqrt{\omega_\xi^2 + \omega_\eta^2}$ around an axis perpendicular to the rod. The explicite time dependence of the Eulerian angles can be obtained by integrating (3.20)

$$\tan\alpha = \tan(\omega t)/\sin\beta_{\text{min}} \tag{3.24a}$$
$$\cos\beta = \cos(\omega t)\cos\beta_{\text{min}} \quad , \tag{3.24b}$$

where β_{min} is the smallest angle between the axis of the rod and the z-axis, which occurs during the rotation.

The falling and rotating rod is also an appropriate example to discuss basically what happens during an impact. To demonstrate more clearly the essential idea we simplify the motion and assume that the rod rotates in the same plane in which its center of mass moves. This means $\alpha = 0$. To be consistent with later notation we introduce the angle $\varphi = 90° - \beta$ for the orientation of the rod. Fig. 3.5 shows the situation at the moment of impact.

The motion is completely described by

$$x_c = v_{cx0}t + x_{c0} \tag{3.25a}$$
$$z_c = -\frac{1}{2}gt^2 + v_{cz0}t + z_{c0} \tag{3.25b}$$
$$\varphi = -\omega_y t + \varphi_0 \quad . \tag{3.25c}$$

With x_e, z_e we denote the Cartesian coordinates of the lower impacting end of the rod, which are geometrically related to the coordinates x_c, z_c, φ by

$$x_e = x_c - \frac{l}{2}\cos\varphi \tag{3.26a}$$
$$z_e = z_c - \frac{l}{2}\sin\varphi \quad . \tag{3.26b}$$

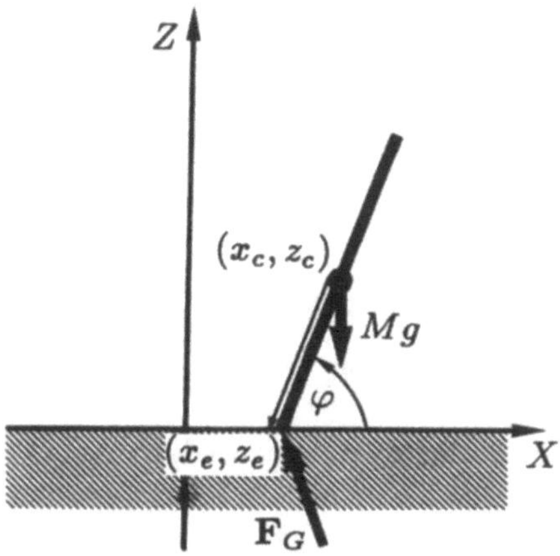

Fig. 3.5. Coordinates and external forces of a rigid rod during impact

The time derivative of (3.26) yields for the corresponding velocities

$$\dot{x}_e = \dot{x}_c + \frac{l}{2}\sin\varphi\dot{\varphi} \tag{3.27a}$$

$$\dot{z}_e = \dot{z}_c - \frac{l}{2}\cos\varphi\dot{\varphi} \quad . \tag{3.27b}$$

As a further notation we introduce the upper indices *impact* for the values of the quantities at the time of the impact, *before* for immediately before and *after* for immediately after the impact.

Assuming the rod and the bottom to be infinitely rigid the duration of the impact is infinitely short and the ground reaction force $\boldsymbol{F}_G$ is a δ-peak. The integration of the equations of motion

$$M\ddot{x}_c = F_{Gx}(t) = c_x\delta(t^{\text{impact}}) \tag{3.28a}$$

$$M\ddot{z}_c = -Mg + F_{Gz}(t) = -Mg + c_z\delta(t^{\text{impact}}) \tag{3.28b}$$

$$\Theta\ddot{\varphi} = (x_e^{\text{impact}} - x_c)F_{Gz} - (z_e^{\text{impact}} - z_c)F_{Gx} \tag{3.28c}$$

over the infinitesimally short impact time leads to the relations between the changes of the linear and angular momenta and the integral of the impact forces and torques

$$M(\dot{x}_c^{\text{after}} - \dot{x}_c^{\text{before}}) = M\Delta\dot{x}_c = \int_{t^{\text{impact}}-\epsilon}^{t^{\text{impact}}+\epsilon} F_{Gx}(t')dt' = c_x \tag{3.29a}$$

$$M(\dot{z}_c^{\text{after}} - \dot{z}_c^{\text{before}}) = M\Delta\dot{z}_c = \int_{t^{\text{impact}}-\epsilon}^{t^{\text{impact}}+\epsilon} [-Mg + F_{Gz}(t')]\, dt' = c_z \tag{3.29b}$$

$$\Theta(\dot{\varphi}^{\text{after}} - \dot{\varphi}^{\text{before}}) = \Theta\Delta\dot{\varphi} = (x_e^{\text{impact}} - x_c)c_z - (z_e^{\text{impact}} - z_c)c_x \quad . \tag{3.29c}$$

To calculate explicitly these changes further information on the mechanical properties of the ground is necessary. Two limiting cases are on the one hand a totally elastic behaviour and on the other hand a totally inelastic behaviour. In the first case the z-component of the velocity of the impacting end $\dot{z}_e$ of the rod alters its sign and the second equation for determining the constants c_x and c_z is the conservation of the total energy during the impact. In the second case the end of the rod comes to rest immediately after the impact, which yields the two additional equations desired.

Let us first look to the totally elastic case. The equation of the reversal of the z-velocity reads

$$\begin{aligned}
\dot{z}_e^{\text{after}} &= -\dot{z}_e^{\text{before}} \quad \Longrightarrow \\
\Delta\dot{z}_e &= \dot{z}_e^{\text{after}} - \dot{z}_e^{\text{before}} \\
&= \dot{z}_c^{\text{after}} - \frac{l}{2}\cos(\varphi^{\text{impact}})\dot{\varphi}^{\text{after}} - \dot{z}_c^{\text{before}} + \frac{l}{2}\cos(\varphi^{\text{impact}})\dot{\varphi}^{\text{before}}
\end{aligned} \tag{3.30a}$$

$$\Longrightarrow \quad \Delta\dot{z}_c - \frac{l}{2}\cos(\varphi^{\text{impact}})\Delta\dot{\varphi} = -2\dot{z}_e^{\text{before}} \quad , \tag{3.30b}$$

and the conservation of the total energy during the impact leads to

$$\begin{aligned}
&E^{\text{after}} - E^{\text{before}} = 0 \quad \Longrightarrow \\
&\frac{1}{2}M\left[(\dot{x}_c^{\text{after}})^2 + (\dot{z}_c^{\text{after}})^2\right] + Mgz_c^{\text{impact}} + \frac{1}{2}\Theta(\dot{\varphi}^{\text{after}})^2 \\
&-\frac{1}{2}M\left[(\dot{x}_c^{\text{before}})^2 + (\dot{z}_c^{\text{before}})^2\right] - Mgz_c^{\text{impact}} - \frac{1}{2}\Theta(\dot{\varphi}^{\text{before}})^2 \\
&= \frac{1}{2}M\left[\Delta\dot{x}_c(\Delta\dot{x}_c + 2\dot{x}_c^{\text{before}}) + \Delta\dot{z}_c(\Delta\dot{z}_c + 2\dot{z}_c^{\text{before}})\right] \\
&\quad + \frac{1}{2}\Theta\left[\Delta\dot{\varphi}(\Delta\dot{\varphi} + 2\dot{\varphi}^{\text{before}})\right] = 0 \quad .
\end{aligned} \tag{3.30c}$$

Eqs. (3.30b,c) and (3.29c) determine the changes of the velocities during the impact. The values of the quantities immediately before the impact can be calculated from the solution (3.25) and depend uniquely on the initial conditions. Having the changes at hand the values of the positions at the impact and the values of the velocities immediately after the impact serve as initial conditions for the further motion until the next impact.

In the second case of a totally inelastic impact with $\dot{x}_e^{\text{after}} = 0$ and $\dot{z}_e^{\text{after}} = 0$ the equations read

$$\begin{aligned}
\Delta\dot{x}_e &= \dot{x}_e^{\text{after}} - \dot{x}_e^{\text{before}} = -\dot{x}_e^{\text{before}} \quad \Longrightarrow \\
\Delta\dot{x}_e &= \dot{x}_c^{\text{after}} + \frac{l}{2}\sin(\varphi^{\text{impact}})\dot{\varphi}^{\text{after}} - \dot{x}_c^{\text{before}} - \frac{l}{2}\sin(\varphi^{\text{impact}})\dot{\varphi}^{\text{before}}
\end{aligned}$$

$$\Longrightarrow \quad \Delta\dot{x}_c + \frac{l}{2}\sin(\varphi^{\text{impact}})\Delta\dot{\varphi} = -\dot{x}_e^{\text{before}} \quad , \tag{3.31a}$$

$$\begin{aligned}
\Delta\dot{z}_e &= \dot{z}_e^{\text{after}} - \dot{z}_e^{\text{before}} = -\dot{z}_e^{\text{before}} \quad \Longrightarrow \\
\Delta\dot{z}_e &= \dot{z}_c^{\text{after}} - \frac{l}{2}\cos(\varphi^{\text{impact}})\dot{\varphi}^{\text{after}} - \dot{z}_c^{\text{before}} + \frac{l}{2}\cos(\varphi^{\text{impact}})\dot{\varphi}^{\text{before}}
\end{aligned}$$

$$\Longrightarrow \quad \Delta\dot{z}_c - \frac{l}{2}\cos(\varphi^{\text{impact}})\Delta\dot{\varphi} = -\dot{z}_e^{\text{before}} \quad , \tag{3.31b}$$

From (3.31a,b) and (3.29c) with the same procedure as above the motion can further be monitored. Of course, in this case the total energy is not conserved. In Fig. 3.6 three stroboscopic time series of a falling rod are shown for different elastic behaviour of the ground.

In the above considerations the impact is a point event in time. If one is interested in details during the impact the mechanical properties of the colliding parts must be taken into account. This requires the knowledge of the relation between the reaction

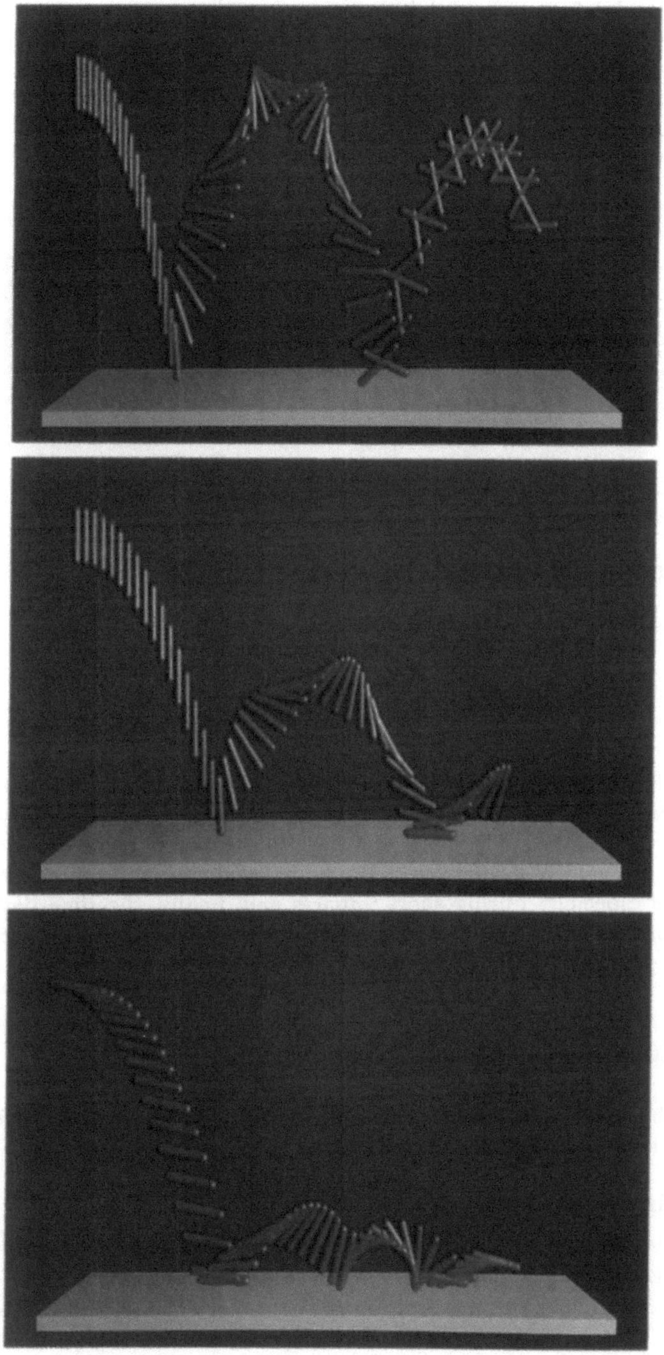

Fig. 3.6. Three stroboscopic time series of a falling rod for an increasing (top to bottom) damping component in the ground reaction force.

force and the local deformation and, if damping elements are present, the instantaneous deformation velocity. Inserting a realistic relation $\boldsymbol{F}_G(\boldsymbol{r}_{\text{deform}}, \dot{\boldsymbol{r}}_{\text{deform}})$ into the right hand sides of (3.28) and integrating numerically these equations yield all quantities as continuous functions of time even in the impact region, which is now extented in a small time interval. As an example for a specific ground behaviour the following relations could be used as components of the ground reaction force:

$$F_{Gz} = a\,(z_{\text{deform}})^b + d\,\dot{z}_{\text{deform}} \quad ; \quad F_{Gx} = \mu F_{Gz} \quad . \tag{3.32}$$

The vertical component of the ground reaction force depends on the deformation and on the deformation velocity of the ground; a, b and d are material constants. The horizontal component of the ground reaction force is usually determined by friction and therefore proportional to F_{Gz}.

4 Mechanics of multi-linked models for biomechanical simulations

For the modelling of human beings or animals with legs and arms multi-linked systems of extended bodies connected by joints are necessary. Developing a satisfactory model is by no means a trivial problem. The joints and their constraints must be correctly described as well as the mechanical properties of the body segments. Important is the action of external forces especially during short impacts and, finally, the time development of the internal torques in the joints, which are generated by the skeletal muscles and thus reflect the free will of the being to control its motion.

4.1 Description of a multi-linked system

In principle, the mechanical problem of a multi-linked system has been solved for a long time. We will recapitulate some general facts.

4.1.1 Coordinates and degrees of freedom

Let us consider a system with n segments and $n-1$ joints. At first, we will assume that the motion takes place in a plane. Then, each segment is defined by three coordinates, two cartesian coordinates for the position of the center of mass and one angle for the orientation (cf. Fig. 4.1a).

All together we have $3n$ coordinates and, therefore, we need $3n$ equations. In the plane case each joint yields two conditions, namely that the coordinates of the two end points of corresponding segments coincide. Taking into account these conditions we end up with $3n - 2(n-1) = n+2$ degrees of freedom. The number $n+2$ is also the minimal number of coordinates needed for a unique description. These coordinates are free from any restrictions. Additionally, we have three equations of motion, two for the center of mass of the whole system and one for the motion relative to it. Thus, there remain $n+2-3=n-1$ quantities undetermined, the torques in the $n-1$ joints, the free will of the individual.

An other way to consider the same subject is to regard each segment separately. In our plane case we need 3 coordinates $(x_{ci}, z_{ci}, \varphi_i)$ for each segment and, with known forces and torques acting on the segment, the motion of its center of mass and relative to it can be obtained by numerically integrating the 3 equations of motion

$$M_i \ddot{x}_{ci} = \sum_j F_{ijx} \tag{4.1a}$$

$$M_i \ddot{z}_{ci} = \sum_j F_{ijz} \tag{4.1b}$$

$$\Theta_i \ddot{\varphi}_i = \sum_j (x_{ij} F_{ijz} - z_{ij} F_{ijx}) - \sum_j T_{ijy} \quad . \tag{4.1c}$$

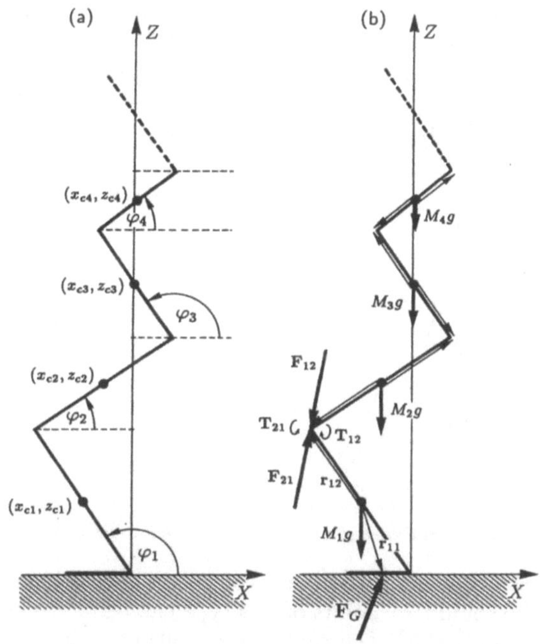

Fig. 4.1. (a) Coordinates of a plane multi-linked system. Each segment is defined by the Cartesian coordinates x_{ci}, z_{ci} of its center of mass and an angle φ_i determining its orientation relative to the horizontal line. (b) Forces and torques acting on the segments. Beside the external forces like gravitation and ground reaction force additionally, for the first joint, the internal forces and torques are shown.

$\sum_j \boldsymbol{F}_{ij}$ and $\sum_j \boldsymbol{T}_{ij}$ contain all forces and torques, external and internal, acting on the segment. The external forces such as gravitation, friction or contact forces must be given, the internal forces are caused by the constraints of the joints. Due to *actio* = *reactio* there are two unknown force components at a joint acting in opposite direction on the two segments connected by this joint. Since the condition of a joint yields two equations, the $2(n-1)$ internal forces are uniquely determined by the $2(n-1)$ equations of the joint conditions. These forces are necessary to keep the segments together. The standard method to deal with such problems is the Langrangian formalism. Solving the $3n + 2(n-1)$ equations, the motion of the n connected segments and the internal joint forces are obtained simultaneously. The $(n-1)$ torques, of course, are free again and determine the active behaviour of the model.

The same counting rhymes can be applied to a three dimensional model. To determine the degrees of freedom we note that one segment needs six coordinates and the $n-1$ joints yield $3(n-1)$ conditions thus, the minimal number of free coordinates is given by $6n - 3(n-1) = 3n + 3$. Taking into account the six equations of motion for the whole system, we end up with $3(n-1)$ freely choosable internal torques. This number, however, is only valid for freely movable spherical ball joints.

4.1.2 Joints and constraints

In the simulation of the motion of animals or human beings the modelling of joints is an essential part. Simple cases are hinge joints, which are movable around definite axes, or spherical ball joints, which are freely movable in three dimensions. For such joints the conditions for the connection of the two segments can easily be formulated as algebraic equations. An example for a ball joint is the human hip, one for a hinge joint is the human knee. The last is true only in a first approximation, a closer inspection exhibits a complex structure shown in Fig 4.2.

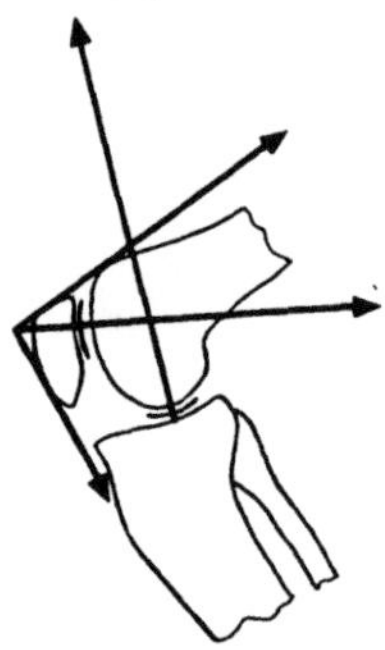

Fig. 4.2. Skeletal structure of the human knee joint with the different muscle and joint forces.

Far more complicated are joints without axes or points of rotation. Biological examples of such joints are the shoulders. Joints of this type can be modelled by introducing appropriate trunk-fixed and arm-fixed surfaces, which roll and slide on each other. These surfaces must be individually determined with the help of film analysis.

A further important aspect in modelling joints is the range of mobility. Each joint possesses a definite range of angles for flection depending on the structure of the skeleton. During the course of animation sequences care must be taken that the joint angles do not exceed these biological limits. Of course, the most promising way is to imitate nature. When approaching the limiting angle in the joint an internal torque is built up which decelerates the motion and prevents an overshooting. This torque must depend on the difference of the actual joint angle and the limiting angle φ_{limit} and on the angular velocity of the joint angle. This velocity dependence is necessary to include a damping mechanism and thus to avoid an unnatural elastic reflection from the stop. A reasonable form of this torque is

$$T(|\varphi_{\text{limit}} - \varphi_{\text{joint}}|, \dot{\varphi}_{\text{joint}}) = \begin{cases} [a(|\varphi_{\text{limit}} - \varphi_{\text{joint}}|)^b + c]^{-1}(1 + d\dot{\varphi}_i) & \text{for } |\varphi_{\text{limit}} - \varphi_{\text{joint}}| \leq \varphi_{\text{on}} \\ 0 & \text{for } |\varphi_{\text{limit}} - \varphi_{\text{joint}}| > \varphi_{\text{on}} \end{cases}, \qquad (4.2)$$

where a, b, c, d and φ_{on} are adjustable parameters. For a certain joint the angle φ_{on} denotes how many degrees before φ_{limit} the limiting torque starts to act. Typical values for φ_{on} are of the order of a few degrees.

4.2 The wobbling mass

In trying to simulate motion with high accelerations with a multi-linked system consisting of rigid bodies as segments the limits of such a model soon become obvious. The reasons for this failure are easily recognized by considering a high-speed movie of a jump or of an impact. The segments of the human body, trunk, thigh, lower leg, arms are far away from reacting like rigid bodies during an impact. Therefore, it is necessary to take into account the different composition of the body, namely the rigid skeletal part and the soft components like tendons, muscles, organs, and last but not least fat.

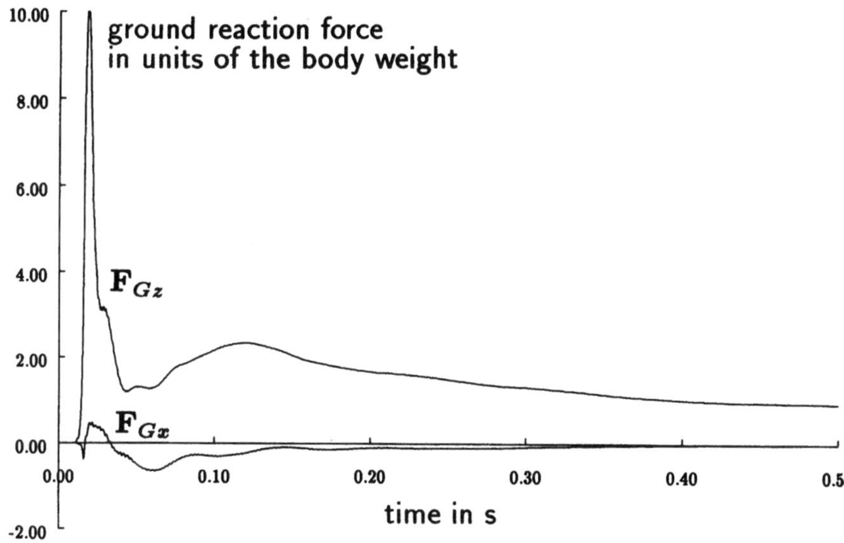

Fig. 4.3. Measured ground reaction force as a function of time for a down jump with landing on the heel.

For a better understanding of this requirement we roughly estimate what happens during the impact after a down jump of a human body from a height of 1 meter. The landing velocity is about 4.4 m/s. The heel is stopped within about 1 cm. Assuming for simplicity a constant deceleration this stopping length leads to a deceleration of 100 times the acceleration of gravity and it acts for about 5 milliseconds. During this time the skeletal part of the lower leg comes to rest. The wobbling mass of the body, however, remains almost in free fall, covers 3 to 4 cm and is then smoothly decelerated by the forces coupling it to the skeleton which is already at rest. The measurement of the time evolution of a typical ground reaction force, shown in Fig. 4.3, clearly exhibits this behaviour. The height of the impact peak is about eight times the body weight and not 100 times and the width is about 20 ms and not 5 ms. A model consisting only of rigid bodies yields totally wrong results, especially, if the internal forces, which are of special interest in biomechanical research, are calculated. The further course of the ground reaction forces, the active phase, is determined by intentionally produced torques in the joints. In this region of the motion with smaller accelerations the wobbling mass is of secondary importance.

A correct modelling of the human body, e.g. with finite element methods, is extremely expensive and an animation based on this level nearly hopeless. A simple, practicable and very successful method to model the essential properties is to introduce a *wobbling mass* (Gruber et al., 1987, 1991), which summarizes all the soft parts of a segment and which is coupled quasi-elastically and strongly damped to the skeletal part. This wobbling mass can be moved and rotated relative to the skeleton as shown in Fig. 4.4.

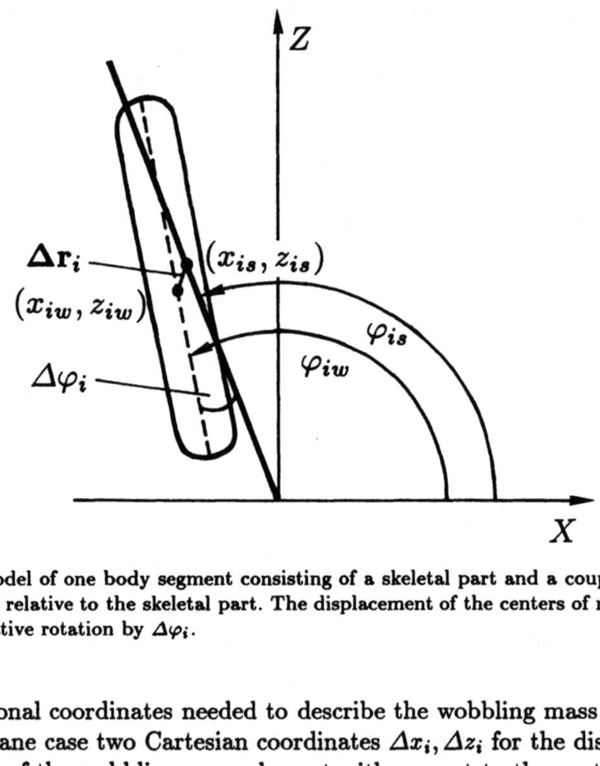

Fig. 4.4. Plane model of one body segment consisting of a skeletal part and a coupled wobbling mass, which is movable relative to the skeletal part. The displacement of the centers of mass is described by $\Delta\boldsymbol{r}_i$ and the relative rotation by $\Delta\varphi_i$.

The additional coordinates needed to describe the wobbling mass are for each segment in the plane case two Cartesian coordinates $\Delta x_i, \Delta z_i$ for the displacement of the center of mass of the wobbling mass element with respect to the center of mass of the corresponding rigid element and the angles $\Delta\varphi_i$ for the torsion relative to the orientation of the skeletal part. In three dimensions six coordinates are necessary, three for the displacement $\Delta x_i, \Delta y_i, \Delta z_i$, and three $\Delta\alpha_i, \Delta\beta_i, \Delta\gamma_i$ for the torsion. The motion of each wobbling mass is determined by the six (or three in the plane case) equations of motion for an extended body analogously to eqs. (3.1), (3.18a) and (3.20). The forces and torques acting in addition to gravity are given by the coupling mechanism between skeletal and wobbling part and depend on the displacement coordinates. Via *actio* = *reactio* the same forces and torques act on the skeletal part in the opposite direction.

Therefore, a multi-linked system with wobbling masses possesses the same number of internal torques reflecting the free will.

To adjust as well as possible the coupling between the skeletal part and the wobbling mass experimental input is necessary. In general, for a small displacement the coupling is very loose and it becomes stiff in a narrow range. Such a behaviour can be described by a dependence of the form (displacement)^m with an exponent $m \approx 3 \ldots 4$. Furthermore, the motions of the wobbling masses are strongly damped and come to rest after some few oscillations. This is described by a dependence of the velocities on the displacements. Additionally, it must be taken into account that the coupling constants of the wobbling masses are different for displacements parallel or perpendicular to the skeletal parts. The relative torques of the angular displacements $\Delta\varphi_i$ can be treated in an analogous manner. After a long period of biomechanical experiments together with fitting procedures we have found that the following relations for the coupling forces seem to be (for the plane case) the best approximations in the framework of our modelling.

$$T_{wi} = a_{wi}\Delta\varphi_i + b_{wi}\Delta\dot{\varphi}_i \tag{4.3a}$$

$$F_{wi,l} = c_{wi,l}\mathrm{sign}(\Delta r_{il})|\Delta r_{il}|^3 + d_{wi,l}\Delta\dot{r}_{il} \tag{4.3b}$$

$$F_{wi,t} = c_{wi,t}\mathrm{sign}(\Delta r_{it})|\Delta r_{it}|^3 + d_{wi,t}\Delta\dot{r}_{it} \quad . \tag{4.3c}$$

The longitudinal and transversal components $F_{wi,l}$ and $F_{wi,t}$ of the coupling forces are then decomposed onto the space-fixed axes and yield the Cartesian components $F_{wi,x}$ and $F_{wi,z}$, which enter into the equations of motion. The coupling constants $a_{wi}, b_{wi}, c_{wi,l}, d_{wi,l}, c_{wi,t}$ and $d_{wi,t}$ must be adjusted individually.

To avoid confusion it should be stated that in the model presented here only the skeletal parts are connected by joints and, therefore, only they couple via the internal reaction forces, but each wobbling mass is only coupled to its corresponding skeletal part.

To become more concrete, we will discuss a three-linked wobbling mass model in detail and demonstrate some animation sequences.

4.3 The three-linked wobbling mass model

The minimum number of segments to simulate a human being is three: one segment for the trunk, a second for the two (parallel) thighs and a third for the two lower legs.

A wobbling mass element is coupled to each segment. Even this simplest model possesses $n + 2 + 3n = 4n + 2 = 14$ (for $n = 3$) coordinates (see Fig. 4.5) in the plane case and 14 second order differential equations must be integrated for the dynamic simulation. Furthermore, for an explicit calculation the geometrical and mechanical parameters of the model must be fixed.

4.3.1 Geometrical and mechanical parameters

As geometrical quantities we have the three lengths l_i of the segments

lower leg including foot $l_1 = 0.43$ m,
thigh $l_2 = 0.45$ m,
trunk including head $l_3 = 0.75$ m

and the biologically possible ranges of the two angles

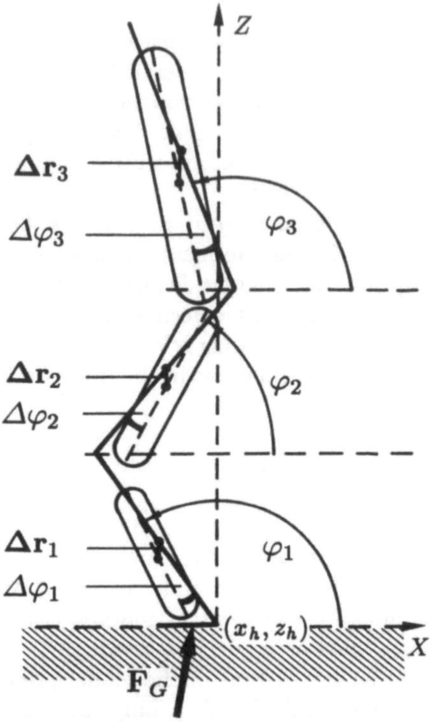

Fig. 4.5. Coordinates of the three-linked wobbling mass model. The position of the heel is described by the Cartesian coordinates (x_h, z_h), the orientations of the skeletal segments by the angles $\varphi_1, \varphi_2, \varphi_3$ and the positions of the wobbling masses relative to their corresponding skeletal parts by the vectors of displacement and the angles of rotation (cf. Fig. 4.4).

$$15° \le \varphi_{\mathbf{knee}} = 180° - \varphi_2 + \varphi_1 \le 182°,$$
$$15° \le \varphi_{\mathbf{hip}} = 180° + \varphi_3 - \varphi_2 \le 210°.$$

The mechanical quantities of the model for each segment are the mass m_i, the disposition in a skeletal part with mass m_{is} and a wobbling part m_{iw}, and the corresponding moments of inertia Θ_{is} and Θ_{iw}. (The index s stands for *skeletal* and w for *wobbling*.)

The masses of the segments can be taken from the medical literature and are given in units of the total mass m:

mass of a lower leg including foot $m_1 = 0.06\ m$,
mass of a thigh $m_2 = 0.11\ m$,
mass of the trunk including head and arms $m_3 = 0.66\ m$.

To obtain numbers for the percental disposition of each segment into a skeletal and wobbling part is much more difficult. Our experimental studies together with fitting procedures yield as reasonable percentages:

lower leg: skeletal part 25%, wobbling mass 75%,
thigh: skeletal part 25%, wobbling mass 75%,
trunk: skeletal part 50%, wobbling mass 50%.

Experimental data for the moments of inertia of the segments relative to their centers of mass although are not available in the literature, therefore, we approximately calculate these quantities by means of the relation for the moment of inertia of a cylinder with mass m_i, length l_i, and average radius r_i perpendicular to its axis

$$\Theta_i = m_i \left(\frac{l_i^2}{12} + \frac{r_i^2}{4} \right) \quad . \tag{4.4}$$

Using the lengths l_i of the segments and experimentally determined radii we obtain from (4.4) the following values for the six moments of inertia divided by the total mass:

$$\begin{array}{ll} \Theta_{1s}/m = 0.00023\ \mathrm{m}^2 & \Theta_{1w}/m = 0.00037\ \mathrm{m}^2 \\ \Theta_{2s}/m = 0.00047\ \mathrm{m}^2 & \Theta_{2w}/m = 0.00152\ \mathrm{m}^2 \\ \Theta_{3s}/m = 0.00845\ \mathrm{m}^2 & \Theta_{3w}/m = 0.03380\ \mathrm{m}^2 . \end{array}$$

4.3.2 Equations of motion

To obtain an impression of the form and complexity of the problem, in the following the equations of motion for the three-linked wobbling mass model using the coordinates from Fig. 4.5 are explicitly given (after a lengthy but elementary calculation):

$$\begin{aligned} & m\ddot{x}_h - (m_1 + 2m_2 + 2m_3)\frac{l_1}{2}\sin\varphi_1\ddot{\varphi}_1 - (m_2 + 2m_3)\frac{l_2}{2}\sin\varphi_2\ddot{\varphi}_2 \\ & \quad - m_3\frac{l_3}{2}\sin\varphi_3\ddot{\varphi}_3 + m_{1w}\Delta\ddot{x}_1 + m_{2w}\Delta\ddot{x}_2 + m_{3w}\Delta\ddot{x}_3 \\ & \quad = (m_1 + 2m_2 + 2m_3)\frac{l_1}{2}\cos\varphi_1\dot{\varphi}_1^2 + (m_2 + 2m_3)\frac{l_2}{2}\cos\varphi_2\dot{\varphi}_2^2 \\ & \quad + m_3\frac{l_3}{2}\cos\varphi_3\dot{\varphi}_3^2 + F_{Gx} \end{aligned} \tag{4.5a}$$

$$\begin{aligned} & m\ddot{z}_h + (m_1 + 2m_2 + 2m_3)\frac{l_1}{2}\cos\varphi_1\ddot{\varphi}_1 + (m_2 + 2m_3)\frac{l_2}{2}\cos\varphi_2\ddot{\varphi}_2 \\ & \quad + m_3\frac{l_3}{2}\cos\varphi_3\ddot{\varphi}_3 + m_{1w}\Delta\ddot{z}_1 + m_{2w}\Delta\ddot{z}_2 + m_{3w}\Delta\ddot{z}_3 \\ & \quad = (m_1 + 2m_2 + 2m_3)\frac{l_1}{2}\sin\varphi_1\dot{\varphi}_1^2 + (m_2 + 2m_3)\frac{l_2}{2}\sin\varphi_2\dot{\varphi}_2^2 \\ & \quad + m_3\frac{l_3}{2}\sin\varphi_3\dot{\varphi}_3^2 + F_{Gz} - mg \end{aligned} \tag{4.5b}$$

$$\begin{aligned} & -\Theta_{1s}\ddot{\varphi}_1 + m_{1s}\frac{l_1}{2}\sin\varphi_1\Delta\ddot{x}_1 - m_{1s}\frac{l_1}{2}\cos\varphi_1\Delta\ddot{z}_1 \\ & \quad = T_G - \frac{l_1}{2}\sin\varphi_1\left[F_{Gx} + \frac{m_1}{m_{1w}}F_{w1x}\right] \\ & \quad + \frac{l_1}{2}\cos\varphi_1\left[F_{Gz} + \frac{m_1}{m_{1w}}F_{w1z}\right] + T_{12} - T_{w1} + T_{corr\,1} \end{aligned} \tag{4.5c}$$

$$\begin{aligned} & -\Theta_{2s}\ddot{\varphi}_2 + m_{1s}l_2\sin\varphi_2\Delta\ddot{x}_1 - m_{1s}l_2\cos\varphi_2\Delta\ddot{z}_1 \\ & \quad + m_{2s}\frac{l_2}{2}\sin\varphi_2\Delta\ddot{x}_2 - m_{2s}\frac{l_2}{2}\cos\varphi_2\Delta\ddot{z}_2 \\ & \quad = -l_2\sin\varphi_2\left[F_{Gx} + \frac{m_1}{m_{1w}}F_{w1x} + \frac{1}{2}\frac{m_2}{m_{2w}}F_{w2x}\right] \\ & \quad + l_2\cos\varphi_2\left[F_{Gz} + \frac{m_1}{m_{1w}}F_{w1z} + \frac{1}{2}\frac{m_2}{m_{2w}}F_{w2z}\right] - T_{12} + T_{23} - T_{w2} + T_{corr\,2} \end{aligned} \tag{4.5d}$$

$$-\Theta_{3s}\ddot{\varphi}_3 - m_{3s}\frac{l_3}{2}\sin\varphi_3\Delta\ddot{x}_3 + m_{3s}\frac{l_3}{2}\cos\varphi_3\Delta\ddot{z}_3 \qquad (4.5e)$$
$$= [\frac{l_3}{2}\sin\varphi_3\frac{m_3}{m_{3w}}F_{w3x} - \frac{l_3}{2}\cos\varphi_3\frac{m_3}{m_{3w}}F_{w3z}] - T_{2\,3} - T_{w3} + T_{corr\,3}$$

$$\ddot{x}_h - \frac{l_1}{2}\sin\varphi_1\ddot{\varphi}_1 + \Delta\ddot{x}_1 = \frac{l_1}{2}\cos\varphi_1\dot{\varphi}_1^2 - \frac{1}{m_{1w}}F_{w1x} \qquad (4.5f)$$

$$\ddot{z}_h + \frac{l_1}{2}\cos\varphi_1\ddot{\varphi}_1 + \Delta\ddot{z}_1 = \frac{l_1}{2}\sin\varphi_1\dot{\varphi}_1^2 - \frac{1}{m_{1w}}F_{w1z} - g \qquad (4.5g)$$

$$\ddot{x}_h - l_1\sin\varphi_1\ddot{\varphi}_1 - \frac{l_2}{2}\sin\varphi_2\ddot{\varphi}_2 + \Delta\ddot{x}_2$$
$$= l_1\cos\varphi_1\dot{\varphi}_1^2 + \frac{l_2}{2}\cos\varphi_2\dot{\varphi}_2^2 - \frac{1}{m_{2w}}F_{w2x} \qquad (4.5h)$$

$$\ddot{z}_h + l_1\cos\varphi_1\ddot{\varphi}_1 + \frac{l_2}{2}\cos\varphi_2\ddot{\varphi}_2 + \Delta\ddot{z}_2$$
$$= l_1\sin\varphi_1\dot{\varphi}_1^2 + \frac{l_2}{2}\sin\varphi_2\dot{\varphi}_2^2 - \frac{1}{m_{2w}}F_{w2z} - g \qquad (4.5i)$$

$$\ddot{x}_h - l_1\sin\varphi_1\ddot{\varphi}_1 - l_2\sin\varphi_2\ddot{\varphi}_2 - \frac{l_3}{2}\sin\varphi_3\ddot{\varphi}_3 + \Delta\ddot{x}_3$$
$$= l_1\cos\varphi_1\dot{\varphi}_1^2 + l_2\cos\varphi_2\dot{\varphi}_2^2 + \frac{l_3}{2}\cos\varphi_3\dot{\varphi}_3^2 - \frac{1}{m_{3w}}F_{w3x} \qquad (4.5j)$$

$$\ddot{z}_h + l_1\cos\varphi_1\ddot{\varphi}_1 + l_2\cos\varphi_2\ddot{\varphi}_2 + \frac{l_3}{2}\cos\varphi_3\ddot{\varphi}_3 + \Delta\ddot{z}_3$$
$$= l_1\sin\varphi_1\dot{\varphi}_1^2 + l_2\sin\varphi_2\dot{\varphi}_2^2 + \frac{l_3}{2}\sin\varphi_3\dot{\varphi}_3^2 - \frac{1}{m_{3w}}F_{w3z} - g \qquad (4.5k)$$

$$-\Theta_{1w}(\ddot{\varphi}_1 + \Delta\ddot{\varphi}_1) = T_{w1} \qquad (4.5l)$$
$$-\Theta_{2w}(\ddot{\varphi}_2 + \Delta\ddot{\varphi}_2) = T_{w2} \qquad (4.5m)$$
$$-\Theta_{3w}(\ddot{\varphi}_3 + \Delta\ddot{\varphi}_3) = T_{w3} \quad . \qquad (4.5n)$$

In addition to the symbols already explained in the previous sections in Eq. (4.5) some further new quantities occur, namely the x- and z-component of the ground reaction force F_{Gx} and F_{Gz}, the torque T_G, which is transmitted at the foot by the ground reaction force (cf. Fig. 4.5) the torques T_{12}, T_{23}, which are generated by skeletal muscles in the knee and hip joints. T_{corri} is an additional torque in each joint, which is necessary to correct the violation of the angular momentum caused by the coupling of the wobbling mass. These latter quantities are tiny and only of theoretical interest.

It should be mentioned that the structure of the equations is always the same as in Eq. (4.5). This is valid for two and three dimensions and for an arbitrary number of segments. Denoting the vector of independent coordinates with $\boldsymbol{x}$, the mass matrix with $\underline{\underline{M}}$, the vector of the generalized Coriolis and centrifugal forces with $\boldsymbol{C}$ and the vector of the generalized forces and torques acting on each segment with $\boldsymbol{F}$ the equations of motion can be generally written in the form

$$\underline{\underline{M}}(\boldsymbol{x}) \cdot \ddot{\boldsymbol{x}} + \boldsymbol{C}(\boldsymbol{x}, \dot{\boldsymbol{x}}) = \boldsymbol{F}(\boldsymbol{x}, \dot{\boldsymbol{x}}) \quad , \qquad (4.6)$$

to which standard integration routines can be applied.

4.4 Inverse and direct dynamics

The equations of motion can be considered from two basically different points of view. On the one hand the motion can be regarded as known, then the left hand sides of the equations are determined and the forces and torques on the right hand side can be calculated. This procedure requires experimental input either by film analysis or by measurements of accelerations. On the other hand with all external forces and internal torques given the integration of the equations of motion leads to the physically correct motion of the system. We will now discuss in some detail these two aspects.

4.4.1 Inverse dynamics

The simplest case is to fix markers at the body and to follow the space-time trajectory of these points with the help of a high-speed camera or other adequate systems. Ideally, as a result all coordinates describing the system are given on a discret time grid with typical time steps of the order of milliseconds. In order to obtain the forces and torques these time sequences have to be differentiated twice (cf. Eq. (4.5) and (4.6)). This numerical differentiation leads to an artificially oscillating behaviour and to a reduced accuracy in the time resolution. An additional complication results from the fact that the markers are fixed at the skin which shows a displacement with respect to the skeleton especially by motions with high accelerations. However, for slow motions the method of film analysis works well and is successfully applied in gait analysis in biomechanical research (e.g. Aleshinsky and Zatsiorsky, 1978; Zajac and Gordon, 1989).

In order to experimentally investigate motions with high acceleration like impacts during contact with the ground we have developed an alternative method to determine the internal forces and torques. To avoid the problems introduced by the numerical differentiation the external forces are directly measured by means of force platforms and a sufficient number of accelerations by appropriately placed accelerometers. These devices can be operated at higher frequencies of about 4 kHz yielding experimental data with a far better time resolution. As follows from the general considerations in Sect. 4.1.1 concerning the degrees of freedom of a multi-linked model and as can be explicitly seen from Eq. (4.5) in the case of a plane three-linked model the two internal torques are unknown quantities even if all external forces and torques are measured. These two (or $n-1$ in the general plane or $3(n-1)$ in the most general threedimensional case) internal torques are not accessible to a direct measurement without invasive operations. This problem can unbloodily be solved by measuring the corresponding number of accelerations. Then, the internal torques are gained from these experimental input not by twofold differentiating but by integrating the equations of motion, a procedure, which is numerically far more stable and yields a much higher degree of accuracy.

With the external and internal forces and torques at hand the physically correct continuous motion can be calculated in a reproducible way. Furthermore, at each arbitrary plane of intersection of the body the forces and torques transmitted in this plane can be determined at any moment, which is of special interest in biomechanical problems.

4.4.2 Controlling direct dynamics

The ultimate goal of producing animation sequences for human beings and animals is the physically realistic simulation of the motion taking into account the biomechanical constraints, the correct mechanical properties of the objects and a behaviour controlled feedback for the building up of the internal torques. This means that all forces and torques, which enter the equations of motion, are determined either by a relation between the force, the deformation and the deformation-velocity or by a self-controlling mechanism.

4.4.2.1 External reaction forces

These forces arise when a body segment collides with objects in its environment. For almost all possible situations a relation of the form

$$F = a\,(z_{\mathbf{deform}})^b + d\,\dot{z}_{\mathbf{deform}} \tag{4.7}$$

for each component of the force with appropriately adjusted parameters is a sufficiently good approximation. The parameters can be determined either empirically or in the frame of an elasto-mechanical theory. To give an example, in Fig. 4.6 the experimental force-deformation relation of the human heel is shown for the static and a dynamic case.

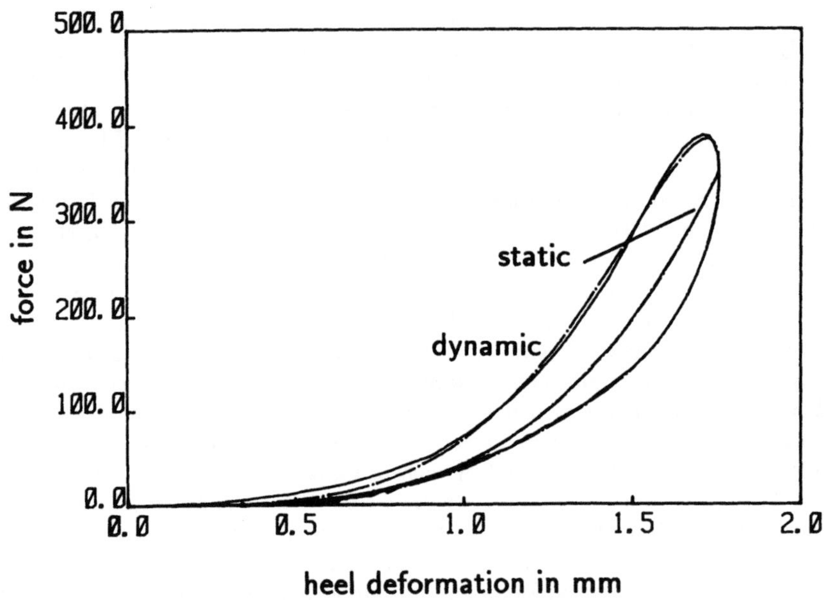

Fig. 4.6. Empirical force-deformation relation of the human heel for the static and a dynamic case.

In general, the relation for the reaction force is a superposition of the mechanical properties of the body and the object. An example is a down jump on a plank, where as well the elastic properties of the heel enter as the bending of the plank (cf. Sect. 4.5). In the presence of friction as a further constraint the component of the reaction force tangential to the striking surfaces must be smaller than the component perpendicular to the surface times the coefficient of friction otherwise sliding sets on.

4.4.2.2 Active internal torques

As discussed previously the internal torques produced by the muscles determine the controlled part of the motion. One way to find the torques for a desired motion as functions of time is the simple trial and error method, e.g. starting from a given initial state, varying the torques and integrating the equations of motion until the desired final state is achieved. A far more sophisticated way is to control the increase and the decrease of the internal torques by an active feedback mechanism. This method shall be demonstrated by the example of the active deceleration phase after a down jump.

During the free-fall phase the joint angles are assumed to be constant. Therefore, the internal net torques must be zero. Shortly after the impact the heels have come to rest, the velocity of the center of mass of the whole body is somewhat reduced by the impact and at the same time the bending of the body segments abruptly starts with definite angular velocities. They have to be stopped by building up the internal torques. Right before the impact the muscles are actively strained, however, without producing net torques. Caused by the bending of the segments the joint angles alter, the strained muscles and tendons are expanded and automatically produce torques, already a few milliseconds after impact. Due to the mechanical properties of the muscles and ligaments the increase of the torques is approximately proportional to the angular velocities $\dot{\varphi}_{ij}$ of the joint angles φ_{ij}. Therefore, in this start phase of increasing torques the internal torque T_{ij} in a joint at the time $t + dt$ can be calculated by

$$T_{ij}(t+dt) = T_{ij}(t) + c'_{ij}\dot{\varphi}_{ij}(t)dt \quad . \tag{4.8}$$

Of course, the torques cannot increase infinitely. Each joint is only able to build up a maximum torque $T_{ij}^{\max}$. Therefore, the increase of the torque will slow down when approaching this limiting torque. Such a behaviour can well be modelled by modifying (4.8) by an additional factor

$$T_{ij}(t+dt) = T_{ij}(t) + c_{ij}\dot{\varphi}_{ij}(t)\left(\frac{T_{ij}^{\max} - T_{ij}(t)}{T_{ij}^{\max}}\right) dt \quad . \tag{4.9}$$

Eq. (4.9) leads to a linear increase of the torque at the beginning and a smooth approaching to $T_{ij}^{\max}$. With appropriate chosen parameters for each joint the torque evolution of the form (4.9) leads, e.g. for a down jump, to a physically realistic hopping of the model.

To produce more and more complex motions more and more control parameters must be introduced in modelling the torques. The alteration of the torques can be controlled either by the coordinates and velocities of the body segments themselves or by external conditions of the environment. A simple example is the controlling of the deceleration phase after a down jump by the z-component of the velocity of the center of mass which can be written as an additional factor in (4.9) of the form

$$\begin{aligned} T_{ij}(t+dt) & \\ &= T_{ij}(t) + c_{ij}\dot{\varphi}_{ij}(t)\left(\frac{T_{ij}^{\max} - T_{ij}(t)}{T_{ij}^{\max}}\right)\cdot\left[1 + a_{ij}\left(\frac{\dot{z}_c}{\dot{z}_c^{\text{impact}}} - 1\right)\right] dt \quad . \end{aligned} \tag{4.10}$$

The choice of the parameter a_{ij} determines at what squat position the body comes to rest.

As an example for the modelling quality which can be achieved within the framework presented, in Fig. 4.7 the measured ground reaction force of a down jump (cf.

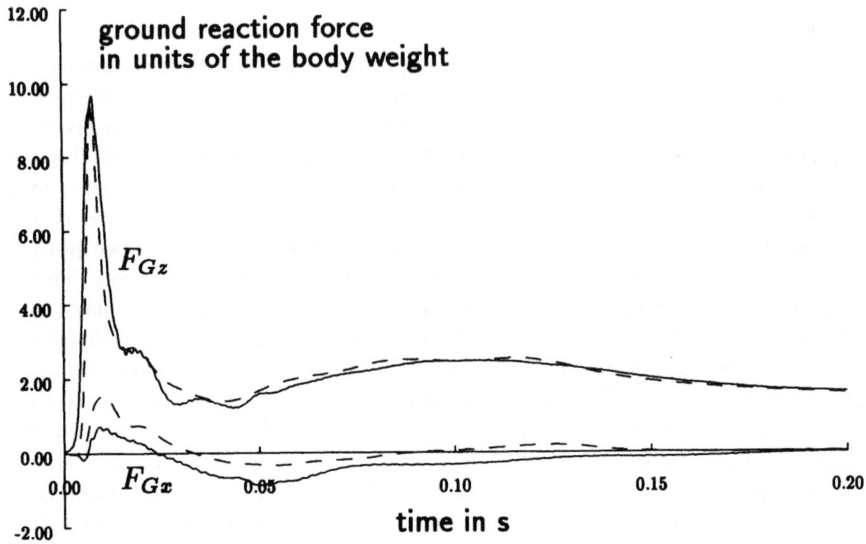

Fig. 4.7. Comparison of the measured and calculated components of the ground reaction forces during the landing on the heel and the following deceleration phase after a down jump. The theoretical curves are produced by integrating the equations of motion (4.5) without any experimental input.

Fig. 4.3) is shown together with the calculated force which was produced without any experimental input. This excellent agreement proves that the whole motion is physically correct described within an error of a few percents.

To remain realistic for actively motivated torques the finite reaction time of a human being, which is of the order of 0.1 s, must be taken into account. This means a retardation of this amount in using coordinates and velocities for the calculation of those changes in the torques which are caused by reactions of external conditions. Studies of such kind are also of great interest for biomechanical and behaviour research. At this stage modern methods of controlled learning must be applied. Besides these things a retardation is also not a trivial problem for the numerical treatment of the integration of the equations of motion.

4.5 Jumps and impacts

The best way to demonstrate the capabilities of our dynamic simulation are, of course, animation sequences. In the following Figs. 4.8 and 4.9 snapshots of two down jumps of an extended five-linked model are shown. In the first example the internal torques are controlled in such a way that the model comes to rest in a squat position and in the second example that the model jumps off again and performs a somersault.

Fig. 4.8. Snapshots of a down jump of a five-linked model with landing on a bending plank. The internal torques are controlled in such a way that the model comes to rest in a squat position.

Fig. 4.9. Snapshots of a down jump of a five-linked model with landing on a stiff plank. The internal torques are here controlled in such a way that the model jumps off again and performs a somersault.

Fig. 4.9. (continued)

5 Symbolic and numerical computation

The methods presented in the previous chapter can canonically be extended to multi-linked systems with more than three links or to three-dimensional models. However, the complexity of the equations of motion describing the planar three-link system with wobbling mass makes it obvious that the equations for much more complicated structures are hard to derive manually. Therefore, symbolic manipulation packages need to be used for an automatic derivation of the equations of motion.

Basically, there are two different approaches: The most common one is the following. In the first step the equations of motion are formulated for every single rigid body assuming it to be unconstrained. Each rigid body has six degrees of freedom, three for translation, and three for rotation. Corresponding to this number of degrees of freedom there are six equations of motion: The three Newtonian equations describe the translation of the centre of mass and the three Eulerian equations describe the rotation with respect to the centre of mass (Sect. 3.2). In a multi-linked system the n segments yield $6\,n$ equations of motion. While assembling the segments to a system the initially unknown forces and torques of constraint that effect the coupling between the segments are added to the external forces and torques. Additionally, the m constraints give an adequate number of further equations resulting in an exactly determined system of $6\,n + m$ equations. Unknown quantities in this case are the second derivatives of the segmental coordinates and the components of the forces and torques of constraint. The coordinates themselves and their first derivatives are known from the initial conditions.

In a second step the components of the forces and torques of constraint are eliminated from the equations of motion by the usual procedures for the symbolic manipulation of systems of linear equations. If there are m constraints the number of equations of motion is reduced to a set of $6\,n - m$. Using these constraints all of the $6\,n$ coordinates and their derivatives are replaced by the $6\,n-m$ generalized coordinates and derivatives of the system. Thus, the whole procedure results in $6\,n-m$ equations containing $6\,n-m$ unknown quantities, i.e. the second derivatives of the generalized coordinates. Again, the system of equations is uniquely determined.

As an example for this approach we discuss the plane two-linked rigid model (cf. Fig. 5.1). Here, we have 8 unknowns, the 6 coordinates $x_{c1}, z_{c1}, \varphi_1, x_{c2}, z_{c2}, \varphi_2$ and the 2 constraint forces F_{12x}, F_{12z}. The equations of motion can be easily derived:

$$m_1 \ddot{x}_{c1} = F_{Gx} + F_{12x} \tag{5.1a}$$

$$m_1 \ddot{z}_{c1} = -m_1 g + F_{Gz} + F_{12z} \tag{5.1b}$$

$$\Theta_1 \ddot{\varphi}_1 = (\boldsymbol{r}_{11} \times \boldsymbol{F}_G)_y + (\boldsymbol{r}_{12} \times \boldsymbol{F}_{12})_y + T_{12} \tag{5.1c}$$

$$m_2 \ddot{x}_{c2} = -F_{12x} \tag{5.2a}$$

$$m_2 \ddot{z}_{c2} = -m_2 g - F_{12z} \tag{5.2b}$$

$$\Theta_2 \ddot{\varphi}_2 = (\boldsymbol{r}_{21} \times \boldsymbol{F}_{12})_y - T_{12} \quad . \tag{5.2c}$$

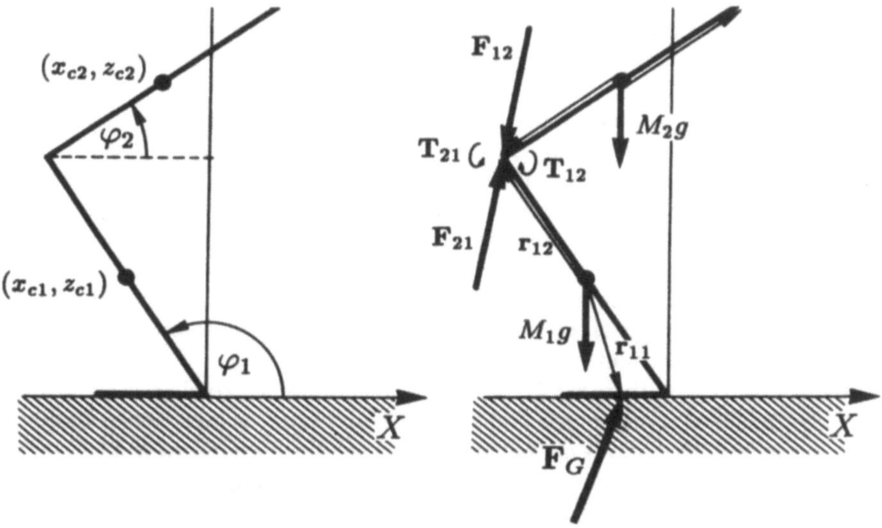

Fig. 5.1. The plane two-linked rigid model.

In addition, we have the joint conditions, which require that the upper end of the lower segment is connected to the lower end of the upper segment:

$$x_{c1} + \frac{l_1}{2}\cos\varphi_1 = x_{c2} - \frac{l_2}{2}\cos\varphi_2 \tag{5.3a}$$

$$z_{c1} + \frac{l_1}{2}\sin\varphi_1 = z_{c2} - \frac{l_2}{2}\sin\varphi_2 \quad . \tag{5.3b}$$

Using those, we can introduce 4 independent coordinates $x_h, z_h, \varphi_1, \varphi_2$ and eliminate the 2 unknown constraint forces and we get the minimum set of differential equations for 4 independent coordinates:

$$\begin{aligned}(m_1 + m_2)\ddot{x}_h &- (m_1 + 2m_2)\frac{l_1}{2}\sin\varphi_1\ddot{\varphi}_1 - m_2\frac{l_2}{2}\sin\varphi_2\ddot{\varphi}_2 \\ &= (m_1 + 2m_2)\frac{l_1}{2}\cos\varphi_1\dot{\varphi}_1^2 + m_2\frac{l_2}{2}\cos\varphi_2\dot{\varphi}_2^2 + F_{Gx}\end{aligned} \tag{5.4a}$$

$$\begin{aligned}m\ddot{z}_h &+ (m_1 + 2m_2)\frac{l_1}{2}\cos\varphi_1\ddot{\varphi}_1 + m_2\frac{l_2}{2}\cos\varphi_2\ddot{\varphi}_2 \\ &= (m_1 + 2m_2)\frac{l_1}{2}\sin\varphi_1\dot{\varphi}_1^2 + m_2\frac{l_2}{2}\sin\varphi_2\dot{\varphi}_2^2 + F_{Gz} - mg\end{aligned} \tag{5.4b}$$

$$-\Theta_1\ddot{\varphi}_1 = T_G - \frac{l_1}{2}\sin\varphi_1 F_{Gx} + \frac{l_1}{2}\cos\varphi_1 F_{Gz} + T_{12} \tag{5.5a}$$

$$-\Theta_2\ddot{\varphi}_2 = -l_2\sin\varphi_2 F_{Gx} + l_2\cos\varphi_2 F_{Gz} - T_{12} \quad . \tag{5.5b}$$

However, serious problems occur when manipulating the equations symbolically following the course of this procedure. Huge algebraic terms are produced during the symbolic elimination of the forces and torques of constraint and the replacement of the segmental coordinates by generalized coordinates. With an increasing number of degrees of freedom the size of these terms exceeds the capabilities of symbolic manipulation programs. Also, the generated source code may reach dimensions which are very hard to handle.

These problems can be avoided by utilizing a method, that requires the solution of a system of more equations, but whose terms are of a much simpler structure. The first step is the same as the one, described at the top of this section. The resulting system of linear equations at the end of this step, however, consists of $6n + m$ equations instead of $6n - m$. At this point the unknown quantities are the $6n$ second derivatives of the segmental coordinates and the m components of the forces and torques of constraint. It is possible to solve the system already at this stage and one obtains the second derivatives of the segmental coordinates and additionally the components of the forces and moments of constraint.

Using this method there are $6n$ differential equations of second order to be integrated instead of the $6n-m$ ones of the first approach. Moreover, at every integration step now there has to be solved a $6n+m$ system of linear equations compared to a $6n-m$ system. The particular terms of the equations, however, are quite simple and therefore easy to be generated automatically. Despite an increased number of equations the cpu-time needed for the second approach may decrease because of the highly simplified terms.

If we use this approach for the plane two-linked rigid model, we first have to differentiate the constraint conditions twice:

$$\ddot{x}_{c1} - \frac{l_1}{2}(\cos\varphi_1\dot{\varphi}_1^2 + \sin\varphi_1\ddot{\varphi}_1) = \ddot{x}_{c2} - \frac{l_2}{2}(\cos\varphi_2\dot{\varphi}_2^2 + \sin\varphi_2\ddot{\varphi}_2) \tag{5.6a}$$

$$\ddot{z}_{c1} + \frac{l_1}{2}(-\sin\varphi_1\dot{\varphi}_1^2 + \cos\varphi_1\ddot{\varphi}_1) = \ddot{x}_{c2} + \frac{l_2}{2}(-\sin\varphi_2\dot{\varphi}_2^2 + \cos\varphi_2\ddot{\varphi}_2) \quad . \tag{5.6b}$$

Together with eq. 5.1, we now have 8 linear equations for 6 second derivatives of the coordinates $\ddot{x}_{c1}, \ddot{z}_{c1}, \ddot{\varphi}_1, \ddot{x}_{c2}, \ddot{z}_{c2}, \ddot{\varphi}_2$ and 2 constraint forces F_{12x}, F_{12z} which have a much more simple structure than the minimum number eqs. 5.3 and 5.4.

Once, the equations of motion are derived in the general form of Eq. 4.6, they have to be integrated numerically. The first step in order to use one of the existing integration procedures is to split each of the second order equations into two first order equations by introducing a new independent variable. Preferably, the symbolic package already does this for you, before the equations are output in a form which can be easily integrated into the source code of your favourite programming language.

According to the forward formulation of the dynamic simulation the numerical problem can be characterized as an initial-value problem for a system of coupled ordinary differential equations:

$$\dot{\boldsymbol{x}} = \boldsymbol{f}(t, \boldsymbol{x}) \quad , \quad \boldsymbol{x}(t_0) = \boldsymbol{f}_0 \quad . \tag{5.7}$$

There are many excellent integration routines for initial-value problems available (for an overview of the area see Press, 1986) and one should definitely not start with implementing the Runge-Kutta algorithm again. For a good tradeoff between accuracy and efficiency a variable order, variable stepsize method should be chosen. We made good experiences with a code called DE (Shampine and Gordon, 1975), which is based on an Adams-Bashford predictor-corrector method. Especially when trying to resolve very sharp impacts the equations tend to appear stiff. This is a result of the predictor step which obviously cannot predict the correct behaviour after the impact. For this case, implicit BDF-methods (Gear, 1968) can be used.

The difference between eq. 4.6 and eq. 5.7 shows that the mass matrix has to be inverted for each evaluation of the right hand side. We use a routine from LINPACK for this part, but any other matrix solver will probably do the job. In order to reduce execution time an algorithm was suggested where it is not necessary to invert the mass matrix for each evaluation of the right hand side, but only, if it resulted in a significant change.

In the last chapter we tried to show that in our view the only reasonable way to reach a set of given end conditions (positions and velocities in the next keyframe) is to do a direct dynamic simulation with behavioural control through feedback from vision or other senses. However, there is still much more research to be done before this method will become computationally feasable. Until then, there is a need for being able to compute backwards. For a simple rigid body (like the rod from Sect. 3.3) this leads to a boundary-value problem. Numerical methods which can be used for this are either shooting algorithms or relaxation methods. We used extensively a relaxation procedure called Hemodes (Nobili and Turolla, 1988) which is based on the Henyey method (Henyey et al., 1964). For multi-linked models there is no unique solution for the boundary value problem. Solutions can only be found by optimizing additional constraints like form stability etc.

Once the dynamic behaviour of the skeleton is computed, there is much more to be done in order to generate a realistic looking human body, like the animation of the body surface and its reaction to deformations, hair, skin, and facial expressions, but all this is far beyond the scope of this tutorial.

6 A survey of commonly used computer animation approaches

Numerous articles on computer animation can be found in the proceedings of the SIGRAPH conferences and in the proceedings of the Computer Animation Workshops. A survey of the state of the art in synthetic actors and motion control was given by Thalmann (1989) and Magnenat-Thalmann (1990). This chapter tries to relate some of the work done by other authors in the field of kinematic and dynamic animation to the concepts presented in this tutorial and defines some of the commonly used notions.

Usually, the basic structure for a human animation is a skeleton consisting of a connected set of rigid segments, corresponding to the limbs with joints at each intersection of the limbs. The animation of the skeleton is therefore determined by one position and all of the joint angles. The *direct kinematic* problem consists in computing the positions of the ends of the segments as a function of time while not taking into account the forces or the moments that cause the motion. This can be done without problems since the transformations from joint angles and angular velocities to Cartesian coordinates and velocities of the end points of the limbs are well behaved.

This is not true for the reverse transformation which is needed in *inverse kinematics* (Featherstone, 1983). Here, the animator is allowed to specify the desired end point positions and the sequence of joint angles is computed automatically. However, several special arrangements of the joint axes have been suggested for which closed form solutions exist (Badler et al., 1985; Forsey and Wilhelms, 1988). In addition, the animator is required to impose internal constraints in order to obtain a unique orientation of the body. A system which allows to specify only one constraint at a time is not a very efficient way to solve. Therefore, iterative algorithms for satisfying multiple constraints according to a priority scheme in inverse kinematics were developed (Badler et al., 1987).

The problem with kinematic motion specification is how to determine a sequence of positions that result in a realistic looking animation. The basic alternatives are either getting the data from real world experiments (like film analysis) or finding them by trial and error, which both can be very tedious and therefore unacceptable in certain situations. The use of dynamic simulation avoids these limitations at a much higher cost and complexity of computation.

The major advantage of dynamics is, that given the time sequence of controlling torques and forces the predicted motion is accurate for the specified conditions and it would occur under these conditions in the real world. This means that the result of a dynamic simulation can be used as a basis for a perfect animation automatically taking into account the reaction to internal and external constraints like fields, collisions, torques and forces. Dynamical analysis couples the field of computer animation with research in the area of robotics, biomechanics and sports.

Like in kinematics, a direct and an inverse formulation can be stated. The *direct dynamics problem* consists of finding the trajectories of the end-point positions of the skeleton with regard to the forces and torques that describe the motion, whereas in *inverse dynamics* one looks for the forces and torques that produce a predefined motion. Inverse dynamics is mainly used for motion analysis, verification of direct dynamic simulations by comparison with experimental data or computing forces and torques for steering manipulators. The goal of animation, however, the production of movement, can only be reached with a direct dynamic simulation.

Numerous papers have been published during the last couple of years dealing with various aspects of the dynamic simulation. Wilhelms and Barsky (1985) have used the Gibbs-Appell formulation instead of Newton's law resulting in an algorithm with computational cost $O(n^4)$ where n is the number of joints. Armstrong and Green (1985) proposed a method which reduces the computational cost to $O(n)$ for the special case of tree-like skeletons, where rotation about the principal axes can be neglected. Kunii and Sun (1990) achieve a similar performance by deriving typical forces and torques for human movement from a database and by moving each segment unlinked from the others. They have to introduce another step of inverse dynamics in order to meet the constraints at the joints. A complete modelling system based on dynamic constraints was presented by Barzel and Barr (1988). They also use inverse dynamics to find the constraint forces which are necessary for the bodies in order to assemble themselves in accordance with the given constraints. Arnaldi et al. (1989) present a motion control system where the animation of a hand writing a letter was achieved with a combination of kinematic and dynamic motion control. Selbie (1989) reproduced a film recording of a running stride by getting the forces and torques from the experiment with inverse dynamics and using those in the forward dynamic simulation. The use of experimental data is quite common for producing realistic looking animation of walking, which is still based on motion analysis and heuristic models (Boulic et al., 1990).

More and more attention is paid to the control of the behaviour of dynamic simulations. With task level control, the animator specifies the broad outlines of a particular movement and the animation system fills in the details. This normally leads to an inverse kinematic or dynamic formulation of the problem with given constraints. Since there are many physical realistic alternatives for generating the in-between-motion, several optimization strategies were developed (Witkin and Kass, 1988; Girad, 1987). An alternative approach, which is much more adapted to forward dynamic simulation is behavioural animation. Here, the motion of an object is generated according to rules which define how the objects react to their environment. This automatic stimulus-response mechanism removes the burden of a detailed motion specification from the animator and leads to realistic behaviour. Reynolds (1987) introduced this method when studying the problem of group trajectories for bird flocks and fish schools. The concept is essentially a particle simulation like the one presented in Sect. 3.2, where the particle interaction is set up in such a way, that they do not come too close together, but do not spread too far apart. Particle animation was also used by Sims (1990) when computing images of waterfalls, snow storms and fire. If the particle interaction can not be defined as clearly as in the previous examples, the behaviour has to be learned. Wilhelms (1990) has described an interactive network for solving a path finding problem.

References

S.Y. Aleshinsky, V.M. Zatsiorsky: J. Biomech. **11** p. 101-108 (1978)
W.W. Armstrong, M.W. Green: The Visual Computer **1**, 4 (1985)
B. Arnaldi et al.: In *Proc. Computer Animation '89* p. 113-124
N.I. Badler et al.: The Visual Computer **1**, 4 (1985)
N.I. Badler et al.: IEEE CG&A **7** (1987)
R. Barzel, A.H. Barr: Computer Graphics **22**, 4 (1988)
R. Boulic et al.: In *Proc. Computer Animation '90* p. 61-80
T. Ertl et al.: Informationstechnologie it **33**, 2 (1991)
R. Featherstone: Int. J. of Robotics Research **2**, 2 (1983)
D. Forsey, J.P. Wilhelms: In *Proc. Graphics Interface '88* p. 8-15
C.W. Gear: Communications of the ACM **14**, 176 (1968)
M. Girad: IEEE CG&A **7**, 6 (1987)
K. Gruber, J. Denoth, E. Stüssi, H. Ruder: In *International Series on Biomecanics 6B* p. 1095-1099 (1987)
K. Gruber, J. Denoth, H. Ruder, E. Stüssi: Z. Orthop. **129**, 3 (1991)
L.G. Henyey, J.E. Forbes, N.L. Gould: Astrophysical Journal **139**, 306 (1964)
T.L. Kunii, L. Sun: In *CG International '90* p. 3-16
N. Magnenat-Thalmann: In *CG International '90* p. 17-36
L. Nobili, R. Turolla: Astrophysical Journal **333**, 248 (1988)
W. Press: *Numerical Recipies*, Cambridge University Press (1986)
H. Ruder et al: In *Supercomputer '90* p. 67-82
C. Reynolds: Computer Graphics **21**, 4 (1987)
L.F. Shampine, M.K. Gordon: *Computer Solutions of Ordinary Differential Equations*, Freeman, San Francisco (1975)
S. Selbie: In *Proc. Computer Animation '89* p. 33-45
K. Sims: Computer Graphics **24**, 4 (1990)
D. Thalmann: In *Proc. Computer Animation '89* p. 3-18
J.P. Wilhelms: In *Proc. Computer Animation '90* p. 95-106
J.P. Wilhelms, B.A. Barsky: In *Proc. Graphics Interface '85* p. 197-204
A. Witkin, M. Kass: Computer Graphics **22**, 4 (1988)
F.E. Zajac, M.E. Gordon: Exercise and sport sciences reviews **17** p. 187-230 (1989)

Dynamic Animation of Deformable Bodies

Marie-Paule Gascuel, Claude Puech

ABSTRACT
The use of mechanical laws is particularly convenient to animate complex objects such as non-rigid bodies, which would be very hard to imitate with key-frames. Moreover, dynamic models can provide natural answers to automatic collision detection and response. In this paper, we review the main existing models, discuss their advantages and limitations, and study the solutions they offer to the highly challenging problem of interactions.

Keywords:

Modeling, Animation, Deformation, Dynamics, Elasticity, Simulation, Collision detection, Collision response.

1 Introduction

To produce natural-looking animation sequences, the fact that each individual frame seems realistic is not sufficient. A coherent succession of images has to be produced in order to give the impression that the actors move and react as if they were part of the real world. They must comply with gravity, avoid interpenetrations, react in a natural way to collisions, and deform as the modeled material.

The classical key-frame animation systems are purely descriptive: the user specifies points of the prescribed trajectories, and controls interactively the possible interactions between objects. With this kinematic method, creating "realistic" animations is quite hard to achieve, particularly when some of the objects involved are non-rigid.

On the opposite, dynamic models generate movement and deformations of the objects according to their physical structure and to simplified physical laws. The movement is generally controlled through external actions (such as forces and torques) specified by the user. As emphasized in [25], the use of fundamental physical principles yields unsurpassed realism. Moreover, such "active models" can provide a natural solution to automatic interaction detection and response. In consequence, the use of dynamic laws to animate deformable bodies has been a topic of wide current interest during the past few years.

The remainder of the paper develops as follows:

Section 2 describes a first class of deformable models used in computer graphics. Based on the physical theory of elasticity in continuous media, these models offer very realistic results.

On the other hand, layered deformable models have been proposed. They integrate discrete mechanical components (such as masses, dampers and springs), which can be combined with purely geometric ones. Those models, listed in Section 3 can achieve interactive natural-looking animations of complex heterogeneous objects.

We present in Section 4 some optimization techniques that can be added to the previous approaches to specify constraints on the behavior of the objects.

As emphasized in Section 5, the automatic detection and response to interactions should be one of the main advantages of dynamic models, but remains a highly challenging problem. Indeed, the solutions advocated are not always generaly applicable; some of them introduce non-intuitive artificial mechanical elements during periods of contact.

Section 6 gives conclusions, and discusses the trends for future research, which include improved solutions for the interaction problem, and better control of the animation through hybrid models integrating dynamic and geometric specifications.

2 Deformable models based on the elasticity theory

This first class of models are derived from mathematical physics. The differential elasticity equations in continuous materials are discretized using finite elements or finite differences methods, and then integrated though time.

2.1 Terzopoulos, Platt, Barr and Fleischer's model

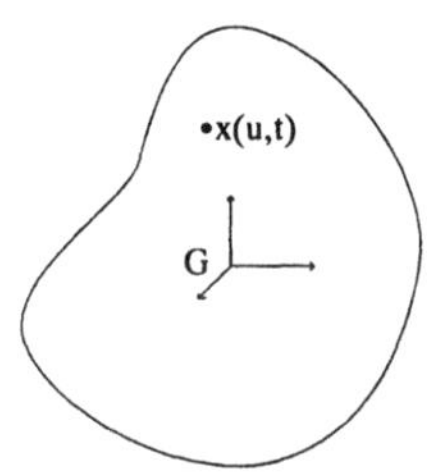

FIGURE 1. Elastically deformable body

The first model based on the elasticity theory was proposed in 1987 by Terzopoulos, Platt, Barr and Fleischer [23]. An elastically deformable body Ω (see figure 1), of parametrization $x(u,t) = (x_1(u,t), x_2(u,t), x_3(u,t))$ (u is a vector of coordinates (u_1, u_2, u_3) for a solid, (u_1, u_2) for a surface), is governed by Lagrange's ordinary differential equation:

$$\frac{\partial}{\partial t}\left(\rho\frac{\partial x}{\partial t}\right) + \gamma\frac{\partial x}{\partial t} + \frac{\partial \epsilon(x)}{\partial x} = f(x,t) \tag{1}$$

- $\frac{\partial}{\partial t}\left(\rho\frac{\partial x}{\partial t}\right)$ models the inertial force.
- $\gamma\frac{\partial x}{\partial t}$ represents the damping force due to dissipation.
- $\frac{\partial \epsilon(x)}{\partial x}$ is the elastic response of the material. It expresses the minimization through time of the functional $\epsilon(r)$, which measures the net instantaneous potential energy of the elastic deformation.
- $f(x,t)$ is the sum of the externally applied forces.

The animation is produced by integrating through time equation (1). More precisely, it involves the following computations:

1. The potential energy ϵ must be constant during a rigid motion, so a non-linear formula holds. Let G be the metric tensor associated with the object (this matrix is 3×3 for a solid, 2×2 for a surface). Let B be the curvature tensor if the body is an elastic surface (n is the unit normal vector at point $x(u,t)$ of the surface):

$$\begin{aligned} G_{ij}(x(u,t)) &= \frac{\partial x}{\partial u_i}\frac{\partial x}{\partial u_j} \\ B_{ij}(x(u,t)) &= n\,\frac{\partial^2 x}{\partial u_i \partial u_j} \end{aligned}$$

   Then,

$$\begin{aligned} \epsilon(x) &= \int_\Omega \|G(r) - G^0(r)\|^2 du_1 du_2 du_3 \quad \text{for a deformable solid} \\ \epsilon(x) &= \int_\Omega \|G(r) - G^0(r)\|^2 + \|B(r) - B^0(r)\|^2 du_1 du_2 \quad \text{for a surface} \end{aligned}$$

   Different types of elastically deformable materials can be obtained by modifying the matrix norm which is used. For instance, for an isotropic solid verifying Hooke's law[1]:

$$\epsilon(x) = \int_\Omega \left[\frac{1}{2}\lambda\left(\sum_i \left(G_{ii} - G^0_{ii}\right)\right)^2 + \mu \sum_{i,j}\left(G_{ij} - G^0_{ij}\right)^2\right] du \tag{2}$$

   where λ and μ are Lamé constants for this material.

2. To compute $\frac{\partial \epsilon(x)}{\partial x}$, a formula from Calculus of Variations must be used:
   If F is such as $\epsilon(x) = \int_\Omega F(u, x, x')\, du$, then:

$$\frac{\partial \epsilon(x)}{\partial x} = \frac{\partial F}{\partial x} - \frac{d}{du}\left(\frac{\partial F}{\partial x'}\right) \tag{3}$$

3. Then, the sum of the external forces must be evaluated (these forces can include gravity, friction, simulation of collision with rigid bodies, and users' actions).

4. Equation (1) is discretized in space, in order to obtain a system of coupled ordinary differential equations.

5. Finally, the previous system is integrated through time. At each time step, we obtain a linear system:

$$A_t\, x_{t+dt} = g_t \tag{4}$$

   where A_t is a matrix representing the state of the deformable material at time t (the size of A_t is proportional to the number of reference points in the body), x_{t+dt} is the unknown vector-position, and g_t includes the sum of the external forces acting on the deformable body at time t. Equation (4) is solved using classical techniques.

This dynamic model yields realistic animation of various deformable materials, such as elastic clothes, sheets of paper, flexible metal bars, or rubber.

Nevertheless, it has several drawbacks:

- The system is not easy to handle, because it involves a large amount of computations. As a matter of fact, a precise control of the effects is difficult to achieve with a non-interactive system.

---

[1]Hooke's law states that the force on an object is linear in the displacement from a rest state.

- Global properties of the material (such as non-compressiveness for instance) cannot be specified.
- It is difficult to find a good spatial discretization if the shape of the object is non-trivial.
- The discrete equations become ill-conditioned when rigidity increases (see [25]). For instance, the movement of a piece of inextensible cloth could not be obtained (notably the apparition of folds).

2.2 Hybrid deformable model

As mentioned previously associating a nil deformation energy to a pure rigid motion gives of a non-linear formula for this energy. But such a model involves a great amount of computations, and the equations become ill-conditioned when rigidity increases. To cope with these problems, Terzopoulos and Witkin [25] propose an hybrid model combining rigid and deformable components.

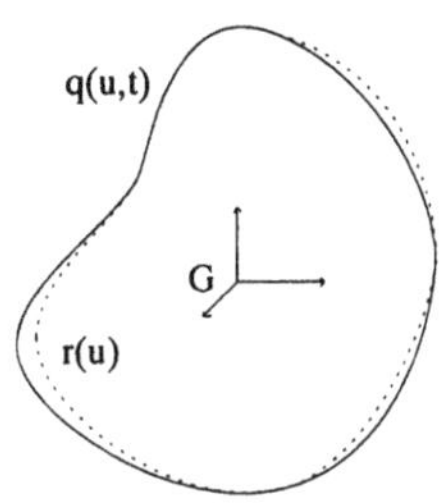

FIGURE 2. Hybrid deformable model with a rigid component

The body (which is parametrized by $q(u,t) = (q_1(u,t), q_2(u,t), q_3(u,t))$ in a referential linked to its center of mass) is divided in two interrelated levels (see figure 2):

$$q(u,t) = r(u) + e(u,t) \tag{5}$$

where :

- $r(u)$ is the rigid "reference component", which evolves according to the laws of rigid bodies dynamics.
- $e(u,t)$ is the "displacement component", which models the difference between the actual shape of the body and its reference shape. Globally still with respect to the reference component, $e(u,t)$ is animated with a linear formula for the deformation energy:

$$\epsilon(e) = \int E(\omega, e, e_u, e_{uu} \ldots .) du \tag{6}$$

where the density of elastic energy E is a linear combination of the $e(u,t)$'s partial derivatives (see [25]).

After spatial discretization, and numerical integration through time, the linear system which must be solved at each time step if of the form:

$$A \; e_{t+dt} = g_t \tag{7}$$

Note that contrary to what happened in the first model (equation (4)), the matrix A which appears hear is not a function of time. So it only needs to be factorized at $t = 0$. This saves substential computation.

Let us make some further comparisons between the two models[2]:

- We just underlined that the use of a linear formula to compute the energy is less time-consuming than a non-linear one. In addition, the equations for the hybrid model stay well conditioned when rigidity increases.
- Linear elasticity is less realistic than non-linear one, but proves to be sufficient for small deformations.
- This implies that the hybrid model is well adapted to animate deformable solids, but, contrary to the first model, cannot be applied to flexible surfaces such as clothes: the rigid reference component defines a rest-shape, and only small deformations from this shape are allowed.

2.3 Inelastic deformations

The equilibrium-shape of an object experiencing inelastic deformations is not only function of its initial shape and of the external forces which are applied. It also depends on all the history of deformations. In general, the object never recovers its original shape.

Terzopoulos and Fleischer [22] generalize the hybrid model of [25] in order to model some inelastic deformations. The reference component r becomes a function of time, and is slowly distorted.

- Viscoelasticity is obtained by letting:

$$\frac{dr}{dt}(u,t) = \frac{1}{\eta(u)}\, e(u,t) \tag{8}$$

  where $\eta(u)$ is the viscoelasticity constant at point u.

- During a plastic deformation, the reference component absorbs all the deformations which exceed a given limit.
- Fractures are modeled by introducing discontinuities when the local distortion exceeds a critic value. The points of possible fracture are preselected in the body description. A special process can be used for automatic propagation of fractures where the distortion is the most important.

Notice that these methods work by adding special processings for each inelastic deformation. So, the view of the different behaviors which is given is far from unified.

3 Layered models with discrete mechanical components

As a general rule, dynamic equations in continuous media don't seem well fitted to the animation of complex models imitating the real world, except perhaps if a very specific structure is designed[3]. Nevertheless, these complex objects, figures, animals, parts of the human body remain animation subjects of choice.

[2] Another discussion of these models can be found in [22].

[3] We will describe in Section 5 Gourret, Thalmann, and Magnénat-Thalmann's model, which simulates the contact between a human hand and a deformable ball.

Many authors choose approaches which still use some dynamic laws but are not based on any physical theory. Deformable objects are constructed by combining very simple mechanical elements (such as elementary masses linked by springs and dampers), with the possible addition of purely geometric components. These models are animated by integrating through time the differential equations of movement ($\Sigma\vec{f} = m.\vec{a}$) associated to each elementary mass of the system.

Sometimes specific to a fixed purpose, layered models are outstanding for the simplicity and efficiency of control they offer, and can yield quite convincing and natural-looking effects in interactive environments.

3.1 Luciani's standpoint: the system "CORDIS-ANIMA"

The "mass-damper-spring" formalism

The work of Luciani and Cadoz is derived from the following idea [17]: it is not always necessary to simulate the real physical structure of an object to reproduce its movement. The most important is to build a "mechanical representation" of the objects or phenomena to animate.

So, the authors describe their deformable objects as some elementary masses linked together by "conditional connections" (such as damped springs) whose parameters can change through time. The resulting system CORDIS-ANIMA [15, 17, 16] is both a modeling system and a simulation module for deformable objects.

Some advantages of this formalism are:

- An unified treatment of interactions inside an object and between the object and the external world (we will describe more precisely the interaction processing in Section 5),
- Real time animation, with enables direct manual intervention of the user. He manipulates an input/output device, which conveys the applied forces to the models, and feeds back their reactions.

Hybridization with geometric components

Some parts of a complex deformable object (a figure's skin for instance) play a insignificant part in the dynamic of movement. Luciani and Cadoz [17] propose to neglect the influence of these components, for which purely geometric models are sufficient.

In CORDIS-ANIMA, geometric points are modeled by zero-mass mechanical points. Three types of links are proposed to connect these components to the dynamic part of the objects (see figure 3)[4]:

- Rigid connections in a referential defined by three dynamic points,
- Geometric hinges: point P is computed from two other points by conservation of two distances,
- Plastic behavior: point P is computed from two other points in such a way that the surface of the triangle stays constant.

Geometric points are totally passive. Influenced by mechanic points, they can't react on them.

This idea of a geometric hybridization has been used again and generalized in a large proportion of the models described below. The main advantages of hybridization are:

[4]These connections were designed for a first version of CORDIS-ANIMA, which was 2-dimensional.

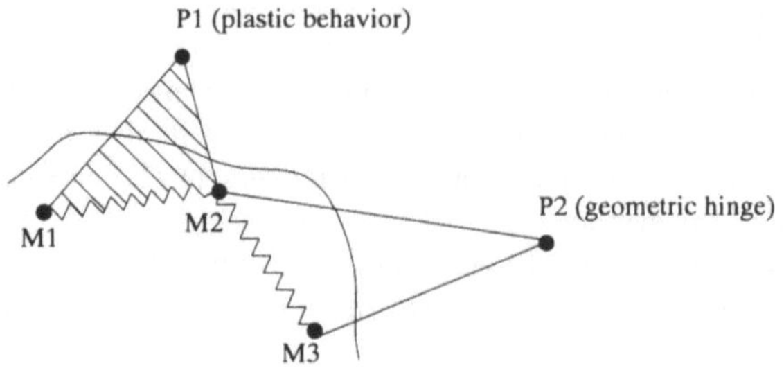

FIGURE 3. Geometric connections

- Optimization of movement control through suppression of useless degrees of freedom.
- Possible use of continuous representations for geometric components (parametric surfaces for instance).
- Better control of the animation. In particular, purely geometric deformations can be added to act on the geometric components[5].

3.2 Heating and melting deformable models

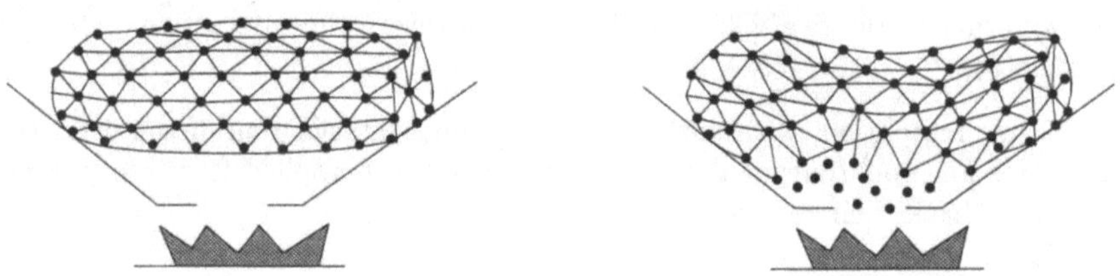

FIGURE 4. Melting a deformable model

In [24], Terzopoulos et al. use discrete elementary masses to model a deformable material which conducts heat, and has a fluid-like behavior in the molten state. The transition from solid to fluid is achieved by modifying the interactions between the masses:

- In the solid state, the material is a lattice of elementary masses linked by thermoelastic springs. These springs propagate the heat according to the "heat equation" (parabolic partial differential equation). Their stiffnesses are functions of the temperature of the connected masses. So, the material becomes less and less rigid while the heat increases. When their temperature reaches a fixed limit, the springs melt and disappear. See figure 4.
- As soon as an elementary mass is disconnected from its neighbours, its movement is computed by using molecular dynamic laws. Two types of interactions are used in the fluid state: long-range attraction forces and short-range repulsion forces.

[5]For instance, Chadwick, Haumann, and Parent use the "Free Form Deformations" of [21] in their model described in Section 3.4.

3.3 Animation of snakes and worms

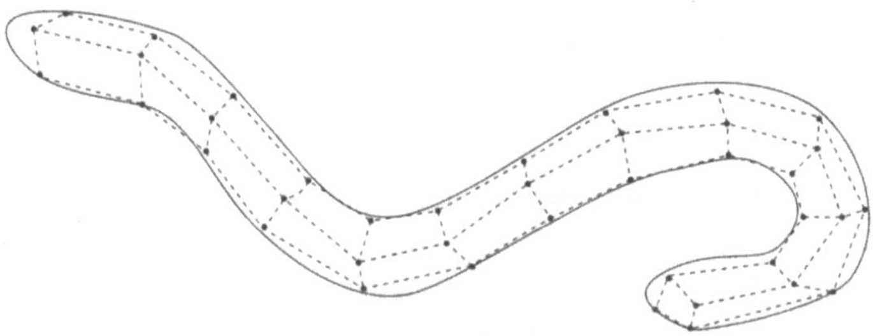

FIGURE 5. A deformable snake

Miller [18] uses an hybrid layered model with dynamic and geometric components to animate snakes and worms (see figure 5):

- The first layer is a mechanical module. The body of a snake is composed of a chain of paralellepipeds, whose vertices are elementary masses and whose edges and diagonals are damped-springs.
- The second layer is a purely geometric surface, which models the skin of the snake. It is generated by sweeping from the positions of the elementary masses.

The interpenetrations between the snakes and the rigid obstacles of the scene are avoided by moving the penetrating masses backward, while inverting their radial speeds.

To achieve realistic animations of creeping animals, Miller must find forces which can be applied on the springs to simulate the action of muscles. He chooses sinusoïdal contraction forces. Directional friction forces are added to model the scales which prevent the snake from moving backward.

3.4 Modeling muscles and fatty tissues for figure animation

In 1976, Burtnyk and Wein [6] presented a method for putting a geometric skin on a skeleton animated with key-frames. Chadwick et al. [8, 7] implement a model of that kind for figure animation. Dynamic layers are integrated to simulate various types of muscles and fatty tissues.

The model is constituted of three interrelated layers:

- The first layer is an articulated rigid skeleton, whose movement is precomputed. It may be a dynamic skeleton governed by rigid bodies physical laws or a geometric one animated with key positions.
- The second layer models the deformable flesh of the figure. Geometric deformations are used to model muscles, while dynamic ones are applied to fatty tissues:
  - Each muscle is modeled with two Free Form Deformations (or FFDs) defined in [21]. The displacement of the FFD lattice's control vertices are computed from the angle at the articulation join associated with the muscle. Notice that it is not the muscles which govern the movement of the skeleton, but the contrary !

   – Visco-elastic deformations of fatty tissues are obtained by connecting together the control vertices of a FFD with damped springs. The properties of FFD lattices insure that these dynamic deformations are automatically translated into deformations of the tissues they contain.

  The user can apply lower level control by moving manually the control vertices of the FFDs.

- The skin of the figure is represented by a purely geometric surface, deduced from the position of the second layer.

The authors emphasize on the interest of partially dynamic and partially geometric models in order to animate very complex objets. The use of a layered structure provides simple and efficient control of movement and deformations.

3.5 Animation of "articulated deformable objects"

Gascuel, Verroust and Puech [9, 27, 11] propose a somewhat general model for complex deformable objects whose elastic flesh coats an articulated skeleton.

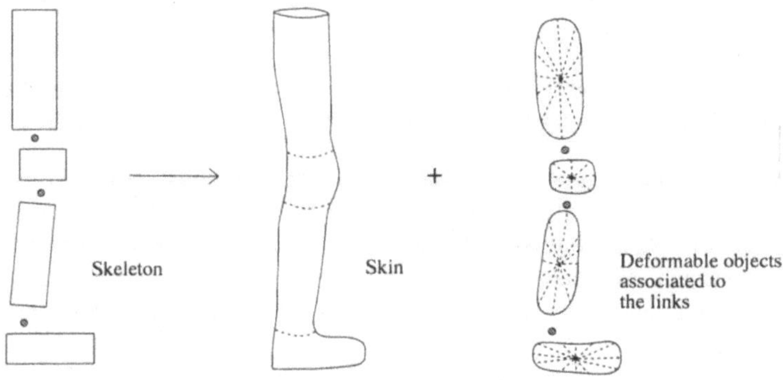

FIGURE 6. Automatic coating of a skeleton

The model is structured into three dynamic and geometric layers (see figure 6):

- The first layer is a rigid articulated skeleton composed of links connected by hinges. The movement of this skeleton is not precomputed as in Chadwick et al.'s method, but generated from dynamic laws during the animation of the articulated deformable object.

- Deformable components are associated to each link of the skeleton, in order to model deformable flesh. Each deformable component is structured into two modules:

   – The "basic mechanical module" simulates the axial deformations of the flesh. It is designed by cones of deformable flesh arranged in a star-shape way around the center of mass of the link. The deformations of these cones are governed by damped-springs.

   – A second layer models the propagation of deformations from one flesh cone to the others. This can be achieved by using dynamic criteria as well as geometric ones (such as constant volume, or constant surface area deformations).

These deformable components are particularly convenient to process automatic detection and response to collision (we will come back to that point in Section 5).

- A purely geometric skin represented by a Bspline surface covers the deformable elements. The control vertices of this surface are located at the extremities of the axial springs. In consequence, deformations of flesh components immediately translate into skin deformations.

An "automatic coating method" is provided [11] to construct very easily articulated deformable objects from a skeleton described by the user.

The animation sequence is computed by applying a simultaneous dynamic simulation of the interrelated levels of the model. In consequence, the movement of skeleton can be modified after a collision (by applying the response forces computed at the flesh level).

4 Controlling flexible models with behavior constraints

When we deal with dynamic animation, one of the main difficulties is to obtain a convenient and efficient control of movement and deformations:

- If the objects deform according to continuous elasticity laws, it is rather impossible to specify any global constraint on the material which is simulated (such as constant volume deformations for instance). The same problem occurs for most of the layered models.

- It is often useful to move a deformable object along a predefined path. Finding which forces and torques must be applied to do so is not easy.

Let us look at some constraint methods that have been proposed to cope with these problems.

4.1 Penalty methods

Total energy of moving bodies is a decreasing function through time (for all dissipative models). In consequence, dynamic animation can be viewed as an energy minimization problem. Penalty methods consist in adding "constraint terms" to this energy, in order to penalize the violations of the constraints.

Such methods have been applied in the field of dynamic animation of articulated rigid objects [5, 29], and also for object reconstruction [26]. They can be used as well to constrain deformable models.

In [20], Platt and Barr list the advantages they offer:

- Several constraints can be applied at the same time;

- Penalty method compromise between constraints, even if they are not compatible;

- No extra differential equation is required.

They also emphasize on several drawbacks:

- The constraints are never completely reached,

- The equations become ill-conditioned when constraint strengths are increased (through the associated coefficients in the energy formula).

We will study now two other constraint methods that were introduced by Platt and Barr [20] to cope with these limitations.

4.2 Reaction constraints

This is a compromise between projection methods and inverse dynamics. At each time step, the system computes the force which must be added to each finite element or each elementary mass of the model in order to fulfill the constraint. Let $D = \vec{M_0M}$ be the vector representing deviation between the next position of the element (eventually violating the constraint) and the position it should have. After suppressing the component of the applied forces which is parallel to D, we add the exact "constraint force" which will force the element to fulfill the constraint at the next time step.

This technique is different from the method used by Barzel and Barr [3, 2, 4] in the case of articulated rigid bodies. Here, the added force is not aimed at slowly minimizing the distance to the constraint, but prevents constraint violations in a single time step.

The reaction constraints enable to enforce mass elements to follow a predefined path, parametrized by time (then, the object will move as if it was dragged by these points). They can also been used to avoid the interpenetrations between a deformable body and a rigid polyhedron. This application will be discussed in Section 5.

Let us list some advantages of reaction constraints:

- These constraint are immediately and perfectly verified,
- Adding constraint forces is not time consuming (for the very simple constraints given behind, these forces are easy to compute).

Nevertheless, the method shows some limitations:

- You can't apply several constraints at the same time to the same mass element,
- This technique does not enable to simulate high-level properties of the deformable material (such as uncompressibility).

4.3 Augmented lagrangian constraints

Lagrange multipliers (noted λ) can be introduced to transform a constrained optimization problem into a simple one. To do so, extra differential equations are added.

More precisely, let $x = (x_1, x_2, ..., x_n)$, and $f(x)$, $g(x)$ be two real functions. The problem:

$$\text{minimize } f(x) \text{ with the constraint } g(x) = 0 \tag{9}$$

leads to the following Lagrange equations:

$$\dot{x}_i = -\frac{\partial f}{\partial x_i}(x) - \lambda \frac{\partial g}{\partial x_i}(x) - cg(x)\frac{\partial g}{\partial x_i}(x) \tag{10}$$

$$\dot{\lambda} = g(x) \tag{11}$$

These equations can be generalized to the cases of multiple constraints and inequality constraints (see [20] for more details).

The augmented lagrangian technique proves to be useful to specify global properties of the deformable material:

- Constant volume deformations are designed by making each finite element uncompressible,
- Plastic materials are modeled by using inequality constraints.

In conclusion, the augmented lagrangian method is time consuming (because of the addition of new differential equations and new unknowns), but is farther more general than the reaction constraint method:

- Several constraints can be applied at the same time,
- These constraints can be non-linear, or given by inequalities.

5 Collision detection and response

Automatic treatment of collisions is an important topic in order to understand the real usefulness of the deformable models for animation purposes.

Most animation systems do not offer automatic detection of collisions. After having specified the trajectories of the objects, the user may see, to his/her surprise, two of them passing quietly through each other.

In addition to the purely kinematic problem of interaction detection, dynamic models are facing a more fascinating challenge: they must respond automatically and in a realistic way to possible collisions. A dynamic system which does not include these abilities, such as Chadwick et al.'s model [8, 7], is therefore limited to the animation of a single isolated object. In some systems, tricks are used to prevent the objects from penetrating rigid still obstacles. For instance, Terzopoulos suggests in [23] that they be surrounded by exponential force fields. Miller [18] avoids the penetrations of the snakes under the floor by displacing some elementary masses and inverting their radial speeds. He emphasizes that this solution would not work for stair-shaped obstacles, or for contacts between several snakes: the detection would become too inaccurate.

Finding a good response to collisions is especially difficult for deformable models. Contrary to the rigid case, collisions are not instantaneous nor conservative, a portion of the energy being consumed in deformations. Furthermore, it is not sufficient to compute the new speeds and accelerations of the objects: we also need their new shapes during and after the contact. The physical elasticity theory only describes the behavior of deformable material during small oscillations around equilibrium states. No real answer is given to the collisions problem. Moreover, up to now, the amount of computation needed deterred anyone from solving the systems of coupled elasticity equations for all the objects involved in a collision. So, even for models based on the elasticity theory, treatment of interactions can be applied only after spatial discretization. This increases collision detection problems as the objects are represented by networks of sample points.

Nevertheless, several interesting solutions have been introduced during the past few years:

- In 1988, an attempt is made by Platt and Barr to use a constraint method to simulate interactions. Nevertheless, this technique is restricted to the collision between a deformable model and a rigid polyhedron.
- The same year, Moore and Wilhelms present a general solution, based on artificial springs introduced during collisions.
- In 1989, Gourret, Thalmann, and Magnénat-Thalmann simulate a hand in a grasping task with a finite element model.
- Luciani proposes two ways of optimizing interaction detection and response for discrete mechanical systems (1988,1989).

- A new method is associated to the articulated deformable objects of Gascuel, Verroust and Puech (1990).

The remainder of this Section describes these models and discusses their advantages and limitations.

5.1 Simulating interactions with constraint methods

In [20], Platt and Barr propose the use of constraints to compute the interactions between a deformable model and a rigid polyhedron, mobile or not. The deformable model can be built with a continuous deformable material (as in [23]), or with discrete mechanical components. The method uses the "reaction constraints" described in Section 4. When a mass element of the deformable model attempts to penetrate the rigid polyhedron, its externally applied forces are modified. The added force moves the mass to the surface of the polyhedron, and so the constraint stays fulfilled (this method doesn't work with non-polyhedral rigid obstacles, because computing the associated constraint forces would become too difficult). An opposite force is applied to the rigid polyhedron (if it is a dynamic model), in accordance to the action and reaction principle.

The reaction constraint method is not based on any physical law: The force which is arbitraryly added does not look like a "reaction force" (in spite of the name of the method): it appears before contact; it is not computed from the parameters of a collision (such as speed, kinetic energy just before the impact, local stiffness of the deformable object...), but depends on all the external forces that are already applied on the elementary mass.

This technique has been employed by Terzopoulos et al. [24] to avoid that the particles of a melting material pass through the rigid container in which it is heated (this application involves contacts rather than collisions). The results are quite natural-looking.

Nevertheless, the reaction constraint technique is not very general. Only a single constraint can be applied at the same time to each elementary mass. Moreover, this method does not seem easy to generalize to a collision between two deformable objects, or with a non-polyhedral solid, the constraints becoming too complex.

5.2 Moore and Wilhelms' methods for collision detection and response

Moore et Wilhelms describe in [19] a set of methods for interaction detection and response. Some of them can be applied to deformable models based on the elasticity theory as well as to discrete models.

Collision detection

Suppose that the deformable bodies are described by a lattice (whose vertices can be elementary masses of finite elements' nodes). Their external surfaces are then defined by a set of triangles constructed on some of these vertices.

The detection algorithm (see figure 7) consists in testing if the trajectory of each point of an object during the last time step did not pass through a triangle not containing this point (so, auto-intersections are detected as well). If n is the number of triangles and m the number of points, the basic detection is in $O(nm)$.

A choice can be made according to the accuracy of detection which is needed:

- If we consider than the triangles are fixed during the time step, the method consists in testing intersections between triangles and segments (which represent the trajectories of points during the time step). This is done by solving a system of three equations and three unknowns, u, v (barycentric coordinates defined by the

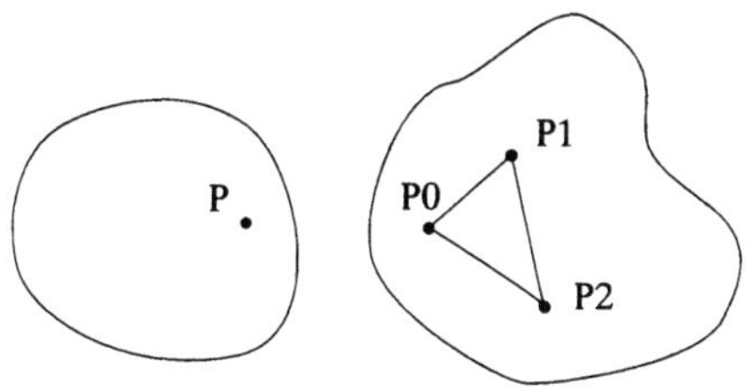

FIGURE 7. Collision detection

triangle) and t (date of the collision) :

$$P + (P' - P)t = P_0 + (P_1 - P_0)u + (P_2 - P_0)v \tag{12}$$

Then, the following conditions must be verified:

$$\begin{cases} 0 \leq t \leq 1 \\ u \geq 0 \\ v \geq \\ u + v \leq 1 \end{cases} \tag{13}$$

However, in most cases, the simplification stipulating that the triangles don't move while the points move is not justified.

- If the triangles move, equation (12) becomes:

$$P + Vt = P_0 + V_0 t + ((P_1 - P_0) + (V_1 - V_0)t)u + ((P_2 - P_0) + (V_2 - V_0)t)v \tag{14}$$

  where V, V_0, V_1, and V_2 are the speeds of the vertices.

  By eliminating u and v in (14), we obtain an equation of degree 5 in t. The actual time of the impact is computed by binary search; then, u and v are evaluated.

Several solutions are proposed to improve these methods: the use of bounding boxes/-spheres, hierarchical representations with octrees, etc.

Anyhow, it is impossible to escape the inefficiency inherent in a point-wise detection.

When a collision is detected, an interpenetration has already occurred between the two objects. Moore and Wilhelms do not say if we must go back in time to the date of the impact before continuing the simulation.

Collision response

From the techniques proposed by Moore and Wilhelms to compute the response to collisions, only one can be applied to deformable objects. It consists in putting a temporary spring between the closer points of the two objects. The contraction of this spring will simulate a kind of response force (see figure 8).

The authors do not precise when this spring must be introduced (before or after the interpenetration), when it must be removed, nor how its stiffness k must be chosen. Nevertheless, they say that if deformable objects are involved, the value k_r of the stiffness after the impact must be smaller than the stiffness k_a used before:

$$k_r = \epsilon k_a \tag{15}$$

where ϵ (chosen between 0 and 1) is a function (to be specified) of the stiffness of the material.

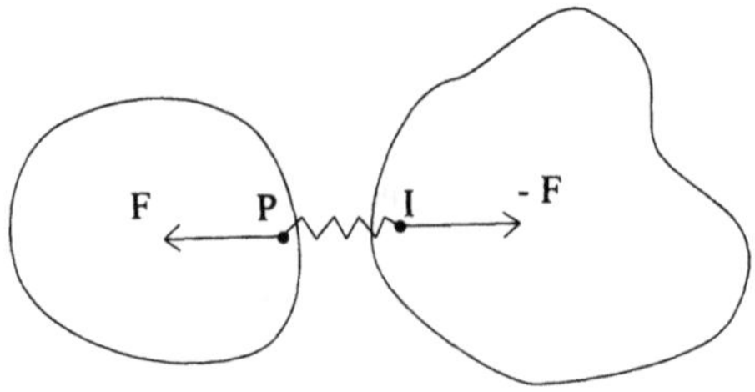

FIGURE 8. Collision response

According to [28] this model of collisions is time consuming especially if stiff springs are used (time steps must be very small to avoid divergences). In addition, if we want to use this solution to model a contact which lasts in time, the use of a spring could produce unwanted oscillations.

5.3 Simulation of a human hand in a grasping task

The system developed by Gourret, Thalmann, and Magnénat-Thalmann [12] [13] is aimed at simulating the equilibrium deformations due to the contact between a hand and a deformable ball. It is based on the elasticity theory and finite element methods.

First of all, notice that this is not a classical dynamic simulation. The displacements of the hand are not computed from externally applied forces. At the contrary, they are governed by the skeleton's key positions specified by the user.

Description of the model

The simulation is based on the principle of virtual displacements. Let R represent the internal forces, and let V, S and F respectively be the volume, surface, and pinpoint external forces. Then, the virtual works of these forces obey the equation:

$$wR = wV + wS + wF \tag{16}$$

Equation (16) is discretized by splitting the hand flesh and the deformable ball into finite elements. Some of the hand finite elements are attached to its rigid skeleton (designed with a very realistic shape). At equilibrium, or during small oscillations, the relation between deformations and the internal elasticity force is:

$$KU = R \tag{17}$$

where K is the stiffness matrix (its size is proportional to the number of finite elements), and U is the displacement vector from the unloaded configuration.

Simulation module

The computation is based on the following idea: when two objects are in contact, they can be viewed as a single object. Thus, equation (17) can be used to simulate the global behavior of the set on finite elements representing the hand and the ball.

The algorithm used can be decomposed as follows:

1. Displace the hand's flesh according to a position of the skeleton specified by the user (without considering interpenetrations with the ball).

2. Start a series of iterations:

(a) Deform the ball from its rest shape to avoid interpenetrations. This is achieved by displacing each reference vertex of the ball which is located inside the hand.

(b) Compute the displacements of the finite elements inside the ball, using equation (17). Compute the reaction forces applied by the ball onto the hand.

(c) These forces being fixed, solve globally equation (17), for the set of finite elements corresponding to both objects. Compute the reaction forces that are applied onto the bones. Displace the flesh of the hand.

Stop :

- If the forces applied onto the bones are too strong to be physically realistic (then, the user must change the position he specified),
- If the finite elements are close enough to an equilibrium state (eg. if the displacement computed during the last iteration is very small).

Discussion

Let us emphasize some of the advantages of this method:

- The control technique is clever: the user can more easily describe a precise movement of the hand by specifying skeleton key-positions rather than forces to apply. Moreover, the system detects unrealistic movements.
- The user can cut from all the parameters that make the movement very complex, eg. the deformable nature of the ball and of the hand flesh. In addition, he is sure that the animation will be much more realistic than if he had designed it himself.
- All in all, a very natural-looking and impressive animation of a complex unhomogeneous object (a hand) which interacts with the external world is obtained.

Nevertheless, this method does not seem suitable for a current use in animation systems:

- A finite element model is very realistic, but also very complex. It must be reconstructed for each particular scene. This also includes the search for suitable limit conditions.
- For each frame, the amount of computations before reaching an equilibrium state seems quite important. In particular, each iteration (steps (a) to (c)) includes a point-wise detection (and displacement) of the ball's node that have penetrated inside the hand. The authors do not give the approximative number of iterations before converging. Anyhow, we can believe that the animation is not computed in real time, particularly because of the number of finite elements used.
- Finally, and above all, the method is restricted to a soft and lasting contact between two objects. In particular, it would not work to model a collision, which cannot be simulated through a succession of equilibrium states. In consequence, an animation system using the previous technique would have to integrate another method especially devoted to collisions, and an artificial limit would have to be fixed between "true collisions" and contacts. This problem, which also occurs for rigid objects [1], can be especially tricky in the limiting cases.

5.4 Interactions in discrete systems: Luciani's approach

We saw in Section 3.1 that the objects used in CORDIS ANIMA are based on conditional connections linking elementary masses. In such a model, interactions between objects can be viewed as particular kinds of connections. Indeed, each couple of mass points belonging to different objects is always linked by a spring-like connection. The stiffness of this spring is zero when the masses are far enough from each other. It increases when the masses gather, in order to simulate the reactive force due to a collision.

"Transmitter elements"

When dealing with discrete objects, an accurate detection of interactions can be difficult to achieve, particularly when geometric components are added:

- Geometric points are often used to model the "skin" of an object, but as mentioned previously, are purely passive. They cannot be used to detect interactions, because they cannot influence the movement of the mechanical components.
- Moreover, the mechanical components are themselves unadapted to interaction detection: they can be rather far apart, and very distant from the external shape of the object.

This problem rises in all layered models based on discrete mechanical elements. For instance, Miller in the snakes animation system cannot use the geometric skin to detect contacts, by lack of feedback from the skin to the mechanical components; a detection with the elementary masses, which is not very accurate, has to be used instead (see [18]).

To cope with this problem, Luciani [16] introduces a third kind of components, the "transmitter elements", which are sorts of "access points" through which the objects interact. They can be chosen within the mechanical points, or simply dynamically connected with these points (because a collision must modify the movement of the mechanical part of the objects). An interaction will be detected if two transmitter points of different objects become close enough. So, an accurate detection near the geometric components can be obtained by associating transmitter elements with them.

The use of a third type of point complicates the parameters left to the user during the modeling phase, but increases the richness and versatility of the models. Moreover, it is a way of minimizing the number of interaction tests, by limiting them to transmitter points located on the surface of the objects.

"Agglomerates" of elementary particles

Jimenez and Luciani [14] proposed in 1989 another method for optimizing interaction detection. The objects are modeled by agglomerates of elementary spheric particles (see figure 9).

Each agglomerate includes three successive layers of deformable material, characterized by the interaction laws between their particles:

- The "kernel", formed by a few large particles, represents the more rigid internal part of the object.
- The "derm" imitates the deformable flesh. It is modeled by particles attracted by the kernel, but two by two repulsive. These interaction laws produce an uniform distribution of the derm around the kernel.

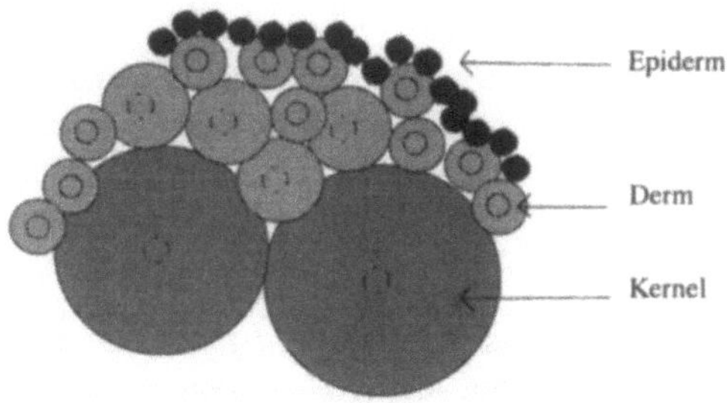

FIGURE 9. Agglomerate

- The "epiderm" insures the cohesion of the agglomerate. The attractive interaction law which is used simulates the tension of the skin. All the interactions between the agglomerate and the external world are treated at the epiderm level (except if we want to enable fractures).

Let us list the main advantages of this model:

- Numerous physical phenomena - such as flexibility, plasticity, collisions, and fractures - can be modeled with agglomerates. The different behaviors are obtained by playing with the interaction laws between the different kinds of particles.
- Based on point-wise physics, this model does not introduce any complex computation (no rotation, no vector product, no projection...). Moreover, the equations of movement can be solved in parallel for each particle (once the applied forces due to interactions are known). This allows the real time animation of complex agglomerates.

5.5 Interactions between articulated deformable objects

The structure of articulated deformable objects proposed by Gascuel, Verroust and Puech (and described in Section 3.5) is particularly well adapted to interaction detection and response. As mentioned, that each link of the skeleton is coated with a deformable component, constituted of deformable cones (which are modeled by springs and arranged in a star-shape way). Interactions are detected and treated independently for each of these components. The resulting reaction forces are transmitted to the associated links, in order to adequately modify the movement of the skeleton.

Let us describe the algorithm more precisely:

1. Detect interactions:
   - Predetection with bounding boxes/spheres,
   - Test if the extremities of the springs associated to the deformable components are inside another object, deformable or not.
2. Avoid interpenetrations by computing the new shapes of the deformed objects (use their local relative stiffness on the contact zone).
3. Respond to collisions:
   Compute the reaction forces that must be applied to the skeleton's links according to the deformations of the flesh cones touching another object (this computation is especially simple, because the cones are modeled by springs).

Of particular interest are the following remarks:

- This method offers a simple and efficient control of the angle constraints imposed at articulation points: if an angle becomes too small, a collision will be detected between two neighbouring deformable elements, and the response forces will prevent the angle from becoming smaller (see [10, 9] to find a technique for precise angle constraint control).
- A succession of small collisions is not a good model for contacts: equilibrium positions can be hard to reach. For instance, unwanted oscillations can appear when an object is resting on the floor. So, as the contact lasts, we introduce reaction forces computed with the associated rigid skeleton. The progressive introduction of these forces can lead easily to an equilibrium state, while the deformable component flattens on the floor (see [27] for more details).

6 Conclusion

Deformable models based on pure simulation of dynamic equations offer unsurpassed realism. Nevertheless, their use is not evident for a layman:

- The physical parameters are often non-intuitive. A good knowledge in physics is needed to understand them (for instance, the effects of the Lamé parameters on an elastically deformable body are not obvious).
- They do not fit exactly with the notions we would want to control. In particular, specifying global properties of a deformable material —such as uncompressibility— is not easy.

In fact, these models seem unadapted to the simulation of heterogeneous complex objects from the real world, except perhaps if a specific structure is built for each animation sequence (as was done by Gourret et al. for a hand in a grasping task). However, this solution would be computer intensive and time consuming.

On the other hand, modular models combining discrete mechanical components and geometric layers are less "realistic", but simplify the modeling and the animation of complex objects. The fact that the parameters from different layers can be controlled independently can be very convenient for the precise tuning of the structure. Discrete models are not suitable for the simulation of existing materials. However, this limitation is also their richness: they can imitate behaviors for which no adequate answer is given by physics (it would be difficult to imitate a creeping snake, muscles, or a collision between two articulated deformable objects with mathematicals physics!). Furthermore, very simple dynamic equations enable the interactive computation of animation sequences. So, the user can modify immediately his parameters according to the desired effect, realistic or not.

This state of the art emphasized on two highly challenging problems:

- The control of movements and deformations for active models:
  It can be improved through optimization techniques, but these methods are often computer intensive. In addition, the constraints must be pre-programmed before being used, and this can be quite difficult for a non-specialized user.
- The automatic detection and response to interactions:
  Some interesting solutions were proposed to deal with interactions between several

deformable models. However, they are not always generaly applicable. Besides, some of them are based on the introduction of non-intuitive mechanical elements during periods of contact.

In the next few years, these two problems will probably remain important scopes of research, especially through the apparition of new hybrid models where geometric specifications will collaborate with dynamic components.

7 References

[1] D. Baraff. Analytical Methods for Dynamic Simulation of Non-penetrating Rigid Bodies. *Computer Graphics*, 23(3):223–232, July 1989.

[2] A. Barr, B. Von Herzen, R. Barzel, and S. Snyder. Computational Techniques for the Self Assembly of Large Space Structures. In *8th Princeton/SSI Conference on Space Manufacturing*, Princeton New Jersey, May 1987.

[3] R. Barzel and A. Barr. Modeling with Dynamic Constraints. *State of the Art in Image Synthesis (SIGGRAPH'87 course notes Number 17, Anaheim, Ca)*, 1987.

[4] R. Barzel and A. Barr. A Modeling System Based on Dynamic Constraints. *Computer Graphics*, 22(4):179–188, August 1988.

[5] L. Shapiro Brotman and A. N. Netravali. Motion Interpolation by Optimal Control. *Computer Graphics*, 22(4):309–315, August 1988.

[6] N. Burtnyk and M. Wein. Interactive Skeleton Technique For Enhancing Motion Dynamics in Key Frame Animation. *Communications of the ACM*, 19(10):564–569, October 1976.

[7] J.E. Chadwick, D.R. Haumann, and R.E. Parent. Layered Construction for Deformable Animated Characters. *Computer Graphics*, 23(3):243–252, July 1989.

[8] J.E. Chadwick and E. Parent. Critter Construction: Developping Characters for Computer Animation. In *PIXIM 88*, pages 283–305, Paris, France, October 1988.

[9] Marie-Paule Gascuel. Déformations de surfaces complexes : techniques de haut niveau pour la modélisation et l'animation. *Thèse de doctorat*, Université Paris XI, October 1990.

[10] M.P. Gascuel, A. Verroust, and C. Puech. Animation with collisions of deformable articulated bodies. In *Eurographics Workshop on Animation and Simulation*, September 1990.

[11] M.P. Gascuel, A. Verroust, and C. Puech. A modeling system for complex deformable bodies suited to animation and collision processing. *Journal of Visualization and Computer Animation*, 2(3), August 1991.

[12] J.P. Gourret, N. Magnenat Thalmann, and D. Thalmann. Simulation of Object and Human Skin Deformations in a Grasping Task. *Computer Graphics*, 23(3):21–29, July 1989.

[13] J.P. Gourret, N. Magnenat Thalmann, and D. Thalmann. The Use of Finite Element Theory for Simulating Object and Human Body Deformations and Contacts. In *Eurographics 89*, pages 477–487, September 1989.

[14] S. Jimenez and A. Luciani. Une vue unifiée des comportements de multitude, flexibilité, plasticité et ruptures : Billes, bulles et agglomérats. *Rapport de Recherche ACROE*, 89(15), November 1989.

[15] A. Luciani. Un Outil Informatique de Création d'Images Animées. *Thèse de docteur ingénieur d'électronique*, Institut National Polytechnique de Grenoble, November 1985.

[16] A. Luciani. Modèles pour la synthèse d'images animées. *Rapport de Recherche ACROE*, 88(5), January 1988.

[17] A. Luciani and C. Cadoz. Utilisation de Modèles Mécaniques et Géométriques pour la Synthèse et le Contrôle d'Images Animées. In *Deuxième Colloque Image, CESTA*, Nice, April 1986.

[18] Gavin S.P. Miller. The Motion Dynamics of Snakes and Worms. *Computer Graphics*, 22(4):169–177, August 1988.

[19] M. Moore and J. Wilhelms. Collision Detection and Response for Computer Animation. *Computer Graphics*, 22(4):289–298, August 1988.

[20] J.C. Platt and A.H. Barr. Constraint Methods for Flexible Models. *Computer Graphics*, 22(4):279–288, August 1988.

[21] T.W. Sedeberg and S.R. Parry. Free-form Deformations of Solid Geometric Models. *Computer Graphics*, 20(4):151–160, 1986.

[22] D. Terzopoulos and K. Fleischer. Modeling Inelastic Deformations: Viscoelasticity, Plasticity, Fracture. *Computer Graphics*, 22(4):269–278, August 1988.

[23] D. Terzopoulos, J. Platt, A. Barr, and K. Fleischer. Elastically Deformable Models. *Computer Graphics*, 21(4):205–214, July 1987.

[24] D. Terzopoulos, J. Platt, and K. Fleisher. Heating and Melting Deformable Models (From Goop to Glop). In *Graphics Interface'89*, pages 219–226, London, Ontario, Canada, June 1989.

[25] D. Terzopoulos and A. Witkin. Physically Based Model with Rigid and Deformable Components. *IEEE Computer Graphics and Applications*, pages 41–51, December 1988.

[26] D. Terzopoulos, A. Witkin, and M. Kass. Energy Constraint on Deformable Models. *State of the Art in Image Synthesis (Siggraph'87 course notes Number 17)*, July 1987.

[27] Anne Verroust. Etude de problèmes liés à la définition, la visualisation et l'animation d'objets complexes en informatique graphique. *Thèse d'état*, Université Paris XI, December 1990.

[28] J. Wilhelms, M. Moore, and R. Skinner. Dynamic Animation : Interaction and Control. *The Visual Computer*, 2(4):283–295, December 1988.

[29] A. Witkin and M. Kass. Spacetime Constraints. *Computer Graphics*, 22(4):159–168, August 1988.

Stochastic Methods and Non-Fractal Applications

Huw Jones

1. Introduction

Our everyday environment abounds with examples of stochastic phenomena, objects or activities that are governed by probabilistic laws [COX65]. These range from observations evident to any observer, such as the number of people in a supermarket checkout queue or the time taken to drive to work on a particular day, to more latent situations, such as the energy levels of subatomic particles. Practitioners of statistics and operational research have, for decades, used computers to create models of such activity in order to gain useful insights into the behaviour of systems that depend on statistical or probabilistic laws. More recently, stochastic methods have been used to model certain natural phenomena in a visually convincing way. Images depicting simulations of the structures of, for example, plants [PRUS90] and other life forms [KAAN91], marble [PERL85], clouds [VOSS85], mountainous terrain [SAUP88] and the boundaries of cities [BATT91] have become familiar. Many researchers use standard "random number generators" to reproduce such effects; not all of them appreciate the implications of what they are doing. The purpose of this tutorial is to describe some of the underlying statistical theory and to show its application to a selection of techniques in computer graphics. The development will be explanatory rather than theoretically rigorous. The intention is to give end users an understanding of the methods they are using without converting them into statistical experts. Statistics is similar to many other technical subjects in that much of its mystique is concerned with its terminology. Many terms will be highlighted when introduced.

2. Random Variables

Random variables (**r.v.'s**) result from **statistical experiments** whose **outcomes** are in some way uncertain. Repetitions of an experiment will not necessarily yield the same value for the r.v. - different **realisations** of the r.v. may take different values. The set of all possible realisations of a r.v. is called the **sample**

space of the experiment. We shall deal with numerical or quantitative r.v.'s, although they can occur in qualitative form - for example the eye colour of a person chosen at random from the population of a certain country. Numerical r.v.'s can be **discrete,** when the sample space can be mapped onto a set of integers, or **continuous**, having an interval of real values as the sample space. Typically, discrete r.v.'s are the result of counting procedures, whereas continuous r.v.'s are produced by measuring activities.

The uncertainty concerned with statistical experiments does not imply complete inability to predict the outcomes of those experiments. Random variables are governed by probabilistic laws, which give the experimenter some indication of their more likely values. Continuous r.v.'s are generally specified by a **probability density function** (p.d.f.), whose integral over a particular range defines the probability of occurrence of that range. Thus, if f(x) is the p.d.f. of some continuous r.v. X, we have

$$P[a \leq X \leq b] = \int_a^b f(x)dx,$$

where a and b are constants such that $a \leq b$. Thus, we can define probabilities of occurrence of any range within the sample space of the experiment. One consequence of this is that the total area below any p.d.f. must be one unit and that the p.d.f. cannot take negative values.

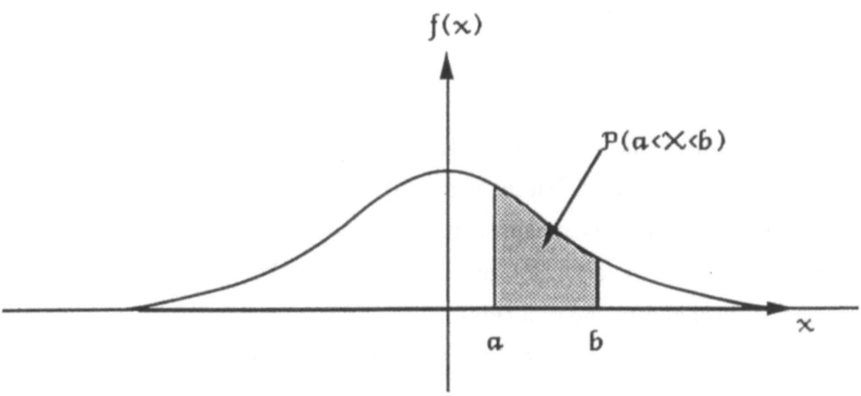

Fig 1 A typical probability density function for a continuous random variable

Discrete r.v.'s are completely specified by listing or defining by formula the probabilities of all possible values of the r.v. within the sample space, giving the **probability distribution** of the r.v. Thus, if X is a random variable, we define $P[X = x]$ for all values x of the sample space of the r.v. X. The notation here is standard with capital letters for r.v.'s and the equivalent lower case letters for their realisations. Thus, X is a r.v. and x is a constant from the sample space of the r.v. Probabilities can be found using a discrete summation instead of a continuous integral. For example, if a and b are values within the sample space of some discrete r.v. X such that $a \leq b$, then

$$P[a \leq X \leq b] = \sum_{x=a}^{b} P[X = x].$$

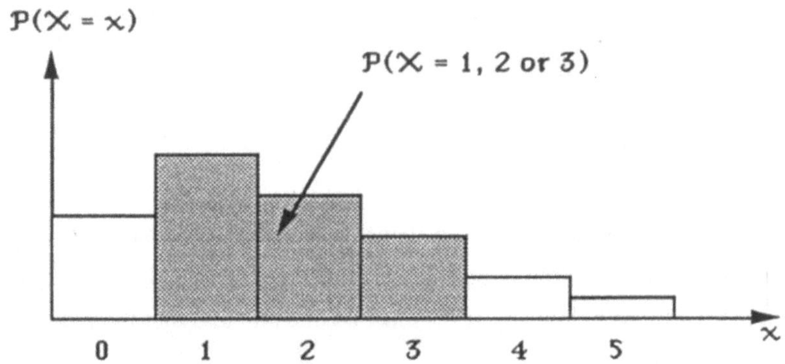

Fig 2 A typical probability distribution for a discrete variable

3. Concepts of Probability

The word **probability** has been used boldly above without giving it a proper definition. It has been assumed that readers have some concept of probability that will enable them to cope. Attempts to make a more precise definition often result in more confusion, but we shall try to clarify this. There are two relatively simple, popular "definitions" of probability, the first being:

> If an experiment has N equally likely outcomes and an event E results from R of these, then the probability of the event E is P[E] = R/N.

For example, a roll of a fair die has 6 equally likely outcomes and the event "score greater than 4" can result from two of these outcomes, so P[score greater than 4 on roll of a die] = 2/6 = 1/3. This seems reasonable until you examine the wording of the "definition" in detail. The words "equally likely" really mean "of equal probability", so we are using the concept of probability in its own definition. The attempted definition is circular, yielding it invalid. The other form, the "frequentist" definition, may seem a more promising experimentally based method.

> If an experiment is repeated n times and the event E occurs on r of these occasions, then the ratio r/n approaches a limiting value as n increases, this limiting value being the probability of E.

If I toss a coin many times, the result "heads" will occur on about half of those occasions. This suggests that the probability of the result "head" on tossing a coin is 1/2.

Fig 3 illustrates the convergence of the sequence representing the number of heads per toss for the sequence (t, h, t, t, t, h, h, t, h, h, h, h, h, t, t, t, h, t, t, t). The fluctuations appear to be diminishing to a narrower amplitude around the value 1/2. This may seem to be more satisfactory than definition 1, but it is still problematic. The limit used in the definition is not the relatively familiar mathematical limit, as there is no precise formula linking the values of r and n. In our example above, there is no guarantee that the sequence will remain close to the value 1/2, but it is likely to do so. The limit has to be defined as a "limit in probability", so this attempt at definition is also circular.

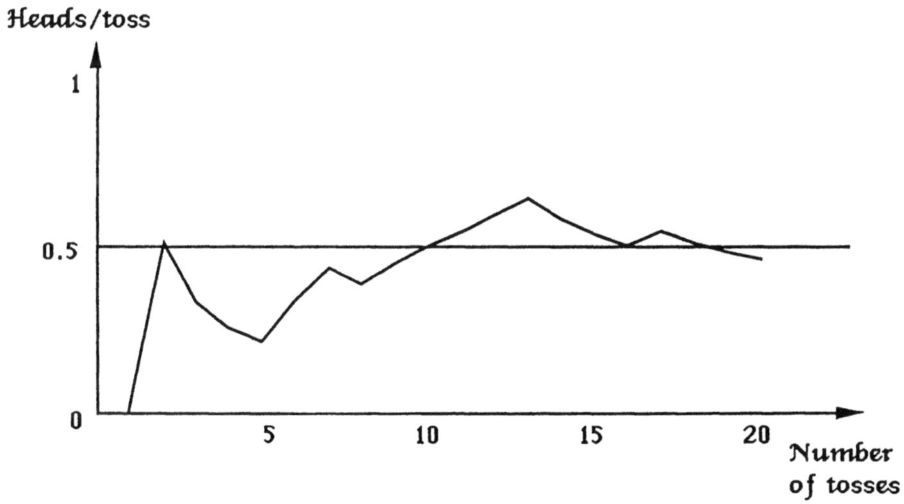

Fig 3 Convergence of ratio of number of heads per toss of a coin

We appear to be stuck in an impossible position - we want to use the concept of probability, but cannot define it. Do not despair - both the above methods may be philosophically inadequate, but they produce values that work. That will be enough of a foundation for us - as it is for many working statisticians. Those who are not satisfied can take a diversion of a year or two's study of measure theory in order to attempt to come up with a well formulated definition [CRAM46], but we shall accept these limitations in the knowledge that the system has produced adequate results for generations of researchers.

Many of the problems of probability involve evaluating probabilities of complicated combinations of events. These have many parallels with mathematical set theory and symbolic logic. If A and B are events, typical laws are

P[A **or** B] = P[A] + P[B] - P[A **and** B],

P[A **and** B] = P[A].P[B], when A and B are statistically independent,

P[A|B] = P[A **and** B]/P[B], where P[A|B] indicates the probability that A occurs given that B has occured.

If A and B are mutually exclusive, then the event A **and** B cannot occur. In this case, we have

P[A **or** B] = P[A] + P[B].

These laws are equivalent to the set theoretic results concerning the numbers of elements in sets and can be illustrated using Venn diagrams, where the Union operator is equivalent to **or** and the Intersection operator is equivalent to **and**. Great care has to be taken in solving such problems as probability is a non-intuitive subject. Instincts often prove to be wrong in probability theory!

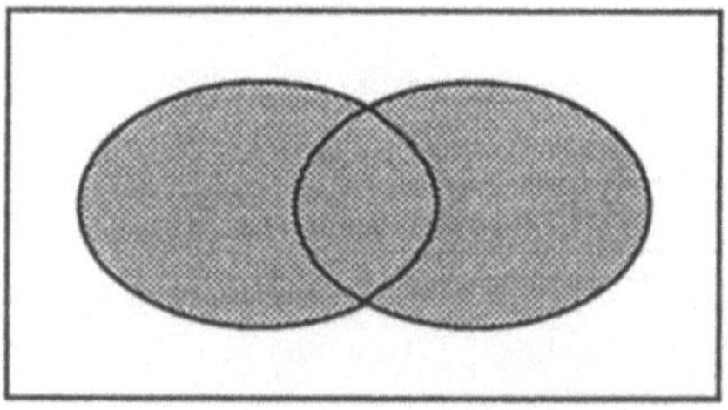

Union

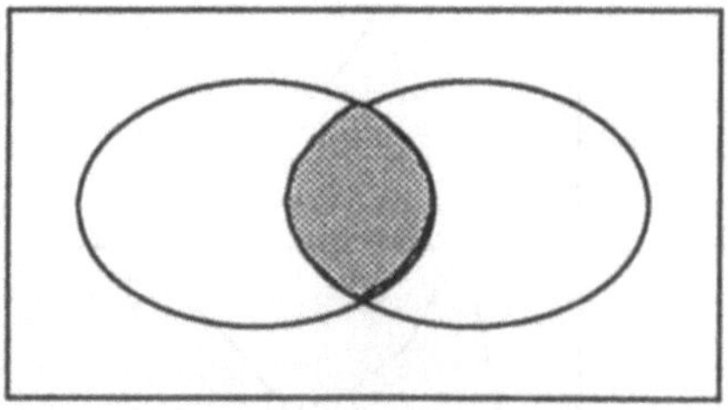

Intersection

Fig 4 Venn diagrams

4. Measures of Random Variables

If we collect the results of a number of statistical experiments, we obtain a list of values. If the r.v. concerned is continuous, those values can be plotted on a real line. Suppose we could know all such results for a particular experiment, giving a scatter of points on the line. Our knowledge of such **distributions** is probabilistic. It is often useful to define values describing the properties of such distributions, such as the location on and dispersion along the axis. **Parameters** defining such values are often used to specify different forms of r.v.'s, so it is important to understand their meanings when using r.v.'s in simulation exercises. We have seen that there are different types of r.v.'s, so the definition of a measure involving such variables will need to take account of these different forms. The concept of **expectation** of a r.v. can be used to unify such definitions. Suppose g(X) is a function of a r.v. X with sample space S. If X is discrete, it can be specified by defining P[X = x] for all x in S. If X is continuous, it is fully defined by its p.d.f. f(x), known for all x in S. We define the expectation of g(X) or the expected value of g(X) as

$$E[g(X)] = \sum_{S} g(x)P(X = x)$$

for the discrete case and

$$E[g(X)\} = \int_{S} g(x)f(x)dx$$

for the continuous case.

These formulae may seem a little daunting, but have a very familiar interpretation. They are no more than the familiar average or **mean** of g(X). If g(x) is replaced by x in the formulae, we obtain the expected value of the random variable X, E[X], which is simply the mean or average of X, often denoted by the symbol μ. This is the most frequently used **measure of location** of the distribution of a random variable. The **mode**, the value that occurs most frequently in the population, and the **median**, the value below which (or above which) exactly half of the population lies, are other measures of location which are less frequently used.

The most obvious **measure of dispersion** or spread of a population is its **range**, simply calculated as the difference between the highest and lowest occuring values. Although it is easy to calculate, it is not particularly useful as a single outlying value in a population can have a major effect on its value. The **standard deviation** (s.d.) is less volatile and more frequently used, although more complicated to calculate and to understand. Suppose the r.v. X has expectation or mean μ. The deviation of a particular value of X from its mean is $(X - \mu)$. The mean deviation from a central value would give a good measure of spread, but we find that $E[X - \mu]$ is identically zero, as $(X - \mu)$ is sometimes positive, sometimes negative, making it useless as a measure of spread. The mean or average value of the squared deviation from the mean is more useful, $E[(X - \mu)^2]$. This value is known as the **variance**, and is a very good measure of spread. Its only drawback is that its dimension is the square of the original variable. Thus, the variance of a distribution of lengths, for example, is an area. The standard deviation is simply the square root of the variance, $\sqrt{\{E[(X - \mu)^2]\}}$, often denoted by σ. This can be interpreted as the root mean square deviation from the mean. Those familiar with alternating current theory will understand that the mean voltage supplied by a normal alternating mains supply is zero. The "root mean square" or r.m.s. voltage often quoted is the standard deviation of the voltage about that mean.

5. Types of Distribution

Many forms of distribution can be used to describe random variables in naturally occuring processes. We shall concentrate on a few which can be useful in visual simulation. It is often found that substituting more simple and familiar forms for some of the more esoteric forms of distributions of r.v.'s has no appreciable effect on the visual effectiveness of the simulation. The simplest distribution is the **uniform distribution**. Random variables from other forms of distribution can also be derived from uniformly distributed variables, so they lie at the core of all forms of simulation. All values within the sample space of a uniformly distributed r.v. are equally likely to occur. Thus, a discrete uniform r.v. X with sample space $a \leq X \leq b$ can be completely specified by the probabilities

$$P[X = x] = 1/(b - a + 1) \quad \text{for } a \leq x \leq b,$$

as there are (b -a + 1) equally likely values within the sample space of X. The score on one throw of a fair die gives a familiar example of such a r.v., with a = 1 and b = 6. Similar considerations for a continuous uniform r.v. X with sample space $a \leq X \leq b$ show that its p.d.f. is defined as

$$f(x) = 1/(b - a) \quad \text{for } a \leq x \leq b.$$

This is also known as a rectangular distribution, from the shape of the pdf (Fig 5). For both discrete and continuous cases, the mean or expected value lies in the middle of the sample space at $\mu = (a + b)/2$ and the range is (b - a). The standard deviation can be calculated as $(b - a)/\sqrt{12}$ for the continuous case.

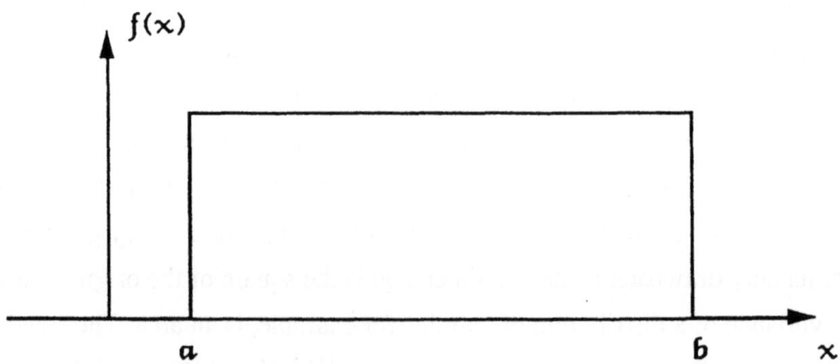

Fig 5 The pdf of a Uniform distribution

A discrete distribution which is widely encountered in statistical theory is the **binomial distribution**. Suppose that the probability of occurrence of an event E as the result of a particular repeatable experiment is p, that this probability does not vary for repetitions of the experiment and that the result of one performance of the experiment does not have any influence on the next performance. Then, if the experiment is repeated n times, and we count X, the number of times on which E occured, then the probability distribution of the r.v. X is given by

$$P[X = x] = \frac{n!}{(n - x)!\, x!} q^{(n - x)} p^x, \text{ where } q = (1 - p), \text{ for } x = 0, 1, 2, \ldots n.$$

Here, the symbol n! refers to the factorial of n, which is n(n - 1)(n - 2)...1 when n is a positive integer with 0! = 1. If X is defined in this way, the mean or expectation of X is $\mu = np$ and the standard deviation of X is $\sigma = \sqrt{\{npq\}}$ - these results can be derived from the definitions of expectation and standard deviation given above.

The **Poisson distribution** is another commonly occuring discrete distribution, often used in queueing theory. Suppose events are occuring at a mean rate of ν per unit time in such a way that the occurrence of events at any particular time is equally likely (emissions of radio-active particles or arrivals of customers in some forms of queue can be modelled in this way). The expected number of occurences in a total time of t units will be $\lambda = \nu t$. If we count the number X of events to occur in t time units, the sample space of X is the set of non-negative integers and we have

$$P[X = x] = \lambda^x e^{-\lambda} /x!\ , \quad \text{for } x = 0, 1, 2, \ldots$$

This distribution has mean $\mu = \lambda$ and standard deviation $\sqrt{(\lambda)}$. It can be derived as the limiting form of the binomial distribution when n becomes large and p becomes small in such a way that $np = \lambda$. As well as describing sequences of events in time, known as Poisson processes, the distribution can be used to simulate the spatial distribution of objects within one, two or three dimensional universes.

The same underlying situation can be modelled by a continuous random variable representing the time interval between successive occurrences of the event. If the mean number of events to occur in unit time is ν, then the mean time between successive events is $1/\nu$. The distribution of inter-event times is given by the **exponential distribution** (sometimes known as the negative exponential distribution) with p.d.f.

$$f(x) = \nu \exp(-\nu x) \quad \text{for } x \geq 0.$$

This distribution has mean $\mu = 1/\nu$ and standard deviation $\sigma = 1/\nu$ and can be useful in simulating sequences of events in time and space.

The most important continuous distribution in statistical theory is the **normal** or **Gaussian distribution**. This can be used to model many situations where the continuous r.v. is the result of accumulation of a large number of values which are prone to random "error". Normal variables can be defined to have any mean or any positive standard deviation. The p.d.f. of a normal variable with mean μ and standard deviation σ is

$$f(x) = \frac{1}{\sigma\sqrt{2\pi}} \exp(-\{x-\mu\}^2)/\{2\sigma^2\}) \quad \text{for } -\infty < x < \infty.$$

This has a symmetric bell shaped p.d.f., centred on its mean μ with 95% of the population lying within 1.96 standard deviations of the mean. A **standard normal distribution** has mean $\mu = 0$ and s.d. $\sigma = 1$. The symbol Z is often used for the r.v. of a standard normal distribution which has p.d.f.

$$f(z) = \frac{1}{\sqrt{2\pi}} \exp(-z^2/2) \quad \text{for } -\infty < z < \infty.$$

The pdf of the standard normal distribution has a shape similar to that of the curve in fig 1. Any member of the family of normal r.v.'s for all possible values of μ and σ can be transformed into a standard normal r.v. by the transformation

$$Z = (X - \mu)/\sigma,$$

showing that Z is a measure of how many standard deviations the variable lies away from the centre of its distribution. Thus, all problems on probability of normal r.v.'s can be reduced to a problem concerning the standard normal r.v. For example, we find that

$$P[X > a] = P[Z > (a - \mu)/\sigma].$$

Similarly, the reverse transformation

$$X = \mu + \sigma Z$$

can be used to generate a Normal r.v with mean μ and standard deviation σ from a standard normal r.v.

For those familiar with the transformations used in computer graphics, the p.d.f. of a Normal r.v. with mean μ and standard deviation σ can be found by applying a scaling of factor σ in the x-direction and $1/\sigma$ in the y-direction followed by a translation of μ in the x-direction to the p.d.f. of Z. The double scaling ensures that the area beneath the p.d.f. remains one unit.

The deceptively simple function for the p.d.f. of a standard normal variable cannot be integrated analytically, so the evaluation of probabilities for Normal r.v.'s can only be achieved through numerical methods, usually by computer approximation or by using tables of the integral concerned.

We shall investigate how to generate standard normal r.v.'s in a later section. The major importance of the normal distribution is shown by the **Central Limit Theorem** (C.L.T.), which states that the sum of a set of identically distributed independent r.v.'s of any form approaches a normal r.v. as the number of independent r.v.'s contributing to the sum is increased. This gives one way of generating normal r.v.'s from other forms of distribution.

There are many other forms of random variable used in statistical simulation, when the exact form of the distribution may be important. In many forms of visual simulation, the simulation is adequate if the scene depicted is visually satisfying, so the same form of rigour is often not needed. The distributions outlined above will be adequqate for many forms of visual simulation.

6. Simulation of Random Variables

Suppose you wish to play a game of chance involving dice but do not have a die at hand. Given paper and pencil, you can mark six identical pieces of paper with the numbers 1 to 6 and draw one piece at random to simulate a single throw. If this piece is replaced, the process can be repeated (sampling with replacement) to simulate a sequence of throws. This is a true simulation in that the sequence of numbers read off the slips of paper has exactly the same properties as the numbers that could be observed from the throws of a die. If two people produced a stream of digits, one by throwing a die and the other by the paper drawing method, no one could distinguish which method had been used by investigating the numbers alone. Other equally valid methods could be devised, for example taking the last digit of telephone numbers from a page of a telephone book and discarding those not in the range 1 to 6. Tables of random numbers could be used similarly. These have been published to help researchers to generate sequences of random digits, particularly for the purposes of selection of random samples. The two properties reuired of such sequences are

1. the integers 1 to 6 occur with equal probability;
2. successive values are independent.

The sequence 1, 2, 3, 4, 5, 6, 1, 2, 3, ... satisfies condition 1, but it clearly violates condition 2 which implies a "lack of memory" in the sequence.

The methods described above would be suitable for small scale simulations, but suppose that the game involves several thousand throws of the die. Even the most avid game fan would become tired of such repetitive activity. This is why computers can be most valuable in general simulations. However, computers are generally machines that can be programmed to convert particular inputs into the same output for each repetition of the programme - this predictability is usually highly desirable, but seems to be contrary to the principles of generation of random sequences of numbers. A computer random number generator really generates a sequence of "pseudo-random numbers" which can be evaluated by formula, but which display many of the properties of true random numbers. A pseudo-random number generator is successful if the sequence of results it produces cannot be distinguished from those produced by the true random number generator that it is intended to replace or simulate.

Consider the algorithm:

1. Input two integers of two digits, x and y.
2. Output z, the integer consisting of the two central digits of the four digit product of x and y.
3. Replace x by y and y by z.
4. Return to step 2.

Suppose we start this procedure off with x = 29 and y = 67. This gives x*y = 1943, giving z = 94. The values of x and y are then reset to 67 and 94 respectively, giving z = 29 (from x*y = 6298). The procedure generates a sequence

94, 29, 72, 08, 57, 45, 56, 52, 91, 73, 64, 67, 28, 87, 43, 74, 18, 33, 59, 94, 54, ...

This appears to have a sense of randomness, although it is calculated from a deterministic rule. There may be a preponderence for higher numbers in the allowed range (from 00 to 99), but there are too few values yet calculated to be sure. There seems to be a sensible mix of even and odd numbers and there does not appear to be any predictive pattern about the values obtained.

If we start this algorithm off with x = 27 and y = 66, we obtain x*y = 1782, giving z = 78. Now, with x = 66 and y = 78, x*y = 5148, so z = 14. Continuing in this mode gives a stream of values for z:

78, 14, 09, 12, 10, 12, 10, 12, 10, 12, ...

that is clearly not random.

The above example illustrates some of the drawbacks and advantages of pseudo-random number generators. A simple deterministic formula has been used to generate sequences which, under some circumstances, have random-like properties. However, this sometimes breaks down in that an obviously non random repetitive cycle of values may be generated. A little thought shows that repetition is bound to occur with all such formula based generators. The domain of values input to the function is inevitably limited, if only by the precision of the computer system. This means that at some stage of the process, a value or set of values will be encountered that was previously used as an input to the formula, so the same cycle will be restarted. The skill of devising random number generators is in ensuring that no short cycles can be generated - minimum cycle lengths of several millions are usually obtained with high precision generators. However, the ability to regenerate the same sequence can be an advantage. If you have generated a particularly interesting figure where the spatial layout was arranged according to some random number sequence and wish to experiment with, for example, colour changes, then you need to be able to repeat the same "random" sequence.

We have not really considered the type of random number to be generated. If we are to simulate nature in some way, the first priority is to describe what is going on in nature, to describe the forms of random numbers that will be needed in terms of their distributional forms and parameters. Having established this using expert knowledge of descriptive statistics, a suitable type of generator must be used, one which has been tested for reliability against the theoretical model. The sources of two streams of random numbers, one produced by a pseudo-random number generator, the other resulting from the natural process that the generator is attempting to simulate, should be undetectable for a "good" simulation, within the cycle length of the pseudo-random generator. A necessary condition is that the parameters, such as mean and standard deviation, of the pseudo-random sequence are acceptably close to those of the theoretical distribution. But this is not enough. Suppose we wish to produce a stream of uniform random digits in the range 0 to 9. Theoretical considerations give such values a mean of 4.5 and will give each value in the range equal frequencies of occurence in the stream. The sequence

0, 3, 6, 9, 2, 5, 8, 1, 4, 7, 0, 3, 6, 9, 2, 5, ...

satisfies these conditions, but is clearly not random. The independence of successive

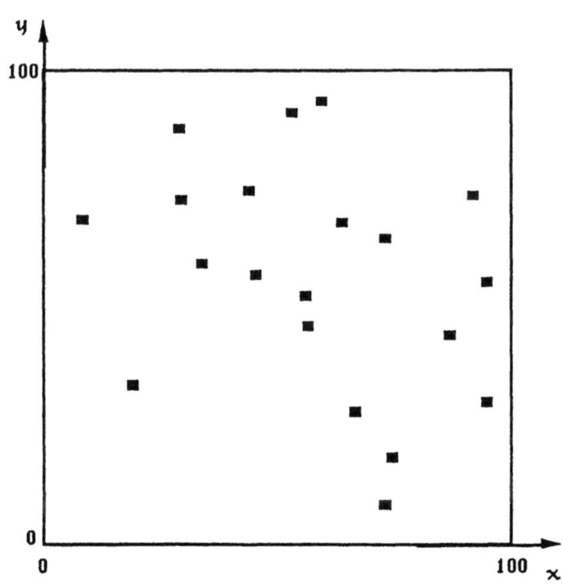

Fig 6 Plotting successive pairs of values

values is of major importance. There are sophisticated statistical tests for such independence that will not be discussed here - it is sufficient to know that they exist and that experts can be consulted if needed. Less formal methods can also be useful, for example, plotting pairs of successive values in a Cartesian coordinate plane may show up hidden patterns in the forms of clusters of points that will not be evident from simple observation of the number sequences. For example, the first sequence generated in this section, when plotted in this way, shows an almost complete void in the lower left hand quarter of the plot, with points quite evenly scattered in the rest of the figure, supporting the suspicion that there is a bias away from lower values. The sample size is too small for this suspicion to be conclusive here.

7. Generation of Uniform Random Variables

Uniform random variables can be converted into random variables of any form, so their generation is the essential first step in any form of simulation using random variables. Large scale simulation involves the generation of thousands or even millions of r.v.'s, so use of dice or paper drawing methods is impractical. A number of specialist machines were used (for example the early versions of ERNIE in the UK - Electronic Random Number Indicator Equipment) [TOCH63], dependent on the monitoring of some randomly occurring natural phenomenon. Most of these had faults, often due to wear or of cyclic activity related to the frequency of sampling, which showed up in long term use. Similar methods can been used in digital computers by monitoring the clock time and taking some high frequency change component as a random number. This can lead to cyclic faults if the sampling cycle is in phase with the clock change cycle,so is generably undesirable, especially as r.v. generators are often used within loops which are fairly regular in their repetitions.

Most computer random number generators are pseudo-random in their operation, depending on a formula which generates a repeatable random-like sequence of values. The most popular forms - due to their simplicity, reliability and relatively good speed properties, are **linear congruential generators**, based on the formula

$$x_{i+1} = a x_i + b \pmod{m}, \text{ for } i = 0, 1, 2, \ldots ,$$

where a, b and m are suitably chosen integer constants ("mod m" means that you divide the value obtained by m and retain the remainder, so, for example, 7 (mod 3) = 1). A stream of numbers is generated by entering a **seed** value x_0. This form of generator can be sub-categorized into **mixed** ($b > 0$) and **multiplicative** ($b = 0$) forms. The values of a, b and m are extremely important in determining the potential cycle length of the generator and the range of values supplied by it. The maximum possible cycle length is m, as the formula can only output integer values within the sample space

{0, 1, ... m-1} which will then be re-entered into the formula. It is sensible to set m to a positive integer power of the number base of the system being used to simpify the calculation of the mod function, so in a binary digital computer system it is natural to make m a power of 2 (for hand calculator based human operators, the values a = 1573, b = 19 and m = 10^3 give a satisfactory stream of uniform pseudo-r.v.'s with sample space {0, 1, ..., 999}). Rules have been devised for the generation of suitable combinations of a, b and m to obtain the maximum possible cycle length, for example [HULL62, KNUT81],

1. b and m have no common factors other than 1;
2. (a - 1) is a multiple of every prime number that divides m;
3. (a - 1) is a multiple of 4 if m is a multiple of 4.

Thus, if $m = 2^k$, where k is a positive integer large enough for the range of values required but not so large as to overload the storage capacity of the machine being used, m will be a multiple of 4, so condition 3 gives a = 4c + 1 where c is some positive integer. This also satisfies condition 2 as the only prime that divides m is 2, so b can be chosen to be any odd positive integer to satisfy condition 1. Generating a long cycle

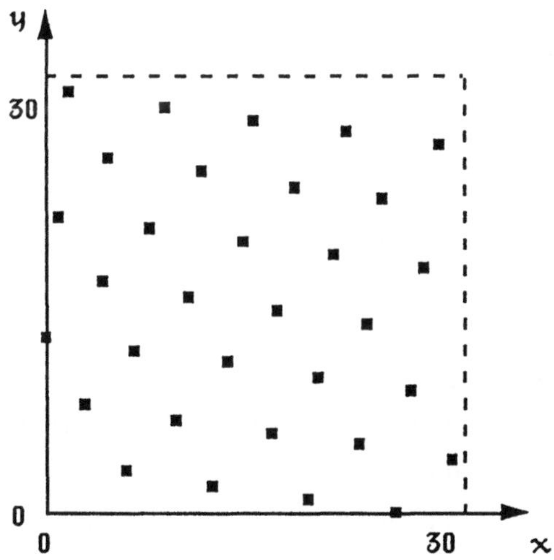

Fig 7 Regular pattern indicates a non-random sequence

does not necessarily produce satisfactory properties in other respects, such as correlation between successive values obtained. For example, the mixed congruential generator

$$x_{i+1} = 9x_i + 13 \pmod{32}$$

produces a full 32 number cycle length. Seeding the process with $x_0 = 0$ gives the sequence

0, 13, 2, 31, 4, 17, 6, 3, 8, 21, 10, 7, 12, 25, 14, 11, 16, 29, 18, 15, 20, 1, 22, 19, 24, 5, 26, 23, 28, 9, 30, 27, 0, 13, 2, ...

A distinct pattern is observable in the behaviour of the even values in this sequence. A good discussion of tests for such problems can be found in Dagpunar's book [DAGP88], but this is beyond the scope of this tutorial. The visual display suggested above, plotting successive pairs of values as (x, y) coordinates, gives a most regular pattern, indicating non-randomness in the sequence.

A number of generators whose properties have been found to be satisfactory are given below.

The multiplicative form, with $b = 0$, involves less arithmetic, so is faster in operation, but has a shorter potential cycle - with $m = 2^k$, a cycle length of 2^{k-2} can be achieved [MORG84]. Suitable choices for a and k are given as $a = 5^{13}$ when $k = 36$ or 39 and $a = 5^{17}$ when $k = 40$, 42 or 43. Dagpunar [DAGP88] recommends $a = 13^{13}$ when $k = 59$ (this is the generator used in the NAG subroutine G05CAF) and a = 630 360 016 when $m = 2^{31} - 1$ (as used in the Simscript II language). For mixed models, a = 69 069 for $k = 32$ and $a = 293$ for $k = 16$ are recommended. The IBM produced multiplicative generator RANDU, using $a = 2^{16} + 3$ when $k = 31$, is criticised as having poor distributivity. Some such criticisms can be overcome by using generators whose output value is based on the last two or more values (X_{i+1} is made to depend on $X_i, X_{i-1}, ...$) or by taking an output stream of given length (100 or 500 values have been tried [EGGE79], [ATKI80], [ANDR72]) and "shuffling" those values to produce the final output stream. This form of shuffling can improve poor generators, but has no significant effect on good generators.

Most of the generators above will produce pseudo-random uniform integers X in the range 0 to $2^k - 1$. Close approximations to uniform continuous r.v.'s in the range [0, 1] can be obtained by outputting $U = X/(2^k - 1)$. Uniform continuous r.v.'s in any range [p, q] can be generated from $p + (q - p)U$. Uniform discrete r.v.'s in any range can be found by equal sub-partitioning of the range of a more extensive generator or by taking the integer part of suitable multiples of continuous uniform random variables.

Most users will have access to a stream of uniform random variables from their own computer systems and will be satisfied with the results obtained from such generators. The explanation given above is intended to help users to understand the processes used by such pseudo-random number generators, their limitations and advantages. Those who do not have ready use of such generators can write simple routines using constants suggested above and will obtain sensible streams of values, subject to the precision of the equipment they are using. The same applies to those who are not happy with the output received from their standard packages who want to try other methods.

8. Generation of Other Forms of Random Variables from Uniform Variables

Suppose that we have an adequate source of continuous uniform random variables, U, with sample space [0, 1], whether from a properly random or a pseudo-random source. Such a source can be used to generate random values from any form of discrete or continuous distribution. Consider first the discrete case.

Suppose we wish to simulate a discrete r.v. with sample space {0, 1, 2, ... } defined by the probabilities

$$p_x = P[X = x] \quad \text{for } x = 0, 1, 2, \ldots$$

Note that the sample space could be bounded above, as in the binomial case, or unbounded as in the Poisson case.

Let
$$P_x = \sum_{i=0}^{x} p_i = P[X \leq x].$$

As x increases from x = 0 through all the values allowed in the sample space, P_x forms a non decreasing sequence of values (as the probabilites accumulated must all be non-negative) with the property that

$$P_x - P_{x-1} = p_x = P[X = x] \quad \text{for } x = 1, 2, \ldots$$

with $P_0 = p_0$

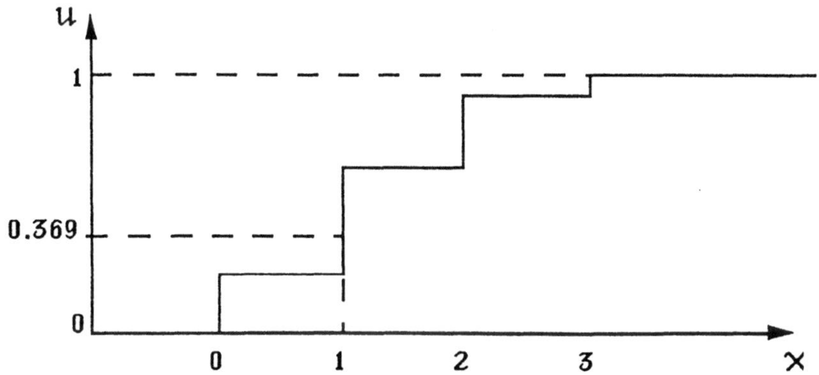

Fig 8 Generation of a discrete r.v. from a Uniform r.v.

When plotted against x, the values of P_x form a rising series of uneven stairs with the final step at level 1. The height of the riser for stair x is the probability of obtaining the value x from the distribution. Given a realised value u of the uniform r.v. U as described above, a value from the distribution of X can be obtained by identifying which stair's riser passes through the value u. This is equivalent to finding the value of x such that

$$P_{x-1} \leq u < P_x.$$

Any awkwardness at the lower end of the scale can be eliminated by setting P_{-1} to zero, making the condition valid for x = 0, 1, 2, ..., that is for the whole of the sample space. The required value of x can be found using a look-up table. For example, the probabilities for a binomial distribution with n = 3, p = 0.4 can be calculated as

$$p_0 = 0.216, \ p_1 = 0.432, \ p_2 = 0.288, \ p_3 = 0.064,$$

giving $P_{-1} = 0.000, \ P_0 = 0.216, \ P_1 = 0.648, \ P_2 = 0.936, \ P_3 = 1.000.$

Suppose our first simulated uniform r.v. is evaluated as 0.369. This gives our first simulated binomial r.v. the value 1 as $P_0 \leq 0.369 < P_1$. This process is illustrated in fig 8.

The simulated uniform sequence

0.369, 0.994, 0.091, 0.812, 0.940, 0.422, 0.938, 0.123, 0.970, 0.291, 0.360, 0.041, 0.371,

generates a simulated binomial sequence

1, 3, 0, 2, 3, 1, 3, 0, 3, 1, 1, 0, 1.

Note that the probabilites used to generate the lookup table for the conversion could come directly from a formula, as in the above example, or by estimation through observation of physical phenomena.

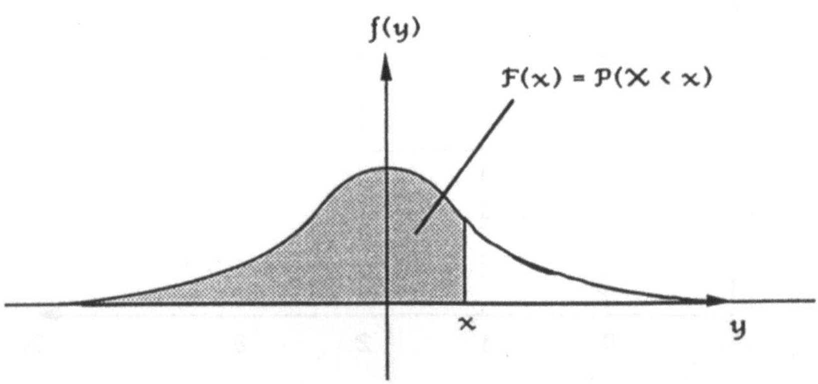

Fig 9 The cumulative distribution function of a continuous r.v.

The transformation of uniform r.v.'s into other forms of continuous r.v. can be obtained by a method with similar theoretical basis, although operational difficulties may be discovered. For a continuous distribution with p.d.f. f(x), the equivalent of the staircase diagram is the graph of the **cumulative distribution function** (c.d.f)

$$F(x) = \int_{-\infty}^{x} f(y)\, dy = P[X \le x].$$

The graph of F(x) is sometimes called an ogive, as its shape often resembles this form of curve familiar to architects (fig 10). The value of F(x) lies in [0, 1] and it can be shown that if X is a continuous r.v. with p.d.f. f(x) then F(X) is a continuous uniform r.v. in [0, 1]. Thus, the function F(X) converts the r.v. X into a uniform r.v. U. The problem we have set ourselves is the opposite, to convert U into X. This can be done using the inverse function $F^{-1}(U)$. That is, if

$U = F(X)$,

then $X = F^{-1}(U)$.

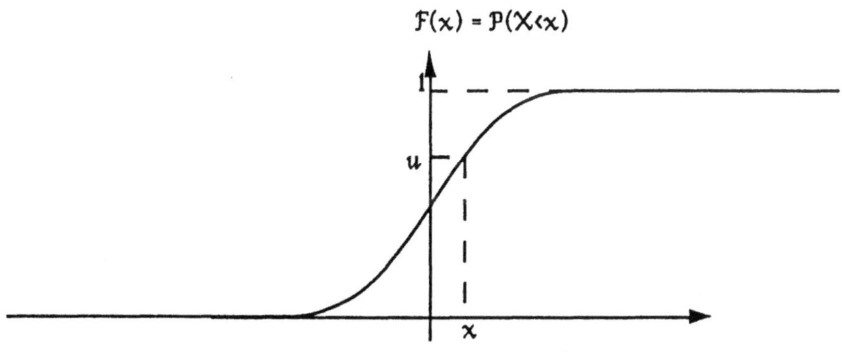

Fig 10 Generation of a continuous r.v. from its c.d.f

As an example, consider the exponential distribution with p.d.f.

$f(x) = \nu \exp(-\nu x)$ for $0 \le x < \infty$.

This integrates to give the c.d.f.

$$F(x) = \int_{-\infty}^{x} (\nu) \exp(-\nu y)\, dy = 1 - \exp(-\nu x)$$

The inverse of this function, expressed with argument u, takes form

$F^{-1}(u) = -\ln(1 - u) / \nu$.

This can be used to generate exponential r.v.'s from uniform r.v.'s. A little thought should convince the reader that if U is a continuous uniform r.v. in [0, 1], then its "mirror" (1 - U) will have the same distribution. The formula can thus be simplified to give the conversion formula

$$x = -\ln(u) / \nu$$

for generating a realisation of a r.v. from an exponential distribution with parameter ν. A stream of such variables can be used to simulate the spatial or time distribution of a sequence of events.

An alternative method of generating such exponential streams within a fixed time or space interval depends on the property that, given the number of events to occur within a given time interval, the distribution of the variables within that interval is uniform [COX65]. Thus, to generate such a sequence, first use a simulated Poisson variable to determine how many events, N say, should occur within the given interval and then generate N uniformly distributed variables within that interval. This may be less time consuming that the direct method given above as the calculation of the logarithm is relatively expensive.

Given a stream of uniform r.v.'s, the inverse of the c.d.f. can be used to convert them into continuous r.v.'s of any form. This is valid in principle, but practical difficulties can arise in implementation. Many p.d.f.'s f(x) cannot be integrated analytically to give their c.d.f.'s F(x) - this is the case for the normal distribution. Even if this can be done, the inverse function $F^{-1}(X)$ may also prove analytically intractable or computationally expensive. Both problems lead to the use of numerical methods which can be relatively slow. Even if analytical forms can be found, they may involve functions such as exponentials (as in the above example) and trigonometric functions which are also notoriously slow to evaluate, leading to time difficulties in complicated simulation exercises requiring the generation of several thousands of r.v.'s. This may be offset against the knowledge that each uniform r.v. used will generate exactly one r.v. of the required distributions. None of the "costly" uniform r.v.'s generated is wasted.

The rejection method is more wasteful in this sense, using more than two uniform r.v.'s on average to generate a single r.v. from the required continuous distribution. However, it can be more efficient if the function f(x) is not too costly to evaluate compared with the numerical methods that may be required for the inversion and integration of the above technique. Suppose the r.v. X has p.d.f. f(x) for a given interval of values of x, [a, b], and that it is known that $f(x) \leq c$ for all x in this range - c is an upper bound for f(x). For this method to work precisely, a and b need to be finite real values. For the normal distribution, we should really set them to $-\infty$ and ∞ respectively, so an approximate method is required. For most purposes, upper and lower limits for standard normal variables can be set to -3 and 3, as

$P[-3 \le Z \le 3] = 0.9973$. This method distorts the generation of extreme values of the distribution and would be of little use to statisticians who are particularly interested in the "tails" of distributions for significance testing. For the generation of streams of random variable for computer graphics uses, the "error" caused is imperceptible - one in about every 370 values will be "missing".

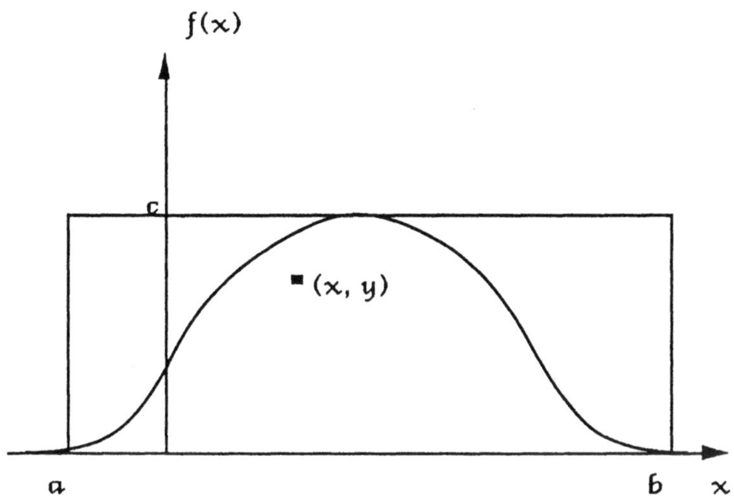

Fig 11 The rejection method - x would be accepted in this case

Given that we can set sensible upper and lower bounds a and b for the domain of the r.v. X and that an upper bound c is known for the p.d.f. f(x), the generating procedure is as follows.

1. Generate a realisation x of a uniform r.v. in [a, b].
2. Generate a realisation y of a uniform r.v. in [0, c].
3. If $y \le f(x)$, output x as a realisation of the r.v. X.
4. If more r.v.'s are needed, return to step 1.

The point (x, y) is a realisation of a uniformly random point within a rectangular area enclosing the p.d.f. of X, the most "popular" values of X lying below the regions for which f(x) takes relatively large values. The procedure converts two uniform r.v.'s into a point, tests to see if the point concerned lies below the curve of the p.d.f., outputting x if that is the case. If [a, b] represents an exact domain or sample space for X, this will be an exact method.

It is relatively easy to assess the efficiency of this method in terms of the numbers of uniform r.v.'s required on average to generate one r.v. of the required form. The area under the p.d.f. is one (or approximately one if a truncated form is used as in the normal case) by a fundamental property of p.d.f.'s. The area of the region in which the point (x, y) can lie is c(b - a). As such points are evenly distributed within this area, the probability of a point being accepted and a value from the required distribution being generated from a particular pair of uniform r.v.'s (x, y) is

$$1/\{c(b - a)\} = p, \text{ say.}$$

The number of pairs required before finding an acceptable value has a geometric distribution which has mean or expected value

$$1/p = c(b - a).$$

Clearly, it is sensible to set c as low as possible, so if the maximum value of f(x) is known, c should be set to this value. Thus, the mean number of uniform r.v.'s that will be required to generate one r.v. from the distribution required is

$$2c(b - a).$$

This method of simulating random variables is similar to "Monte-Carlo" methods used in Numerical Analysis for estimating integrals [HAMM64]. The ratio of points so generated that lie below a given curve can be used to estimate the integral of the curve, within certain statistical error bounds. Extensions of the technique can be used to estimate multivariate integrals and can be used when such methods are needed in Computer Graphics. A possible candidate for such methods is in calculation of the "form factors" used in radiosity calculations [COHE85][FOLE90].

9. Special Methods for Normal Variable Generation

Special methods have been devised for the generation of specific r.v.'s, in particular the standard normal r.v. due to its central importance to statistical theory and to the inadequacy of the standard methods described above in providing an exact simulation of the normal distribition. These methods have the disadvantage of being relatively more expensive in terms of generation time, but are particularly important when the exact statistical behaviour of systems are being investigated. This is seldom the case with Computer Graphics applications of stochastic simulation, so we will only give a brief outline of such methods here. Image generators are too often advised to use precise methods, when a "quick and dirty" method could give indistinguishably acceptable visual results.

A simple method for producing an approximate normal r.v. is to find the sum of several r.v.'s from another distribution. The Central Limit Theorem of statistics says that such a sum will tend towards a normal distribution as the number of r.v.'s used increases. We have seen above how a stream of uniform r.v.'s can be generated, particularly continuous uniform r.v.'s in the range [0, 1]. These can be shown to have mean 0.5 and variance 1/12. The sum of n such independent variables will have mean

0.5n and variance n/12. Thus an approximate standard normal r.v. with mean 0 and standard deviation 1 (remember the variance is the square of the standard deviation), can be found from

$$Z = (Y - 0.5n)/\mathrm{sqrt}(n/12)$$

where Y is the sum of n continuous uniform r.v.'s in [0, 1], where n is an acceptably large value. For most purposes, n = 12 is large enough for a reasonable approximation to the distributional form and this has the added advantage of making the variance equal to one, avoiding the costly square root calculation and an extra division in the evaluation. The formula above then reduces to

$$Z =(y - 6)$$

Dagpunar [DAGPUNAR88] comments "This method should not be used. It is an approximation only, and the fit is poor in the tails of the distribution." This is a sensible criticism in the context of statistical simulations where it is important to consider the occurrence of rare events, but, as stated above, is usually perfectly acceptable in producing visually convincing results. The method requires the evaluation of 12 uniform r.v.'s for each standard normal r.v. generated, but has no more costly functions to evaluate.

An exact method is provided by the Box-Muller technique, which generates one normal r.v. for each uniform r.v. generated at the cost of logarithmic and trigonometric function evaluation. If U_1 and U_2 are independent continuous uniform r.v.'s in [0, 1], then

$$Z_1 = \sqrt{-2 \ln U_1} \cos(2\pi U_2)$$

and $$Z_2 = \sqrt{-2 \ln U_1} \sin(2\pi U_2)$$

Although this method should produce a pair of independent standard normal variables, use of certain forms of pseudo-random generators for U_1 and U_2 may produce some irregular effects, as discussed in [DAGPUNAR88]. However, this should be adequate for visual simulation, although its effectiveness should be compared with the less exact methods suggested above.

There are many other methods specified in more specialist texts, but the above should be adequate for those interested in using random variables in the simulation of natural processes for visual simulation.

10. Stochastic methods used to enhance the quality of images

Most of the methods described in the remainder of this tutorial use stochastic methods to generate convincing geometric models. A number of techniques are used for enhancing the depiction of images, two of which are briefly outlined here.

Most readers will be familiar with the ray casting paradigm in which rays from an eye position are sent out through pseudo-pixel positions in a view window to intersect the scene (fig 12). The equivalent pixel in the display device viewport is then coloured according to the properties of the nearest object intersected by the ray, if any. Rays are normally cast through the centre of the window pixels, but such regularity often produces "staircase" effects in the image. An effective method of anti-aliasing such images is to use "distributed ray casting" [COOK84]. This involves super-sampling each pixel - typically casting four or nine rays for each pixel - and colouring the pixel according to the mean colour value obtained. Aliasing can still occur if the rays are cast in a regular grid. The technique of "jittering" displaces each ray by small independent random displacements in the x and y directions, thus improving the antialiasing effect. If the objects comprising the scene are in motion, a similar technique can be applied to the time variable to produce motion blur effects [COOK86]. Each of a pixel's rays are evaluated at times that are slightly randomly disturbed from the "true" time at which the image is computed [FOLEY90].

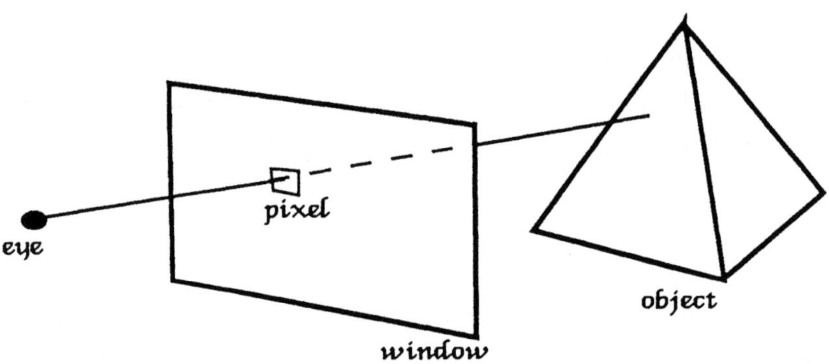

Fig 12 The ray casting method

Dithering is a stochastic method that effectively enlarges the range of colours or tones available to a display device without producing unpleasant side effects such as repetitive patterns. Take the most extreme case of a monochrome device which has two levels per pixel, black (0) or white (1). Suppose we wish to show a shade of grey at a level g, where g is a real value between 0 and 1. Generate a uniform r.v. U in the range [0, 1] and then colour the pixel black if $U < g$, white otherwise. The net effect over an area of pixels is to produce the mean intensity of illumination required, the randomness of the generation ensuring lack of repetitive patterns. The method can be applied to all three guns of an eight colour display and can be used for interpolating between levels of more precise displays. A pre-calculated look up table can improve the performance of the algorithm, but this can lead to unwanted patterns. Although it produces good visual effects, the method is less popular than deterministic methods which use relatively irregular patterns for blocks of pixels.[BURG89]

11. Solid Texturing

Texture mapping is a widely used method for producing the effect of texture on objects. A previously digitised texture is mapped onto the surface of an object, as if the object were wrapped or painted with the pattern of the texture. This method produces texture on the surface only, so the object cannot be successfully subdivided, and can give irregular effects at the join line of the pattern, as in the join between wallpaper sections. Solid texturing [PERL85] avoids both these drawbacks. A randomly produced scalar field is generated by defining field function values at the vertices of a regular three dimensional grid which is assumed to surround the object to be depicted. This grid is effectively part of the object and would move with it if the object were to move. When the object is being depicted, points on its surface are identified as visible, for example, by an algorithm such as the ray casting algorithm of section 9. For each point so identified, the field variable at that point must be evaluated. To maintain continuity and smoothness of the variable, its gradients or rates of change in the x, y and z directions also need to be defined, usually by some random process. These comprise the gradient vector of the scalar field variable. To generate the field value for some point, the grid cube within which it lies is identified, cubic spline interpolation along the four edges in the x direction then reduces the cube to a square, similar interpolation along the remaining two edges in the y direction reduce this to a line and a final cubic spline interpolation along this line, now in the z direction, evaluates the field function for the

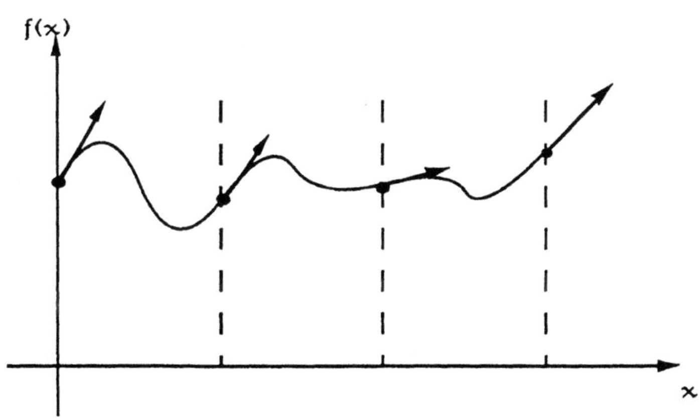

Fig 13 Using positive gradients to generate an irregular wave form

required point. The function value can be used to define or adapt the colour value for the point concerned, or to change the gloss or transparency coefficients for the point on the object. Also, the gradient vector can be used to amend the surface normal at the point concerned, giving a textured effect to the object's depiction. By controlling the type of random variable used, semi-regular effects can be produced. Fig 13 gives a two dimensional illustration of how an irregular wave can be produced by generating random, but always positive, gradients in the x-direction. Applying this in one of the main three dimensional directions can produce semi-regular fluctuations such as seen in wood grain or marble. Images from Perlin's work are also shown to great effect in Foley [FOLE90].

There are other examples of stochastic methods used in Computer Graphics,but the above should serve to give the reader a foundation strong enough to tackle the major methods of using stochastic methods in the modelling of fractal forms, discussed in the second section of this tutorial.

References

[ANDR72] Andrews, D.F., P.J. Bickel, F.R. Hampel, P.J. Huber, W.H. Rogers, J.W.Tukey, (1972) *Robust Estimates of Location*, Princeton University Press, Princeton, N.J.

[ATKI80] Atkinson A.C., (1980) Tests of pseudo-random numbers, *Appl Stats*, 29(2), 164-171.

[BATT91] Batty, M., (1991) Cities as Fractals: Simulating Growth and Form, in *Fractals and Chaos*, Crilly, A.J., R.A. Earnshaw, H. Jones (eds), Springer-Verlag, New York, N.Y.

[BURG89] Burger, P., D. Gillies, (1989) *Interactive Computer Graphics*, Addison-Wesley, Wokingham, England.

[COHE85] Cohen, M.F., D.P. Greenberg, (1985) The Hemi-Cube: A Radiosity Solution for Complex Environments, *SIGGRAPH 85*, 31-40.

[COX65] Cox, D.R., H.D.Miller, (1965) *The Theory of Stochastic Processes*, Methuen, London, England.

[CRAM46] Cramer, H., (1946) *Mathematical Methods of Statistics*, Princeton University Press, Princeton, N.J.

[DAGP88] Dagpunar, J., (1988) *Principles of Random Variate Generation*, Clarendon Press, Oxford, England.

[EGGE79] Egger, M.J., (1979) Power transformations to achieve symmetry in quantal bioassay, *Technical Report No 47*, Division of Biostatistics, Stanford, Cal.

[FOLE90] Foley, J.D., A. van Dam, S.K. Feiner, J.F. Hughes, (1990) *Computer Graphics: Principles and Practice (2 ed)*, Addison-Wesley, Reading, Mass.

[HAMM64] Hammersley, J.M., D.C. Handscomb, (1964) *Monte Carlo Methods*, Methuen, London, England.

[HULL62] Hull, T.E., A.R. Dobell, (1962) Random Number Generators, *SIAM Rev.*, 4, 230 - 254.

[KAAN91] Kaandorp, J., (1991) Modelling Growth Forms of Sponges with Fractal Techniques, in *Fractals and Chaos*, Crilly, A.J., R.A. Earnshaw, H. Jones (eds), Springer-Verlag, New York, N.Y.

[KNUT81] Knuth, D.E., (1981) *The Art of computer Programming*, Vol 2, *Seminumerical Algorithms*, Addison-Wesley, Reading, Mass.

[MORG84] Morgan, B.J.T., (1984) *Elements of Simulation*, Chapman and Hall, London, England.

[PERL85] Perlin, K., (1985) "An Image Synthesizer," *SIGGRAPH 85*, 287-296.

[PRUS90] Prusinkiewicz, P., A. Lindenmayer, (1990) *The Algorithmic Beauty of Plants*, Springer-Verlag, New York, N.Y.

[SAUP88] Saupe, D., (1988) Algorithms for Random Fractals, in *The Science of Fractal Images*, Peitgen, H.O., D. Saupe (eds), Springer-Verlag, New York, NY.

[TOCH63] Tocher, K.D., (1963) *The Art of Simulation*, Hodder and Stoughton, London, England.

[VOSS85] Voss, R., "Fractals in Nature: Characterization, Measurement and Simulation," in *Course Notes 15 for SIGGRAPH 87*, Anaheim, CA July 1987.

State of the Art in Volume Visualization

Arie Kaufman

ABSTRACT
This paper is a state of the art report on 3D volume visualization. It includes a survey of the field and over 100 references. Volume visualization provides mechanisms to peer inside volumetric objects in order to view that which is not ordinarily viewable and to probe into the voluminous and complex structures and their dynamics to comprehend that which is not ordinarily comprehensible. It encompasses an array of techniques, a technology, and a nomenclature, and holds substantial challenges.

1 Introduction

Volume visualization is a method of generating 2D images from 3D volumetric data. Volume data are 3D entities that have information inside them, may not consist of surfaces and edges at all, and/or too voluminous and complex to be represented geometrically. Volume visualization is emerging as a key field of computer graphics and imaging. Its techniques provide ways to explore the inner structures of volumetric data, allowing visual insight into complex data sets. Volume visualization as a technology brings a revolution to computer graphics and promises important breakthroughs in the applications of volume visualization. Just as raster graphics in the seventies superseded vector graphics for visualizing surfaces, volume visualization now has the potential to supersede surface graphics for handling and visualizing volumes. Furthermore, just as raster graphics has been dominant for rendering both surfaces and lines, volume visualization coupled with the progress in hardware has the potential to liberate computer graphics from the limitations of surface graphics and to prevail in the nineties for rendering volumes, as well as surfaces and lines.

Volume visualization is related to visualization in scientific computing and has been identified by the Visualization in Scientific Computing report [67] as an emerging visualization environment. The report claims that software and hardware for volume graphics and imaging are still rudimentary. Nevertheless, volume visualization is available **today** to scientists and engineers as a partner in their scientific discoveries and engineering tasks.

The field of volume visualization can be traced back to the mid-70's when the use of volumetric data, particularly in 3D medical imaging, had been reported. By now the field has matured with several breakthroughs and seminal projects. The interest and enthusiasm of the cohort of experts and the perplexed users of volume visualization have sprung a series of workshops and tutorials devoted to the topics of volumetric data, the associated visualization techniques, and the related applications: *Chapel Hill Workshop on Volume Visualization* [15, 19, 29, 32, 34, 39, 58, 62, 80, 82, 88, 95, 99], ACM SIGGRAPH video review on "Volume Visualization - State of the Art" [28], a special issue of *IEEE Computer* on Visualization in Scientific Computing [7, 12, 23, 30, 56, 65, 79], a special issue of *Computer & Graphics* on "3D Voxel-Based Graphics" [14, 38, 57], and a special issue of *The Visual Computer* on "Volume Visualization" [6, 10, 33, 64, 94], IEEE Press tutorial titled "Volume Visualization" [46], San Diego Workshop on Volume visualization [13, 22, 59, 66, 72, 73, 75, 83, 84, 87, 96, 97, 98], and Boston Workshop on Volume Visualization to be held in October 1992. The proliferation of conferences and literature on volume visualization demonstrates that this area is developing into a major computer technology of the 1990's.

2 Taxonomy

In a relatively new field such as volume visualization a consensus has not been reached yet on the taxonomy. Nevertheless, this section attempts to define the basic taxonomy for volume visualization.

The primary source of volume data is empirical, generated by D or a 2D sampling device or by a computer model. Both generate discrete sampling points of a real or simulated object, usually as a sequence of cross-sectional scans, or as samples on a regular or irregular grid. These data sets are being processed by 2D or 3D image processing and computational geometry techniques and being *3D reconstructed* into a 3D volume data set by usually interpolating between the cross-sections or the sample points. For example, real human organs sampled experimentally with medical scanners, like Computer Tomograms (CT), Magnetic Resonance Imaging (MRI), or ultrasonography, are often reconstructed from the 2D cross-sectional scans and stored and manipulated as a 3D volume data set. The 3D volume data set in *3D discrete/digital voxel space* is usually stored in a *cubic frame buffer* (volume buffer) which is a 3D array of unit volume cells or elements (called *voxels*).

An alternative source of volume data is by *voxelizing (3D scan-converting)* a 3D continuous geometric model commonly represented as a display list of polygons or surfaces. A *voxelization (3D scan-conversion) algorithm* generates a set of voxels that "best" represents the synthetic model within the discrete voxel space. The digital synthetic model may also be intermixed with the sampled data set forming a *hybrid voxel model* [55, 63].

In order to visualize the volume data set, the volume primitives are projected onto discrete pixel space and stored as a raster image in a frame buffer. This process, which is termed *volume rendering*, usually contains the viewing and the shading stages in one step. Alternatively, the volume data can be first converted into geometric primitive in a process called fitting involving either *iso-contouring*, *iso-surfacing*, *surface extraction/tracking*, or *border following*. Then, the geometric primitive is rendered to the screen by a process called *surface rendering*. This process again involves both the viewing and the shading stages. Surface rendering is an indirect technique for visualizing volume primitives by first converting them into an intermediate surface primitive and then employing conventional computer graphics techniques to render them to the screen. Volume rendering, on the other hand, is a direct display of the volume primitives without any intermediate conversion of the volume data to surface primitives.

3 Representation

Many objects and natural phenomena in our spatial surroundings and in computational models are 3D volumes of data. Unlike traditional techniques, which represent 3D objects in terms of surfaces and edges approximated by polygons and lines, volume data are 3D entities which might not consist of surfaces and edges. A volumetric object is typically represented as a large 3D grid of voxels. A voxel is the 3D counterpart of the 2D pixel.

Each voxel is a quantum unit of volume and has a numeric value, or values, associated with it representing some measurable properties or independent variables (e.g., color, opacity, density, material, coverage proportion, refractive index, velocity, strength, deformation, time) of the real objects. A voxel is commonly represented as a unit cube centered at a discrete address in 3D space, and the aggregate of voxels tessellating the volume forms the volumetric data set.

The voxels may be derived from discrete samples of the physical phenomenon as in medical imaging, may be computed by a computer simulation as in computational fluid dynamics, or may be synthesized by a computer model as in solid modeling. The physical phenomenon, the computer simulation, and the computer model may generate 3D or multi-dimensional lattices of tensor fields, where the lattice is either regular (even), rectilinear, or general (random or deformed) [82]. The tensor field may vary in rank; for example, a tensor of rank zero is a scalar field in which every voxel has a single value (magnitude), while a tensor field of rank one is a vector field in which each voxel has a value as well as a direction.

Regardless of the origin of the data set, it can be stored, manipulated, and displayed using a variety of display primitives. The display primitives range from zero-dimensional points or particles, one-dimensional curves, lines, vector, ribbons, or contours, two-dimensional polygon meshes or curved surfaces, to three-dimensional volume cells or voxels. Although volume visualization focuses on the latter primitive, the volume visualizer may capitalize on the advantages of the more traditional, lower-dimensional primitives to represent and visualize the various aspects of the same data set (see also [85, 92]).

Similarly, there is a large number of data structures, closely related to the display primitives to be exploited, that are used to represent the volume data set. Those include spatial enumeration using a voxel matrix, a sparse matrix, or a flat matrix, cell decomposition as in octrees [37], constructive solid geometry, primitive instancing, sweep methods, and boundary models.

4 Viewing

A critical step in volume visualization is to the image presentation and rendering that captures the contents of the voxels outside and inside the volume data set by projecting them onto a 2D display. Volume viewing algorithms create a 2D projection from the 3D volumetric data set using volume rendering. The algorithms are classified according to three categories:

- whether the algorithm operates in 3D object (voxel) space (e.g., [95]), in 2D image (pixel) space (e.g., [32]), or in both (e.g., [8]);
- whether the voxel value is represented by a binary (e.g., [89]) or graded (multi-valued, percentage) function (e.g., [8, 61, 81, 91]). In the latter category the multi-value function may be classified as representing either partial coverage, variable densities, or graded opacities; and
- whether the traversal for visibility is performed back-to-front (e.g., [11]) or front-to-back (e.g., [20]).

Based on these categories a vocabulary of volume rendering has been established, and thus, for example, one may refer to ***binary-field volume rendering***, and ***graded-field volume rendering***. The special case of rendering by combining graded opacities/translucencies is termed ***volume compositing***.

5 Shading

Another related aspect of volume rendering is the shading of the projected volume, termed *discrete shading* or *volumetric shading*. The ultimate goal in shading is to provide a 2D image that is practically indistinguishable from a photograph of the real object, while retaining all the minute details of the original object which might be of great scientific, engineering, or medical value. Unlike shading of geometric objects where the normals are calculated directly from the geometric information, in discrete shading these normals are not available and have to be recovered from the volume data.

The shading techniques are classified either as pixel (image) based, in which the surface gradient is recovered from the depth (z) buffer of the visible voxels, or as voxel (object) based, in which the gradient is computed directly from the 3D voxel information. The primary pixel-based techniques are *block/constant shading* [25], in which the visible voxel faces are shaded as a polygon mesh; *distance-only (depth-only) shading* [16, 93], in which the color of the surface varies only as a function of the distance between the observer and the surface point; *distance/depth gradient shading* [20, 77], in which the gradient is approximated from the 2D distance map of the visible voxels; and *congradient shading* [6], which is a hybrid of the contextual and gradient techniques. The voxel-based techniques are *contextual shading* [4, 26], in which the normal is estimated from the adjoint faces; *gray-level/density gradient shading* [31], in which the voxel values (e.g., densities) in a neighborhood are used to indicate the surface inclination; *composting shading* [8, 61, 81], in which blended colors and opacities along a projection ray appear as a shaded pixel; and *local surface interpolation shading* [94], in which a biquadratic surface is approximated for each voxel based on a 3 x 3 x 3 neighborhood of the densities.

6 Voxelization Algorithms

Both the synthesis and analysis of voxel models require a substantial mathematical and theoretical foundation. These include studies in the field of 3D discrete space, its topology, and the use of 3D discrete topology in the development of 3D scan-conversion algorithms. Many theoretical studies have been conducted to characterize the 3D discrete space, where the primary goal is to devise a framework for discrete space that is a close analog of the continuous space, in which case the discrete space is labeled as well-behaved. A particular interest in well-behaved spaces is related to voxelization algorithms and iso-surfacing. A voxelization algorithm generates from a geometric representation of an object a connected set of voxels in 3D voxel space that best represent that object [5, 42, 43, 44, 53, 71]. The generated digital representation has to conform to fidelity, thickness, minimization, efficiency, and connectivity requirements. For example, a digital surface formed by a scan-conversion process might have a certain "thickness" which is characterized by the absence of tunnels or holes of certain connectivity. In other words, the connectivity of the surface determines which type of projection rays may or may not penetrate it during ray casting on ray tracing [101, 102].

7 Architectures

Volume images are huge 3D matrices of the order of giga bits for moderate spatial resolution (e.g., 128M bytes for a resolution of 512^3), with voxel granularity as fine as that of the pixel. These sizes place new demands on graphics systems for more memory, faster computing and communications, and new breeds of processing and display. About a decade ago the notion that computers or special-purpose hardware could be efficiently used for volume processing of 512^3 resolution or higher, was merely a dream. Nowadays, with the rapid progress in parallel processing and in microelectronics (especially in memory compactness), the dream is closer to reality. The following special-purpose innovative hardware architecture for volume visualization are briefly reviewed (see also [41, 52]): the GODPA/Voxel processor, the Cube architecture, $3DP^4$ system, the PARCUM architecture, and the Insight system.

GODPA [16], designed for medical applications, is a derivative of the Voxel processor [17] which has been used as the underlying architecture for a physician workstation [18]. GODPA is a hierarchical pipelined hardware organization, in which the 256^3 voxel memory is divided into 64 symmetric equal sub-cubes, each processed by a separate concurrent processing element. Two projects, similar to GODPA, have been proposed in Japan, one is a prototype system, SCOPE [90], and the other is the $3DP^4$ architecture [76].

The *Cube architecture* [48] is a versatile volume visualization system which handles both sampled and synthetic data. The Cube architecture is centered around a full cubic frame buffer of voxels. In order to cope with the huge quantity of voxels and still perform in real time, special features were incorporated within the architecture: parallel processing [50], a unique skewed memory organization which permits the retrieval and storage of voxels in parallel [40], and a multiple-write bus which speeds up the viewing process. The cubic frame buffer is accessed to input synthetic [43, 44, 53]. and sampled volume data [2], to manipulate the volume images [47], to view the volume images from an arbitrary direction [51], and to render them [6].

In the PARCUM system [35, 36] the memory cube is divided into 4^3 macro voxels each of which is 4^3 voxels, one bit each. The read access fetches a macro voxel which is sorted in an output dataword. Two hardware implementations for the projection process are proposed: a surface detection technique with ray stepping using a binary rate multiplier, and an analytical approach using matrix multiplication.

A commercial voxel-image system, Insight [70], has combined hardware and software employing octree encoding [68], mainly for solid modeling and medical applications. It can display complex objects at a near real-time rate [69]. The current system is being marketed by Octree Corporation.

Several general-purpose systems, like the AT&T Pixel Machine, the HP Turbo VRX, the Pixar machine, the Pixel Planes, the Silicon Graphics 4D, the Stardent Machine, and the Sun TAAC-1, provide software for volume visualization, relying on partial hardware support.

8 Applications

Three-dimensional medical imaging has been the primary application of volume visualization and a driving force in the development of this field (e.g., [2, 3, 9, 12, 24, 27, 49, 74, 78, 86, 93]). Voxel representation is very effective for the traditional applications employing empirical 3D voxel imagery, such as in medical imaging, in which the acquired data is almost in a volumetric form. Other empirical applications include: biology (e.g., confocal microscopy) [1, 54] earth science [30, 81, 100], industry (e.g., industrial inspection [60]), meteorology [21, 91], and molecular systems (e.g., electron density maps) [19].

Volume visualization has a great potential beyond its original goal to observe internal human organs. It is also effective for model-based volumetric applications like computer aided design (e.g., solid modeling [45], finite elements, material stress patterns), simulation and animation (e.g., flight simulation), and scientific visualization (e.g., astrophysical simulation, fluid flow [65, 82]). With the advent of voxelization algorithms, which form a bridge between geometric models and volume representation, the new model-based applications become common place. The Visualization in Scientific Computing report [67] predicted that "in the future animated and interactive presentation and analysis of volume imagery will play a central role in medical imaging, geoscience, astrophysics, computational fluid dynamics, and finite element analysis, as well as many other scientific and engineering fields of research".

Volume visualization has recently emerged as a key research and development area of computer graphics. Volume visualization is a technical reality today and imperative tomorrow. The progress in volume visualization and computer development, coupled with the desire to reveal the inner structures of volumetric data sets guarantees that volume visualization will develop into a dominant field in computer graphics and the associated applications.

Acknowledgements:

This work was supported by the National Science Foundation under grants MIP-8805130 and IRI-9008109, and grants from Hughes Aircraft Company, Hewlett Packard, and Silicon Graphics. I wish to thank the many students of mine who have worked on 3D volume visualization, voxelization algorithms, and the Cube project. Among them, special thanks are due to Dany Cohen and Roni Yagel.

9 References

[1] D. A. Agard. Optical Sectioning Microscopy. *Annual Review of Biophysics and Bioengineering*, 13:191–219, 1984.

[2] R. Bakalash and A. Kaufman. MediCube: a 3D Medical Imaging Architecture. *Computers & Graphics*, 13(2):151–157, 1989.

[3] L. J. Brewster, S. S. Trivedi, H. K. Tuy, and J. K. Udupa. Interactive Surgical Planning. *IEEE Computer Graphics and Applications*, 4(3):31–40, March 1984.

[4] L. Chen, G. T. Herman, R. A. Reynolds, and J. K. Udupa. Surface Shading in the Cuberille Environment. *IEEE Computer Graphics and Applications*, 5(12):33–43, December 1985.

[5] D. Cohen and A. Kaufman. Scan Conversion Algorithms for Linear and Quadratic Objects. In A. Kaufman, editor, *Visualization*, pages 280–301. IEEE Computer Society Press, Los Alamitos, CA, 1990.

[6] D. Cohen, A. Kaufman, R. Bakalash, and S. Bergman. Real-Time Discrete Shading. *The Visual Computer*, 6(1):16–27, February 1990.

[7] T. A. DeFanti, M. D. Brown, and B. H. McCormick. Visualization: Expanding Scientific and Engineering Research Opportunities. *IEEE Computer*, 22(8):12–25, August 1989.

[8] R. A. Drebin, L. Carpenter, and P. Hanrahan. Volume Rendering. *Computer Graphics*, 22(4):64–75, August 1988.

[9] E. J. Farrell, W. C. Yang, and R. A. Zappulla. Animated 3D CT Imaging. *IEEE Computer Graphics and Applications*, 5(12):26–32, December 1985.

[10] C. Frederick and E. L. Schwartz. Brain Peeling: Viewing the Inside of a Laminar 3D Solid. *The Visual Computer*, 6(1):37–49, February 1990.

[11] G. Frieder, D. Gordon, and R. A. Reynolds. Back-to-Front Display of Voxel-Based Objects. *IEEE Computer Graphics and Applications*, 5(1):52–60, January 1985.

[12] H. Fuchs, M. Levoy, and S. M. Pizer. Interactive Visualization of 3D Medical Data. *IEEE Computer*, 22(8):46–51, August 1989.

[13] M. P. Garrity. Raytracing Irregular Volume Data. *Computer Graphics*, 24(5):35–40, November 1990.

[14] D. Geist and M. W. Vannier. PC-Based 3-D Reconstruction of Medical Images. *Computers & Graphics*, 13(2):135–144, 1989.

[15] L. Gelberg, D. Kamins, and J. Vroom. VEX: A Volume Exploratorium. In *Chapel Hill Workshop on Volume Visualization*, pages 21–26, Chapel Hill, NC, May 1989.

[16] S. M. Goldwasser. A Generalized Object Display Processor Architecture. *IEEE Computer Graphics and Applications*, 4(10):43–55, October 1984.

[17] S. M. Goldwasser and R. A. Reynolds. Real-Time Display and Manipulation of 3-D Medical Objects: The Voxel Processor Architecture. *Computer Vision, Graphics and Image Processing*, 39:1–27, 1987.

[18] S. M. Goldwasser, R. A. Reynolds, T. Bapty, D. Baraff, J. Summers, D. A. Talton, and E. Walsh. Physician's Workstation with Real-Time Performance. *IEEE Computer Graphics and Applications*, 5(12):44–57, December 1985.

[19] D. S. Goodsell and A. S. Olson. Molecular Applications of Volume Rendering and 3-D Texture Maps. In *Chapel Hill Workshop on Volume Visualization*, pages 27–32, Chapel Hill, NC, May 1989.

[20] D. Gordon and R. A. Reynolds. Image Space Shading of 3-Dimensional Objects. *Computer Graphics and Image Processing*, 29(3):361–376, March 1985.

[21] R. Grotjahn and R. Chervin. Animated Graphics in Meteorological Research and Presentation. *Bulletin of American Meteorological Society*, 65:1201–1208, 1984.

[22] P. Hanrahan. Three-Pass Affine Transforms for Volume Rendering. *Computer Graphics*, 24(5):71–78, November 1990.

[23] J. Helman and L. Hesselink. Representation and Display of Vector Field Topology in Fluid Flow Data Sets. *IEEE Computer*, 22(8):27–36, August 1989.

[24] G. T. Herman. Special Issue on Computerized Tomography. *Proceedings of the IEEE*, 71, 1983.

[25] G. T. Herman and H. K. Liu. Three-Dimensional Display of Human Organs from Computed Tomograms. *Computer Graphics and Image Processing*, 9(1):1–21, January 1979.

[26] G. T. Herman and J. K. Udupa. Display of Three Dimensional Discrete Surfaces. *Proceedings of SPIE*, 273:90–97, 1981.

[27] G. T. Herman and J. K. Udupa. Display of 3D Digital Images: Computational Foundations and Medical Applications. *IEEE Computer Graphics and Applications*, 3(5):39–46, August 1983.

[28] L. Herr. Volume Visualization - State of the Art. *ACM SIGGRAPH Video Review*, Issue 44, 1989.

[29] W. Hibbard and D. Santek. Interactivity is the Key. In C. Upson, editor, *Chapel Hill Workshop on Volume Visualization*, pages 39–44, Chapel Hill, NC, May 1989.

[30] W. Hibbard and D. Santek. Visualizing Large Data Sets in the Earth Sciences. *IEEE Computer*, 22(8):53–57, August 1989.

[31] K. H. Hoehne and R. Bernstein. Shading 3D-Images from CT Using Gray-Level Gradients. *IEEE Transactions on Medical Imaging*, MI-5(1):45–47, March 1986.

[32] K. H. Hoehne, M. Bomans, A. Pommert, M. Riemer, C. Schiers, U. Tiede, and G. Wiebecke. 3-D Visualization of Tomographic Volume Data Using the Generalized Voxel-Model. In *Chapel Hill Workshop on Volume Visualization*, pages 51–58, Chapel Hill, NC, May 1989.

[33] K. H. Hoehne, M. Bomans, A. Pommert, M. Riemer, C. Schiers, U. Tiede, and G. Wiebecke. Visualization of Tomographic Volume Data Using the Generalized Voxel Model. *The Visual Computer*, 6(1):28–37, February 1990.

[34] X. Hu, K. K. Tan, D. N. Levin, S. G. Galhotra, C. A. Pelizzari, G. T. Y. Chen, R. N. Beck, C. T. Chen, and M. D. Cooper. Volumetric Rendering of Multimodality, Multivariable Medical Imaging Data. In *Chapel Hill Workshop on Volume Visualization*, pages 45–50, Chapel Hill, NC, May 1989.

[35] D. Jackel. The Graphics PARCUM System: A 3D Memory Based Computer Architecture for Processing and Display of Solid Models. *Computer Graphics Forum*, 4(1):21–32, January 1985.

[36] D. Jackel and W. Strasser. Reconstructing Solids from Tomographic Scans - The PARCUM II System. In A. A. M. Kuijk and W. Strasser, editors, *Advances in Computer Graphics Hardware II*, pages 209–227. Springer-Verlag, Berlin, 1988.

[37] C. Jackins and S. L. Tanimoto. Octrees and Their Use in Representing Three-Dimensional Objects. *Computer Graphics and Image Processing*, 14(3):249–270, November 1980.

[38] G. J. Jense and D. P. Huijsmans. Interactive Voxel-Based Graphics for 3D Reconstruction of Biological Structures. *Computers & Graphics*, 13(2):145–150, 1989.

[39] E. R. Johnson and C. E. Mosher. Integration of Volume Rendering and Geometric Graphics. In *Chapel Hill Workshop on Volume Visualization*, pages 1–8, Chapel Hill, NC, May 1989.

[40] A. Kaufman. 'Memory Organization for a Cubic Frame Buffer. In *EUROGRAPHICS '86*, pages 93–100, Lisbon, Portugal, August 1986.

[41] A. Kaufman. Voxel-Based Architectures for Three-Dimensional Graphics. In *IFIP'86, 10th World Computer Congress*, pages 361–366, Dublin, Ireland, September 1986.

[42] A. Kaufman. An Algorithm for 3D Scan-Conversion of Polygons. In *EUROGRAPHICS '87*, pages 197–208, Amsterdam, Netherlands, August 1987.

[43] A. Kaufman. Efficient Algorithms for 3D Scan-Conversion of Parametric Curves, Surfaces, and Volumes. *Computer Graphics*, 21(4):171–179, July 1987.

[44] A. Kaufman. Efficient Algorithms for 3D Scan-Converting Polygons. *Computers & Graphics*, 12(2):213–219, 1988.

[45] A. Kaufman. Voxel-Based Solid Modeling. In *International Conference on CAD/CAM and AMT*, Jerusalem, Israel, December 1989.

[46] A. Kaufman. *Volume Visualization.* IEEE Computer Society Press Tutorial, Los Alamitos, CA, 1990.

[47] A. Kaufman. The voxblt Engine: A Voxel Frame Buffer Processor. In A. A. M. Kuijk and W. Strasser, editors, *Advances in Graphics Hardware III.* Springer-Verlag, Berlin, 1991.

[48] A. Kaufman and R. Bakalash. Memory and Processing Architecture for 3-D Voxel-Based Imagery. *IEEE Computer Graphics and Applications*, 8(6):10–23, November 1988. Also translated into Japanese, Nikkei Computer Graphics, 3, No. 30, March 1989, pp. 148-160.

[49] A. Kaufman and R. Bakalash. The CUBE System as a 3D Medical Workstation. In *SPIE'89 Symposium on 3D Visualization of Scientific Data*, pages 189–194, Los Angeles, CA, January 1989.

[50] A. Kaufman and R. Bakalash. Parallel Processing for 3D Voxel-Based Graphics. In R. A. Earnshaw P. M. Dew and T. R. Heywood, editors, *Parallel Processing for Computer Vision and Display*, pages 471–478. Addison-Wesley, 1989.

[51] A. Kaufman, R. Bakalash, and D. Cohen. Viewing and Rendering Processor for a Volume Visualization System. In R. L. Grimsdale and W. Strasser, editors, *Advances in Graphics Hardware IV*, pages 171–178. Springer-Verlag, Berlin, 1991.

[52] A. Kaufman, R. Bakalash, D. Cohen, and R. Yagel. Architectures for Volume Rendering - A Survey. *IEEE Engineering in Medicine and Biology*, 9(4):18–23, December 1990.

[53] A. Kaufman and E. Shimony. 3D Scan-Conversion Algorithms for Voxel-Based Graphics. In *ACM Workshop on Interactive 3D Graphics*, pages 45–76, Chapel Hill, NC, October 1986.

[54] A. Kaufman, R. Yagel, R. Bakalash, and I. Spector. Volume Visualization in Cell Biology. In *Visualization '90*, pages 160–167, San Francisco, CA, October 1990.

[55] A. Kaufman, R. Yagel, and D. Cohen. Intermixing Surface and Volume Rendering. In H. Fuchs K. H. Hoehne and S. M. Pizer, editors, *3D Imaging in Medicine: Algorithms, Systems, Applications*, pages 217–227. June 1990.

[56] N. Kluksdahl, A. Kriman, and D. Ferry. The Role of Visualization in the Simulation of quantum Electronic Transport in Semiconductors. *IEEE Computer*, 22(8):60–67, August 1989.

[57] T. Y. Kong. A Digital Fundamental Group. *Computers & Graphics*, 13(2):159–166, 1989.

[58] W. F. Kraske, F. W. George III, and J. M. Halls. Morphological Description in 3D Volumetric Biomedical Visualization. In *Chapel Hill Workshop on Volume Visualization*, pages 59–66, Chapel Hill, NC, May 1989.

[59] W. Krueger. Volume Rendering and Data Feature Enhancement. *Computer Graphics*, 24(5):21–26, November 1990.

[60] R. P. Kruger and T. M. Cannon. The Application of Computerized Tomography, Boundary Detection, and Shaded Graphics Reconstruction to Industrial Inspection. *Materials Evaluation*, 36:75–80, April 1978.

[61] M. Levoy. Display of Surfaces from Volume Data. *IEEE Computer Graphics and Applications*, 8(5):29–37, May 1988.

[62] M. Levoy. Design for Real-Time High-Quality Volume Rendering Workstation. In *Chapel Hill Workshop on Volume Visualization*, pages 85–92, Chapel Hill, NC, May 1989.

[63] M. Levoy. A Hybrid Ray Tracer for Rendering Polygon and Volume Data. *IEEE Computer Graphics and Applications*, 10(3):33–40, March 1990.

[64] M. Levoy. Volume Rendering by Adaptive Refinement. *The Visual Computer*, 6(1):2–7, February 1990.

[65] M. B. Long, K. Lyons, and J. K. Lam. Acquisition and Representation of 2D and 3D Data from Turbulent Flows and Flames. *IEEE Computer*, 22(8):39–45, August 1989.

[66] N. Max, P. Hanrahan, and R. Crawfis. Area and Volume Coherence for Efficient Visualization of 3D Scalar Functions. *Computer Graphics*, 24(5):27–34, November 1990.

[67] B. H. McCormick, T. A. DeFanti, and M. D. Brown. Visualization in Scientific Computing. *Computer Graphics*, 21(6), 1987. edited special issue.

[68] D. J. Meagher. Geometric Modeling Using Octree Encoding. *Computer Graphics and Image Processing*, 19(2):129–147, June 1982.

[69] D. J. Meagher. Interactive Solids Processing for Medical Analysis and Planning. In *NCGA'84 Conference*, pages 96–106, Anaheim, CA, May 1984.

[70] D. J. Meagher. Applying Solids Processing Methods to Medical Planning. In *NCGA'85 Conference*, pages 101–109, Dallas, TX, April 1985.

[71] W. Mokrzycki. Algorithms of Discretization of Algebraic Spatial Curves on Homogeneous Cubical Grids. *Computers & Graphics*, 12(3/4):477–487, 1988.

[72] C. Montani and R. Scopigno. Rendering Volumetric Data Using the STICKS Representation Scheme. *Computer Graphics*, 24(5):87–94, November 1990.

[73] H. Neeman. A Decomposition Algorithm for Visualizing Irregular Grids. *Computer Graphics*, 24(5):49–56, November 1990.

[74] D. P. Ney, E. K. Fishman, D. Magid, and R. A. Drebin. Volumetric Rendering of Computed Tomography Data: Principles and Techniques. *IEEE Computer Graphics and Applications*, 10(2):24–32, March 1990.

[75] K. L. Novins, F. X. Sillion, and D. P. Greenberg. An Efficient Method for Volume Rendering Using Perspective Projection. *Computer Graphics*, 24(5):95–100, November 1990.

[76] T. Ohashi, T. Uchiki, and M. Tokoro. A Three-Dimensional Shaded Display Method for Voxel-Based Representation. In *EUROGRAPHICS '85*, pages 221–232, Nice, France, September 1985.

[77] Horn B. K. P. Hill Shading and the Reflection Map. *Geo-Processing*, 2:65–146, 1982.

[78] M. Rhodes. Computer Graphics in Medicine. *IEEE Computer Graphics and Applications*, 10(2):20–23, March 1990.

[79] L. Rosenblum. Scientific Visualization at Research Laboratories. *IEEE Computer*, 22(8):68–69, August 1989.

[80] J. R. Rossignac. Considerations on the Interactive Rendering of Four-Dimensional Volumes. In *Chapel Hill Workshop on Volume Visualization*, pages 67–76, Chapel Hill, NC, May 1989.

[81] P. Sabella. A Rendering Algorithm for Visualizing 3D Scalar Fields. *Computer Graphics*, 22(4):51–58, August 1988.

[82] P. Shirley and H. Neeman. Volume Visualization at the Center for Supercomputing Research and Development. In *Chapel Hill Workshop on Volume Visualization*, pages 17–20, Chapel Hill, NC, May 1989.

[83] P. Shirley and A. Tuchman. A Polygonal Approximation to Direct Scalar Volume Rendering. *Computer Graphics*, 24(5):63–70, November 1990.

[84] D. Speray and S. Kennon. Volume Probes: Interactive Data Exploration on Arbitrary Grids. *Computer Graphics*, 24(5):5–12, November 1990.

[85] S. N. Srihari. Representation of Three-Dimensional Digital Images. *ACM Computing Surveys*, 4(13):399–424, December 1981.

[86] U. Tiede, K. H. Hoehne, M. Bomans, A. Pommert, M. Riemer, and G. Wiebecke. Investigation of Medical 3D-Rendering Algorithms. *IEEE Computer Graphics and Applications*, 10(2):41–53, March 1990.

[87] K. D. Toennies and U. Tronnier. 3D Modeling Using an Extended Cell Enumeration Representation. *Computer Graphics*, 24(5):13–20, November 1990.

[88] J. M. Torson. Interactive Image Cube Visualization and Analysis. In *Chapel Hill Workshop on Volume Visualization*, pages 33–36, Chapel Hill, NC, May 1989.

[89] H. K. Tuy and L. T. Tuy. Direct 2-D Display of 3-D Objects. *IEEE Computer Graphics and Applications*, 4(10):29–33, October 1984.

[90] T. Uchiki and M. Tokoro. SCOPE: Solid and Colored Object Projection Environment. *Transaction of the Institute of Electronics and Communication Engineers of Japan*, 68-D(4):741–748, April 1985. in Japanese.

[91] C. Upson and M. Keeler. V-BUFFER: Visible Volume Rendering. *Computer Graphics*, 22(4):59–64, August 1988.

[92] C. Upson and D. Kerlick. Volumetric Visualization Techniques. In *Two and Three Dimensional Visualization Workshop, ACM SIGGRAPH'89 Course Notes*, volume 13, pages 1–86, Boston, MA, August 1989.

[93] M. W. Vannier, J. L. Marsh, and J. O. Warren. Three Dimensional Computer Graphics for Craniofacial Surgical Planning and Evaluation. *Computer Graphics*, 17(3):263–273, July 1983.

[94] R. E. Webber. Ray Tracing Voxel Based Data via Biquadratic Local Surface Interpolation. *The Visual Computer*, 6(1):8–15, February 1990.

[95] L. Westover. Interactive Volume Rendering. In *Chapel Hill Workshop on Volume Visualization*, pages 9–16, Chapel Hill, NC, May 1989.

[96] J. Wilhelms, J. Challinger, N. Alper, S. Ramamoorthy, and A Vaziri. Direct Volume Rendering of Curvilinear Volumes. *Computer Graphics*, 24(5):41–48, November 1990.

[97] J. Wilhelms and A. Van Gelder. Octrees for Faster Isosurface Generation. *Computer Graphics*, 24(5):57–62, November 1990.

[98] J. Wilhelms and A. Van Gelder. Topological Considerations in Isosurface Generation - Extended Abstract. *Computer Graphics*, 24(5):79–86, November 1990.

[99] S. E. Wixson. True Volume Visualization of Medical Data. In *Chapel Hill Workshop on Volume Visualization*, pages 77–84, Chapel Hill, NC, May 1989.

[100] R. H. Wolfe and C. N. Liu. Interactive Visualization of 3D Seismic Data: A Volumetric Method. *IEEE Computer Graphics and Applications*, 8(7):24–30, July 1988.

[101] R. Yagel, D. Cohen, and A. Kaufman. Discrete Ray Tracing. *IEEE Computer Graphics and Applications*, pages 19–28, September 1992.

[102] R. Yagel, A. Kaufman, and Q. Zhang. Realistic Volume Imaging. In *Visualization '90*, pages 226–231, San Diego, CA, October 1991.

On the Theory and Application of Stereographics in Scientific Visualization

Eric Hibbard, Michael Bauer, Margaret Bradshaw,
Glenn Deardorff, Ken Hu, and David Whitney

ABSTRACT
Extracting useful insights from complex three-dimensional (3D) data sets requires an effective means of three-dimensional visualization. Stereographic, or binocular, 3D data visualization enables scientists to understand the spatial relationships and topological structures inherent in complex data sets. This paper reviews the basic physiological theory of the stereoptic effect and the geometric foundations for generating stereographic images. Algorithms are presented for the creation of stereographic images and for manipulating images to the best 3D effect. Sufficient detail is provided to enable readers to generate stereo animations on a workstation. Also discussed are the different types of stereo display hardware and the viewing techniques involved. The paper concludes with the discussion of several current projects that are applying stereographics in the fields of fluid dynamics, virtual environments, space science, and geology.

1 Introduction

The number of scientists performing large-scale numerical simulations has increased by an order of magnitude in the last few years, generating overwhelming amounts of data to be processed and analyzed. Gaining a physical understanding of this complex data often involves novel and innovative visualization methodologies, algorithms, and hardware. The challenge is to display the information in a manner that conveys the essential science and structure of the simulated phenomena and, at the same time, uses the most effective and efficient method of conveying this complex information to the scientist. Of the many graphical display methods available with current workstations, stereo imaging, or stereographics, is emerging as one of the most useful methods for gaining topological understanding of complex numerical simulations.

Just as stereophonics fools the brain into hearing multi-dimensional sound from two single sounds, stereographics makes the brain believe that pairs of flat images are actually three-dimensional scenes. The brain processes the two flat images seen separately by each eye and fuses the images to create a single scene with depth. This effect is known as stereopsis, and understanding the physiology of stereopsis is crucial to the development of accurate and effective stereographic algorithms. There are many other issues involved in the creation of stereographic images including special effects, viewing techniques, and hardcopy. This paper explores these issues as they relate to scientific visualization and discusses how these issues have been addressed in applications created at the National Aeronautics and Space Administration's Ames Research Center (NASA ARC).

2 Physiology of Stereopsis

The following brief review of some current theories of the neurophysiology of stereopsis will provide background for the subsequent discussion of stereo image generation.

2.1 Depth Cues

Perception of depth is influenced by both monocular and binocular depth cues. A depth cue is any visual information that helps convince the brain that it is seeing a three-dimensional image. Traditional 3D images create the effect of depth by employing monocular depth cues. For example, large bright objects appear to be closer than small dark objects; an object overlapping another object will appear closer; and shaded objects and objects drawn in perspective will appear to have depth. The visual system processes these monocular depth cues and attempts to interpret single flat images as 3D images. Stereographic 3D, on the other hand, takes advantage of the way the human visual system actually sees everyday scenes, as two images instead of one. This technique exploits the main binocular depth cue – stereopsis.

2.2 Stereopsis

The sensation of depth occurs when the visual system fuses the nearly identical flat images from each eye into a three-dimensional model of the viewer's world. When objects vary in depth from the viewer, their relative positions on the retina of each eye differ slightly. This difference is called disparity. Calculation of depth through geometric triangulation using disparity information is a relatively easy task for the brain[11] . A more difficult problem involves selecting a particular point on one retinal image and finding its corresponding point on the other retinal image. The evaluation of many possible matches and the elimination of false matches is a very demanding task. The mechanism that the human visual system uses to solve the correspondence problem is not completely understood. A proposed solution involves the matching of primitive symbolic representations composed of oriented edges[4]. The following paragraph describes the processes involved.

In the retina of each eye, cells are arranged in groups called receptive fields. Each field supplies a single retinal ganglion cell. Receptive fields are characterized by excitatory centers and inhibitory surrounding areas, making their ganglia most sensitive to circular patterns of light of a particular size and location. Retinal ganglia communicate through the optic nerve with the visual cortex of the brain. Inputs from retinal ganglia that respond to stimulation in a particular location and orientation are processed by cortical neurons. These neurons, arranged in a hierarchy from simple cells to complex cells, transform the retinal stimuli into representations of line segments and boundary contours. Left- and right-eye line segment information is then input to the complex binocular neurons. When similar attributes (similar orientation and size) are found in approximately corresponding locations on each retina, the visual system assumes that they represent corresponding regions of the scene. Given this information, the disparity-specific complex binocular neurons provide local depth information.

The mechanism proposed above works for stereo pairs containing oriented lines and edges that produce locally discernible patterns. It fails, however, to account for the visual system's ability to perceive depth in cases such as a random dot stereogram [9] where all features are identical except for a small shift in a particular region of the pattern. In this case, disparity information is extracted from a very ambiguous visual field containing many identical points. The result is that the shifted region appears in depth (see figure 1).

Gian Poggio and colleagues found that complex binocular neurons are more likely than

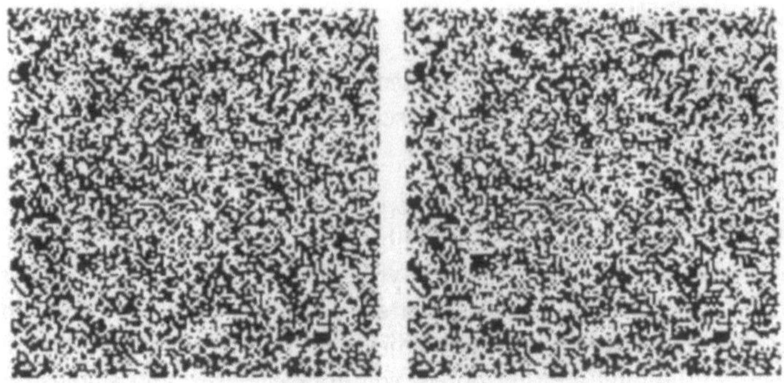

FIGURE 1. Random Dot Stereogram. To see the raised image, use a stereo viewer to look at the right square with the right eye and the left square with the left eye.

simple cortical neurons to respond to random dot stereograms[14]. It was suggested that complex cells must match left- and right-eye inputs very precisely to accomplish globally correct binocular correspondence. The proposed mechanism for finding the correct match in a multiply-ambiguous field involves gated retinal subfields. (Further discussion can be found in [15])

2.3 Parallax

The reason that the correspondence problem is important to the generation of stereographic images is that one must make sure that all the lines in a left-eye image can be fused to the corresponding lines in the right-eye image. This correspondence can be assured by the calculation of a correct parallax shift. The parallax shift for a particular object point is the apparent distance that the point moves when the viewing angle for the object is changed. The distance the point moves from side to side is called horizontal parallax, and the up and down distance is called vertical parallax.

Horizontal parallax, related to retinal disparity, is what creates the illusion of depth. Many early stereo pair generating algorithms created both horizontal and vertical parallax. Unfortunately, the stereo effect was often lost because the brain cannot fuse images that have too much vertical parallax. The most common of these stereographic algorithms created horizontal parallax by rotating the image around its vertical axis [17]. The effect of rotation in conjunction with a perspective transformation caused corresponding lines to be shifted vertically from each other. Lines appeared to be different sizes to each eye, yet the brain tried to fuse the lines assuming they were identical. The resulting confusion often negated the 3D effect. The correct parallax generating algorithm, involving shifting the perspective viewpoint, is described in the following section. In further discussion, parallax will mean only horizontal parallax.

3 Creating Stereographic Images

Generating simple stereo pairs is not difficult, but creating effective stereo pairs requires more effort. Many factors come into play that affect how a viewer perceives a stereo image. For example, different amounts of parallax, different eye separations, and the use of monocular depth cues can change an image drastically. Before making a pleasing image, however, it is necessary to have a method to create a correct image.

3.1 Creating a Stereo Image on a Workstation

To create the effect of stereopsis with software, one needs only to induce retinal disparity by calculating the correct parallax shift for each point in a particular scene. By presenting the shifted images to the left and right eyes, a realistic stereoptic effect can be achieved.

Although the concept of generating stereo images is simple and can be found in the literature[7], much less work has been reported on algorithms that take advantage of workstation hardware. This section describes the geometric foundations of stereo transformations and the correct projection and transformations for applications on a typical workstation.

The basic theory behind generating stereo pairs is the simulation of binocular vision. Figure 2 shows the position of the eyes relative to a point in 3D space, and where each eye would see this point on a 2D screen.

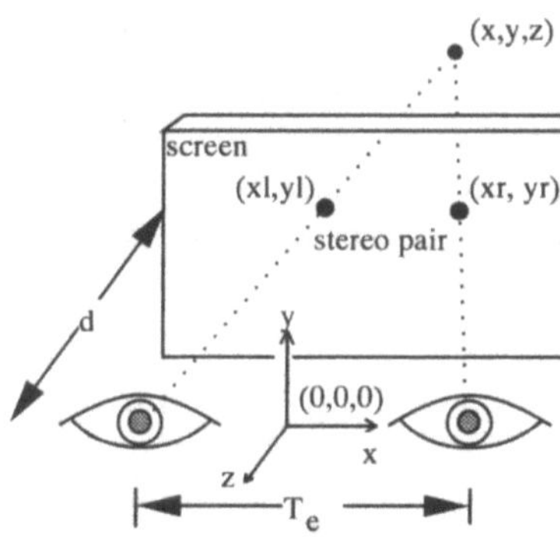

FIGURE 2. Determining 2D Screen Coordinates from a 3D Point.

The transformation matrix for the left eye can be derived by multiplying a translation of $T_e/2$ along the x-axis (the coordinate system is shown in Figure 2) followed by a perspective projection[3] and then a translation back. The transformation matrix for the right viewpoint can be formulated similarly by reversing the translation directions. The resultant transformation matrix for the left- and right-eye perspective projections can be expressed in the following form, where T_e is the eye separation, and d is the distance from the viewer's eye to the screen:

$$\mathbf{L} = \begin{bmatrix} 1 & 0 & 0 & 0 \\ 0 & 1 & 0 & 0 \\ T_e/2d & 0 & 1 & -1/d \\ T_e/2 & 0 & 0 & 0 \end{bmatrix} \quad \mathbf{R} = \begin{bmatrix} 1 & 0 & 0 & 0 \\ 0 & 1 & 0 & 0 \\ T_e/2d & 0 & 1 & -1/d \\ -T_e/2 & 0 & 0 & 0 \end{bmatrix}$$

While these two matrices can be used to demonstrate the basic concept and perhaps create some simple stereo pairs, they do not take into account all the factors required for practical applications on a 3D graphics workstation.

A typical workstation provides a perspective transformation rather than a perspective projection. The transformation turns the viewing frustum into a cubic volume bounded by -1 and 1 in all three dimensions. The cubic volume is then projected to a monitor through a scaling transformation. This scaling and normalization to dimensionless units makes the stereo viewing computation more complex. In addition, the interocular distance (T_e) must be scaled to a proportional value based on the graphical object's world coordinates. For example, using $T_e = 2.5$ inches for the viewing of a molecule modeled in angstroms is clearly inappropriate. To resolve all the scaling factors involved and to take advantage of the hardware features of the workstation, the following, alternate approach is proposed.

In a right-hand coordinate system, with the line of sight and the viewing frustum toward the negative $(-z)$ direction, a typical perspective transformation matrix ($\mathbf{P}$) is:

$$\mathbf{P} = \begin{bmatrix} \frac{cot\left(\frac{v}{2}\right)}{a} & 0 & 0 & 0 \\ 0 & cot\left(\frac{v}{2}\right) & 0 & 0 \\ 0 & 0 & -\frac{f+n}{f-n} & -1 \\ 0 & 0 & -\frac{2fn}{f-n} & 0 \end{bmatrix}$$

In this matrix, v is the vertical field viewing angle, a is the aspect ratio, and n and f are the near and far clipping planes in the world coordinate system. Note that this matrix will transform a viewing frustum into a cubic volume. The transformation matrix for the perspective projection for the left viewpoint can be expressed as $\mathbf{L'} = \mathbf{T_1 P T_2}$:

$$\mathbf{L'} = \begin{bmatrix} 1 & 0 & 0 & 0 \\ 0 & 1 & 0 & 0 \\ 0 & 0 & 1 & 0 \\ \frac{T_e}{2} & 0 & 0 & 1 \end{bmatrix} \begin{bmatrix} \frac{cot\left(\frac{v}{2}\right)}{a} & 0 & 0 & 0 \\ 0 & cot\left(\frac{v}{2}\right) & 0 & 0 \\ 0 & 0 & -\frac{f+n}{f-n} & -1 \\ 0 & 0 & -\frac{2fn}{f-n} & 0 \end{bmatrix} \begin{bmatrix} 1 & 0 & 0 & 0 \\ 0 & 1 & 0 & 0 \\ 0 & 0 & 1 & 0 \\ -\frac{T_e}{w} & 0 & 0 & 1 \end{bmatrix}$$

Note that the T_e/w (where w is the screen width) in T_2 is the normalized term of $Te/2$ in T_1 . The final form of both left and right transformation matrices is :

$$\mathbf{L'} = \begin{bmatrix} \frac{cot\left(\frac{v}{2}\right)}{a} & 0 & 0 & 0 \\ 0 & cot\left(\frac{v}{2}\right) & 0 & 0 \\ \frac{T_e}{w} & 0 & -\frac{f+n}{f-n} & -1 \\ \frac{T_e cot\left(\frac{v}{2}\right)}{2a} & 0 & -\frac{2fn}{f-n} & 0 \end{bmatrix} \mathbf{R'} = \begin{bmatrix} \frac{cot\left(\frac{v}{2}\right)}{a} & 0 & 0 & 0 \\ 0 & cot\left(\frac{v}{2}\right) & 0 & 0 \\ -\frac{T_e}{w} & 0 & -\frac{f+n}{f-n} & -1 \\ \frac{-T_e cot\left(\frac{v}{2}\right)}{2a} & 0 & -\frac{2fn}{f-n} & 0 \end{bmatrix}$$

From these perspective transformation matrices, the horizontal parallax can be computed by:

$$H = (1/z)(T_e \cot(v/2)/a) + 2T_e/w,$$

To examine the value of H, the following typical values in a workstation environment can be used:

T_e	interocular distance (eye separation)	= 2.5 in	(6.3 cm)
d	distance from the viewer's eye to the screen	= 32 in	(81 cm)
w	width of the screen (using a 19-inch monitor)	= 15 in	(38 cm)
h	height of the screen	= 11.25 in	(28.6 cm)

By expressing the aspect ratio and the field viewing angle as $a = w/h$, and $\cot(v/2) = d/(h/2) = 2d/h$, and substituting these values and scaling to normalized dimensions, the horizontal parallax equation becomes

$$H = T_e(d/z + 1).$$

Note that on the plane of convergence ($z = -d$), the parallax is zero. At infinity, the parallax is equal to the eye separation. This equation is the basis for the discussion in section 3.2 on parallax and the determination of object placement in 3D space.

As a practical guideline, the steps necessary for generating stereo images can be summarized as follows:

1. Compute the centroid and the maximum dimension of the graphical object under consideration.

2. Translate the centroid of the graphical object(s) to $(0, 0, -d)$ (same as the distance from the viewer to the monitor) and normalize the size of the object by its maximum dimension. Then, scale the object to a reasonable size on the screen (a typical value is $0.7w$).

3. Most graphics workstations provide the perspective transformation matrix ($\mathbf{P}$) or its equivalent form. Specify the field of view (v) such that $\cot(v/2) = 2d/h$ to account for the screen size and the distance from the viewer to the screen. Using the correct v is very important in generating high quality images.

4. The final perspective transformation matrices, $\mathbf{L}'$ and $\mathbf{R}'$, can be created by inserting the two T_e terms directly into the workstation's perspective transformation matrix ($\mathbf{P}$), as shown. This method is usually simpler and faster than performing the two translations to create the matrices.

3.2 Controlling Parallax

At NASA ARC, stereo graphics animation software has been developed by using the above described guidelines. The equations defined in section 3.1 allow fine control over parallax for generating effective stereo animations. When viewing objects in stereo, one can create special effects by controlling the placement of objects within z-depth, i.e., objects can be placed in front of the screen (theater space) as well as behind the screen (screen space) by changing the parallax. When placing objects in space, several cases of parallax are encountered (see figure 3).

Negative (or crossed) *parallax* ($|z/d| < 1$) occurs when an object appears in theater space. The eyes' line of sight must cross in front of the screen to fuse the two images (see also figure 7).

Zero parallax ($|z/d| = 1$) occurs when the left- and right-eye images lie exactly on top of each other on the screen, i.e., the horizontal parallax value is equal to zero. The eyes converge and focus on the plane of the screen (see also figure 8).

Positive (or uncrossed) *parallax* ($|z/d| > 1$) occurs when an object appears behind the screen. The eyes converge at a point behind the screen yet are still focused on the plane of the screen (see also figure 9). When an object is at infinity ($|z/d| = \infty$), the left- and right-eye axes are parallel and the horizontal parallax value is equal to T_e.

Parallax should be used in moderation to create the best effect of depth and to minimize eye strain. Excessive negative parallax will cause the eyes to cross past a comfortable angle of convergence, and excessive positive parallax will cause the eyes to diverge past

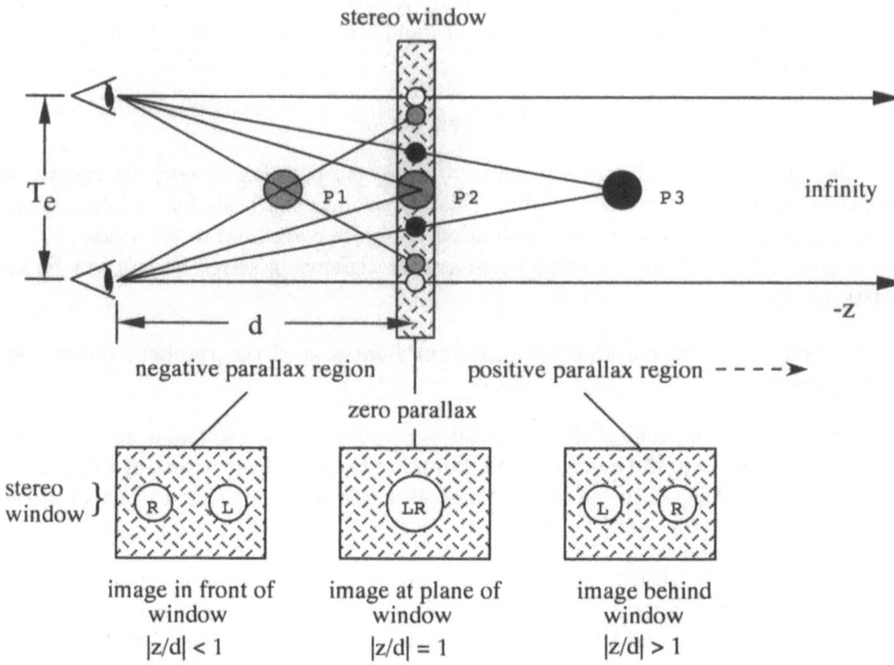

FIGURE 3. Appearance of Stereo Pairs in Different Parallax Regions.

the parallel. Neither action is natural and will usually result in discomfort for the viewer. While this limits the impact of special effects, there are other techniques that have been used at NASA ARC to make viewing comfortable while still attempting to create a wide range of depth.

3.3 Adjustments Due to Excessive Parallax

Normally the eyes converge on particular points in space, and each eye adjusts to focus on these same points. In stereographics, the eyes are forced to focus on the display screen, while at the same time the eyes must converge on points that are not on the plane of the screen. This departure from the usual coordinated response of the muscles that focus and converge the eyes may become a source of discomfort to the viewer if the parallax becomes excessive. To minimize this discomfort, the eye separation Te may be artificially reduced in these regions to keep the parallax from getting too large. Large parallax values, however, do not always cause eye strain, because it is actually the angle to which the eyes must converge that causes discomfort. This means that, while parallax values should be kept small on a monitor viewed from a few feet away, the parallax can be made very large on a distant projection screen with little difference in resultant eye strain.

At NASA ARC, tests were conducted to determine values of the eye separation, as a function of z-depth, which would provide comfortable parallax while maintaining strong stereoscopic depth cues. A group of observers were shown stereo slides of objects with varying z-depth and varying eye separation. They were asked which slides provided the best perceived stereo effect and which slides were uncomfortable to view. From this analysis various functions were established. To determine which set of functions provided the best results, several animation sequences were filmed and shown to the observers. A best fit curve of the empirical results yielded a set of functions that compute the eye separation based on the value of z. This set is described in figure 4.

It should be noted that changing the eye separation as a function of object distance (z) may introduce problems, such as slight distortions on very long, z-oriented objects. Ideally the eye separation should remain constant, but the eye strain this causes can negate any positive effects. These and other problems are under continuing investigation.

While these functions are not physiologically "correct," empirical data indicate that these functions offer a better solution than a constant 2.5 inch eye separation. Even with a diminished stereoptic effect, monocular depth cues can take over and be used to create extreme perceptions of depth. Monocular cues are often as powerful as the stereoptic cue at influencing depth perception. Therefore, close-up zooming and far-away fading effects can still be employed without causing undue eye strain.

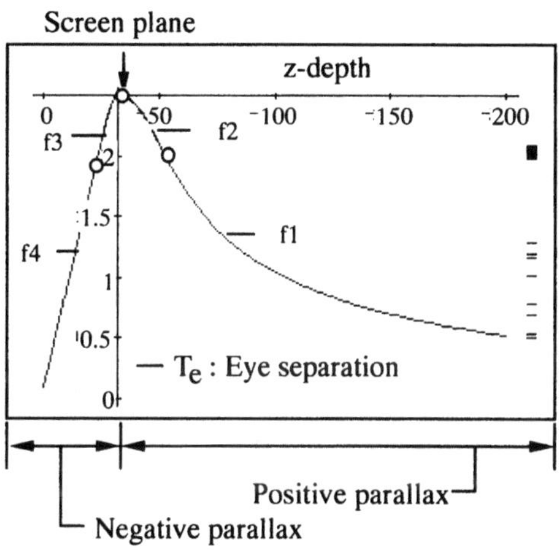

FIGURE 4. Change in T_e as a function of z-depth

Function description:	Range of z-depth (inches):
f1: $T_e = -105/z$	$z = (-\infty, -51.5]$
f2: $T_e = 2.5(0.2)[(z+32)^2/3000]$	$z = (-51.5, -32.0]$
f3: $T_e = 2.5(0.2)[(z+32)^2/500]$	$z = (-32.0, -26.0]$
f4: $T_e = (-1.726z + 1.89)/21$	$z = (-26.0, 0]$

3.4 Maintaining Consistent Depth Cues

Another important issue is to make sure that the monocular depth cues and the binocular depth cues are not conflicting. For example, if an object approaches the viewer into theater space, the object should not be clipped on the screen. If the object is clipped it will appear as if the object is behind the window of the screen because of the depth cue of interposition. Meanwhile, the depth cues of negative parallax and relative size will lead the viewer to believe that the object is in front of the screen. These contradictory cues will lead observers to describe the image as blurry, fuzzy, or confusing in some other way.

4 Stereographic Viewing Technology

Once a stereo pair is created, there are many directions in which one can proceed in order to view it. Several techniques exist for ensuring that the left eye sees only the left image and that the right eye sees only the right image. There are also many types of hardware that take advantage of these techniques. While there are many viewing methods, the proper way to view a stereographic image depends mostly upon the intended forum. The advantages and disadvantages of each technology are often a trade between how expensive the hardware is and how many people are going to see the images. This section is a presentation of the current technology in stereographic viewing techniques and hardware.

4.1 Stereographic Viewing Techniques

There are many ways to view stereo pairs so that the stereoptic effect is clear and precise. One problem in many viewing techniques is that of "ghosting." Ghost images appear when one image of the stereo pair bleeds into the opposite eye's field of view. Other problems include eye strain, color consistency, and hardware expense. Some of the more popular techniques involve viewing the scenes as polarized images, anaglyphs, stereograms, or autostereoscopic images.

Polarized Stereo Viewing

In the technique of polarization, the left image is polarized orthogonally to the right image, and both images are displayed simultaneously or in rapid succession on the screen (as described in section 4.2). Viewed through a polarized lens, only one of the two images will be visible. A viewer wearing glasses polarized in phase with the image polarization will see both images, but only one image will be visible per eye. The result is a single stereo image. If the polarization is incomplete or incorrect, ghost images may appear. For example, in the use of projected images, a highly reflective metallic screen must be used to prevent the dispersion of the polarized light.

Anaglyph Stereo Viewing

Anaglyphs are similar to polarized images except that different colors are used in place of different polarizations. Stereo pairs are generated with complementary colors (e.g., red and blue) and viewed through glasses with corresponding color filters[5]. The subtractive property of the filters will cause the red colored image to turn to black when viewed through the blue colored filter. Also, the overlapping sections of the left and right images must be created using the correct mixed color so both eyes can see these sections.

The anaglyph technique is particularly well suited for wire frame objects and translates well to hardcopy. The technique is also inexpensive to use because no special hardware other than colored glasses is required for viewing. Anaglyphs, however, are not very versatile in what they can show. Some experiments have been conducted using red and blue colors, and it was found that minimum parallax should be used. Also, the purity of the filter colors must be very precisely matched to the image colors or else ghosting will occur. To lessen the ghosting, the intensity of the colors should be at a reduced level. Another drawback of the technique is that it is very difficult to make any use of extra colors due to the filtering effect of the glasses. Problems also arise when complex solid surfaces are viewed without any shading. Shading will enhance depth perception, but there is little range of color left to use in shading due to the necessarily low intensity colors.

Autostereoscopic Viewing

One of the biggest complaints with stereographics is that 3D glasses, stereoscopes, or other peripherals are required to view the images. Autostereoscopic systems create a 3D effect without these peripherals. To date, only a few vendors have developed autostereoscopic display systems that allow the viewer to see both the left- and right-eye images on a single screen. The technique uses precisely positioned left- and right-eye columns of pixels, simultaneously displayed on a rear-illuminated screen. Through the use of masking or the spacing of the columns, each eye sees only the columns intended for it and a black background on the others. Because both eye versions must be displayed simultaneously, the resolution of the display system is often significantly reduced. On static systems, this low resolution can be compensated for by displaying as many as 18 stereo pairs. One stereo pair is visible at a time to each viewer, and all pairs can be viewed in sequence by shifting the viewing angle.

4.2 Stereo Display Hardware

When using the techniques described in section 4.1 to display stereographic images, one often needs specialized hardware[8]. A stereographic monitor can be used for interactive viewing and editing, or a hardcopy can be created on various media, including film, video tape, and print. The following are the most common monitor and hardcopy methods.

Stereographic Monitor Display Systems

Most stereographic monitor display systems today consist of a display screen with two modes, standard and stereographic. The polarization technique is used for viewing the images. To create the stereo effect, a stereographic monitor must display both left- and right-eye scenes fast enough to create a non-flickering image. A typical 60 Hz, non-interlaced monitor that alternately displays the left and right images will only display 30 images per second to each eye. This slow rate will result in a flickering image. To solve the problem, the alternation rate must be doubled to 120 Hz.

To make a stereo image on the screen, the left image and the right image must be placed in opposite viewports of the standard screen. To properly map the stereo pair images, the left- and right-eye viewports must be defined as in Figure 6. When displaying on a non-interlaced monitor at 120 Hz, the left-eye image is refreshed in such a way that the left-eye viewport maps to the entire screen. This mapping is accomplished through the accelerated vertical refresh rate and a reduction in the screen resolution. After displaying the left-eye viewport, the alternating process is repeated for the right eye viewport. With the monitor in the standard non-stereo mode (60 Hz), both images appear on the screen at once, appearing to be compressed into the top and bottom halves of the screen. To channel the appropriate image to the appropriate eye, a liquid crystal modulator provides different polarizations for the alternating images. Thus, each eye sees only every other image.

Currently, there are two monitor display systems in common use at NASA ARC. The first system uses a screen-sized liquid crystal stereoscopic modulator with a built-in polarization controller. "Passive" polarized glasses are worn by the user to view the circularly polarized images created by the screen modulator.

The second system incorporates so-called "active" glasses. These glasses are battery powered with liquid crystal modulators in the lenses to select the appropriate stereo pairs for the appropriate eye. An infrared emitter at the monitor is used to communicate with the glasses, so its lenses open and close in exact synchronization with the video field rate. For systems that are not stereo-ready, a separate controller is required to double the computer's video signal and provide a timing signal for the liquid crystal glasses. This system also requires a special monitor that can show 120 pictures/sec.

The primary difference between the two systems is that the first has a switching polarizer on the monitor and the latter has a switching device in the glasses.

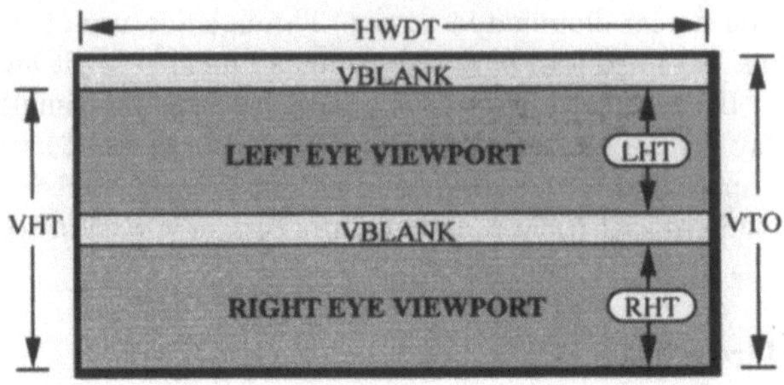

FIGURE 5. Position of Left- and Right-Eye Images on the Screen of a 60Hz Monitor (non-stereo mode)[10].

Definitions:

VHT	= The number of lines of the visible display running at 60 Hz
HWDT	= Width of the visible display
VBLANK	= Normal vertical blanking field (system dependent)
VTOT	= Total number of lines per frame
LHT = RHT	= Heights of the left- and right-eye viewports
	= (VHT - VBLANK) / 2

For example, a monitor with 1280 x 1024 resolution and (0, 0) in the lower left corner may have:

VHT = 1023, VBLANK = 41, hence LHT = RHT = 491

The left-eye viewport would be: (0, 491+41) x (1279, 1023).

The right-eye viewport would be: (0, 0) x (1279, 491).

Stereo Hardcopy

In conducting scientific research, the perception and understanding of a complex visual problem is only part of the work. It is also part of the scientific discovery process to discuss one's findings with colleagues and present the results at scientific meetings. The ability to present these research results in stereo has become extremely important. Three types of media have emerged to facilitate stereo presentations: film, video, and print.

The use of slides and movies (16mm, 35mm, and 70mm) as presentation media has been very attractive in stereo scientific visualization because of its high quality and relatively low cost. The polarization method described in section 4.1 is the most common method employed, and it requires the use of two projectors with polarized filters on the lenses, a highly reflective metallic screen to preserve the polarization, and polarized glasses for the viewers. In the case of movies, the projectors must be capable of frame-by-frame synchronization.

Video has not been a very effective stereographics presentation medium because of its low resolution and problems with simultaneously displaying left- and right-eye images.

The anaglyph and Pulfrich methods are the most commonly used because only one image needs to appear on the screen to create the 3D effect. Anaglyphs, however, have many problems, as described in section 4.1, and the Pulfrich effect only works on objects in motion. The Pulfrich effect is created by wearing a pair of glasses with one lens darker than the other. Objects moving across the screen will appear to be in 3D because of the slow reaction time of the eye under the darkened lens, thus inducing a primitive form of parallax. Recently, the introduction of field sequential stereoscopic videos[20], using active liquid crystal glasses, appears to have provided a solution to this lack of quality 3D video. As with the display system described in section 4.2, the active glasses are employed to view the left-eye images recorded on the odd video fields and the right-eye images recorded on the even video fields.

Stereograms or stereo pairs recorded on paper are an effective and efficient medium for mass producing stereo results. An assortment of viewers are available and most consist of a pair of magnifying lenses with an opaque separator. Articles in scientific and technical journals often include printed stereograms[21, 19, 13]. Several examples are included at the end of this paper.

5 Applications of Stereographics at NASA ARC

This section discusses several current projects within the NASA ARC research community that are using applied stereographics.

5.1 16mm Stereo Movie on Turbulence Production

A fifteen-minute stereo movie, *Turbulence Structures in a Simulated Boundary Layer*, was created by using some of the techniques described above. The enormous quantity of data the scientists provided to visualize one image was overwhelming. Over 200 CRAY X-MP CPU hours were required to generate the 54.7 gigabytes of data for the simulation [16]. It was clear that traditional means of visualization would not suffice for interpretation of these results.

The objective of the project was to study vortical structures internal to the boundary layer and to establish their attributes and spatial relationships. Establishing their spatial relationships with standard visualization techniques was nearly impossible. Stereo imagery provided the researchers with a key tool to accomplish this task. As a result, the study has led to new and much more complete conceptual models of boundary layer kinematics and dynamics. This knowledge will be used to help develop a structural approach for predictive mathematical models of turbulence. A sample frame from the movie is shown in figure 10.

5.2 ASHFRD Virtual Environment Display System

The Aerospace Human Factors Research Division (ASHFRD) has developed a head-mounted stereoscopic display system for use in an interactive virtual environment[2]. Controlled by operator position, voice, and gesture, the system provides a multisensory, interactive display environment in which a user can explore and manipulate a 360-degree synthesized or remotely sensed environment. Presently, the primary applications are in the areas of telerobotics, management of large-scale information systems (e.g., for use on board the U.S. space station *Freedom*), and human factors research.

The current virtual environment display system consists of a wide-angle stereoscopic display unit, a glove-like device for providing 3D tactile input, connected speech recognition technology, gesture tracking devices, computer-generated graphics, video image generation equipment, 3D sound-location cueing, and speech synthesis technology.

The prototype display unit is helmet-mounted and consists of high-resolution, monochrome liquid crystal display screens presented to each eye of the user through wide-angle optics. Disparate viewpoints from a pair of remote video cameras, or of computer-generated images, are used for the stereoscopic imaging. Head position and orientation data, provided by a helmet-mounted real-time tracking device, is used to update the displayed stereo images in coordination with the user's activity, enabling the user to explore the objects of the virtual environment from multiple viewpoints in real-time.

5.3 Virtual Planetary Exploration Project

A commercial version of the helmet-mounted stereoscopic display, called the eyephone, is employed in a development project which seeks to provide researchers with the ability to interactively explore the terrain of Mars and, in the future, Venus[6]. The on-board imaging cameras of the Mars Viking orbiters provided the raw image data, which was processed and enhanced at NASA Goddard Space Flight Center. Using the eyephone and a means of motion control, astrogeologists can explore the structural geology of Mars in real time. This tool can also be used by mission planners as an aid in determining optimal paths that a future Mars rover might take.

During a roaming session, a viewer can interactively select his light source, position, and orientation with a mouse or with a six-degree-of-freedom controller. The images can be displayed as a stereoscopic pair on the monitor itself (requiring the user to manually focus), or they can also be converted to NTSC video with dual dedicated scan converters and displayed using the LCD monitors of the eyephone. Viewer motion can be controlled with a control stick. Alternatively, the viewer can use an eyephone attached to a boom which provides head position and orientation tracking data.

5.4 Numerical Studies of Galaxy Collisions

Researchers in the Theoretical Space Science Division have used stereoscopic visualization in their study of galaxy collisions (see figure 11). In this case, numerical experiments were performed on the collision and merging of two disk galaxies embedded in haloes, using various combinations of initial orbital energy, angular momentum, and disk orientations[18]. Three-dimensional n-body programs on a CRAY X-MP/48 supercomputer were used to investigate the dynamics of the simulated disk galaxies, from initial interpenetration to the point of final merging.

The particles were color-coded according to their population type (disk or halo), and monocular depth cues were provided by making farther particles appear dimmer. A stereo 35mm film recording was made to show to other researchers, and to validate the usefulness of this technique for viewing by a large audience. Future extensions to this work include the modeling of galaxy formation and will employ stereographics as an important tool in the analysis and interpretation of the numerical results.

5.5 Earthquake Studies

Stereographics is also being used in geophysical research. Seismologists from the United States Geological Survey (USGS), working in conjunction with NASA ARC, have used stereographic imaging to study the seismicity patterns of the Hawaiian volcanoes[1]. Earthquake locations of the last 40 years were plotted in 3D space and colored according to magnitude. The resulting distribution clearly demarcates the mantle plume presently underlying and forming the large island of Hawaii, as well as several auxiliary magma conduits. These features can easily be seen in a static stereographic image. The images were viewed with the passive polarizing glasses technique described in section 4.1.

Currently, these researchers are applying stereoscopic imaging to the study of the 17th October, 1989 Loma Prieta earthquake[12]. The epicenter of this magnitude 7.1 earthquake was located 40 kilometers from NASA ARC. Main shock and aftershock location, time, magnitude, and focal mechanisms (stress and slip directions) will be analyzed stereographically, in a visualization environment which allows interactive selection of subsets of the earthquakes based on these parameters. One of the goals of this project, apart from increased scientific insight into this particular tectonic event, is to demonstrate to other seismologists the usefulness of stereoscopic visualization in the hopes of promoting and expanding its use in this field.

6 Conclusion

In summary, this paper conveys the fundamental elements necessary to applying stereographics to a wide field of applications. Through an understanding of the physiological and geometric foundations of stereographics, effective techniques for creating and viewing stereo images have been developed. This paper serves as a basis for understanding and expanding upon current theories in stereographic image generation, manipulation, and projection.

At NASA ARC, the Computer Graphics Group has developed a stereographics environment, utilizing both hardware and software components, and has used these tools to visualize complex fluid dynamics data. The additional visual cues generated by stereographics allow the perception of true three-dimensionality, and this perception provides the redundancy necessary for the unambiguous interpretation of complex data. The algorithms presented here are the results of practical experiences in the use of stereographics in scientific visualization. The stereo images created with these algorithms have been found to be effective in conveying complex relationships and allowing topological understanding of the computed data sets.

Acknowledgements:

For their discussion, comments, and suggestions we would like to thank Val Watson, Bill Barhydt, Joel Antipuesto, Diana Choi, Randy Kaemmerer, and Jeff Hultquist from NASA, Pete Paluzzi and Marilyn Rogers from Sterling Software, Stephanie Sabato from the Kansas City Art Institute, and all the referees.

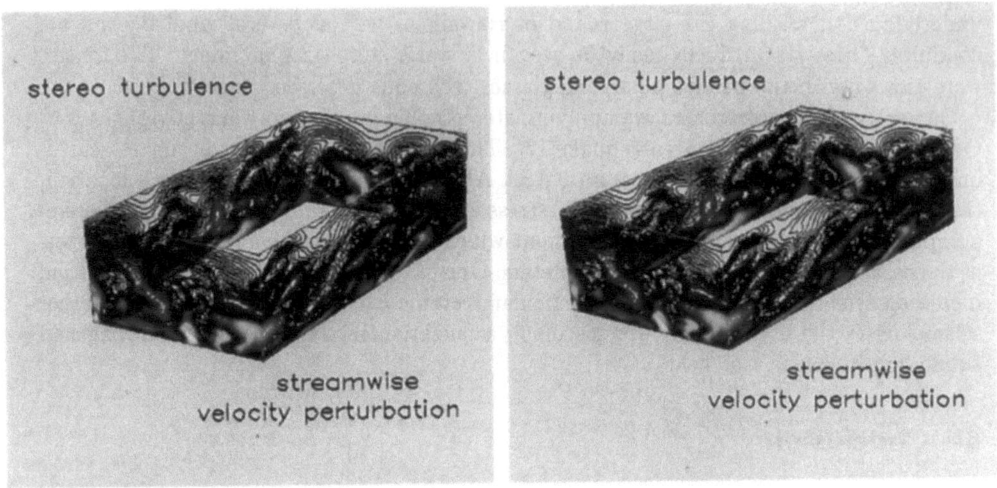

FIGURE 7. This figure shows the fluctuating component of the streamwise velocity (velocity perturbation). Cyan represents a high velocity perturbation, yellow a low velocity perturbation. The image appears in front of the screen, illustrating negative parallax.

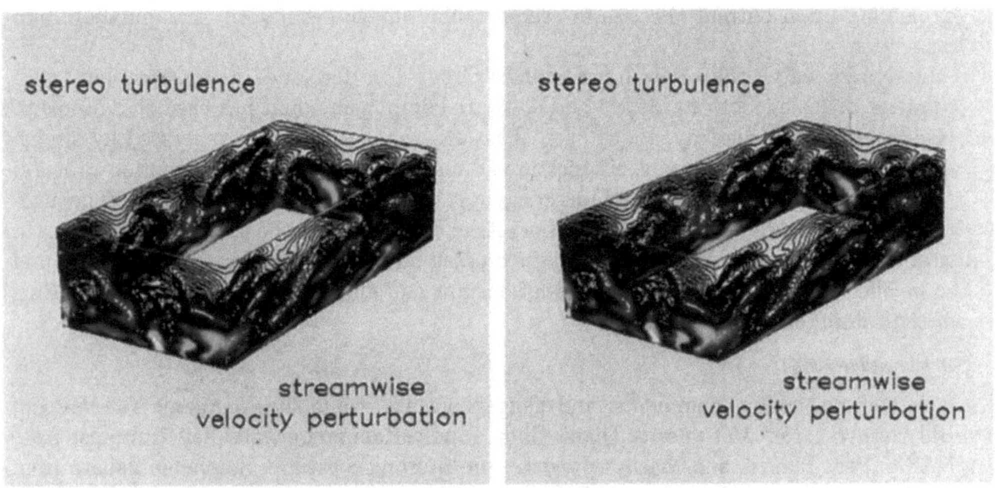

FIGURE 8. This image appears on the plane of the screen.

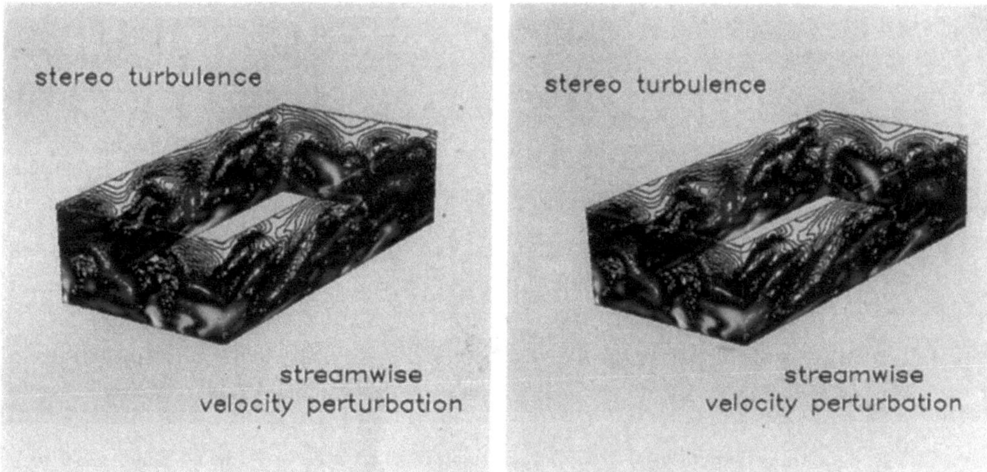

FIGURE 9. This image appears behind the screen, illustrating positive parallax.

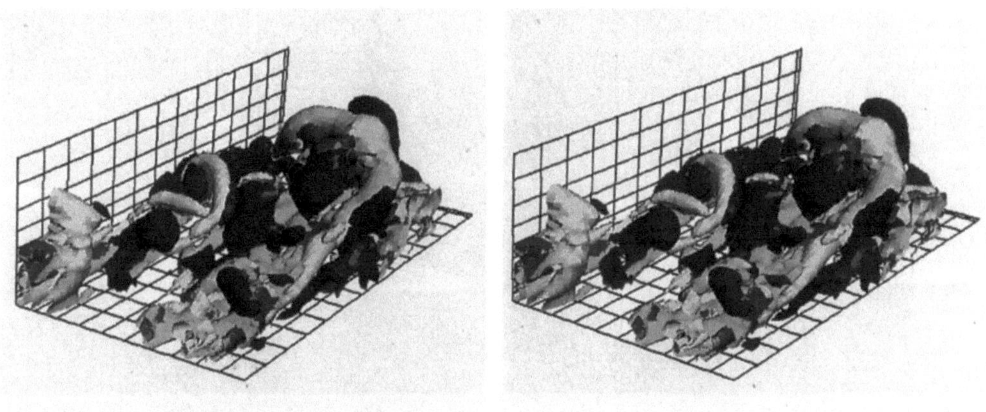

FIGURE 10. This image illustrates one of the frames from the animation of a simulated boundary layer. White surfaces identify the cores of tornado-like vertices, and yellow surfaces represent low streamwise velocity. The red surfaces identify low-speed fluid moving away from the wall while blue surfaces show high-speed fluid moving toward the wall. The green surfaces represent high pressure regions which are local stagnant regions.

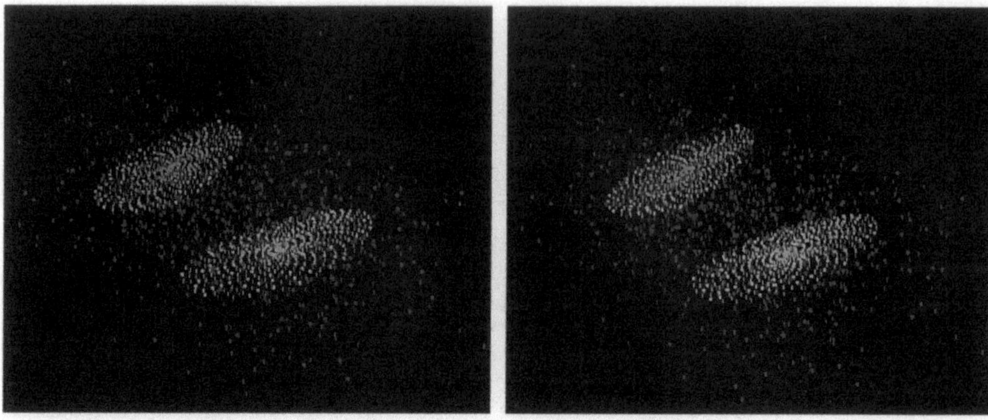

FIGURE 11. This image illustrates one of the frames from the galaxy collision sequence. Yellow particles depict stars from the galactics disks, and blue particles depict the surrounding halo stars.

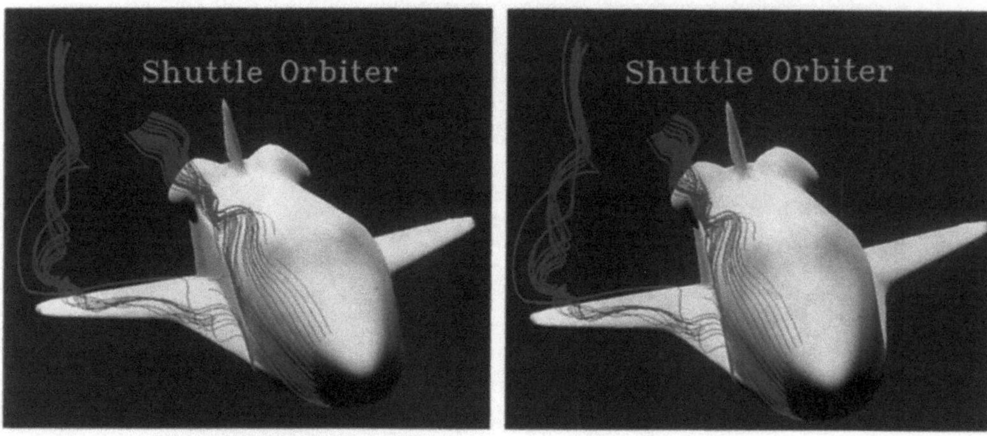

FIGURE 12. Particle traces around the space shuttle orbiter.

7 References

[1] William Acevedo. Personal communication. United States Geological Survey.

[2] S. S. Fisher, M. McGreevy, J. Humphries, and W. Robinett. Virtual Environment Display System. In *ACM SIGGRAPH Workshop on Interactive 3D Graphics, Chapel Hill*, October 1986.

[3] J. D. Foley and A. Van Dam. *Fundamentals of Interactive Computer Graphics.* Addison-Wesley, 1983.

[4] S. Grossberg. Cortical Dynamics of Three Dimensional Form, Color and Brightness, Perception, II: Binocular Theory. *Perception and Psychophysics*, 41:117–158, 1987.

[5] E. F. Hiser. Drawing in Three Dimensions for Animation and Stereoscopic Process. *Journal of the SMPTE*, 59, 1952.

[6] Lewis Hitchner. Personal communication. RIACS Corporation.

[7] L. F. Hodges, S. Love, P. Johnson, D. F. McAllister, L. D. Sher, and L. Noble. Stereoscopic and Multiplanar Computer Graphics. Course Notes no 21, ACM SIGGRAPH, 1988.

[8] L. F. Hodges and D. F. McAllister. Stereo and Alternating-Pair Techniques for Display of Computer-Generated Images. *IEEE CG and A*, pages 38–45, September 1985.

[9] B. Julesz. Binocular Depth Perception of Computer Generated Patterns. *Bell System Technical Journal*, pages 1125–1162, 1960.

[10] L. Lipton. The Creation of Software for Stereoscopic Computer Graphics. In *Programmer's Guide*, pages 24–25. Stereographics Corporation, 1988.

[11] D. Marr and T. Poggio. A Computational Theory of Human Stereo Vision. In A. Collins and E. E. Smith, editors, *Readings in Cognitive Science*, pages 534–547. Morgan Kaufman, 1978.

[12] D. Marr and T. Poggio. A Computational Theory of Human Stereo Vision. In A Collins and E E Smith, editors, *Readings in Cognitive Science*, pages 534–547. Morgan Kaufman, 1978.

[13] T. V. Papathomas, J. A. Schiavone, and B. Julesz. Stereo Animation for Very Large Data Bases: Case Study Meteorology. *IEEE CG and A*, pages 18–27, September 1987.

[14] G. F. Poggio, B. C. Motter, S. Squatrito, and Y. Trotter. Responses of Neurons in Visual Cortex (V1 and V2) of the Alert Macaque to Dynamic Random Dot Stereograms. *Vision Research*, 25:397–406, 1985.

[15] G. F. Poggio and T. Poggio. The Analysis of Stereopsis. *Annual Review of Neuroscience*, 7:379–412, 1984.

[16] S. K. Robinson. *The Kinematics of Turbulent Boundary Layer Structure.* PhD thesis, Stanford University, April 1990.

[17] J. A. Roese and L. E. McCleary. Stereoscopic Computer Graphics for Simulation and Modeling. *Computer Graphics*, pages 41–47, 1979.

[18] B. F. Smith and R. H. Miller. Collisions and Merging of Disk Galaxies. In *International Astronomical Union Symposium, Internal Kinematics and Dynamics of Galaxies*, pages 353–354. D. Reidel Publishing Company, 1983.

[19] S. Sprang, E. Goldsmith, and R. Fletterick. Structure of the Nucleotide Activation Switch in Glycogen Phosphorylase A. *Science*, 237, August 1987.

[20] M. Starks. Portable Low Cost Devices for Videotaping, Editing and Displaying Field Sequential Stereoscopic Motion Pictures and Video, Stereoscopic Displays and Applications. *Proceedings of the Society of Photo-optical Instrumentation Engineers*, 1256, 1990.

[21] K. Wu and L. Hesselink. Computer Display of Reconstructed 3-D Scalar Data. *Applied Optics*, 27(2):395–404, January 1988.

User Interface Management Systems: Present and Future

Michel Beaudouin-Lafon

ABSTRACT
This report presents the current state of the art, ongoing work, and future research directions in the domain of User Interface Management Systems (UIMS). We first define what a UIMS is, a task made difficult by the overloading of this term over the past ten years. We then present two major categories of UIMSs: those based on a language approach, and those dedicated to direct manipulation techniques. Finally, we present the active areas of research.

1 Defining a UIMS

1.1 A Bit of History

The term User Interface Management System (UIMS) is now 10 years old; it first publicly appeared in an article entitled "A User Interface Management System" [52], published by Kasik in the July 1982 issue of ACM Computer Graphics. It also appeared in the summary of the workshop on Graphical Input Interaction Techniques (GIIT), held in Seattle in June 1982 [81, page 7]. The term was coined after Data Base Management System (DBMS); in the same way a DBMS is a tool that helps to create and access a database, a UIMS should be a tool that helps to create and utilize user interfaces. The following sentence is quoted from GIIT [81, page 17]:

> "The analogy was drawn between the UIMS and a database management system. The DBMS frees the application programmer from detailed concern with the management of data storage and retrieval, and provides for the specific skills of the database designer and administrator to be applied to this task."

Buxton et al. [16] draws the following comparison:

> "The DBMS mediates between programmer and data, enforcing consistency of technique among all programmers in accessing that data. It provides portability because only the lowest-level DBMS routines are hardware-dependent. Similarly, the UIMS mediates between the applications programmer and the input events, encouraging a consistency both of graphical layout representation and of input processing mechanisms."

The notion of UIMS is older than the word itself: the Seillac II workshop on the Methodology of Interaction, held in 1979 [39], already evidenced the need for a specific component of an interactive application, in addition to the graphics system and the application program. Buxton et al. [15], states that the run-time support of their UIMS was put together in 1979. The idea of a UIMS became natural as soon as the interest turned from *graphical*

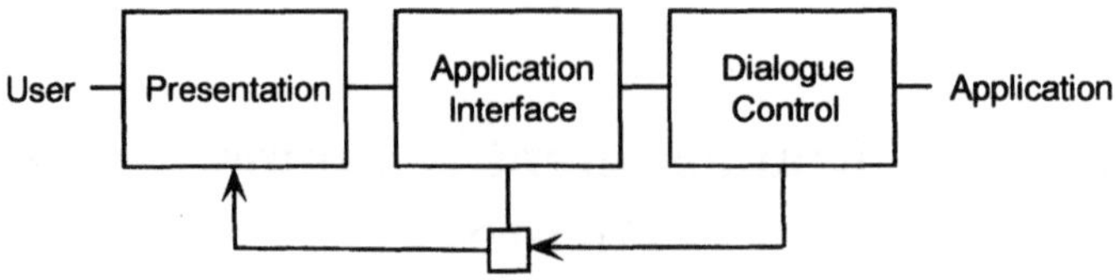

FIGURE 1. The Seeheim model, as presented by Green at Seeheim.

applications to *interactive* applications. Most graphical applications at that time were CAD applications concerned primarily with graphical output, ie. visualization. In effect, the standards for graphical applications, such as GKS [45] had little support for managing complex user input. Basically, user input was always requested by the application in a conversational mode: the user was prompted to enter a value when that value was needed by the application.

Moving from graphical to interactive applications meant giving more control to the user, and recognizing that human-computer interaction is a two-way process. Hence, it is not surprising that the notion of UIMS emerged at a workshop on interaction techniques: issues like feedback for user actions and control of the application by the user are at the very heart of human-computer interaction.

Indeed the first people who tried to create interactive applications, in particular those who experimented with direct manipulation [76] were faced with difficult problems. Some were solved by introducing new primitives in the graphics systems (such as segment identification in GKS), but this was far from sufficient. It then became obvious that a new component of the application had to be devoted to managing the dialogue between the user and the application: this is known as the *Seeheim Model.*

1.2 The Seeheim Model

Seeheim, West Germany, was the site of a workshop on UIMS's held in November 1983. The results of this workshop were published in book form in 1985 [70]. The main contribution of this workshop was to define what is now known as the Seeheim Model. Until then, traditional graphical applications were built from a graphics system that ensured some degree of device independence, plus an application program that managed the display of objects, the user input and the application specific computation. Typical applications were CAD systems for mechanics, civil engineering, or VLSI.

The Seeheim workshop proposed a new model, which can be characterized by two principles:

- the application program shall be separated from the user interface;
- the user interface shall be decomposed into three components: the presentation component, the dialogue component, and the application interface component (see figure 1, from [36, page 9]).

The presentation component is responsible for the low-level input and output, and can be implemented with a graphics system. The application interface component appears because of the separation between the interface and the application; it provides the interface with a view of the application, and manages communication with the application. Finally the dialogue component manages the user dialogue and the mapping between user input and application commands on the one hand, application data and graphical objects on the other.

The three components of the Seeheim model were interpreted for some time as the lexical, syntactic and semantic components of a language analyzer. In effect, the presentation handles low-level aspects comparable to tokens (at least for user input), while the dialogue component ensures that proper commands are specified by a set of tokens, and the application interface describes the semantics of the application. This interpretation has been the motivation for using language description techniques to build user interfaces: we will describe a number of UIMSs which use such techniques. However, this interpretation falls short when trying to create direct manipulation applications. Hence, we can identify two trends in user interface construction: the language-based approach, which tries to describe a user dialogue in terms of a (computer) language, and the approach which tries to use specific tools and techniques to describe the *whole* user interface, not just the dialogue.

1.3 What is a UIMS ?

Within the context we have just outlined, a UIMS is a tool, or a set of tools, which helps to specify, implement, test and maintain a user interface. However, it turns out that each author of a UIMS has their own definition of what a UIMS is (or should be). Instead of trying to synthesize a definition from these different authors, we will outline the definitions that were given in several working group reports.

According to the Graphical Input Interaction Techniques workshop [81, page 16]:

> "The role of a UIMS is to mediate the interaction between a user and an application; satisfying user requests for application actions, and application requests for data from the user. It accepts as input a dialogue specification, describing the detailed structure of the interaction."

The same workshop identifies the following advantages of constructing user interfaces with a UIMS:

- a UIMS improves the efficiency with which user interface designers can use their skills;
- a UIMS speeds the incremental process of creating a user interface;
- a UIMS makes it possible to create prototypes that can be discussed with the end user;
- a UIMS can adapt to different user profiles;
- a UIMS makes the integration of new application functionalities easier;
- a UIMS allows the application to be portable, while the user interface can be tailored to the particular environment;
- a UIMS can ease the debugging of interactive applications.

In his paper [52], Kasik defined the *architecture* of a UIMS as follows:

> "The user interface management system contains two components: a special purpose, application-independent dialogue specification language and a run-time interpreter that provides a number of interaction extensions not possible with procedure libraries."

The Seeheim workshop tried to identify models to be used for defining a UIMS. Kasik's UIMS uses a language-based model, but this is not a basic requirement. The most basic requirement is that the UIMS is a tool that takes as input a description of the user dialogue and produces an output used by the run-time component of the UIMS to control the execution of the interaction. In his definition, Kasik puts a slight restriction on the role of the UIMS in that it is only concerned with the dialogue. The Seeheim workshop extended this to the presentation and application interface components, although it recognized that the dialogue component models had the most highly developed notations [70, page 14]. Nevertheless a large number of UIMSs did take Kasik's approach instead of Seeheim's. This had the effect that the dialogue was considered to be modeled by a language, and it took a long time to realize that this was not appropriate. This had been quoted at Seeheim [70, page 6]:

> "The popular linguistic model, which distinguishes a lexical, a syntactic and a semantic level, is not considered appropriate for this purpose. Its main problem stems from the fact that in graphical interactions commands are not necessarily "entered in full" before feedback or action starts."

A more recent workshop gives a better idea about what a UIMS should be: the ACM SIGGRAPH Workshop on Software Tools for User Interface Management, held in November 1986, and reported in the April 1987 issue of ACM Computer Graphics, defines a UIMS as follows [8, page 73]:

> "A User Interface Management System (UIMS) is a tool (or tool set) designed to encourage interdisciplinary cooperation in the rapid development, tailoring and management (control) of the interaction in an application domain across varying devices, interaction techniques and user interface styles."

The domain of a UIMS is much wider in this definition. According to the report, a UIMS must provide a user interface with the following characteristics:

- consistency;
- support for a range of users from novice to expert; and
- support for tailorability and extensibility of the application.

It encourages:

- a consistent user interface between related applications;
- development and use of reusable software components;
- insulation of applications from the complexities of environments;
- shielding of applications from the effects of the end user actions; and
- support for ease of learning and use of applications.

A UIMS is now supposed to address the complete life-cycle of a user interface: requirements, specification and design, implementation, testing, and maintenance. In other words, a UIMS is a CASE tool (Computer-Aided Software Engineering tool) specialized for interactive applications. Applying a software engineering approach to user interfaces is a good idea. However, extending the role of a UIMS to the whole life cycle is questionable, since there are several life cycle models corresponding to at least the same number of design methodologies [9]. Moreover, this view of a UIMS is not of great utility since there does not exist, to our knowledge, any UIMS that really handles all of these aspects. For these reasons, we will restrict our definition of a UIMS in this report to the models and tools used to specify, implement and test the user interface of an interactive application. In a recent article, Myers [62] captures this notion by the term User Interface Development System (UIDS).

2 First Epoch: Dialogue Specification

The first UIMSs to be designed focused on the dialogue component of the Seeheim model. In effect, here lies the heart of user interface management: the presentation layer provides the dialogue layer with tokens which must be analyzed and grouped together to construct application commands. During this construction, some feedback must be sent back to the user.

At the beginning of the eighties, the state of the art of graphics systems with respect to user input did encourage viewing the user dialogue as a language. For instance, GKS [10] provides the client application with logical input devices: locator, valuator, choice, pick, string, stroke. These logical devices are accessed in a request, sample or event mode. *Request mode* means that the user is asked to enter a value with a given device, while *sample mode* makes it possible to retrieve the current state of an input device, for instance, to track the position of a stylus on a tablet. *Event mode* means that the device output is stored as events in a queue so that the application can retrieve them later. GKS's event mode, however, is quite primitive and cannot be compared to events as used in modern window systems like the X Window System [73]: GKS events are triggered by another device, which puts a lot of responsibility on the application.

Given the assumption that the user was seen as an entity sending input tokens, and that the control of the dialogue was mostly in the application, the language-based model of dialogue management was the natural way to proceed. Three models have been particularly popular: context-free grammars, several kinds of finite state automata, and event-response languages.

The three main language-based models have been compared by Green in [38]. Other studies can be found in [49] and [70]. The following sections present these models, with a common example: the interactive specification of a polyline with the mouse, providing rubber-band feedback to the user.

2.1 Context-Free Grammars

Context-free grammars have been used for many years in language theory. Most, if not all programming languages have their syntax described by a context-free grammar. Because the area of programming languages was so crucial to computer science, context-free grammars have a very sound theoretical basis. A context-free grammar describes the syntax of a language by a set of *production rules*. The left hand of a production rule is a non-terminal, while the right hand can contain tokens or non-terminals. In particular, it is possible to use recursive rules, for instance, to specify a list of items of arbitrary length. The theory provides the necessary results to check that a given grammar is well-behaved, and that an analyzer can be built for it. Moreover, well-known techniques exist to generate such analyzers automatically. Under Unix, YACC [50] is such a generator of syntax analyzers.

Within the context of user interfaces, the tokens are user inputs, and the rules describe commands of the system. For instance, assuming the tokens BUTTON for a click and MOVE for a mouse move, the grammar for a command consisting of clicking, dragging the mouse, and clicking again can be described as follows:

line → BUTTON end-point
end-point → MOVE end-point
end-point → BUTTON

The rule for end-point is recursive, which is, unfortunately, not very intuitive compared to the description of the command. Moreover, such rules do not specify any feedback.

For instance, to draw a rubber-band line, we need to add some actions to the rules (the actions are written between braces):

line → BUTTON {register start-position} end-point
end-point → MOVE {draw line from start-position to current position} end-point
end-point → BUTTON {trigger command Line(start-position, current position)}

This approach has several drawbacks:

- the production rules are difficult to write;
- the actions are even more difficult; and
- to work correctly, the feedback must be carried out at the time the tokens are produced by the user.

The latter problem is the most important. It means that most of the technology developed for programming languages analyzers does not apply, because most parsers need some look-ahead tokens. The only parsers that work are descent parsers, which can analyze only a small subset of grammars called LL(1) grammars.

To describe the complete polyline example, we need the following grammar and actions:

polyline → BUTTON {register start-point} next-point {add end-point} polyline
polyline → BUTTON {trigger command Polyline(poly)}
next-point → MOVE next-point
next-point → BUTTON {register end-point}

It is not obvious from this specification that the polyline is finished by two successive clicks without intervening mouse moves. Moreover, this grammar is not suitable for a descent parser, although some transformation techniques could be used to make it an LL(1) grammar.

If we were to add a new token, say BACKSPACE, to allow backtracking in the specification of a polyline, the grammar would become unreadable: there would be many more rules, because a BACKSPACE can happen anywhere, and the actions to undo the polyline would be hard to specify.

Syngraph [67] is one of the first and the most well-known of UIMSs that used context-free grammars. Mike [68] also uses production rules, which are generated from a higher level description of the application commands and functions. Edge [53] provides a graphical notation for the production rules. The examples above reveal the limitations of this model, which nevertheless can still be used for the conversational parts of a user interface.

2.2 Finite State Automata

A finite state automaton is a logical machine composed of *states* and *transitions*. States are usually represented graphically by circles, and transitions by arrows between states. The machine works as follows: if it is in state s_1 and token t arrives, it goes into state s_2 if there is a transition labeled t from s_1 to s_2. There cannot be more than one transition leaving a state with the same label. If there is no transition, depending on the models, the token is ignored, or the machine goes into an error state.

Like context-free grammars, finite-state automata can only specify the valid sequences of input tokens. But the sequence of actions is explicit in an automaton, while it is implicit with a grammar. Feedback and commands still need to be handled by actions. There are two classes of automata with respect to actions. Traditional automata have their actions associated to a state; when that state is entered, the action is executed. Figure 2 shows the specification of the line example with this kind of automaton.

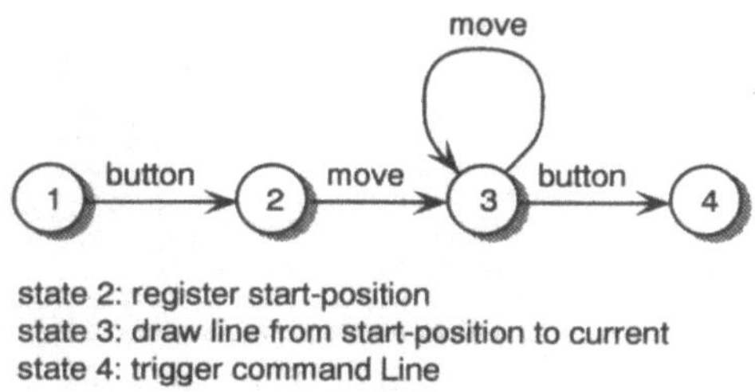

FIGURE 2. Specifying a rubberband with a finite state automaton.

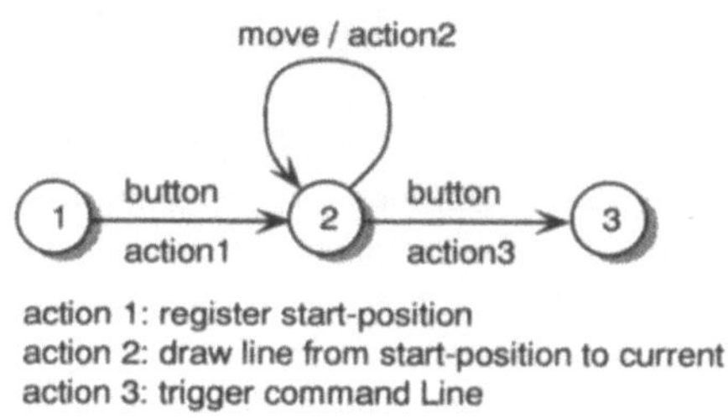

FIGURE 3. Specifying a rubberband with an ATN.

More specialized automata, called Augmented Transition Networks (ATN) associate the actions with the transitions. They have been used in Rapid/USE [85]. Figure 3 describes the line creation example with an ATN, while figure 4 describes the polyline example. The transition can also have a predicate associated with the token: the transition can be traversed only if the predicate returns true. This makes it possible to specify more complex dialogues by augmenting the expressive power of the automata. For instance, the polyline example could be extended to include transitions with the BACKSPACE token. A predicate would use the number of points already entered to decide whether backspacing is allowed.

Another extension of finite state automata, Recursive Transition Networks (RTN) have been used [26]. The University of Alberta UIMS [37] also uses RTNs as a specification formalism, but they are translated into an event-based form. With such networks, a transition can be described by a separate network; if this network reaches a final state, the transition can be fired. The augmented expressiveness comes from the possibility of referencing

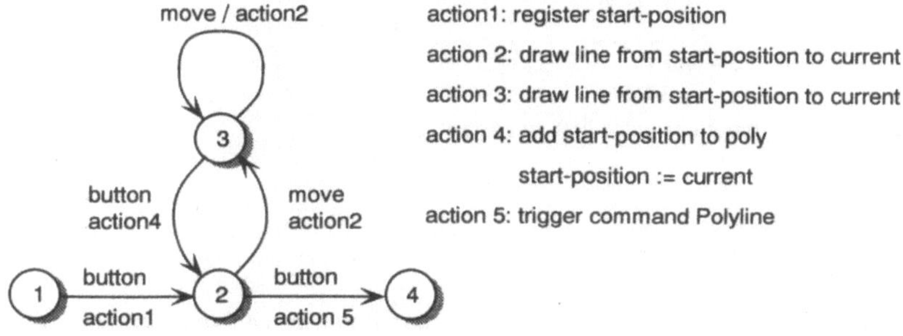

FIGURE 4. Specifying a polyline with an ATN.

a network from itself. This recursive aspect makes it possible to specify the backspace feature of the polyline example, without needing an external predicate as required by an ATN. Unfortunately, such recursive definitions are complex and can be difficult to understand.

Finally, Statecharts [40], which also provide sophisticated hierarchical automata, have been used for user interface specification in Statemaster [86].

All these automata share the same problem: the feedback to the user is specified in the actions, that is, independently of the automaton. When the application grows, the size of the automaton becomes difficult to manage, and proving it becomes impossible.

2.3 Event-Response Languages

Both context-free grammars and finite-state automata suppose that the set of valid input sequences has been predefined by the designer so that, in some sense, the user has no real control over the application. This is not compatible with the advent of event-driven applications and event-based graphics systems: in such systems, the activity of the user is not requested or sampled by the application or by the user interface, but instead, all user activity is reflected by events, stored in an event queue. It is the responsibility of the user interface to handle all of these events.

Event-response languages have been introduced to support event-driven applications. Unlike the other models presented in the previous sections, event-response languages have no theoretical background. This is a problem if their semantics are not precisely defined, which, unfortunately, is often the case.

An event handler is a process that can handle a number of event types. This process is described by a program which contains local variables and the different procedures to handle events of the different types. For instance, the program below is an event handler for the single line creation command:

```
EVENT HANDLER line;
    TOKEN Button, Move;
    VAR
    int state;
    point first, last;
    EVENT Button DO {
        IF state = 0 THEN
            first := current position;
            state := 1;
        ELSE
            last := current position;
            deactivate (self);
    }
    EVENT Move DO {
        IF state = 1 THEN
            draw line from first to current position
    }
    INIT
        state := 0;
END EVENT HANDLER line;
```

A complete program contains several event handlers, which can activate and deactivate each other. In the example above, the handler deactivates itself when the final click has been processed. Several event handlers can be active at the same time, and several active event handlers can process the same event in parallel. Because the data accessible by an event handler is local, there is no conflict. Thus, it is possible to describe multi-threaded dialogues. This is especially useful to handle several devices in parallel, as demonstrated by the Sassafras UIMS [43]. Event response languages have also been used in ALGEA [28]. They are well-adapted to modern graphics systems, which have an input model based on events. For instance, the University of Alberta UIMS [37] uses an event-based language internally, although the dialogue can be specified with RTNs.

An advantage of event handlers and the event model is that new event types can be defined. Event handlers can send synthesized events, which provides a means of communication between event handlers. This is useful in multi-threaded dialogues to coordinate several event handlers. For instance, an event handler can send an event to indicate that he wishes exclusive access to a device, ie. that no other event handler should process events of a given type.

The expressive power of an event language depends on the language used in the procedures, which is typically a general purpose programming language. Although this looks good, this also means that in general it is impossible to prove anything on such a program. On the contrary, context-free grammars and automata make it possible to prove that a given sequence of tokens is or is not recognized. Some languages with well-defined semantics have been created to overcome this problem: Squeak [19], for instance, is dedicated to user interfaces; Esterel [7], on the other hand, is a general purpose reactive language, which has been used successfully for describing interactive objects [20]. Unfortunately, such efforts are more the exception than the rule.

3 Second Epoch: Direct Manipulation

The term "direct manipulation" was introduced by Shneiderman in 1983 [76] as a syntactic and semantic model for user interfaces that has the following properties:

- continuous representation of the objects of interest;
- physical actions instead of complex syntax;
- rapid, incremental, reversible operations whose impact on the object of interest is immediately visible; and
- layered or spiral approach to learning that permits usage with minimal knowledge.

Although the term was coined by Shneiderman, the concept of direct manipulation already existed and some commercial products such as Visicorp's Visicalc already used it. At the same time, Xerox PARC was developing the STAR [78], the first workstation with a graphical user interface, featuring direct manipulation through icons. In 1984 the Apple Macintosh came out, bringing the concept of direct manipulation to the non-specialist through three revolutionary applications: the Finder, MacPaint, and MacWrite.

Since then, direct manipulation has become the standard paradigm for creating natural interfaces. But developing direct manipulation interfaces is still a hard task: even on the Macintosh, most applications are developed directly on top of the Macintosh Toolbox [1]. There are very few tools to aid the development: MacApp, an application framework [75], and Prototyper [77], an interface generator, cannot be considered full-fledged UIMSs.

Although direct manipulation interfaces have been around for almost as long as the concept of UIMS, UIMSs supporting direct manipulation have not been developed until recently. The most likely reason is that direct manipulation breaks the "dialogue as a language" model that was the main motivation for creating UIMSs. Also, because direct manipulation interfaces require the presentation on the screen of application objects,

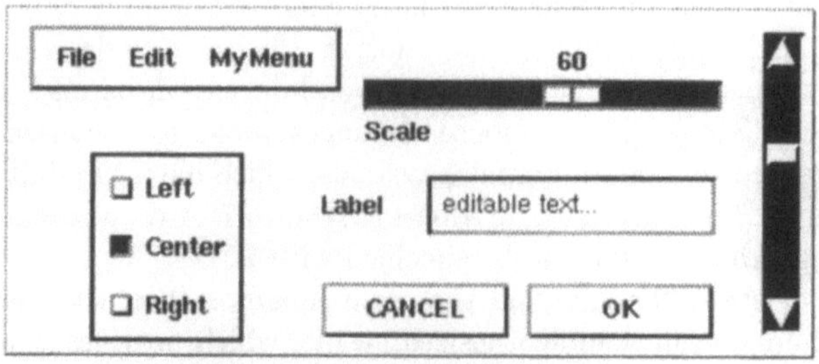

FIGURE 5. Sample MOTIF widgets.

a UIMS that supports direct manipulation must be able to describe the data of the application. Again, the main focus of UIMSs of the first period was on the dialogue, not on the application interface. Finally, direct manipulation works well only if there is a close feedback from user actions on the screen objects. This kind of feedback is often called *semantic feedback* because it is highly dependent on the application.

Semantic feedback breaks the Seeheim model and poses performance problems. Here is an example of semantic feedback: under the Macintosh Finder, when dragging an icon around, some icons highlight when the cursor passes over them while others do not. For instance, when dragging the icon of a document, the icon of the trash and the icons of the folders highlight. The feedback of the icon being dragged is a lexical feedback similar to the echo of characters, but the highlighting of icons is a semantic feedback, because the presentation cannot guess which icons must highlight: this depends on the objects represented by the icon being dragged and the icons being highlighted, which are known only to the application. Hence semantic feedback breaks the Seeheim model because there is a close relationship between the presentation and the application. The dialogue component becomes mixed in with the presentation layer. Moreover, this poses performance problems because asking the application whether an icon must highlight each time the mouse changes position can be very expensive.

3.1 User Interface Toolkits

The first tools to help build direct manipulation applications were *user interface toolkits*. Some managers of the Macintosh Toolbox [1] (menu manager, control manager, dialogue manager), as well as the X Toolkit [60] and InterViews [57] illustrate what a toolkit is: a collection of object types that can be used by applications. Objects of the toolkit are called "widgets" in the X toolkit, "interactors" in InterViews; we call them *reactive objects*. They are defined by an aspect on the screen (their presentation), which can be parameterized by a set of attributes, and a behavior in response to user input. Figure 5 shows some MOTIF widgets: menus, buttons, scrollbars, etc.

Reactive objects correspond to the principles of direct manipulation. For instance, a scrollbar is a reactive object with an aspect on the screen, made of two arrows and a thumb. When the user clicks on the arrows, the thumb moves in one direction or the other; the user can also drag the thumb to a different position. A toolkit provides a means for notifying the application of the user's action on the reactive objects. This can be in the form of *callbacks* (most often), or *logical events* (more rarely).

Callbacks are a primitive way of communicating with the application: the application registers a function in a reactive object, to be called back (hence the name) by the interface when something interesting happens to the object, such as being activated by the user. This makes it possible for an application to monitor the manipulation of a scrollbar by a user.

Logical events are high level events sent by the reactive object themselves, instead of being sent by physical devices. For instance, a scrollbar can send events when it is scrolled up, down, or to a given position. The reactive object is then considered as a logical device, so that event handling techniques can be applied.

A typical toolkit contains a dozen different basic types of reactive objects: scrollbars, push and toggle buttons, menus, labels, editable texts, scrolled windows, confirm boxes, prompt boxes, etc. A toolkit also provides facilities to compose reactive objects, by means of container objects. Such containers can impose some constraints on the layout and behavior of their components; for instance, a container can ensure that its components be of the same size and aligned in rows.

An application that uses a toolkit has to create the reactive objects it needs, and to register the necessary callbacks. This works as long as the toolkit offers the reactive object types needed by the application. But if this is not the case, then the application has to go down one level and use the graphics layer directly. For instance, on the Macintosh, the toolbox does not offer any support for icons like those managed by the Finder. Hence, it is very difficult to create iconic applications on the Macintosh. Similarly, it is impossible to create a drawing tool with an X toolkit such as OSF/MOTIF [69] or Open Look [79] without using the underlying graphics system.

Toolkits are now a necessary, but insufficient, component of a user interface development environment; higher level components are also needed. The next two sections present two families of such components: interactive tools that help to create interfaces from the object classes found in a toolkit, and tools to create new reactive objects.

3.2 Interface Generators

Programming with a toolkit is quite tedious because it means writing programs that use a (usually large) library of procedures. This does not encourage modifying the interface. Interface generators have appeared for several years now: SOS Interface [47], Graffiti [6], and Dialogue Editor [18] were the first research prototypes. Many tools are now commercially available, such as UIMX by Visual Edge, or NeXT's Interface Builder.

Such tools are made of an interactive editor that makes it possible to "draw" the interface much like a drawing tool makes it possible to create drawings. Instead of drawing circles and rectangles, the editor of an interface generator draws reactive objects. Once the interface has been built with the editor, it is saved in a data file. The application can then load this file, which will create the interface at run-time. The interface can be tested from within the editor, saving alot of turnaround time. This process is illustrated in figure 6.

This approach is very satisfying because it uses the very principle of direct manipulation to create direct manipulation interfaces. However, specifying everything by direct manipulation can become a real challenge. FormsVBT [2] overcomes this problem by providing two editable views of the interface under construction: a graphical view and a textual view.

Nevertheless, the problems inherent in the toolkit approach still exist: you will not be able to create an interface for an application if the toolkit does not offer the reactive objects you need. To compare with a drawing tool, you will not be able to draw circles if you only have rectangles and lines in the palette. Moreover, the interfaces constructed with a generator are *static*: there is usually no way to describe the dynamic modification of the interface at run-time, such as a menu containing one item for each opened window. These two problems leave user interface generators ill-adapted to the presentation of the

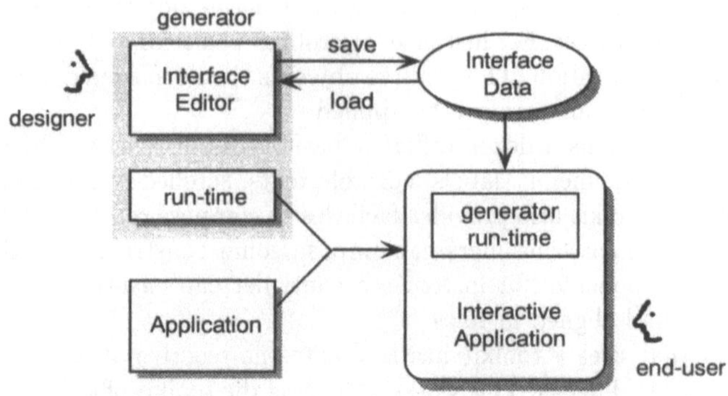

FIGURE 6. Interface generator: sample architecture.

application data, which is by nature domain specific and dynamic. On the other hand, these generators can be used for specifying the control part of the interface, ie. the set of menus, palettes and dialogue boxes that decorate the application data windows.

Another main weakness of interface generators stems from the fact that these tools are oriented towards the presentation part of the interface. Hence, the model for the application interface is usually very poor, mostly limited to callbacks. This does not encourage a clean separation between the interface and the application. Some interface generators such as Graffiti [6] and XFM [66] provide active values, a concept also investigated in Apogee [42]. Active values are shared data between the interface and the application. An active value can be bound to one or several presentation objects, but this mapping is not known to the application. This dramatically increases the independence between interface and application.

3.3 Architectural Models

Smalltalk was one of the first programming environments with a graphical user interface. All the components of the graphical user interface as well as the applications that may be created by the user are built on the Model-View-Controller model (MVC) [34].

Each reactive object is made of three components: the *view*, similar to the presentation, the *controller*, similar to the dialogue, and the *model*, similar to the application interface. Although MVC allows the model to directly communicate with its view, it is comparable to the Seeheim model. The new aspect is that the interface is not monolithic with one presentation component, one dialogue component and one application interface component, but instead made of a set of small MVC triplets.

Taking the example of the scrollbar again, the view would contain the necessary information to display the scrollbar and to capture user input; the model would contain three values: the low and high bounds of the scrollbar and its current value. Finally, the controller would ensure that the current value of the model corresponds to the position of the thumb.

The MVC model is a good framework for creating interactive applications where specific interactive objects are needed. However, the correct use of the MVC model requires much experience, although the existing classes provide a good starting point. No interactive system has been built to date for the creation of new reactive objects: the MVC model requires programming by hand.

Another model, called PAC (Presentation, Abstraction, Control), has been developed

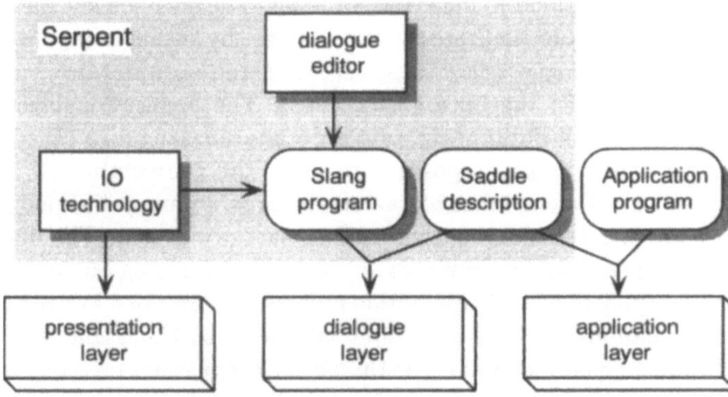

FIGURE 7. The architecture of Serpent.

by Coutaz [22, 3]. PAC provides a framework to decompose a user interface into a set of *agents* that can communicate together in several ways. Unlike MVC, PAC is not bound to an implementation language. It is more a logical model that helps to identify, structure and design interactive applications.

Like MVC, PAC and other user interface tools and models are based on an object-oriented model which has long since been proven to be well-suited to user interface construction. The many variations of the object paradigm apply to the domain of user interfaces as well. Prototype-based approaches can be more appropriate than the usual class-based approach, as will be illustrated with the description of Garnet in the next section; actor-based system can be an implementation model for the agents of PAC; etc.

4 Two Examples

Interface generators are now common tools, widely available on the commercial market. They do, however, solve only a small part of the problem of user interface construction, because they only deal with the part of the interface that can be represented by a set of predefined reactive objects. Many systems have been developed in the research community, and many are under development as well, to overcome this limitation and to address the construction of the whole interface. We now present two of them which are particularly significant and representative of the current state of the art.

4.1 Serpent

Serpent [74, 4] is a UIMS developed at the Software Engeneering Institute, Carnegie Mellon University. It features:

- A language designed for the specification of user interfaces (Slang);
- A language to define the interface between the application and Serpent (Saddle);
- An interactive editor for the specification of dialogues and for the construction and previewing of displays; and
- Provision to integrate new input/output subsystems.

The architecture of Serpent is based on the Seeheim model (see figure 7). The presentation layer is managed by an *IO technology*, ie. a collection of interaction objects visible to the user. The only IO technology currently available is a subset of the Athena or MOTIF

Widgets (form, text, button, label), under the X toolkit. The dialogue layer is described by a mapping between application and presentation layers, by means of application-shared data. For instance, the dialogue tells the presentation the position of a button and its contents, and responds when the button is selected. The application layer consists of the description of the shared data, using a data declaration language called Saddle. An interactive dialogue editor makes it possible to build the presentation of the interface interactively, but most of the work has to be done by programming the dialogue in Slang.

The dialogue component is the most interesting part of Serpent. The dialogue is described by a set of *view controller* templates. A view controller is an object that maps application data into display objects. Presentation objects are described by a set of attributes (e.g. position) and methods (e.g. notify). View controllers can be instantiated and deleted dynamically. They can be nested, and multi-threaded dialogues are possible. Instantiation and deletion of view controllers are triggered by conditions; these conditions are boolean expressions which can use attributes of objects and local variables, as well as state changes in the shared data, like the creation of a new application object. For instance, a condition can instantiate a view controller template when a new data is added to the shared data base. Conversely, the application has only to interact with this shared database to add, modify, and delete objects. When the shared database is changed as a consequence of a user action, the application is notified; this provides a means for sending commands to the application.

The original idea behind Serpent is the fact that it is centered around the application interface, represented by the shared database, instead of the dialogue, as is usually the case in UIMSs. The dynamic aspect of the description is also very powerful; by describing templates instead of particular instances, the user of Serpent can describe how objects are created and deleted. Most often, UIMSs require that the set of objects in the interface is statically defined, so that it is only possible to hide or show presentation objects to allow dynamic behavior.

On the other hand, the current IO technology used by Serpent is very limited, offering only form-based interaction; hence it is difficult to tell how well-suited it is, for instance, to create an iconic interface or a drawing tool. Although the mechanisms can clearly support this, it is not obvious how difficult it is to actually build such interfaces.

4.2 Garnet

Garnet [64, 31], is a User Interface Development Environment (UIDE) developed at Carnegie-Mellon University under the direction of B. Myers. The Garnet system can be separated into two parts: the Garnet toolkit and the Garnet tools (see figure 8). The Garnet toolkit is built on top of CommonLisp and the X Window System. It contains an object system, a constraint system and a graphics system. The Garnet tools include an interface builder, a dialogue box creation system and a spreadsheet. We are now going to present these components in more detail.

The heart of Garnet is an object-oriented system called KR built on top of CommonLisp. This system uses a prototype-based approach instead of the usual class-instance model. Instead of defining classes, a programmer creates ***prototype*** objects, defined as a set of untyped *slots*. The value of a slot can be any Lisp object, including a Lisp expression. New objects are created from existing prototypes. An object inherits the slots (ie. their name and value) of its prototype; it can override inherited slots and define new ones. The advantage of this model is that it provides inheritance of values; if the value of a slot is changed in a prototype, all objects that inherit this slot inherit the new value.

The object model of Garnet is complemented by a constraint system, which is heavily

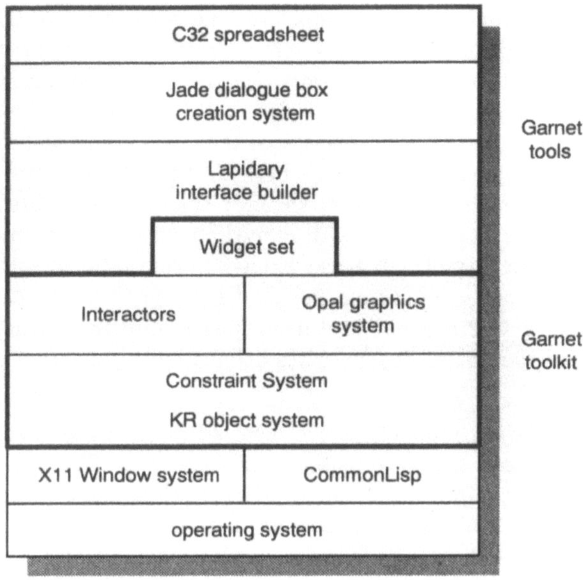

FIGURE 8. The architecture of Garnet.

used throughout the system. When the value of a slot is an expression that references other slots (called dependents), the constraint system reevaluates the expression whenever the value of a dependent slot is changed. This is not a full-fledged constraint system, as these constraints are one-way relationships (they are actually called *formulas* in Garnet), whereas a real constraint system such as ThingLab [11] uses multiway constraints. The authors claim that one-way constraints are sufficient in virtually all cases for user interfaces. Indeed, one-way constraints are much easier to satisfy than general constraints; they require exactly one traversal of the dependency graph.

The originality of the graphics system of Garnet lies in its model for input handling. This model is based on six types of input techniques (called *interactors*): the menu interactor, the move-grow interactor, the new-point interactor, the angle interactor, the trace interactor, and the text interactor. These interaction techniques are independent of the actual graphical objects they use: a menu interactor can be used to pick a command in a menu as well as for radio buttons, graphical palettes, etc. The authors claim that these six interactors cover virtually all possible interaction styles in graphical user interfaces. This is probably true as long as one only considers keyboard and mouse input, but may fall short when considering new input devices like speech recognition, gesture input, eye tracking, etc. as well as multimodal input, ie. the combination of several input devices. Nevertheless, the approach of Garnet is much more open than most conventional toolkits, which tightly bind input techniques to graphical objects.

The first Garnet tool is *Lapidary*, an interface builder. It is similar to other interface builders in that it allows the user to create the interface interactively, by placing graphical objects and specifying their attributes. The differences come from the possibility to define constraints (formulas) between objects, and to bind input techniques to graphical objects freely. This is possible thanks to the underlying constraint system and input model.

The second Garnet tool is *Jade*, a system that automatically creates dialogue boxes from a simple textual description. This description contains the names and types of the fields of the dialogue box. Jade uses a database of presentation rules to decide where to place the fields and buttons, and which input technique to use according to a given look and feel. The obvious advantage over an interactive editor is that the description is look and feel independent, but this can only work if a given look and feel is specified in such a way that it can be described by a set of rules.

The last Garnet tool is *C32*, a browsing tool that uses a spreadsheet metaphor. Any Garnet object can be presented in C32 as a table displaying the names and values of the slots of that object. Whenever the object changes, the table is updated. Conversely, the user can edit the values interactively, with immediate effect on the object. C32 provides a set of facilities to edit formulas in a way similar to conventional spreadsheets: instead of typing a slot name, one can click on the cell displaying that slot, or even click on the graphical object itself. C32 is a powerful debugging tool in the Garnet environment, in order to understand the web of dependencies defined by the thousands of formulas used throughout the system.

As a conclusion, Garnet probably is the most advanced UIDE to date. Nevertheless there are several problems and weaknesses to this approach. The system is oriented toward the presentation component of the interface, with some facilities for the dialogue component, but no tool is aimed at the definition of the application interface component. This component must be developed by hand, in CommonLisp, and chances are that it is intermixed with the other components.

More generally, one would like to give more abstract descriptions of the interface. Instead of this, the programmer is usually at the level of Lisp or the object system. Indeed, prototypes and constraints provide a powerful way to describe an interface, but higher level models would help even more.

5 Ongoing Work and Future Directions

The effort in creating tools to build user interfaces has considerably increased in the last few years. Among the many tools, systems, models and methods that exist, we try in this section to identify a number of current trends and promising directions. We have classified them in two categories. The first category concerns the ability to describe an interface in terms of what it should do rather than how it should do it. The second category concerns the widening of the domain of user interfaces with respect to interaction modes and techniques, and its influence on user interface construction.

5.1 From Imperative to Declarative Descriptions

An ever-present goal of computer science is to provide models and tools that make it possible to describe a system by its properties rather than by the way it works. Let us call the former a declarative description and the latter an imperative description. The domain of user interface construction does not escape from this rule. Three main directions are being investigated to that purpose.

The first direction concerns the use of *constraints*. A constraint is a relationship between a set of variables that must hold at all times. Whenever the value of a variable changes, a *constraint solver* must modify the values of other variables in order to satisfy all the constraints. Several techniques can be used for constraint satisfaction: numerical techniques, as used in Juno [65], propagation techniques as used in ThingLab [58], incremental techniques such as the DeltaBlue algorithm [30], or symbolic techniques as in Bertrand [55]. In all cases, the solver must handle the situations where there is no solution to the constraint system and where several solutions are acceptable. The latter can be handled by a notion of distance that is used to choose the solution closest to the current state, in order to achieve the least-astonishment principle: avoid surprising the user with the result of the resolution. The former situation (over-constrained system) can be handled by introducing a hierarchy of constraints [12]; higher priority constraints are satisfied first, while some lower priority constraints can be left unsatisfied.

Constraints have been used for a long time (ThingLab [13] is ten years old), but surprisingly, they have not been adopted as a standard technique for user interface specification. One reason might be the difficulty to implement efficient constraint solvers. Another reason is that the research has focused mainly on constraint solving, and current systems lack a clean model with well-defined semantics. This is now being investigated, as with the Alien system [21] or the Kaleidoscope programming language [29]. Constraints could then prove to be a very general specification technique, not limited to graphical aspects. For instance, the application interface could be specified with constraints, by replacing active data [42] with constraints. Visual programming environment like Fabrik [48] could also benefit from constraint techniques.

Another direction toward declarative specifications is based on the programming by example paradigm, also called demonstrational interfaces. The principle is to create examples of the desired interface, and have the system infer the whole interface from these examples. Peridot [61] illustrates this approach: the user can create interaction techniques interactively. The system uses a knowledge base to infer the properties of the created objects. For instance, it is possible to build a scrollbar and have the system infer that the thumb must be contained in the scrollbar, and that the thumb can be dragged with the mouse, changing the value of the scrollbar.

Metamouse [59] is similar to Peridot, but applies to the definition of drawing tools. It can infer geometrical relationships between graphical objects. Therefore it is possible to "teach" the system how to align a set of objects along a line, for instance. Eager [24] is another example-based system. It works behind Hypercard [35], watching user actions until it discovers a pattern. At this point, it pops up and proposes to take over the task. While Peridot could be a part of a UIMS, Eager is clearly aimed at the end-user, while Metamouse sits in the middle.

Example-based interface construction is closely related to constraints [63]. These systems can be thought of as a layer on top of a constraint system, trying to recognize which constraints are satisfied, and instantiating these constraints if the user so wishes [?]. Thus, the limits of these systems are the same as any knowledge-based or rule-based system: they will never infer rules (or constraints) that are not in their database. Hence, the construction of the rule database becomes the main problem. In order to have the system "guess the right thing," the rules, and in some cases the inference engine, must be carefully adapted to the domain.

There is no doubt that demonstrational interfaces are going to be an active research area, with some spectacular applications. However, it is not clear whether the main applications will concern user interface construction. As suggested by the examples above, the end user could benefit more from such super-macros facilities.

5.2 New Needs, New Models, New Solutions

A decade of UIMSs have been built around the Seeheim model. But the context of user interfaces has changed significantly since the eighties. WIMP (Window-Icon-Menu-Pointing) interfaces are now generalized, because graphical workstations and PCs with mouse and keyboard are everywhere. The principle of direct manipulation has been applied in a large

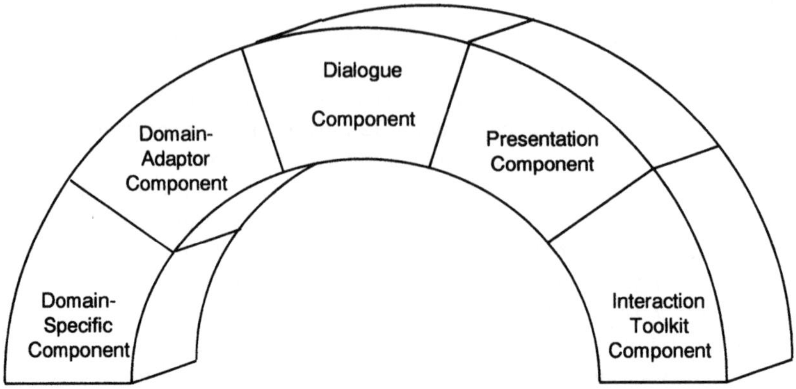

FIGURE 9. The Arch model – Seeheim revisited.

number of applications. The automatization of interface construction already has problems catching up with this evolution; most interactive applications on Unix workstations, Macintoshes and PCs are developed by hand. But the evolution still goes on, with new input devices (dataglove, eye tracking, etc...), new paradigms (computer supported cooperative work, virtual realities), and more computing power (50 Mips workstations today, 100 Mips tomorrow). How can we achieve the challenge of providing tools for user interface construction in such an evolving world ?

The answer lies in our ability to define models that accept a wide range of interactive techniques and application domains. A revision of the Seeheim model has been undertaken by the User Interface Developer's Workshop. The intermediate results of the workshop were presented at a SIG (Special Interest Group) meeting at the last ACM SIGCHI conference [83]. The workshop has defined a new model, called the Arch model, presented in figure 9.

The components of the model can be described as follows:

- *The Interaction Toolkit Component* implements the physical interaction with the user. It corresponds to a user interface toolkit such as OSF/Motif or OpenLook.
- *The Domain-Specific Component* implements the domain functionality, ie. what is called the "application" in the Seeheim model.
- *The Dialogue Component* is the keystone of the Arch model. It provides task-level sequencing, and mapping between domain-specific formalisms and UI-specific formalisms.
- *The Domain-Adaptor Component* implements domain related tasks required for human interaction, not present in the domain component.
- *The Presentation Component* provides a set of toolkit independent objects to the dialogue component.

This model is more realistic than the Seeheim model because it integrates the two components that always exist in an interactive application: the interaction toolkit component and the domain-specific component. But its main feature lies in the branching facility, illustrated in figure 10. The branching facility makes it possible to integrate several toolkit and domain specific components, thus providing extensibility.

Unfortunately, the branching facility has disappeared in more recent works of the User Interface Developer's Workshop [?]. In this article, the Arch model is presented as an instance of the *Slinky* metamodel. This metamodel features the five components that

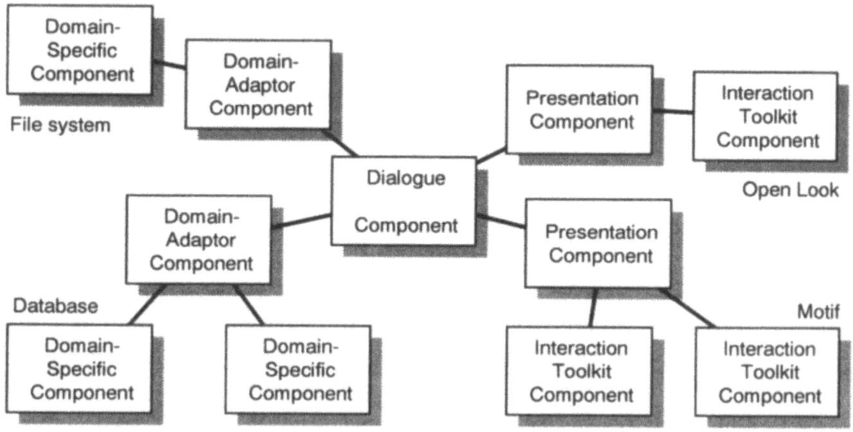

FIGURE 10. Branching facilities in the Arch model.

we have presented above, but does not impose a rigid allocation of functions among these components. The name, "Slinky", was chosen to emphasize this flexibility, as in the popular Slinky^{TM} toy. By changing the balance of functionality between the components, the Slinky metamodel produces a family of Arch models. The Slinky metamodel is different from other models, including Seeheim, PAC, MVC, in that it is evaluative rather than prescriptive. An evaluative model makes it possible to compare existing systems and leads to a better understanding of the architectures that are actually used. On the other hand, the purpose of evaluation does not justify the branching facility that was present in the first Arch model, because such branching is not representative of existing applications.

Nevertheless, the Arch model provides a useful framework for classifying ongoing research in the domain of user interface construction. A first important direction concerns the growing interest in specifying the domain-adaptor component of the interface. We have already seen that Serpent provides some support for specifying the application interface in terms of an active database. The Higgens UIMS [46] uses attribute techniques, which have long been used in compiler construction, in order to describe the semantics of the application. In particular, incremental evaluation techniques are available. The attributed graphs used by Higgens can be thought of as a generic dialogue-adaptor component. The classification of Coutaz [23] is also relevant to the domain-adaptor component as it gives some insights into the way data are exchanged between application and interface.

Humanoid [80] also investigates the application interface, by using templates that map application data to presentation objects. Hence it lies more in the center of the Arch model, with an implicit dialogue component, a presentation component and a generic domain-adaptor component. This approach also appears in other systems. For instance, Hypercard [35] provides an environment to develop applications based on the model of stacks of cards. WISh [5] provides an iconic model based on a client-server architecture that makes it possible to build iconic interfaces that integrate several applications. Unidraw [84] is a framework for building domain-specific graphical editors. TGE [51] is a generic editor for applications that use graphs or trees to represent their data. Although these systems address very different domains, they all provide similar services, ie. a generic interface for applications in the form of a domain-adaptor component, and they implement the other components of the Arch model. If they could share the same dialogue component, then it would be possible to combine them according to the branching facility of the Arch model.

5.3 New Dimensions of Interaction

A common characteristic of the systems we have presented so far is that they deal only with graphical interfaces that use a display and a pointing device, and that interact with a single user. Other dimensions of user interaction deserve more attention, because they represent important directions for the future of user interfaces. Let us present some of them.

Animated interfaces bring animation to the user interface. Animations are already used for the purpose of interaction: for instance, when an icon is double-clicked on the Macintosh Finder, a rectangle grows from that icon to the window being opened. However, with the exception of Animus [25] and Whizz [?], tools for defining animated interfaces have not been investigated very much. Most animation systems only address visualization, for instance algorithm animation [14], whereas animation could be used efficiently as a medium by itself. Robertson et al. [72] assess that an animated display is essential to the understanding of the system response by the user. Adding audio output to interfaces, which to some extent can be considered a problem similar to animation, is known to be effective [32]. Again, as yet no tool exists to include auditory feedback in a user interface.

Multi-user interfaces [54], also known as groupware and CSCW (Computer-Supported Cooperative Work), are systems that allow a group of users to work on a common task in a shared environment. The field of CSCW is becoming a domain of active research, but very few tools exist to develop such systems (see for instance Liza [33]). This domain poses new and unexpected problems to user interface construction: if a document is to be edited by several users at the same time, each user must be aware of what the other users are doing. This raises the issue of feedback of other users actions, which is very different from feedback of the user's own actions. As an example, the Grove editor [?] uses a number of interesting ideas in this domain: text turns from blue to black as it gets aged, and "clouds" indicate the areas of the document where other users are working. Unfortunately, generalizing such techniques and making them available in a UIMS remains to be seen.

Multimodal interfaces have the ability to manage several input channels at the same time. Among others, the Sassafras UIMS [44] can handle multimodal input in the case where the devices are independent: for instance a mouse controls the brush of a painting tool while a slider controls the width of the brush. But composing the input of several input devices in order to specify one application command is by far more complex. For instance, saying the sentence *"put that there"* while the user specifies the object and the location with mouse clicks requires an input and dialogue model which is far beyond the capabilities of today's UIMS models. The difficulty lies in the semantic information which is necessary to interpret the input data, and the real-time feedback that is required. In the example above, the first mouse click must be mapped to an object while the second mouse click specifies a location.

Such problems are even more complex in virtual worlds environments, where a user can potentially use gesture input, eye-tracking, voice recognition, etc. It is encouraging to see that UIMSs are being developed for such systems. The UIMS presented in [56] uses a rule-based kernel, and separate processes to handle low-level input (the system currently uses 7 workstations and 2 PCs). It features several logical levels so that the mapping between input devices and application commands can be redefined transparently, even at run-time.

6 Conclusion: The Future of UIMSs

The goal of creating a UIMS that supports the whole life-cycle of user interface development is still ahead. The engineering of user interfaces is at its very beginning; integrating state-of-the-art techniques for software engineering into human-computer interface engineering is one of the challenges of future UIMSs. Most efforts are currently focused on the implementation and maintenance phases, but specification and test are going to be of particular importance. It is worth noting that these problems are not specific to user interface construction, but apply to software development in general.

The specification of (some parts of) an interface has been addressed by different models, some of which we have described. Unfortunately, the models that are well-suited are generally not formally defined. For instance, most event-response languages have no formal semantics. As a consequence, interfaces cannot be proved, they cannot be tested automatically, and they cannot be reused easily. This will not be overcome until formal models and techniques are defined and widely used.

In addition to traditional software engineering issues, the engineering of user interfaces raises human factors issues that are hard to integrate into a design methodology [17]. For instance, most systems fail to represent the user's task model. This has a tremendous impact on the quality of user interfaces, such as the lack of undoing facilities, context-sensitive help, macros, etc. More and more, the user's model is taken into account when specifying an interface, through techniques like rapid prototyping, scenarios, etc. But the representation and use of this model in the interface itself is far more difficult, because it is not directly reflected in the user's input, which is the only perception of the user by the system.

User interface engineering is subject to a strong "technology pull"; this is not likely to change in the next few years. A positive consequence is the overall effort dedicated to the development of interfaces and the development of tools for building interfaces. A more questionable consequence is the current standardization process; a user interface standard could jeopardize the possibility to create a new generation of UIMSs, in a similar way as GKS made it difficult to create direct manipulation interfaces and multi-threaded dialogues.

We expect future UIMSs to consist of a set of specific tools that address the different aspects of user interface construction, rather than big systems that cover the whole development process. These tools will use different techniques, ranging from traditional programming using libraries to interactive construction and declarative specification. To be effective, these tools will need to be open and interoperable so that they can be integrated into a user interface development environment.

Acknowledgements:

I want to thank Len Bass and Joëlle Coutaz, and the other members of the IFIP WG2.7 working group, for clarifying a number of concepts and ideas. Stéphane Chatty and Solange Karsenty provided useful comments and fruitful discussions during the preparation of this article. I am also grateful to Chris Weikart and Heather Sacco for proofreading the article.

7 References

[1] Apple Computer Inc. *Inside Macintosh.* Addison-Wesley, 1985.

[2] Gideon Avrahami, Kenneth P. Brooks, and Marc H. Brown. A Two-View Approach to Constructing User Interfaces. In *Proc. ACM SIGGRAPH*, pages 137–146, July 1989.

[3] Len Bass and Joëlle Coutaz. *Developing Software for the User Interface.* The SEI Series in Software Engineering. Addison-Wesley, 1991.

[4] Len Bass, Erik Hardy, Reed Little, and Robert Seacord. Incremental Development of User Interfaces. In G. Cockton, editor, *Engineering for Human-Computer Interaction*, pages 155–173. North-Holland, 1990.

[5] Michel Beaudouin-Lafon. User Interface Support for the Integration of Software Tools: an Iconic Model of Interaction. In *Proc. ACM Symposium on Software Development Environments (SIGSOFT)*, pages 187–196, November 1988.

[6] Michel Beaudouin-Lafon and Solange Karsenty. A Framework for Man-Machine Interface Design. In *Proc. European Unix Users Group Conference (EUUG)*, pages 1–10, September 1987.

[7] G. Berry, P. Couronné, and G. Gonthier. The Esterel Synchronous Programming Language and its Mathematical Semantics. In S. D. Brookes, A. W. Roscoe, and G. Winskel, editors, *Seminar on Concurrency, LNCS 197*, pages 389–448. Springer-Verlag, 1985.

[8] Bill Betts et al. Goals and Objectives for User Interface Software. *ACM Computer Graphics*, 21(2):73–78, April 1987.

[9] B. Boehm. A Spiral Approach to Software Development and Enhancement. *IEEE Computer*, 21(5):61–72, 1988.

[10] Peter R. Bono, José L. Encarnação, F. Robert A. Hopgood, and Paul J. W. ten Hagen. GKS – the First Graphics Standard. *IEEE Computer Graphics and Applications*, July 82.

[11] A. Borning and R. Duisberg. Constraint-Based Tools for Building User Interfaces. *ACM Transactions on Graphics*, 5(4):345–374, October 1986.

[12] A. Borning, R. Duisberg, B. Freeman-Benson, A. Kramer, and M. Woolf. Constraint Hierarchies. In *Proc. ACM OOPSLA*, pages 48–60, October 1987.

[13] Alan Borning. The Programming Language Aspects of ThingLab, a Constraint-Oriented Simulation Laboratory. *ACM Transactions on Programming Languages and Systems*, 3(4):353–387, October 1981.

[14] Marc H. Brown. *Algorithm Animation.* PhD thesis, Brown University, 1987.

[15] W. Buxton. Lexical and Pragmatic Considerations of Input Structure. *ACM Computer Graphics*, pages 31–37, January 1983.

[16] W. Buxton, M. R. Lamb, D. Sherman, and K. C. Smith. Towards a Comprehensive User Interface Management System. *ACM Computer Graphics - Proc. SIGGRAPH*, 17:35–42, July 1983.

[17] S. K. Card, T. P. Moran, and A. Newell. *The Psychology of Human-Computer Interaction.* Lawrence Erlbaum Associates, 1983.

[18] Luca Cardelli. Building User Interfaces by Direct Manipulation. In *Proc. ACM Symposium on User Interface Software and Technology (UIST)*, pages 151–166, October 1989.

[19] Luca Cardelli and Rob Pike. Squeak: a Language for Communicating with Mice. *ACM Computer Graphics - Proc. SIGGRAPH*, 19(3):199–204, 1985.

[20] Stéphane Chatty. Integrating Animation with User Interfaces. In J. Larson and C. Unger, editors, *Engineering for Human-Computer Interaction.* North-Holland, 1992. Proc. IFIP WG2.7 Working Conference, Ellivuori, Finland, August 1992.

[21] Dominique Clément and Janet Incerpi. Specifying the Behavior of Graphical Objects Using Esterel. Research Report 836, INRIA, France, April 1988.

[22] Eric Cournarie and Michel Beaudouin-Lafon. Alien: a Prototype-Based Constraint System. In *Second Eurographics Workshop on Object Oriented Graphics*, pages 93–114, June 1991.

[23] Joëlle Coutaz. PAC, an Implementation Model for Dialog Design. In *Proc. Interact'87*, pages 431–436, September 1987.

[24] Joëlle Coutaz and Sandrine Balbo. Applications: A Dimension Space for User Interface Management Systems. In *Proc. ACM SIGCHI*, pages 27–32, May 1991.

[25] Allen Cypher. Programming Repetitive Tasks by Example. In *Proc. ACM SIGCHI*, pages 33–39, May 1991.

[26] Robert A. Duisberg. Animated Graphical Interfaces Using Temporal Constraints. In *Proc. ACM SIGCHI*, pages 131–136, April 1986.

[27] E. A. Edmonds. Adaptive Man-Computer Interfaces. In M. J. Coombs and J. L. Alty, editors, *Computing Skills and the User Interface.* Academic-Press, 1981.

[28] C.A. Ellis, S.J. Gibbs, and G.L. Rein. Groupware, Some Issues and Experiences. *Comm. ACM*, 34(1):38–58, January 1991.

[29] M. A. Flecchia and R. D. Bergeron. Specifying Complex Dialogues in ALGEA. In *Proc. ACM CHI+GI*, pages 229–234, 1987.

[30] Bjorn N. Freeman-Benson. Kaleidoscope : Mixing Constraints, Objects and Imperative Programming. In *Proc. ECOOP-OOPSLA*, pages 77–87, 1990.

[31] Bjorn N. Freeman-Benson, John Maloney, and Alan Borning. An Incremental Constraint Solver. *Comm. ACM*, 33(1):54–63, January 1990.

[32] The Garnet Compendium: Collected Papers, 1989–1990. Technical Report CMU-CS-90-154, School of Computer Science, Carnegie Mellon University, November 1990. Edited by Brad A. Myers.

[33] William W. Gaver, Randall B. Smith, and Tim O'Shea. Effective Sounds in Complex Systems: the Arkola Simulation. In *Proc. ACM SIGCHI*, pages 85–90, May 1991.

[34] S. J. Gibbs. LIZA: An Extensible Groupware Toolkit. In *Proc. ACM SIGCHI*, pages 29–35, May 1989.

[35] Adele Goldberg. *Smalltalk-80 – The Interactive Programming Environment.* Addison-Wesley, 1984.

[36] D. Goodman. *The Complete Hypercard Handbook.* Bantam Books, 1987.

[37] M. Green. Report on Dialogue Specification Tools. In Günther E. Pfaff, editor, *User Interface Management Systems*, Eurographics Seminars, pages 9–20. Springer-Verlag, 1985.

[38] M. Green. The University of Alberta UIMS. *ACM Computer Graphics - Proc. SIGGRAPH*, 19(3):205–213, 1985.

[39] Mark Green. A Survey of Three Dialogue Models. *ACM Trans. on Graphics*, 5(3):244–275, July 1986.

[40] Richard A. Guedj et al., editors. *Methodology of Interaction.* North-Holland, 1980.

[41] D. Harel. Statecharts: A Visual Formalism for Complex Systems. *Science of Computer Programming*, 8(3):231–274, June 1987.

[42] H. Rex Hartson and D. Hix. Human-Computer Interface Development: Concepts and Systems for its Management. *ACM Computing Surveys*, 21:5–92, 1989.

[43] Tyson R. Henry and Scott E. Hudson. Using Active Data in a UIMS. In *Proc. ACM Symposium on User Interface Software and Technology (UIST)*, pages 167–178, October 1989.

[44] Ralph D. Hill. Supporting Concurrency, Communication and Synchronization in Human-Computer Interaction – The Sassafras UIMS. *ACM Trans. on Graphics*, 5(3):179–210, July 1986.

[45] Ralph D. Hill. Event-Response Systems: A Technique for Specifying Multi-Threaded Dialogues. In *Proc. ACM CHI+GI*, pages 241–248, 1987.

[46] F. R. R. Hopgood, D. A. Duce, J. R. Gallop, and D. C. Sutcliffe. *Introduction to the Graphical Kernel System, GKS.* Number 19 in Apic Studies in Data Processing. Academic-Press, 1983.

[47] S. E. Hudson and R. King. Semantic Feedback in the Higgens UIMS. *IEEE Trans. on Software Engineering*, 14(8):1188–1206, August 1988.

[48] Jean-Marie Hullot. SOS Interface, un Générateur d'Interfaces Homme-Machine. In AFCET Informatique, editor, *Actes des Journées Langages Orientés Objet*, pages 69–78, 1986.

[49] Dan Ingalls, Scott Wallace, Yu-Ying Chow, Franck Ludolph, and Ken Doyle. Fabrik: A Visual Programming Environment. In *Proc. ACM OOPSLA*, pages 176–190, September 1988.

[50] R. J. Jacob. Using Formal Specifications in the Design of a Human-Computer Interface. *Comm. ACM*, 26(4):259–264, April 1983.

[51] S. C. Johnson. Language Development Tools on the Unix System. *IEEE Computer*, 13(8), August 1980.

[52] Anthony Karrer and Walt Scacchi. Requirements for an Extensible Object-Oriented Tree/Graph Editor. In *Proc. ACM Symposium on User Interface Software and Technology (UIST)*, pages 84–91, October 1990.

[53] Solange Karsenty, James A. Landay, and Chris Weikart. Inferring Graphical Constraints with Rockit. Research Report #17, Digital Equipment Corporation, Paris Research Laboratory, March 1992.

[54] D. J. Kasik. A User Interface Management System. *ACM Computer Graphics*, 16(3):99–105, July 1982.

[55] Michael F. Kleyn and Indranil Chatravarty. EDGE – A Graph Based Tool for Specifying Interaction. In *Proc. ACM Symposium on User Interface Software and Technology (UIST)*, pages 1–14, October 1989.

[56] K. L. Kraemer and J. C. King. Computer-Based Systems for Cooperative Work and Group Decision Making. *ACM Computing Surveys*, 20(2):115–145, June 1988.

[57] William Leler. *Constraint Programming Languages*. Addison-Wesley, 1987.

[58] J. Bryan Lewis, Lawrence Koved, and Daniel T. Ling. Dialogue Structures for Virtual Worlds. In *Proc. ACM SIGCHI*, pages 131–136, May 1991.

[59] M. A. Linton, J. M. Vlissides, and P. R. Calder. Composing User Interfaces with InterViews. *IEEE Computer*, pages 8–22, February 1989.

[60] J. H. Maloney, A. Borning, and B. N. Freeman-Benson. Constraint Technology for User-Interface Construction in ThingLab II. In *Proc. ACM OOPSLA*, pages 381–388, October 1989.

[61] David L. Maulsby, Ian H. Witten, and Kenneth A. Kittlitz. Metamouse: Specifying Graphical Procedures by Example. In *Proc. ACM SIGGRAPH*, pages 127–136, July 1989.

[62] Joel McCormack and Paul Asente. An Overview of the X Toolkit. In *Proc. ACM Symposium on User Interface Software and Technology (UIST)*, pages 46–55, October 1989.

[63] Brad A. Myers. Creating Interaction Techniques by Demonstration. *IEEE Computer Graphics and Applications*, 1987 1987.

[64] Brad A. Myers. User-Interface Tools: Introduction and Survey. *IEEE Software*, pages 15–23, January 1989.

[65] Brad A. Myers. Creating User Interfaces Using Programming by Example, Visual Programming and Constraints. *ACM Trans. on Programming Languages and Systems*, 12(2):143–177, 1990.

[66] Brad A. Myers et al. Garnet, Comprehensive Support for Graphical, Highly Interactive User Interfaces. *IEEE Computer*, pages 71–85, November 1990.

[67] Greg Nelson. Juno, a Constraint-Based Graphics System. *ACM Computer Graphics - Proc. SIGGRAPH*, 19(3):235–243, July 1985.

[68] NSL. *XFM2 User's Manual.* N.S.L., 57–59 rue Lhomond, 75 005 Paris, France, 1990.

[69] Dan R. Olsen, Jr. SYNGRAPH: a Graphical User Interface Generator. *ACM Computer Graphics - Proc. SIGGRAPH*, 17(3):43–50, July 1983.

[70] Dan R. Olsen, Jr. MIKE: the Menu Interaction Kontrol Environment. *ACM Trans. on Graphics*, 5(4):318–344, October 1986.

[71] Open Software Foundation, Cambridge. *OSF/Motif Programmer's Reference Manual*, 1989.

[72] Günther E. Pfaff, editor. *User Interface Management Systems.* Eurographics Seminars. Springer-Verlag, 1985.

[73] Martin Prime. User Interface Management Systems – A Current Product Review. *Computer Graphics Forum*, 9, 1990.

[74] George G. Robertson, Jock D. Mackinlay, and Stuart K. Card. Cone Trees: Animated 3D Visualizations of Hierarchical Information. In *Proc. ACM SIGCHI*, pages 189–194, May 1991.

[75] R. W. Scheifler and J. Gettys. The X Window System. *ACM Trans. on Graphics*, 5(2):79–109, April 1986.

[76] Serpent Overview. Technical Report CMU/SEI-89-UG-2, Carnegie Mellon University, Software Engineering Institute, August 1989.

[77] K. J. Shmucker. MacApp: An Application Framework. *Byte Magazine*, pages 189–192, August 1986.

[78] B. Shneiderman. Direct Manipulation: a Step Beyond Programming Languages. *IEEE Computer*, pages 57–69, August 1983.

[79] SmetherBarnes. *SmetherBarnes Prototyper User's Manual.* P.O. Box 639, Portland, Oregon, 87.

[80] David Canfield Smith, Charles Irby, Ralph Kimball, Bill Verplank, and Eric Harslem. Designing the Star User Interface. *Byte Magazine*, 7(5), April 1984.

[81] Sun. *OLIT Specifications.* Sun Microsystems, Mountain View, 1990.

[82] Pedro A. Szekely. Template-Based Mapping of Application Data to Interactive Displays. In *Proc. ACM Symposium on User Interface Software and Technology (UIST)*, pages 1–9, October 1990.

[83] J. J. Thomas et al. Graphical Interaction Technique (GIIT) – Workshop Summary. *ACM Computer Graphics*, pages 5–30, January 1983.

[84] User Interface Developer's Workshop. The Arch Model: Seeheim Revisited. Presented at ACM SIGCHI, April 1991.

[85] User Interface Developer's Workshop. A Metamodel for the Runtime Architecture of an Interactive System. *ACM SIGCHI Bulletin*, 24(1), January 1992.

[86] J. M. Vlissides and M. A. Linton. Unidraw: A Framework for Building Domain-Specific Graphical Editors. Technical Report CSL-TR-89-380, Computer Systems Laboratory, Stanford University, July 1989.

[87] A. I. Wasserman. Extending State Transition Diagrams for the Specification of Human-Computer Interaction. *IEEE Trans. on Software Engineering*, SE-11:699–713, August 1985.

[88] Pierre D. Wellner. Statemaster: A UIMS based on Statecharts for Prototyping and Target Application. In *Proc. ACM SIGCHI*, pages 177–182, May 1989.

Trends in Edge Detection Techniques

Eduard Antoniu

ABSTRACT
An overview of several research results in edge detection techniques over the last decade is provided with the present paper. First, the aim of detecting edges is emphasised from gathering various points of view. Main features for edge detectors to be evaluated from are discussed as well. According to just a personal classification, groups of methods are evolutively surveyed. Both software and hardware implementations, along to some performances reported in litterature, are briefly considered. Each group's main features are analyzed, pros and cons included. Future developments are finally anticipated.

Abbreviations

Fields: CG - Computer Graphics; CV - Computer Vision; ED - Edge Detection; EF - Edge Fitting; IP - Image Processing; PR - Pictorial Pattern Recognition.

Filters: DOG - Difference of Gaussians; FIR - Finite Impulse Response; IIR - Infinite Impulse Response; LOG - Laplacian of Gaussian; NSEP - Noise Smoothing Edge Preserving.

1 Introduction

During an early research age, edge detection (ED) had been considered as a distinct topic within image processing (IP). Computer simulation of the human visual perception, processing, storage, transfer, analysis and pictorial data interpretation is what IP deals with. The interaction between pictorial data perceived by humans and machine data structures is essential within IP. If one wants to get a description (analysis) out of an image, one actually deals with the adjacent field of pictorial pattern recognition (PR). Conversely, if one wants to generate an image (synthesis) out of some data suited for, one is now into computer graphics (CG) [68, 128]. These are illustrated in figure 1.

IP and PR were also considered as actually merging into what is now commonly referred to as Computer Vision (CV). By assembling, mathematically modelling and valuating discoveries from Biology, Physics and related sciences, fruitful work has been done within this major topic. Therein, ED is usually a first step. Successful achievement of subsequent CV stages strongly depends on ED's completion. E.g., when looking a scene with moving objects, motion is first detected by the edges and only then it propagates within the observed region [129].

Backtracking the roots in using gradient operators in ED, we reach to Kovasznay and Joseph [138] and Kirsch [91] in the mid-'50s. However, it is Roberts (in 1965) to be commonly considered as having pioneered ED as an investigation field within low-level vision [10, 152].

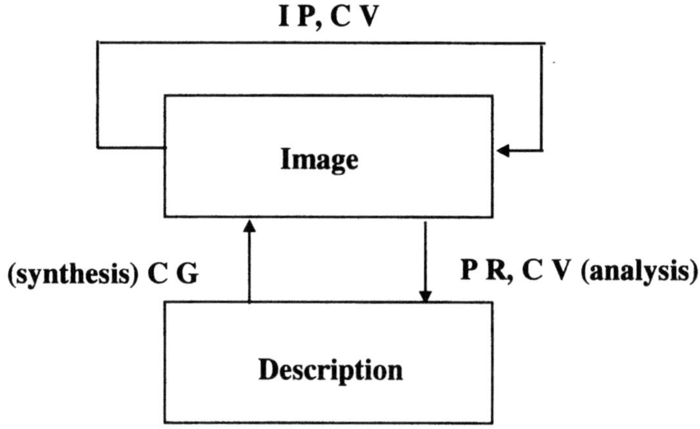

FIGURE 1. Interrelationship among CG, IP, PR, CV.

Our paper tries to overview some in-field works over the last decade. A sketch of the edge concept is aimed first to be etched, out of various acceptances, in the next section. The meanings of contours and of their models are then attempted to be enlightened. Main features that edge detectors might be classified according to, as well as criteria for good detection are discussed. A typical sequence of operations aiming at extracting edges is then futher detailed. Finally, a classification of edge detectors is also attempted to, according to our own point of view. It would be extensively dealt with in sections 3–5. Both hardware and software implementations along to some performances are also briefly mentioned. Main features of each group are underlined, with pros and cons as well. Peculiar applicability within CG is also stressed. We finally dare to anticipate future in-field developments (section 6).

The reference list is not as thorough as the topic is worth of. If compared to minor and major detected edges (to be mentioned in section 2.1), there might be milestone references to have escaped from our view or to have simply missed or to have been not available to us. Whereas, perhaps we have rather emphasised minor contributions instead of at least mentioning major ones supposed to be well-known. Nevertheless, the interested reader could step down as well through different levels of reference lists gathered in an imaginary tree. If this paper were to be the root-node, with references as leaf-nodes, the reader should track those papers or books (aiming to ED) successively referenced at each leaf-node level. Of course, just if he had to complete his knowledge on ED.

2 About the ED Philosophy

First we try to reinforce the concept of edge (also referred to in this paper as boundary, border, frontier, contour or even discontinuity). We also try to enlighten what are contours and their models and to discuss criteria for good detection. A typical edge extraction sequence is then further detailed. Finally, edge detectors are attempted to be classified in terms of their main features.

2.1 The Edge Paradigm

As for CV, the term *edge* is usually referred to as a point lying on a boundary between two regions. Concerning the grey levelled image itself, an edge is a point where an intensity change takes place.

Two simple definitions of edges [91, 138] may already be inferred from these statements:

Definition 1 *If there are two homogeneous regions of different intensity values in an image, there is an edge as the frontier between regions.*

Comment on Definition 1 *It is an overall description, obviously involving a local one.*

Definition 2 *There is an edge element around a local variation of intensity.*

Comment on Definition 2 *Edges are to be detected by examining local neighbourhoods in search of such local variation [138]. However, not all intensity changes are edge elements: they might be detected where no meaningful boundary exists; conversely, there could be no detected edge elements where a boundary yet is.*

One may see there is *fuzziness* involved in defining edges. There were attempts to unify both concepts from mathematical uncertainty (e.g,. Bayesian approach), the *discontinuity* term being used [10, 87, 152].

2.2 Contours and their models

The psychovisual background of ED relies on the fact that ganglion cells of the retina are sensitive only to differences in their receptive fields, ignoring the absolute light intensities [84]. A subjective enhancement of sharp brightness changes because of lateral inhibitions and excitations of these cells (the so called Mach phenomenon) is noticed. The *just noticeable difference* between two adjacent regions, each of homogeneous brightness, might be determined according to Weber-Fechner's law [57, 84]. Brief psychovisual along to computational considerations are in the following.

Explicite image interpolation was found to be performed by the human visual system [117]. Two parallel contour sensitive processes were hypothesised and demonstrated to interact within human vision. They were found to have complementary sensitivities to either orientation and contrast or direction of contrast in scenic edges [30, 58, 59]. While human eyes perform easily the task of identifying boundaries between objects, ED by computer is a difficult task indeed. Noise, blurrings and quantizing effects are the most common burdens to be removed [60].

Contouring may be thought of as particular binary segmentation of image [138], where pixels are assigned just two levels: *edge* or *no-edge*. It seems there is no restriction in thinking just in terms of illumination (brightness, intensity, luminance) and ignoring other physical and surface properties or geometrical criteria. However, researchers still have not agreed about how much pictorial data is enough for an efficient contour detection to be performed on an image. Some of them said that much pictorial data may be recovered from an edge image [60]. Whereas others insisted on gathering as much generic information as possible into what they called the *local structure of image discontinuities* [87].

Edges were also studied in [89]. A review of ideal edge models (step, ramp, staircase, pulse) is in [168].

Different computational approaches for boundary representations: finite element approach [155], Markovian process [73, 87], Bayesian decision problem [169], parameterised templates [183], parametrically deformable [150], neural [94], active [12] and circular autoregressive contour models [45].

2.3 Criteria for good detection

An edge operator should both have good detection characteristics and mark features accurately. These features should be described in terms of their true nature, the types of noise likely to affect that nature included. As for detection characteristics, there are two rough classes of edges:

- edges used e.g., in image segmentation, which are expected just to clearly separate homogeneous regions, while there is no need of their accurate localisation;
- edges used e.g., in stereoscopy, motion detection, where the request of accurate positionning becomes heavier than that of good detection.

Hence, edge detectors used in purposes falling into one class of problems might be not necessarily suited for the other one, whichever trade-offs between performance criteria might be resorted to.

Three such performance criteria were proposed in an attempt of creating an optimal edge detector [18, 19]:

1. **Good Detection** by finding true edges and not falsely marking nonedge points.
2. **Good Localisation** , that is, marked edge points lying in the closest positions to the centre of the true edge.
3. **One-Edge-One-Response** i.e., multiple outputs being not produced as response to just a single edge.

Parameters mathematically reflecting them were embodied by maximizing the product of the former two criteria under the constraint of the third one. Solving this system by calculus of variations and imposing boundary conditions suited for a finite impulse response (FIR) filter led Canny to an expression that was close to the first derivative of a 1D Gaussian:

$$f(x) = -x/(\sigma^2)\exp(-x^2/2\sigma^2) \qquad (1)$$

Ignoring the first – sign, it were as if noise obeyed a Rayleigh distribution law (see e.g., [43]).

Though having introduced useful ideas into developing an edge detector, Canny's approach was found to feature some limitations. There were noticed cases when no clear distinction could have been done between poor detection and localisation. Thus, criteria 1 and 2 became rather useless, since it was only at random that one of them was improved. Furthermore, one's improvement was done on the expense of the other. Leaving nonlinear operations in the decision stage was also also minded on as being not the best way to partition the problem of finding an optimal operator [169]. A further Achile's heel was revealed in the approximation to (1) being done only on examining operator's shape [34].

Considering edge as an event occurring in a grey level sequence, each such a sequence was assigned a value corresponding to the probability that it contained at least one edge [169]. This probability was proved to be possibly inferred from knowing just three other probability distributions: 1) at least one edge or 2) no edge occurrence within a sequence and 3) overall likelihood of edge-within-arange occurrence. These might be respectively compared to criteria 1, 3 and 2, distribution 3 actually playing the part of a control parameter over the other two ones, similarly to Canny's approach. However, no results were provided with this Bayesian formulation of optimal ED.

Edge localisation using extended Kalman filter was found to yield substantially better results than obtained when using Canny's operator [108]. Optimum line detection and localisation filters were developed in [31]. Statistical classification, a recent viewpoint, was found likely to yield results as good as optimal operators [83].

2.4 Typical steps in edge extraction

Merely applying an edge detector over an image yet does not necessarily involve completing the contour extraction process. Both previous and subsequent stages are needed as a general rule: previous ones - since acquisitioned images are usually distorted and noise corrupted; subsequent ones - since edge images are often somewhat meaningless.

Pre-processing

Noise and distortion may be degrading any image, thus alterring the performance of whatever edge detector. Image restoration [1, 53] and, more often, noise smoothing edge preserving (NSEP) filtering are needed against. Various NSEP filters have been proposed: nonlinear product averaging [132, 138], nonlinear homomorphic [132], homomorphic and order statistic [131].

However, adaptive ones, that is, those taking into account the contents in a local neighbourhood before deciding how to perform the filtering, have been found to yield the best NSEP behaviour among filters. They were dealt with in [28, 53, 55, 140, 167]. An evaluation has been provided in [27]. It found median filter and K-Nearest Neighbour averaging as yielding the best results. K-Nearest Connected Neighbour filter was proved more efficient in [96]. Whereas in [81] the Symmetric Nearest Neighbour filter was found excellent within multiresolution techniques. Average smoothing was applied in [116]. A NSEP VLSI filter is in [130].

Contour detection

From either of the definitions in section 2.1 it comes that edges are consequences of changes/variations/differences in parameters which characterize adjacent regions. Supposing image were a 2D continuous function $I(x, y)$, such differences may be depicted by its gradient

$$\nabla I(x,y) = \frac{\partial I(x,y)}{\partial x} + \frac{\partial I(x,y)}{\partial y} \tag{2}$$

which is a vector, thus being characterized by a magnitude

$$\mid \nabla I(x,y) \mid = [(\frac{\partial I(x,y)}{\partial x})^2 + (\frac{\partial I(x,y)}{\partial y})^2]^{1/2} \tag{3}$$

and an orientation

$$\alpha = \arctan(\frac{\partial I(x,y)/\partial y}{\partial I(x,y)/\partial x}) \tag{4}$$

An image actually being a 2D discrete function, whatever edge detector were to be applied it should attempt detecting contours as maxima among magnitudes

$$\mid G(j,k) \mid = [G_h^2(j,k) + G_v^2(j,k)]^{1/2} \tag{5}$$

of the discrete version of gradient (2), where indices h, v denote horizontal and vertical components of the gradient, respectively, and $j = 1 \div m, k = 1 \div n$ denote rows and columns of the I(m x n) image array. The orientation

$$\theta = \arctan(G_v/G_h) \tag{6}$$

should also be taken into account.

However, not all detected maxima point out true edges. Various post-processing techniques should be applied over the resulting image in order to remove spurious edges.

Post-processing

There is no standard post-processing technique to be universally applied over an image in order to improve contour detection's result. It should only be suited for this result. If from the subsequent techniques the former two are IP specific, the remainder are rather tools of CG.

Thresholding is a point dependent segmentation where image is scanned pixel by pixel. Its result is an image having just two grey level subbands, one for the background and one for the objects in the image. By means of a specific technique [53], detected edges are preserved as boundaries between background and objects. A survey of threshold selection techniques is in [166]. Thresholding seems to be necessary when using what we would call local operators (section 3.1) as edge detectors. It was applied in [6, 116, 179]. However, it was given up in [25] in order to preserve connectivity of edge elements. Optimal thresholding sequences, like Lemkin's boundary trace transform [91] have been also proposed.

Extraneous Edge Removal (Non-Maxima Suppression) Since performing ED might be leading to meaningless contours, extra elements have to be suppressed. A dominant neighbour suppression procedure was proposed by Rosenfeld as early as 1970 [132]. Local smoothing as irregularity removal means was used in [25]. Region growing, which is a particular approach to segmentation, was used as spurious edge removal in [116]. Non-maxima suppression and hysteresis thresholding were used in [34, 146].

Approximate Location Searching Boundaries are to be refined given an initial estimate. This might be done using local search, nonlinear correlation or divide-and-conquer techniques [10]. Such approaches seem to be suited for some available a priori knowledge on a shape whose boundary is to be extracted. They were applied in [79, 124]. However, such a method finally led to failure in [11].

Linking (Edge Gap Filling) Since there might be no detected edges where a meaningful boundary yet is, contour closing is to be completed by linking gapped-between edge groups. Linking by means of a chord algorithm [127] was used in [173]. Local connectivity information [91] was used as an edge knowledge base in [22]. Gradient magnitude data were exploited for contour closing and region separation (figure 2) in [37]. Planning [91], a concept originated by Kirsch (in 1957), introduced by Minsky (in 1963) and improved by Kelly (in 1971), was also used as a step in iterative gap filling for edge segment linking in [95]. Linking with analytical contour description was applied in [56]. A Perkins algorithm was used in [179].

Graph Searching is a particular linking approach. Edge elements are viewed as nodes of a graph. A boundary thus consists of a path relying them, as suggested by Kelly [91].

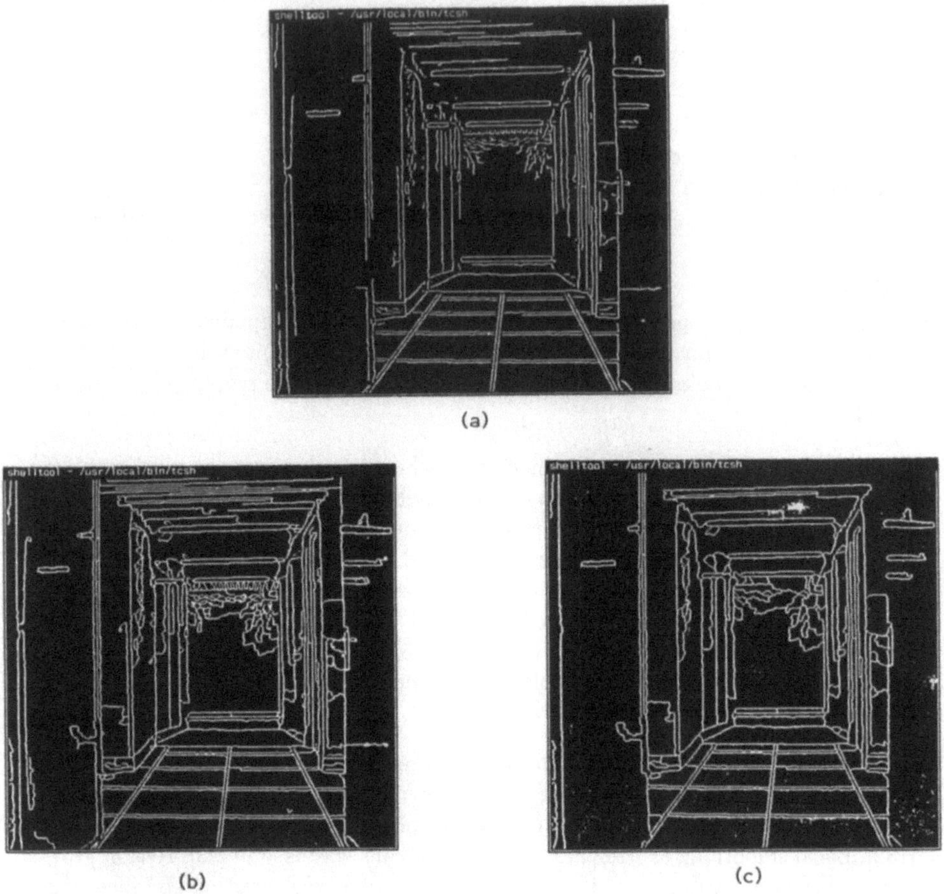

FIGURE 2. Extracted edges: (a) prior to and (b) after contour closing; (c) after region separation ([37], IEEE ©1988, reprinted with permission)

According to Martelli, an edge were a path to be optimally found between a start and a goal node in a graph having weights/costs associated to its arcs. Boundary completion would thus be formulated as searching for the lowest cost path between those nodes [10, 91]. Graph searching theoretical approaches are in [7, 66, 128]. They were applied in [4, 11]. Figure 3 shows a result of graph searching boundary completion.

Contour Following (Tracking) assumes segmentation to have been performed over an image. Contours are then to be recovered by simply following the boundary between two regions. Tracing algorithms are in [128]. A typical sequence of edge extraction operations (figure 4) was included in a feedback system (figure 4) performing a backtracking until a termination criterion was satisfied [25]. Tracking was applied in [79, 120, 174, 180]. Optimal boundary tracers were used in [46, 163]. A result of a contour following is in figure 5.

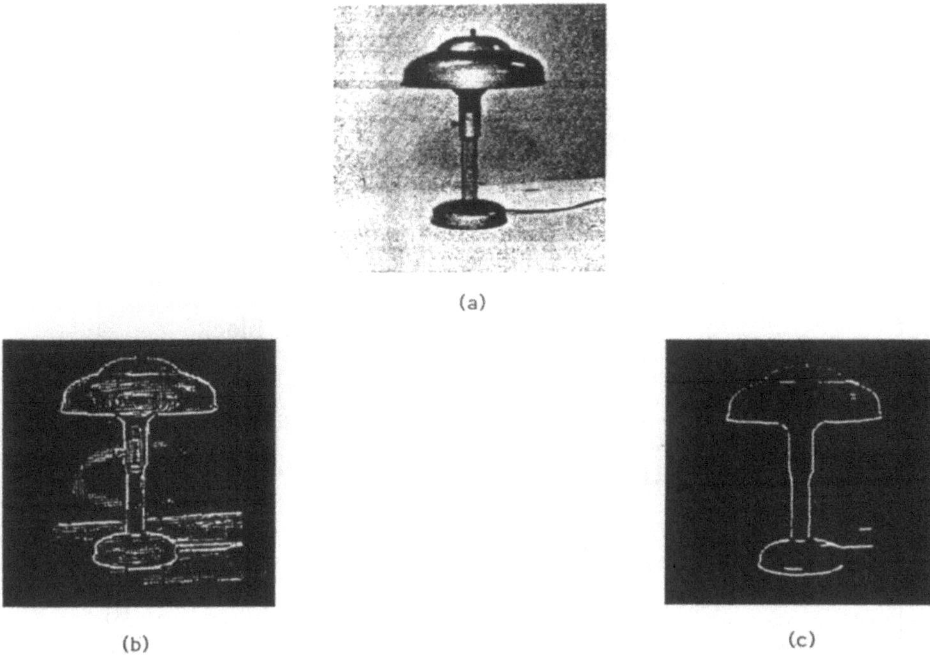

FIGURE 3. Boundary completion by graph searching: (a) image; edges (b) detected by the Hueckel operator and (c) extracted after some graph searching steps ([10], IEEE ©1975, reprinted with permission)

Detected Border's Thinning is the most common extraneous edge removal. Most often, edge elements are joined so that contours are more than a single pixel in their widths. This is typical for gradient operators (section 3.1) which respond with a broad peak at an edge location. Thinning algorithms have been proposed in [26, 128]. They were used in [6, 22, 83, 85, 173, 179].

Nowadays edge extraction processes are sometimes fully built into chips [23]. The best performances are in [151]: durations about $1 \mu s$.

2.5 Features to classify edge detectors

Main performance criteria to be considered when classifying edge detectors [91]:

speed to notice whether an edge is obtained during the required time for the application under consideration;

memory large images and/or computational complexity might involve early memory filling;

isotropy detection regardless of edge orientation (e.g., 2D/3D Gaussian filters and their second derivatives, see section 3.3);

static/dynamic range the grey level map to deal with, also referred to in the literature as quantization;

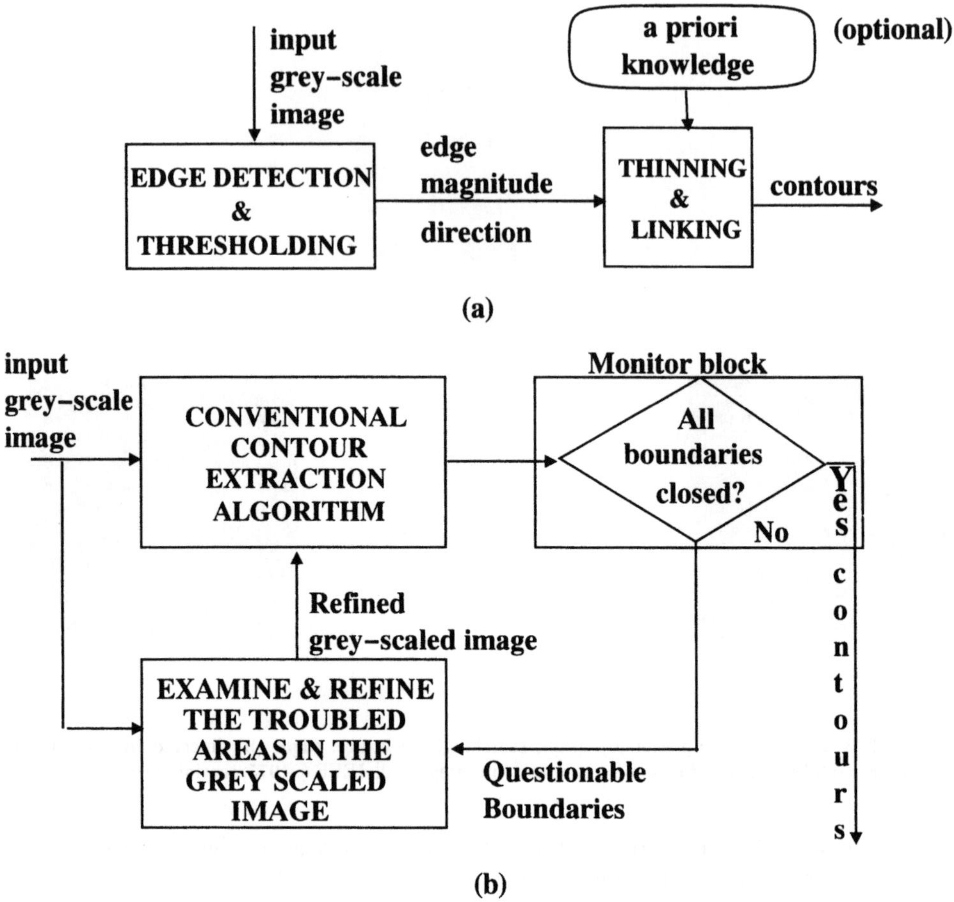

FIGURE 4. Contour extraction algorithms: (a) conventional and (b) with feedback path

noise immunity perhaps the heaviest criterion so far, though hard indeed to be achieved; actually, various noises occur throughout the edge extraction process;

universality the independence from a specific problem, also hard indeed to be achieved since ED is rather a task dependent problem [60, 73];

level the usefulness of the output into interpretation;

quality the geometrical similarity between the virtual edges in the output result and the true edges in the real scene (e.g., in line drawings).

Edge detectors may be clustered according to various features within their intrinsical nature. With regards to the mathematical principle of ED, one might thus see them gathered into two broad classes: gradients and second derivative operators [67]. Or, according to their computational nature, one might think of them as being parallel, sequential or

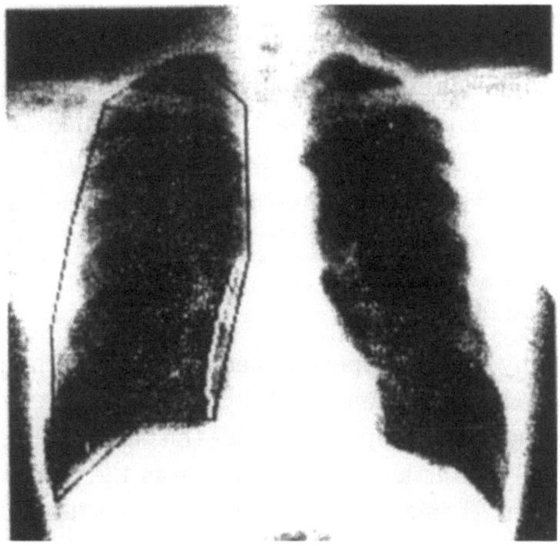

FIGURE 5. A result of contour following ([10], CGIP ©1976, reprinted with permission)

relaxational procedures [40]. As for the level of incorporated parameter set to perform ED, one might separate operators into classes as gradients, matching templates (changing at different orientations) and operators fitting local intensities to parametric edge models [10]. Another classification [91, 131] attempted discriminating specialized features of techniques. Classes of methods were stated as:

local based on the discretization of operators originally applied on continuous functions;

regional aiming to detect straight lines or curved figures (particularly ellipses and circles) and using either analytical expressions or best fit criteria;

global performing ED as an overall image filtering;

heuristic using a priori knowledge and thus being rather inherently sequential in computational nature; suited for finding a path in a graph between two nodes;

dynamic using the mathematical expression of an overall best boundary; suited for more points to start with in a graph search, when no powerful heuristic were available;

relaxation a computational hybride taking advantage of both speed of parallel techniques and powerful, *on-the-fly* learning, adaptive behaviour of sequential methods.

Some of them are subgroups of a new classification that we dare to propose. Edge detectors might be mainly discriminated from their level of using a pictorial context. We reckon that ED techniques might be broadly separated into context either -free or -dependent, as in [60]. We think there is also an intermediate class making just little use of the pictorial context and thus being a matter of edge rather fitting than detection. We agree that the classification is a rough one because certain features are shared by the three of the classes.

Sections 3–5 will try to further detail the above groups as how we think of them. There will be no comparison made in terms of class performances, since these groups use too different criteria of success. Only an estimation of future developments, according to our own point of view on the state-of-art in ED, is what we shall be trying instead.

3 Context-Free ED

First, some classical gradient operators are introduced. Given that applying such an operator over an image area a convolution is actually performed, an intermediate subclass might be called local filtering. Extending the image area up to the whole picture, an overall smoothing is performed. Either of these techniques does not make use of the pictorial context.

3.1 Gradients. Masks. Templates

Some authors called ED by gradient operators as image sharpening by differentiation [53] or linear and non-linear edge enhancement [132].

Many such operators had been proposed during the early age of ED. Usually they came out into the shape of a 3 x 3 array. Such a mask was the practical means of computationally implementing a mathematical expression (usually an algebraic sum) aiming to approximate (2) as a discrete version. Some masks along with their analytical expressions are given in table 1. Only horizontal masks were depicted, the vertical ones being usually recovered from a 90 degrees counterclockwise rotation (exceptions are marked within table 1). All masks were assummed to be applied over a 3 x 3 image array (exceptions being shown in table 1) given by:

$$I = \begin{bmatrix} I(j+1,k-1) & I(j+1,k) & I(j+1,k+1) \\ I(j,k-1) & I(j,k) & I(j,k+1) \\ I(j-1,k-1) & I(j-1,k) & I(j-1,k+1) \end{bmatrix} \tag{7}$$

Actually, as suggested by Kirsch and Compass operators' expressions, the magnitude returned by the operation at pixel I(j,k) will be taken from among all mask's rotated versions applied over the image array (7):

$$\mid G_{out}(j,k) \mid = \max \mid G_i(j,k) \mid \tag{8}$$

It is also $G_{out}(j,k)$'s orientation as an output. Given some symmetry within certain masks, the number of rotations can be reduced (to 4 for P, S, 1 for L_4 and 0 for L_8). Thus, some computational effort is saved. 3 x 3 local operators are subsequently used as in figure 6 [91]. A result of applying a Roberts-like edge detector is given in figure 7.

There were demonstrated useful decompositions of Roberts and Sobel kernels into simpler ones, without any multiplications being needed into [61].

As how one might have already been expecting, nowadays only the most performant among gradient operators are used: Roberts [145, 175], Prewitt [14, 25] and widely spreaded Sobel [6, 11, 22, 48, 93, 116, 173, 175, 179]. The remaining operators are still implemented only into systems deserving learning purposes [15].

A hardware implementation of the Sobel operator [22] exploited mask's separability property

$$S_h = \begin{bmatrix} 1 & 0 & -1 \\ 2 & 0 & -2 \\ 1 & 0 & -1 \end{bmatrix} = \begin{bmatrix} 1 \\ 2 \\ 1 \end{bmatrix} \begin{bmatrix} 1 \\ 0 \\ -1 \end{bmatrix} = V_1 V_2^T \tag{9}$$

$$S_v = \begin{bmatrix} -1 & -2 & -1 \\ 0 & 0 & 0 \\ 1 & 2 & 1 \end{bmatrix} = \begin{bmatrix} -1 \\ 0 \\ 1 \end{bmatrix} \begin{bmatrix} 1 \\ 2 \\ 1 \end{bmatrix} = -V_1 V_2^T \tag{10}$$

so that $G_{h,v}$ from (5) were respectively given by

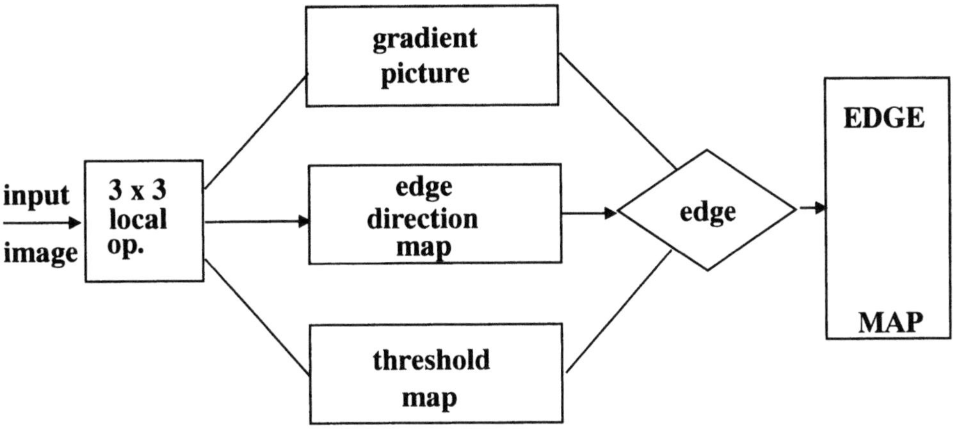

FIGURE 6. A simple ED scheme

(a) (b) (c)

FIGURE 7. *Lena*: (a) 256 x 256 x 8 bit original image; (b) after performing an initial ED using a Roberts-like operator; (c) after 10 iterations of relaxation process ([92], IEEE ©1988, reprinted with permission)

$$G_h = I * S_h = -V_1^T I V_2 \quad (11)$$
$$G_v = I * S_v = V_2^T I V_1 \quad (12)$$

with I given by (7). (11) and (12) were implemented as in figure 8. Resulting data were subsequently feeded on for (5)–(6) to be implemented (figure 8). Edge orientation was determined according to the Freeman code (figure 8) and magnitude was considered over a given threshold (figure 8). Edges were then extracted like in figure 8. A more performant hardware Sobel operator is in [23].

However, using such already old operators has not been impeaching conceiving new ones. Frei and Chen proposed a set of 9 templates performing some thresholding and forming an orthogonal basis for a 3 x 3 image array to be matched to [10, 53]. A statistical mask was proposed in [132] which assummed correlation factors $\rho_{r,c}$ between adjacent row and column pixels, respectively

TABLE 1. Gradient masks [91, 132]

Type of Operator	Mask	Discrete Gradient Approximation Sum	Remarks
Roberts	0 −1 1 0	$R_h(j,k) = \mid I(j,k) - I(j+1,k+1) \mid$	2x2 sized, 3levelled performed over $I = \begin{bmatrix} I(j+1,k) & I(j+1,k+1) \\ I(j,k) & I(j,k+1) \end{bmatrix}$
Prewitt	1 0 −1 1 0 −1 1 0 −1	$P_h(j,k) = \mid \sum_{j-1}^{j+1}(I(i,k-1) - I(i,k+1))$	3 levelled, better than Roberts for step edges
Sobel	1 0 −1 2 0 −2 1 0 −1	$S_h(j,k) = \mid \sum_{j-1}^{j+1}(I(i,k-1) - I(i,k+1)) + I(j,k-1) - I(j,k+1) \mid$	5 levelled, usually with best performances among all 3x3 masks
Kirsch	3 3 −5 3 0 −5 3 3 −5	$K_h(j,k) = \max\{1, \max \sum_0^7 \mid 5S_l - 3T_i \mid \}$ $S_h = \sum_0^2 A_{i+l}, \quad T_h = \sum_3^7 A_{i+l}$ $A_6 \quad A_7 \quad A_0$ $A_5 \quad I(j,k) \quad A_1$ $A_4 \quad A_3 \quad A_2$ i computed mod8; all remaining masks keep all these notations	due to the sensitivity to the magnitude of $I(j,k)$, in practice 5 x 5 masks are used; K_v results from 3 successive anti-clockwise permutations of A_is
Compass	1 1 1 −2 −1 −1 1 1 −1	$C_h(j,k) = \max \mid \sum_0^7 (S_i - T_i) - 2I(j,k) \mid$	3 levelled
Laplacian	0 1 0 1 −4 1 0 1 0	$L_{14}(j,k) = \mid \sum_0^3 A_{2i+1} - 4I(j,k) \mid$	3 levelled, 4 neighbour first version
Laplacian	1 −2 1 −2 4 −2 1 −2 1	$L_{24}(j,k) = \mid \sum_0^3 A_{2i+1} + 4I(j,k) \mid$	3 levelled, 4 neighbour second version
Laplacian	1 1 1 1 −8 1 1 1 1	$L_8(j,k) = \mid \sum_0^7 A_i - 8I(j,k) \mid$	2 levelled

$$M = \begin{bmatrix} \rho_c\rho_r & -\rho_c(1+\rho_r^2) & \rho_c\rho_r \\ -\rho_r(1+\rho_c^2) & (1+\rho_c^2)(1+\rho_r^2) & -\rho_r(1+\rho_c^2) \\ \rho_c\rho_r & -\rho_c(1+\rho_r^2) & \rho_c\rho_r \end{bmatrix} \tag{13}$$

which e.g., for $\rho_r = \rho_c = 1$ would yield L_{24} from table 1. Persoon and Wechsler proposed 5 x 5 sized masks which combined gradients and Laplacians [165]. Higher order polynomial models were used to obtain optimal estimates of neighbourhoods of arbitrary size, up to 9 x 9, by least-squares fitting [114]. A set of masks for extracting thin linear features and an improvement of mask matching by means of confidence measures and probabilistic analysis were proposed in [121]. Each mask from this set could have been optimally associated to a pixel, in a process of pixel pairwise consistent labelling, in order to perform ED [78]. A new set of templates based on confidence measures of a one-response-to-one-ideal-stimulus hypothesis, using optimal linear associative mapping, was proposed in [109]. Another set was conditioned by significant data within imaging process [136].

An image is a 2D discrete function. Performing ED by local operators mainly involves a differentiation. However, it has been noticed that differentiating a discrete function is an ill-conditioned problem [75]. Furthermore, this mathematical operation is intrinsically very sensitive to noise. Thus, since missing useful directional information and, as an approximation to the second derivative, twice enhancing noise in image, Laplacian masks have become actually misused [10, 91].

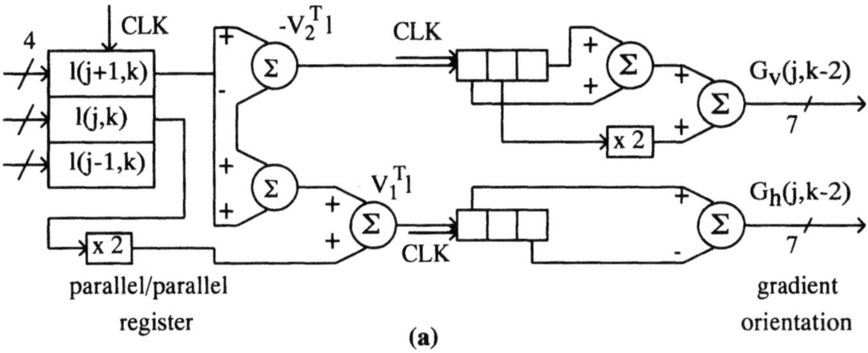

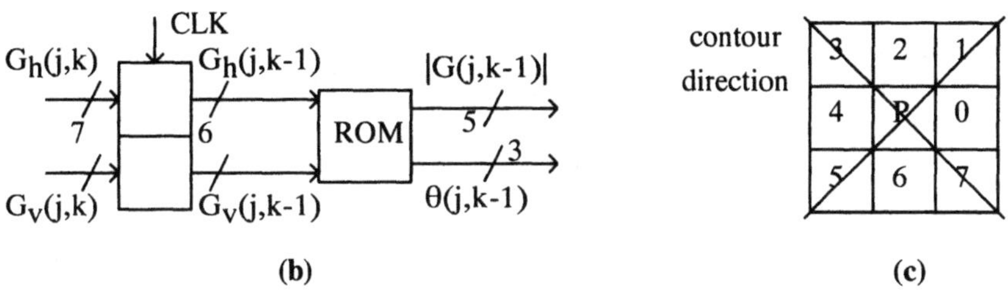

12 bit adress \ Byte	5 bits	3 bits
$G_h^2 + G_v^2 > 4$	$\sqrt{G_h^2 + G_v^2}$	Freeman code of θ
$G_h^2 + G_v^2 \leq 4$	0	0

(d)

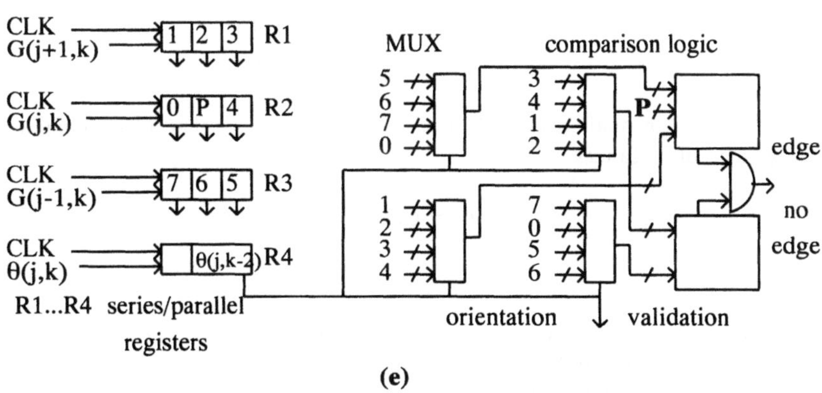

FIGURE 8. Hardware Sobel operator: (a) vertical and horizontal gradient components; (b) magnitude and orientation; (c) Freeman code; (d) coding and thresholding; (e) edge/orientation output

5 levelled masks perform good approximations of partial derivatives along both axes. Usually being 0 center weighted, they help to suppress line jitter. They have a greater sensitivity to diagonal directions than to horizontal and vertical axes, which is different from the human visual response [91]. These explain why Sobel among 3 x 3 masks are still so widely used nowadays.

A comparison of all these operators, whether gradients, Laplacians or templates is difficult. However, some indexes to compare local operators are in [10, 91, 132].

There is still a wide use of these operators within applications. They are mainly encountered within tasks of rather medium both computational complexity and memory availability. Since images which are generated in CG feature less much noise, if at all, than those acquisitioned to be used into IP, PR, CV and since they already provide much better segmentation too, such local operators might be successfully used into CG as well. However, we find no clear perspective for such operators from an evolutionary point of view, since the only approaches focussed on local operators themselves deal with either decomposing them into simpler kernels or creating new sets of templates based on rather sophisticated criteria.

3.2 Local Filtering

Since applying such a 3 x 3 operator to detect edges in an image means convolving 3 x 3 operator and image arrays, one might see it as a local filtering.

3 x 3 mask configurations according to Gaussian patterns were proposed by Argyle and MacLeod [132]. A similar model was considered in [170]. A pixel's normalized new value was taken as being

$$v_0(x,y) = \frac{\Sigma w_n v_n(x,y)}{\Sigma v_n(x,y)} \tag{14}$$

where w_n was a weight to be further detailed below, $v_n(x,y)$ was the brightness value of the (x,y) coordinate pixel, N was the number of elements to be taken into account by the operator.

Instead of just a 3 x 3 convolution array, the operator had $N \in \{5, 9, 21\}$ squared pixels (figure 9) as the discrete approximation of a circle given by

$$(x - x_0)^2 + (y - y_0)^2 = r^2 \tag{15}$$

According to psychovisual criteria, Wojczik expressed w_n as either a rotational symmetric filter or a ratio of distances

$$w_n = \exp(-Pr^2) \tag{16}$$

or

$$w = 1 - r/S \tag{17}$$

where S was said to be the distance from the center of the circle to the closest pixel outside the circle boundary (figure 9). (16) is similar to Argyle's function. We should emphasize that (16) and (17) are just distinct filters: (17) may not be (16)'s approximation since it contains an odd power of r. Such an approximation would feature an even power of r. Actually, it has been already successfully resorted to within overall filtering [35].

Anyway, there were no additional theoretical considerations on P. It was said to have been taken just from experience as being P = 0.18 or P = 0.3 so that w_n would have been close to 1 for lower radii and close to 0 for upper radii (hence a FIR, see e.g.,

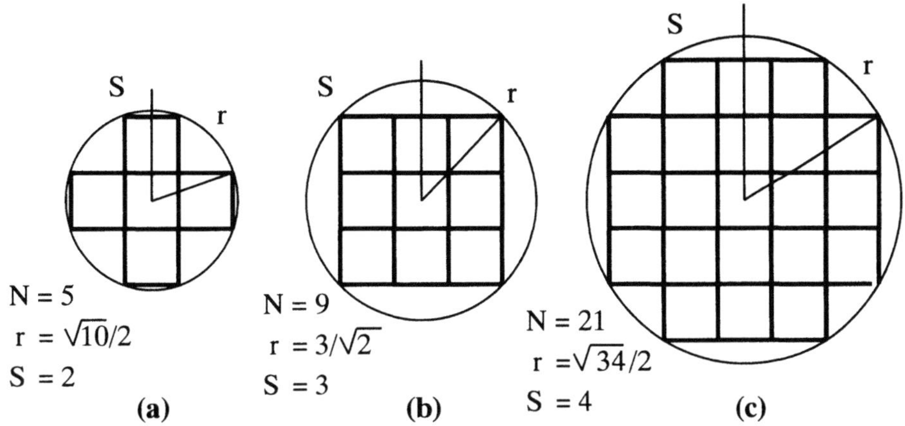

FIGURE 9. Discretized approximation of a circular operator

[2]). Actually, one of the two local Gaussians obtained for the two of the P values had a standard deviation σ_1^2 which was the square of the other's σ_2^2.

An interpolation filter performing convolution over a 7 x 7 image array was proposed in [117]. A surprisingly performant hardware implementation of a 3 x 3 versatile operator, called logical filter, was reported in [142]. Filtering being not common to CG, such methods are not needed therein. However, they still remain a research area within IP, PR, CV, since their mainly using studies of human and/or animal visual systems. Due to such a dependence, other classes of filtering approaches have been actually emerging.

3.3 Overall smoothing

Given an ideal noise-free image I(x,y) alterred by additively superimposed noise N(x,y), the output O(x,y) we get from by convolving it with F(x,y) is

$$O(x,y) = (I(x,y) + N(x,y)) * F(x,y) \quad (18)$$

$$= I(x,y) * F(x,y) + N(x,y) * F(x,y) \quad (19)$$

Whereas the second term in the above sum were to smooth noise, the former one would smear edges. Hence, F(x,y) were desired to be a NSEP one, but implementations of these two features are most often traded off between. A natural assumption would be that noise obeyed a Gaussian distribution law (see e.g., [43] for the 1D case). According to studies from the mid-'60s [104], the human eye performs a Gaussian filtering which in the 2D case is given by

$$F(x,y) = F(x)F(y) = 1/(2\pi\sigma^2)\exp[-(x^2+y^2)/(2\sigma^2)] \quad (20)$$

where σ is called spread/scale/space constant/variance/standard deviation/level of resolution of the Gaussian. Along to separability, featured by the former equality in (20), 2D Gaussian filter's properties were reviewed e.g., in [147, 146]. The opportunity of using (20)-like filters had been noticed since early. For instance, an exponential low-pass filter with cut-off frequency at some σ reminding distance D from the origin of (x,y) plane [53]:

$$F(x,y) = \exp[-(D(x,y)/D_0)]^n \quad \text{with} \quad D(x,y) = (x^2+y^2)^{1/2} \quad (21)$$

It was later extended in terms of various distance measures D(x,y) [148, 21]. As early as 1977 had been also the rather sophisticated filter of Modestino and Fries [91]:

$$\begin{aligned} F(x,y) &= (x^2+y^2)/([(x^2+y^2)+2(1-\rho)^2\lambda^2 \\ &\quad ((x^2+y^2)+(1-\rho)^2\lambda^2)^{1/2}]/[8(1-\rho)\lambda\xi]) \\ &\quad \exp[-(x^2+y^2)/2] \end{aligned} \tag{22}$$

where ρ was a correlation coefficient taken from the spatial evaluation of random amplitudes (degrees of correlation across an edge), $\xi \approx \sigma^2/\sigma_n^2$ was the signal-to-noise ratio of edge structure with respect to background noise and λ was the number of events (edges) per sampled (unit) distance.

To implement this filter, a 2D Z-transform (see e.g., [2]) had been used. Similar methods, connected to recursive filters, were successfully reprised later [34, 35, 36].

ED in O(x,y) given by (18), where F(x,y) given by (20) is used for convolution, means computing local maxima in pixel intensity changes. That is, getting maximum gradient magnitudes, or finding out peaks of the first derivative, of the filtered image O(x,y). This principle may be alternatively stated as detecting zero-crossings in the second derivative (i.e., Laplacian) of the filtered image O(x, y).

First derivative approaches

The most significant contributions in improving the original Canny approach (section 2.3) seem to have been carried out in [34, 39]. First, the infinite impulse response (IIR) instead of the FIR filter were considered, thus different boundary conditions being used. These ones, along to a rigourous performance analysis, finally led him to write the optimal filter as being

$$f(x) = Sx\exp(-\alpha \mid x \mid) \tag{23}$$

where S was the slope of f(x) at the origin and the positive real α was the only parameter to adjust the filter. (23) might be compared to an exponential noise distribution law (see e.g., [43]). Actually, it were a modified one, having x as parameter and α as appropriate exponent variable. Performing integration over it, we get:

$$F(x) = (-S/\alpha^2)(\alpha \mid x \mid +1)\exp(-\alpha \mid x \mid) \tag{24}$$

The next step, to have been crucially achieved, relied on this filter's implementation in a recursive manner by means of Z-transform. A key to this approach was also in avoiding to straightforwardly perform convolution. Just few multiplications and additions were needed instead. Canny had proposed the following operators to be applied over an image in order to detect edges [18, 19]:

$$X(x,y) = f(x)F(y) \tag{25}$$

and

$$Y(x,y) = f(y)F(x) \tag{26}$$

where F and f are to be taken from (20) and (1), respectively. Deriche's ones looked in turn like:

$$X(x,y) = (-S^2/\alpha^2)x[exp(-\alpha \mid x \mid)](\alpha \mid y \mid +1)exp(-\alpha \mid y \mid) \tag{27}$$

$$Y(x,y) = (-S^2/\alpha^2)y[exp(-\alpha \mid y \mid)](\alpha \mid x \mid +1)exp(-\alpha \mid x \mid) \tag{28}$$

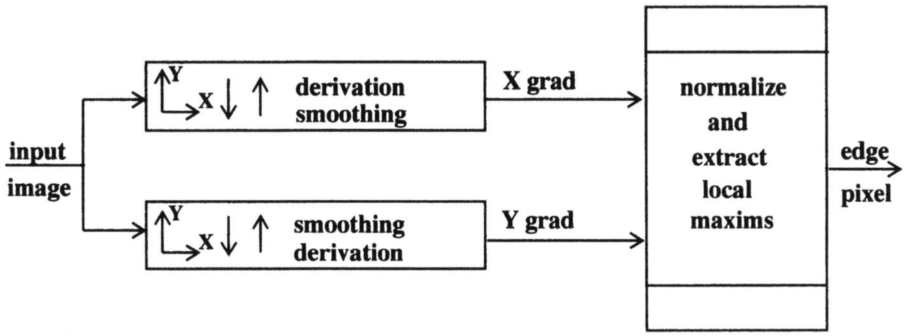

FIGURE 10. The principle of recursive filtering ED

Given the separability featured by (27) and)28), these operators were implemented as a 2D recursive filter. To convolve the image with X(x,y), first a derivation in the horizontal direction was performed using f(x) given by (23). The resulting image was then vertically smoothed with F(y) taken from (24). A reciprocal technique was applied to convolve the input image with Y(x,y) (figure 10). A result is given in figure 11.

Another optimal operator was found in [122]. Its expression is close to one of Deriche's results. The French researcher was led to (23) by getting, among others, the solution of a differential equation as

$$f(x) = (S/\omega)[\exp(-\alpha \mid x \mid)] \sin(\omega x) \tag{29}$$

where S and α are the same from (23) and ω is a positive real. Since he had found that the best trade-off between criteria 1 and 2 (section 2.3) occurred for ω close to zero, Deriche was allowed to put $[\sin(\omega x)]/\omega \approx x$, thus getting (23). Apart from him, the Chinese researchers kept on using the trigonometric function in the filter expression they had got:

$$f(x, \omega_0) = [\exp(-p \mid x \mid)] \cos(\omega_0 x) \tag{30}$$

ED by Canny's approach was applied in [90, 129, 184]. An unexpected application was in ...music feeling analysis: Canny's operator extracted attack note candidates from a time-frequency map [77]. A hardware implementation of Canny's operator using FIRs was reported in [47].

Applications of Deriche's approach are in [38, 37, 62, 111, 111]. It is noticeable that not only proposed Deriche an operator and found he its rather simple algorithmic operation, but also that he thought of its hardware implementation [39]. One version relied on data flow being divided in order to parallelize computation of X and Y (Fig. 12). Two corner turning memory (CTM) blocks were used to exchange rows and columns for image transposing and sequential accessing. Just two instead of four CTM blocks might have been used because of convolution's commutativity. But thus, next modules had to deal with a transposed instead of a true image. The second version gave up data flow concept, using instead a multiple frame memory to store the image (figure 13). Here data moved between filter and memory until ending up image smoothing, while the cross port switches (CPS) deserved interchanging data pathway. The address generator switched rows and

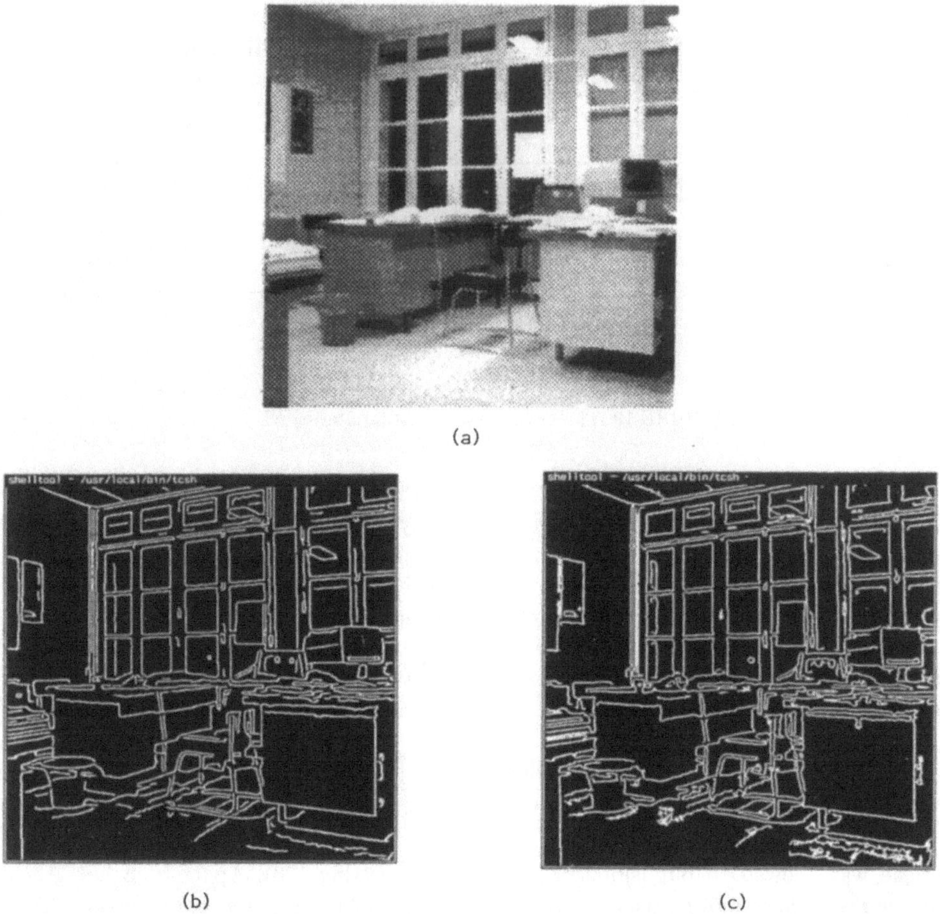

FIGURE 11. Recursive filtering ED: (a) indoor scene; (b) first derivative and (c) zero-crossing approaches ([36], IEEE ©1988, reprinted with permission)

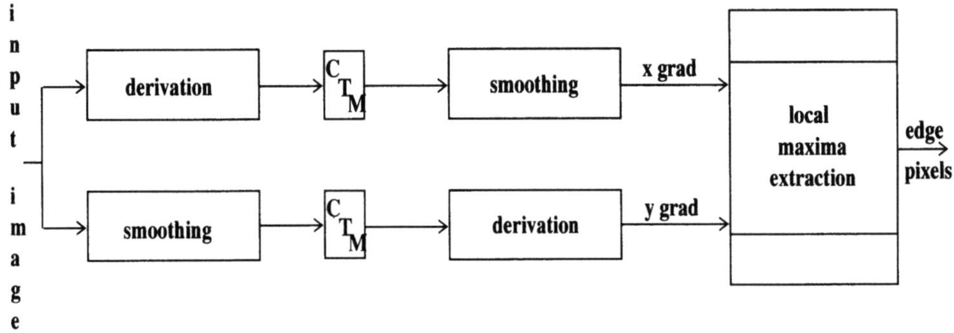

FIGURE 12. Video rate minimal configuration for ED

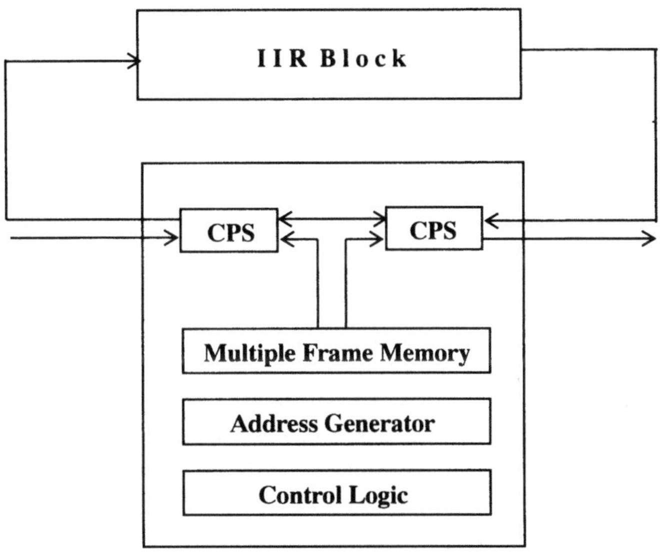

FIGURE 13. ED using MFM

columns. Though cheaper than the former version, this one was found to be not operational at video rate. The former version was subsequently implemented in [159].

New ideas have enhanced the work originated by Canny and carried on by Deriche: a generalization using a spatiotemporal concept [69, 70] and an appropriate spatial width measure for the IIR filter being incorporated into criterion 3 (section 2.3) [141].

Anyway, since we reckon ED rather a task dependent problem, we doubt that looking for optimal operators is the right way. First derivative methods might have no clear future. Not us, but two researchers, themselves having dealt with Canny/Deriche-like techniques, stated it clearly [141]: *We do not recommend using the first derivative of the Gaussian.*

Second derivative techniques

The second derivative of O(x, y) given by (18) is:

$$\begin{aligned} \nabla^2 O(x,y) &= \nabla^2([I(x,y)+N(x,y)]*[F(x,y)]) &(31)\\ &= [\nabla^2(F(x,y)]*[I(x,y)+N(x,y)] &(32)\end{aligned}$$

It follows from (20) that:

$$\nabla^2 F(x,y) = \frac{\partial^2 F}{\partial x^2} + \frac{\partial^2 F}{\partial y^2} = -(1/2\pi\sigma^4)(2 - \frac{(x^2+y^2)}{\sigma^2})\exp(-\frac{(x^2+y^2)}{2\sigma^2}) \qquad (33)$$

ED in (18) smoothed by (20) is equivalent to finding zero-crossings in (31), with the convolution multiplicand (33). (33) yields the Laplacian-of-Gaussian (LOG) operator introduced by Marr and Hildreth in 1980 [104]. Some results on using the LOG are in figure 14. Using the Laplacian in studying edges was found as old an approach as since Ernest Mach's time, that is, back to the turn of the 19th century. However, doubts have been expressed about making zero-crossings, a concept which was found to have both limitations and questions opened to discussion, the core of an ED theory [57].

Zero-crossings are able to detect just edge positions, discarding essential features of the pattern near the edge. Marr and Hildreth anticipated that edge not only position, but also orientation, contrast, length and width should be computed at zero-crossings. However, *What is to be done next?* remained a querry to be answered to by rather researcher than research tool itself [57]. The *local structure of image discontinuities* concept might be considered as refining this theory [87].

Zero-crossings may displace detected edges, or even fail to detect edges, under certain conditions. Points of inflections having also zero second derivatives, spurious edges are detected. Such phenomena are called phantoms (i.e., false visualisations of patterns) and subjective contours [57, 67]. Noise performance of LOG was analyzed in [168, 176].

Were zero-crossings a choice, LOG's straightforward implementation would be rather computationally expensive. LOG's earliest implementation took about 3 hours to perform ED over a 512 x 512 x 8 bit image. One can attempt at least accurately decomposing it into Difference-of-Gaussians (DOG). This was suggested as early as 1966 by Enroth-Cugell and Robson who had been studying the receptive field structure of the ganglion cells [104]. Written as DOG, (33) would look like:

$$\nabla^2 F(x,y) = K_1^2 \exp(-(x^2+y^2)/(2\sigma_1^2)) - K_2^2 \exp(-(x^2+y^2)/(2\sigma_2^2)) \qquad (34)$$

where $K_{1,2}$ and $\sigma_{1,2}$ depend only on that σ from (33). Marr and Hildreth had been finding $\sigma_1/\sigma_2 = 1/1.6$ as an optimum ratio [104]. Following this approach and using a 32 x 32 DOG convolver chip, Nishihara and Larson reported 1s to perform ED over an 1024 x 1024 x 8 bit image [67].

A straightforward decomposition was performed by King in 1982 [67]:

$$\begin{aligned} \nabla^2 F(x,y) &= K(1-x^2/\sigma^2)\exp(-(x^2+y^2)/(2\sigma^2)) &(35)\\ &\quad +K(1-y^2/\sigma^2)\exp(-(x^2+y^2)/(2\sigma^2)) \end{aligned}$$

where $K = -1/(2\pi\sigma^4)$. Though avoiding a mere accurate approximation of (33), as to where (34) attains, though featuring separability, (35) still remains difficult for a computer to perform. For this sake, Huertas and Medioni assummed filtered images to be

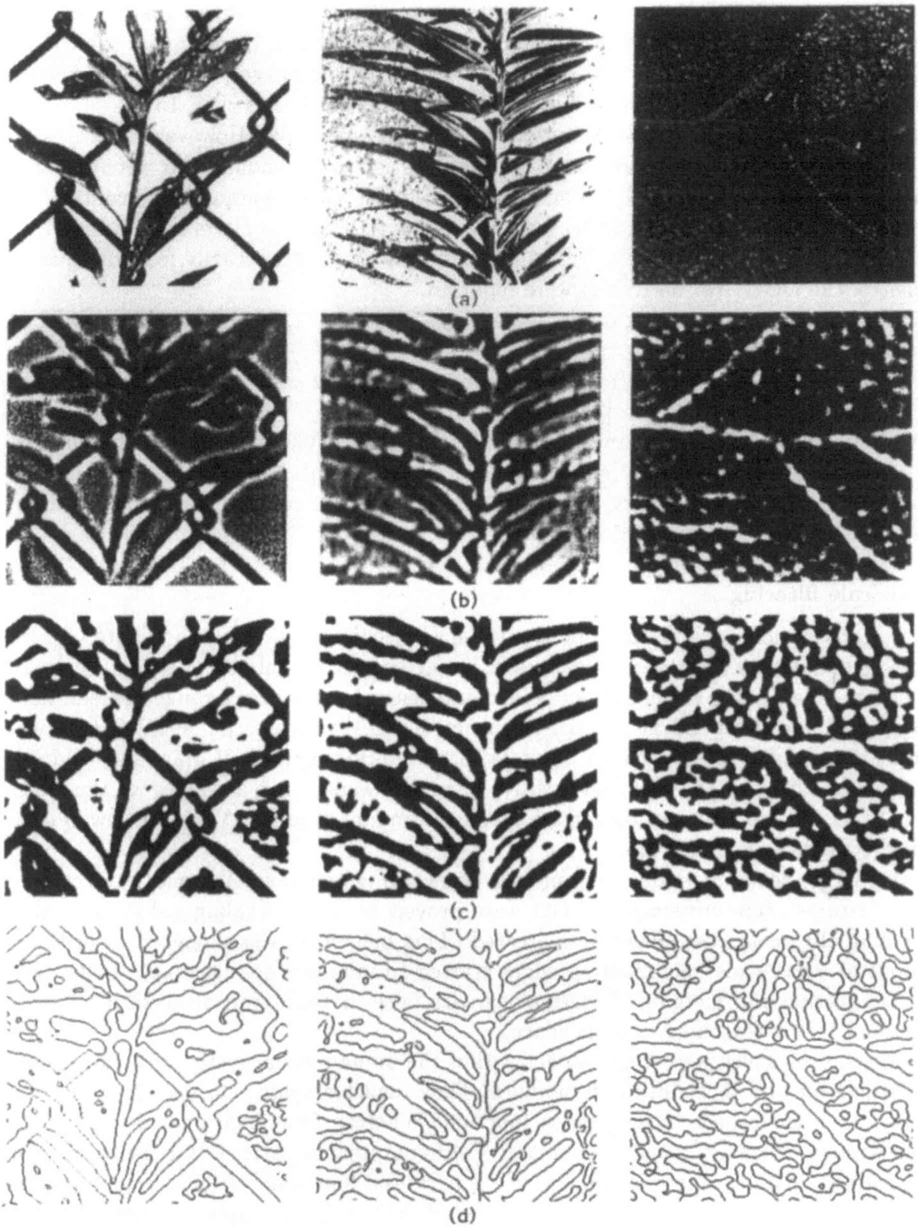

FIGURE 14. ED using LOG: (a) plants (320 x 320 pixels); (b) LOG convolution; (c) positive (white) and negative (black) values; (d) zero-crossings ([104], from VISION, by David Marr, ©1982 by W.H. Freeman and Company. Reprinted with permission)

modelled by polynomials in the neighbourhoods of zero-crossings. 3 x 3 neighbourhoods and 5 x 5 or 9 x 9 convolution Gaussian filters were used, which shows that sometimes overall filters themselves might be considered local filters as well. Durations of a few minutes were reported to perform ED over a 512 x 512 x 8 bit image. Nowadays hardware implementations perform zero-crossing detection within about $1\mu s$ [151, 157].

A DOG (34)-like skillful approximation was worked out in [35]. However, according to the manner the DOG was found into, two further variables depending on σ were involved in filter's adjustment, whereas (34) actually reveals just σ as a parameter to control the filter. A result of applying this DOG implemented with recursive filters is in figure 11.

A refinement was attempted in [5]. A (34)-like result was got, actually featuring just σ to control the DOG. Yet no results were reported.

Applications of zero-crossing detection are in [8, 49, 51, 101, 164]. 3D versions of LOG were used in [64, 100, 181].

New methods of taking edge/no edge decisions when using zero-crossings came out into theory: circular autocorrelation [24] and regularization [52].

We do not expect significant approaches to further occur. What is to be expected instead are gaps' filling in and further refinements of Marr-Hildreth's theory. But these seem to have been started within a new topic that had emerged from zero-crossing approaches: filtering at multiple scales of resolution.

Multi-scale filtering

It was Marr's vision study framework that these ED techniques were also originated by. He stated as early as 1976: intensity changes in pictures must be isolated at several scales of resolution. The human visual system detects intensity changes over a range of resolution, using up to five independent, spatial-frequency-tuned, bandpass channels [104]. It was Witkin to have pioneered research on scale space filtering in 1983. If Marr and Hildreth proposed in 1980 just the first four positive integer powers of two as values for the scales of the LOG, Witkin's suggestion consisted of a continuum of scales. A brief review of later in-field contributions is in [146].

Using larger scales σ, major contours are extracted, whereas smaller ones extract finer image features. Zero-crossings of LOG were proved to have a scaling behaviour: more increasing the scale, less edges were created. This behaviour was analyzed in order to find out at what scale neighbouring edges started to influence the response of the LOG [98]. Dislocation and merging of edges along with false contours were studied. Rules were driven out into a reasoning in scale space.

Two types of scales were found to act within the human visual system [57]. Structural ones reside into its most intimate modules. They depict a system to visualized pattern interaction with respect to a distance function. Whereas functional ones do not reside within system. They are not just properties of either system or pattern. It is the interaction between system and pattern which actually generates a functional scale as a quantization of system's behaviour towards overall features of pattern (e.g., length). A question may now arise: Is not such an interaction actually a context-dependent ED, whereas multi-scale filtering has been called a context-free approach? Our answer is left up to the end of this paper.

The LOG filtered input image can be determined up to a scaling constant, from its zero-crossing set, under certain conditions. Since the zero-crossing set looked like fingerprints in the (x,y,σ) space (see e.g., in [72]), considerations from previous paragraphs were mathematically expressed into what was called fingerprint theorems. These ones stated the conditions for an unique determination to hold [143]. Weaknesses' removal along with improvements on early contributions within this topic were proposed in [110, 172].

A simple scheme of combining edge data at multiple scales of resolution, featuring both noise immunity of larger scaled filters and edge fidelity of smaller scaled ones, was proposed in [146]. This scheme relied on locating edges at local maxima output by the gradient of Gaussian filter. Thus, it was inspired by Canny's work, though being not conceived from an optimality criterion. Since it used local peaks instead of zero- crossings, this multiresolution Gaussian ED approach has been an alternative to the scale space representation of Witkin. Assumming that a set of increasingly ordered scales σ has been chosen so that their corresponding Gaussian filters could be cascaded, the algorithm steps could be:

Algorithm 3.1 (Multiresolution Gaussian ED)

1. *For each σ smooth the input image according to (18).*
2. *For each filtered image compute the gradient magnitude according to (5).*
3. *Compute the product of the gradient magnitudes.*
4. *Compute the gradient orientation (6) for the largest filter and reduce the orientation to one of the four pairs of octants considered counterclockwise from zero.*
5. *Perform non-maxima suppression on the product of the gradient magnitudes, with a neighbourhood size four times the largest σ.*

Also aiming to gather edge knowledge at various scales into unified concepts were: Laplacian multilayer representation [72], also giving up zero-crossings and proposing a nonlinear operator (ideal Laplacian) instead, Gaussian pyramid [16, 17], grouping operations on symbolic shape tokens residing in a scale space blackboard data structure [144], spatiotemporal edge focussing [156], wavelet maxima representation [103], primary raster [86], maxima of absolute curvature of the boundary function featured at all scales [135], scale space tree [160].

Applications of multi-scale filtering are in [33, 41, 54, 80, 119, 143, 158, 174, 185].

A hardware implementation of the scale space has been removing the high cost of previous computational approaches [134]. Four main modules were used (figure 15): LOG(x,y), Gaussian filter F(x,y), normalizer N(x,y) and zero-crossing detector Z(x,y). The LOG block (figure 15) has an operating principle somewhat resemblant to the one in figure 10. The scale space chip fully exploited Gaussian's main properties (symmetry, separability and scaling). It is likely to have been the fastest among those reported in litterature. 12.5 ms were reported to perform ED over a 512 x 512 x 8 bit image. The spatiotemporal concept was already built into hardware too [118].

A considerable research interest has been spawned into both analysis and applications of multi-scale filtering. However, introducing multi-scale approaches, an ambiguity also comes into, since using each time a new scale needs also a different description. This is inherent and unavoidable. Not the removal of ambiguity is the actual goal of providing descriptions (such a purpose being alternatively looked for by approaches in Section 5.1), but to manage and to diminish this ambiguity. And it is to this point that we expect the focussing of future research interests. Multi-scale filtering's shortcomings (in appropriately selecting a scale under certain conditions and in linking edge data recovered at different scales) would still be the topics to concentrate on. One might even expect that works over

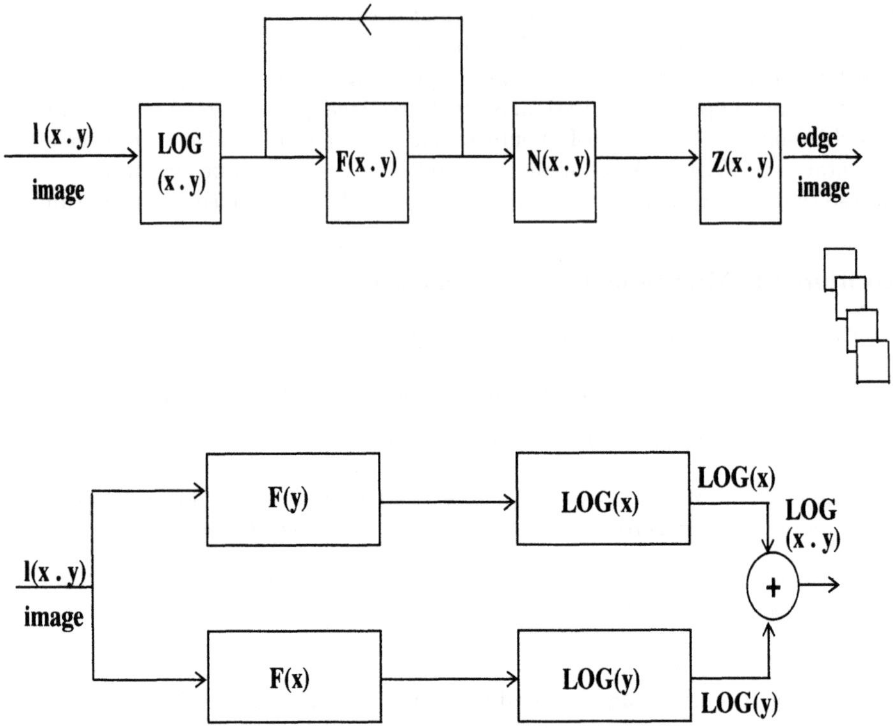

FIGURE 15. ED by scale space filtering: (a) 2D scale space and (b) 2D LOG convolution blocks

the last decade (mainly studies like [98]) would help to build up a modern multi-scale theory of ED.

It almost makes no sense to mention that, given the different intrinsical natures of both filtering approaches and synthesised images, methods in Section 3 are neither suited for, nor even needed into, CG. CV is their main field to fertilize, though a spreading of their applications has been also noticed within PR and IP.

4 Edge fitting using little a priori knowledge

Two major contributions, gapped by almost a decade between, are the roots of edge fitting (EF) methods. It was first Hough's transform to have been pattented in 1962 among other PR methods [10]. It uses analytical expressions and parameterisations of lines and curves. Next, Hueckel's operator, proposed in 1971, determined a certain distance measure from the center of a circular configuration, using a best fit criterion to extract 2D step edges [91].

4.1 Hough transform methods

Line or curve detection may involve a coordinate transformation into a picture, such that all points belonging to that line or curve were mapped into a single location in the transformed coordinate space. Thus, overall features would be mapped into easier to be detected local ones.

Straight line detection assumes points having a high likelihood of lying on linear frontiers to have been selected in a previous stage. By means of the Hough technique, they are organized into straight lines. They are treated at once and rated as a pencil of straight lines: 1) passing through a given point or 2) having a given slope [138].

Straight lines may be written in the *image space (x,y)*

$$y = sx + i, \qquad s - slope, \qquad i - intercept \tag{36}$$

For a fixed point $P_k(x_k, y_k)$ in the image space, (36) becomes the equation of a line in the *parameter space (s,i)*. A second fixed point $P_l(x_l, y_l)$ would have a corresponding associated line in this parameter space too. The intersection of the two lines in the parameter space would be a point that maps the straight line passing through P_k and P_l. Were m so called characteristic points in the image space, $k = 1/m, C_m^2 = m(m-1)/2$ straight line segments from the image space would be mapped.

From the above considerations [10, 97, 138], a line detection algorithm might be derived:

Algorithm 4.1 (Line Detection Using Hough Transform)

1. *Set appropriate maximum and minimum values for s, i to quantize the parameter space.*

2. *Dimension an accumulator array A(i,s) and initialize its elements to zero.*

3. *For each (x_k, y_k) in a gradient image (such that its magnitudes exceed a given threshold) increment all elements in the accumulator array along the appropriate line: $A(i,s) := A(i,s) + 1$, for $i = -sx + y$ within the bounds of digitization.*

4. *Values of the elements in the accumulator providing a measure of the number of points on the line, detect among them local maxima corresponding to collinear points in the image space.*

If a circle given by (15) were to be detected, then elements with x_0, y_0, r lying on a surface of a cone would be incremented in Step 3. If gradient direction is integrated in this algorithm, considerable decreasing in the amount of computation can be fulfilled, since only points near (x_0, y_0) need to be incremented [10]. Differentiating (15) with respect to x and solving for x, y between the result and (15), we obtain after all

$$x = x_0 \pm r \sin\phi \tag{37}$$

and

$$y = y_0 \pm r \cos\phi \tag{38}$$

where $\phi(x)$ is the gradient orientation returned by an edge operator, with $\tan\phi(x) = dy/dx$. A result is given in figure 16.

Step 3 may be changed: 1) convolving gradient image with a circular template of 1s at a fixed radius r and 0s otherwise, a part of $A(x_0, y_0, r)$ resulting; 2) incrementing by a function of gradient, yet giving phantom lines because of few bright points, or missing coherent boundaries since their dimness.

If an ellipse given by

$$\frac{(x-x_0)^2}{a^2} + \frac{(y-y_0)^2}{b^2} = 1 \tag{39}$$

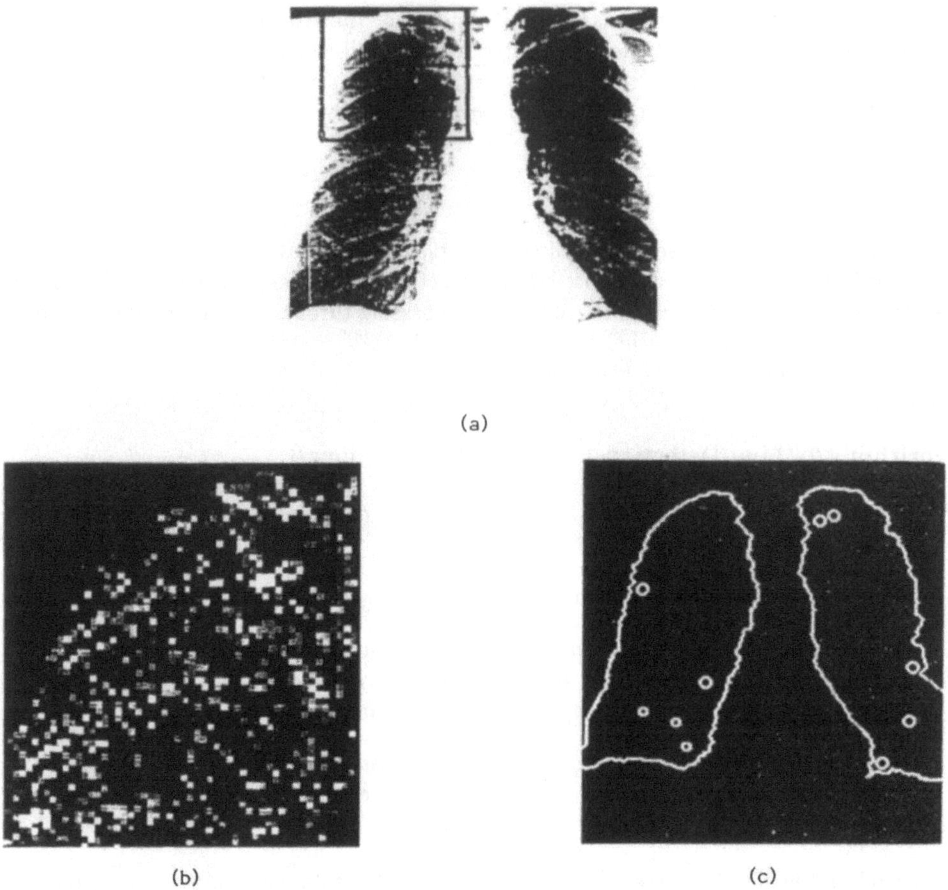

FIGURE 16. Applying Hough technique for circular shapes (tumors in chest radiographs): (a) radiograph; (b) accumulator array for r = 3; (c) maxima detection's result ([10], CGIP ©1976, reprinted with permission)

with (x,y) edge point (and x_0, y_0, a, b parameters) were to be detected, then, as in circle's case, Step 3 might be reformulated like: For each (x,y) taken from

$$x = x_0 \pm \frac{a}{[1 + b^2/(a^2 \tan^2 \phi)]^{1/2}} \tag{40}$$

$$y = y_0 \pm \frac{b}{[1 + (a^2 \tan^2 \phi)/b^2]^{1/2}} \tag{41}$$

increment the element in the parameter space

$$(a, b, x_0, y_0) : A(a, b, x_0, y_0) := A(a, b, x_0, y_0) + 1$$

For all m(m-1)/2 pairwise combinations of edge elements, the four parameters can be exactly found by substituting $(x_k, y_k), (x_l, y_l)$ in (39) and in its first derivative with respect to x.

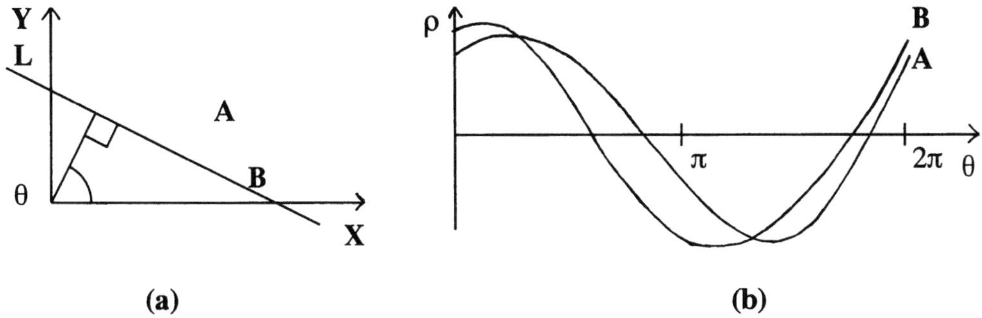

FIGURE 17. Hough transform: (a) (x,y) - image and (b) (ρ, θ) - parameter spaces

The same algorithm is valid when the line is better parameterised as

$$\rho = x\cos\theta + y\sin\theta \tag{42}$$

which avoids the case of s becoming infinite in (36). One might see that $-\pi/2 < \theta < \pi/2$ or $0 < \theta < \pi$ and $-N\sqrt{2} < \rho < N\sqrt{2}$ for an N x N image space could be taken. Straight lines intersecting at an arbitrary point (x,y) in image space (figure 17) are mapped into a sinusoidal, Hough curve, defined by (42), in the (ρ, θ) parameter space (figure 17). One point in the (ρ, θ) parameter space maps exactly one straight line in the image space. Back to our set of m $P_k(x_k, y_k)$ points, $k = 1 \div m$, this fact looks quite clear when substituting successively (x_k, y_k) and (x_l, y_1) in (42) [97]:

$$\theta = \arctan[\frac{(x_k - x_l)}{(y_l - y_k)} \tag{43}$$

$$\mid \rho \mid = \frac{\mid x_k y_l - x_l y_k \mid}{[(x_k - x_l)^2 + (y_k - y_l)^2]^{1/2}} \tag{44}$$

One may see (figure 17) that any pair of Hough curves intersect just once in $\theta \in [0, \pi]$ [115].

Uniqueness of the pedal point (x_r,y_r), figure 17, might also be exploited for a parameter space. The straight line L passing through this point is depicted by

$$y - y_r = -(x_r/y_r)(x - x_r) \tag{45}$$

which could be easily rewritten as

$$(x_r - x/2)^2 + (y_r - y/2)^2 = (x^2 + y^2)/4 \tag{46}$$

Thus, a point (x_k, y_k) in the image space (x,y) would be mapped into a circle having centre $(x_k/2, y_k/2)$ and radius $(x_k^2 + y_k^2)^{1/2}/2$. The point (x_r, y_r) of a given straight line could only be located on this circle. The accumulator array is then incremented at this location either by one or by a given amount [178].

Several developments were reviewed in [10]. As for modified Hough approaches, we noticed: successive decomposition of Hough parameter nets into subnets [161], labelled and hierarchical Hough transforms [20, 133], 3D Hough space decomposition into two 2D spaces, one used for early filtering and one for appropriate peak selection [125], parameterisation generalisation [44], randomized Hough transform [82]. As for applications: convex hull (i.e., minimum convex polygon including all given points inside or on its border in the image space) extraction [115], wheel silhouette detection [90], spatial description [182], document interpretation [63], parametric curve detection [126]. As for Step 3 hardware improvements: image grey level interpretation using registers instead of threshold selection [123], raster system using bitmaps and Boolean operations instead of accumulator array [74], parallel compressed pixels' projection [149]. As for full hardware implementations of Hough approaches: classical [3] and hierarchical [50] which was reported to perform extraction of 256 (ρ, θ) pairs from an 128 x 128 image, using an 128 x 128 multiple/single instruction multiple data machine, within about 4 ms, with about 1 additional ms to combine the results.

The Hough technique is useful in curve detection when there is just few knowledge about boundary location, but shape can be analytically expressed. Prediction of Hough transform's performances was considered in [102].

This method was found earlier to have relative immunity to both gaps in curves and noise [10]. More recently, it was given up after all in an ellipse extraction application [163]. Ellipse contour broken with gaps was noticed. It covered rather a ring area than an ellipse locus. Also the so called bucket array limitation was noticed: either a peak of new feature parameters might have been not found, or accurate parameters fitting an ellipse had been difficultly obtained.

Hough space parameter distribution was proved non-homogeneous and non-equiprobable due to discretization of the image space. Only for the case of detecting parallel straight lines has been a correction provided. Furthermore, Hough method was found suited only for images which were scanned by relatively large windows. However, computational effort increases with the size of its parameter space [97].

For objects having no simple analytical form but a particular silhouette, due to Hough technique's similarity to a template matching, generalized algorithms have been proposed.

4.2 Generalized Hough transforms

A former generalization of the Hough transform, proposed by Merlin and Farber in 1975, was intended for detecting arbitrary shapes. It had an $o(q^2mn)$ computational complexity, where m, n were the number of points of model's and shape's boundaries, respectively, and q the quantization of the parameter space. A later reformulation [99] assummed model's and shape's boundaries to be represented by sets of points like traced chains of boundary pixels M for the model, and N for the shape:

$$M = \{m_i \mid m_i = (x_i, y_i)^T, i = 1/m\} \tag{47}$$

$$N = \{n_i \mid n_i = (u_i, v_i)^T, i = 1/n\} \tag{48}$$

where $(x_i, y_i), (u_i, v_i)$ are points' coordinates, respectively, in the image space.

A set of parameters (S, θ, x_0, y_0) could match every pair (m_i, n_i) of correspondent model set M to shape set N points

$$\mathbf{m}_i = S\mathbf{T}\mathbf{n}_i + (x_0, y_0)^T \tag{49}$$

S being a scale factor, θ a rotation angle and $\mathbf{T}$

$$\mathbf{T} = \begin{bmatrix} \cos\theta & -\sin\theta \\ \sin\theta & \cos\theta \end{bmatrix} \tag{50}$$

Merlin-Farber's algorithm could now be rewritten as:

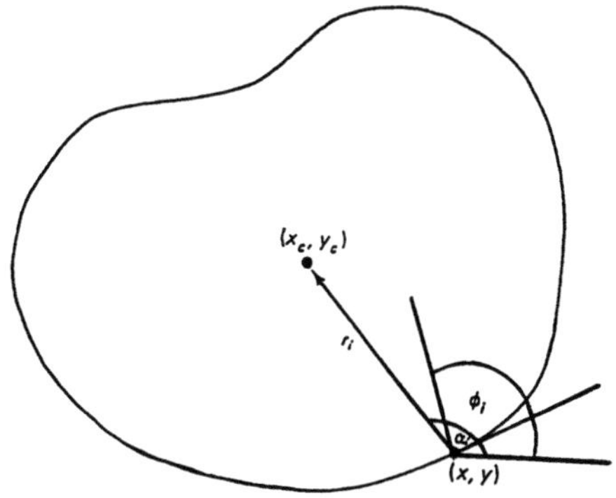

FIGURE 18. Geometric notations for the R-table

Algorithm 4.2 (New version of Merlin-Farber's Algorithm)

1. *For every pair* $(\mathbf{m}_i \in \mathbf{M}, \mathbf{n}_j \in \mathbf{N})$
2. *For any possible* S *assummed to be quantized by* q *steps*
3. *For any possible* θ *assummed to be quantized by* q *steps*
4. *Set up a 2D accumulator array A(x,y). Compute* $(x_0, y_0)^T$ *from (49). Increment* $A((x_0, y_0)^T)$.
5. *Local maxima in* $A((x_0, y_0)^T)$ *point out to instances of the model in the image.*

An early generalization (from 1976) of Ballard had a computational complexity of $o(m^2n)$ [10, 99]. Sklansky (in 1978) found it equivalent to a convolution or cross-correlation between model and shape boundaries.

The location of a reference point within a shape could be computed using both distance r_i from this point to an arbitrary one on the boundary and gradient orientation ϕ_i at the boundary point (figure 18). Thus, an edge point (x,y) having gradient orientation ϕ_i constrains possible reference points to be located at $(x + r_i(\phi_i)\cos(\alpha_i(\phi_i)), y + r_i(\phi_i)\sin(\alpha_i(\phi_i)))$. Indexing all such locations by ϕ_i, a so called R-table could be built (table 2). Therefore, another generalized Hough algorithm could be derived as follows [10]:

TABLE 2. The R-Table

Orientation ϕ_i Measured from Shape Boundary to Reference Point	Set of Radius-Angle Couples (r_i, α_i)
ϕ_1	$(r_1, \alpha_1)^1$, $(r_2, \alpha_2)^1$, $\cdots$, $(r_{n1}, \alpha_{n1})^1$
ϕ_2	$(r_1, \alpha_1)^2$, $(r_2, \alpha_2)^2$, $\cdots$, $(r_{n2}, \alpha_{n2})^2$
$\vdots$	$\vdots$
ϕ_m	$(r_1, \alpha_1)^m$, $(r_2, \alpha_2)^m$, $\cdots$, $(r_{nm}, \alpha_{nm})^m$

Algorithm 4.3 (Ballard's Second Generalized Hough Transform)

1. *Set up table 2 for the shape to be located*
2. *Create an accumulator array of possible reference points* $A(x_{min}/x_{cmax}, y_{cmin}/y_{cmax})$ *and zeroize its elements.*
3. *For each edge point do*
   (a) *Compute* $\phi(x)$
   (b) *For each table entry compute possible centres* $x_c := x + r(\phi)\cos[\alpha(\phi)]$, $y_c := y + r(\phi)\sin[\alpha(\phi)]$
   (c) *Increment accumulator:* $A(x_c, y_c) := A(x_c, y_c) + 1$.
4. *Maxima in A point out to possible locations for shape.*

A result of applying this algorithm is in figure 19. Introducing scale and rotation parameters S and θ, respectively, the algorithm is then modified as follows:

Algorithm 4.4 (Algorithm 4.3 modified)

2. *Accumulator is now* $A(x_{cmin}/x_{cmax}, y_{cmin}/y_{cmax}, S_{min}/S_{max}, \theta_{min}/\theta_{max})$.

3(b). *Becomes: For each table entry* ϕ *do For each S and* $x_c := x + r(\phi)S\cos[\alpha(\phi) + \theta]$ $y_c := y + r(\phi)S\sin[\alpha(\phi) + \theta]$

3(c) *Becomes:* $A(x_c, y_c, S, \theta) := A(x_c, y_c, S, \theta) + 1$

Using Ma and Chen's analytical form, this algorithm could be rewritten as:

Algorithm 4.5 (New Version of Ballard's Second Generalized Hough Transform)

1. *For every pair* $(\mathbf{m}_i \in \mathbf{M},\ \mathbf{n}_j \in \mathbf{N})$
2. *For any possible S*
3. *For any possible* θ
4. *If* $\theta_{\mathrm{mi}} - \theta_{\mathrm{nj}} = \theta + e$, *e being a threshold*
5. *Set up a 2D accumulator array A(x,y). Compute* $(x_0, y_0)^T$ *from (49). Increment* $A((x_0, y_0)^T)$.
6. *Local maxima in* $A((x_0, y_0)^T)$ *point out to instances of the model in the image.*

It was estimated to have had at least an o(qmn) computational complexity [99].

Turney used in 1985 a subtemplate given by a segment of slope/arc length curves instead of simply restricting slope as local property. Ma and Chen exploited in 1987 the edge point pair information which defined possible scale factors and rotation angles. Ballard's 1976 o(m^2n) computational complexity was again attained to. One year later, they fulfilled an algorithm of computational complexity o(mn) [99].

Using slope and curvature as local properties, iterations with respect to S and θ in Algorithms 4.2 and 4.5 were avoided. A parametrical representation of corresponding points $\mathbf{m}_i, \mathbf{n}_i$

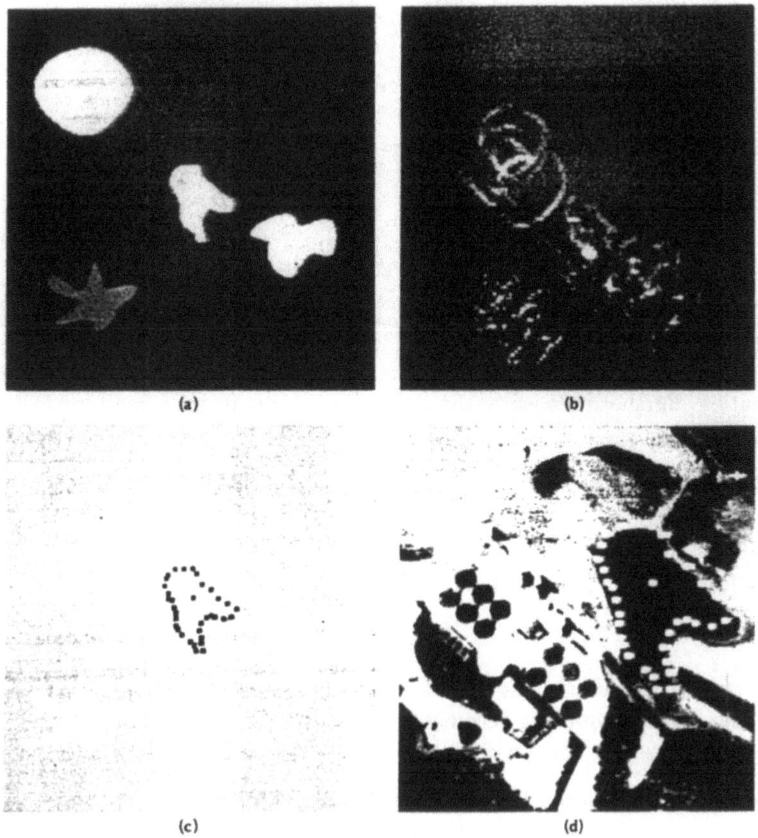

FIGURE 19. Applying generalized Hough technique: (a) synthesised image; (b) generalized Hough transform $A(x_c, y_c)$ for the central shape; (c) detected shape; (d) the same shape in some aerial image ([10], CGIP ©1976, reprinted with permission)

$$\mathbf{m}_i = (x(t_i), y(t_i)^T) \tag{51}$$

and

$$\mathbf{n}_i = (u(t_i), v(t_i)^T) \tag{52}$$

turns (49) into

$$\begin{bmatrix} x(t_i) \\ u(t_i) \end{bmatrix} = S\mathbf{T} \begin{bmatrix} u(t_i) \\ v(t_i) \end{bmatrix} + \begin{bmatrix} x \\ y \end{bmatrix} \tag{53}$$

Taking first/second derivatives of (53) with respect to t

$$\begin{bmatrix} x' \\ y' \end{bmatrix} = S\mathbf{T} \begin{bmatrix} u' \\ v' \end{bmatrix} \tag{54}$$

and

$$\begin{bmatrix} x'' \\ y'' \end{bmatrix} = S\mathbf{T} \begin{bmatrix} u'' \\ v'' \end{bmatrix} \tag{55}$$

and assumming slope angles on $\mathbf{m}_i, \mathbf{n}_i$ to be α_i, β_i, respectively

$$\tan \alpha_i = y'/x' \tag{56}$$

and

$$\tan \beta_i = v'/u' \tag{57}$$

it comes from (56) by (57), (54) and (50) that after all

$$\tan(\alpha_i - \beta_i) = \tan \theta \tag{58}$$

That is, tangent vectors of boundary points of the shape rotate with the same angle of shape's rotation. Furthermore, since the curvatures on $\mathbf{m}_i, \mathbf{n}_i$ are given by

$$\xi_i = (x'y'' -' x'')/(x'^2 + y'^2)^{3/2} \tag{59}$$

$$\gamma_i = (uv'' - v'u'')/(u'^2 + v'^2)^{3/2} \tag{60}$$

it follows from (59) by (60), (54) and (55) that after all

$$S = \gamma_i/\xi_i \tag{61}$$

That is, scaling a circle having radius r (hence curvature 1/r), with a factor S, its radius becomes Sr (its curvature becomes 1/Sr). A new version of the generalized Hough transform could now be written as:

Algorithm 4.6 (Ma-Chen's Generalized Hough Transform)

1. *For every pair* $(\mathbf{m}_i \in \mathbf{M}, \mathbf{n}_j \in \mathbf{N})$
2. *Set up two 2D accumulator arrays:* $A(x, y), B(S, \theta)$.
3. *Compute* (S, θ, x_0, y_0) *from (49), (58) and (61). Increment* $A(x_0, y_0)$ *and* $B(S, \theta)$.
4. *Local maxima in* $A(x_0, y_0)$ *and* $B(S, \theta)$ *point out to instances of the model in the image.*

Applications of Ballard's second generalized Hough transform: shape matching [88], PR in CAD [154], stereo vision [120]. A full hardware implementation is in [3].

Generalized Hough transform is a very robust method when dealing with partially occluded curves or noisy edge pixels, however being drawbacked by severe computational demand.

Given their assumming lines and curves into images, Hough methods may also be applied in CG. Applied either in CG, PR or CV, they request a high computational effort. Advances in Hough transforms themselves will be obtained just by exploiting new curve geometry approaches and analytical descriptions. However, some among such advances might be traded-off by higher computational complexities. So that Hough techniques might be no more a real choice in the near future.

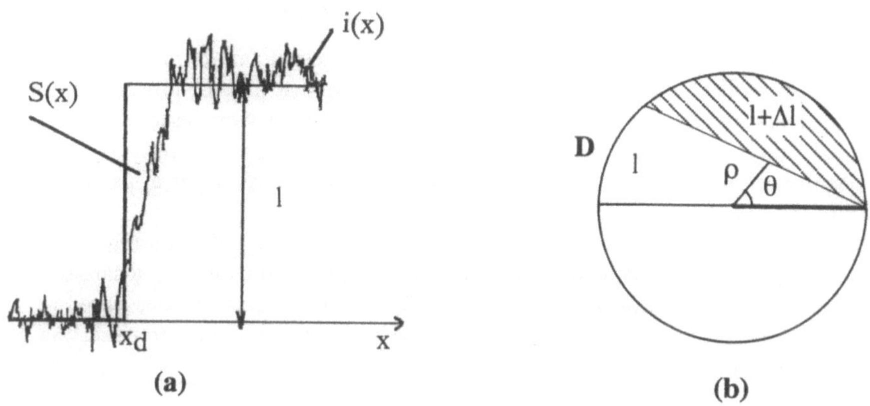

FIGURE 20. Step EF: (a) 1D; (b) 2D and Hueckel's operator

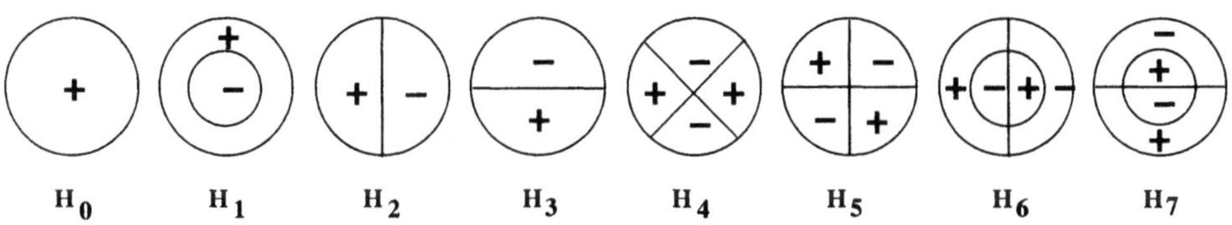

FIGURE 21. H_i functions of Hueckel's operator

4.3 Hueckel operator techniques

(42) was also used to segment a disk D supposed to detect a step edge between two adjacent grey levels l and $l + \delta l$ (figure 20). A 2D step function was defined [91, 132]

$$S(x,y) = \begin{cases} 1 & \text{if } x\cos\theta + y\sin\theta < \rho \\ 1 + \delta 1 & \text{if } x\cos\theta + y\sin\theta > \rho \\ 0 & \text{otherwise} \end{cases} \tag{62}$$

to approximate the image I(x,y) within a least squares error

$$\mathcal{E} = \int_b \int [I(x,y) - S(x,y)]^2 dxdy = min \tag{63}$$

where actually we have abridged $S(x,y) = S(x,y,\mathbf{l},\rho,\theta,\delta\mathbf{l})$.

Hueckel performed as early as 1971 a 2D EF procedure. Image points were expanded within a circle in a set of 2D basic functions $H_i(x,y)$ by a Fourier series, where Fourier coefficients for I(x,y) and S(x,y) were given by:

$$i_i(x,y) = int \int_b H_i(x,y) I(x,y) dxdy \tag{64}$$

$$s_i(x,y) = \int\int_b H_i(x,y)S(x,y)dxdy \tag{65}$$

The H_i functions, $i = 0/7$ (figure 21), were found to be resemblant to models of receptor fields in cat cortex [91]. + and - are signs of functions, whereas lines denote zero-crossings in D area. Thus, it also becomes very interesting that H_1 is very resemblant to LOG [67, 98, 104]. $H_{0,2,3}$ were each found to behave like a Roberts edge detector [137]. Other properties were proved for various neighbourhoods in [13, 138]. A result of using Hueckel operator on an image is in figure 3.

Refinements on fitting lines to edge data were proposed in [71, 139]. Another technique considered EF as two independent consecutive steps: edge direction and localisation. It proposed an edge model invariant to blurring [75]. The edge detector was based on the informative projection choice criterion. A best fit criterion was searched to select the best projection of the rotation

$$I_\alpha(x,y) = I(x\cos\alpha + y\sin\alpha, -x\sin\alpha + y\cos\alpha) \quad \alpha \in [0, 2\pi] \tag{66}$$

of image I(x,y), this one being assummed to be square integrable and vanishing outside the disk D on the real plane R^2. The best projection was to be chosen from a finite set given by the Radon transform of I(x,y):

$$p(\alpha,x) = \int I_\alpha(x,y)dy \tag{67}$$

For a step edge, the error criterion was finally written:

$$\mathcal{E}(I,\alpha) = \int_{-1}^{0} p(\alpha,x)dx - \int_0^1 p(\alpha,x)dx \tag{68}$$

while the edge detector was suggested as being

$$E(I) = 1 - \int_0^\pi \frac{\mathcal{E}(I,\alpha)d\alpha - \min\mathcal{E}(I,\alpha)}{\pi(\max\mathcal{E}(I,\alpha) - \min\mathcal{E}(I,\alpha))} \tag{69}$$

(69) gives magnitudes, whereas orientations are taken from maxima of (68) with respect to α. Yet no results were reported on the implementation of this approach. Hueckel operators were used in [32].

Not only line but also curve fitting using best fit criteria were considered. In [56] parameters to control the shape of the contour were determined by minimizing an appropriate functional called *radial inertia*:

$$\mathcal{P}[I(x,y), D, c(\theta), x_0, y_0] = \sum_{i\in D} I(x_i,y_i)(r_i - c(\theta_i))^2 \tag{70}$$

where polar coordinates r_i and θ_i of pixels (x_i, y_i) are given by (15) and $\theta_i = \arctan[(y_i - y_0)/(x_i - x_0)]$. D is now the set of all values i labelling pixels within a bounded subdomain of the 2D Euclidean space. $c(\theta_i)$ is a sample of a continuous positive 2π periodical function expressed by basic splines.

Only objects having radially connected contours (i.e., crossed once and only once by any radius) were considered. A sinusoidal function simulated a multi-lobe contour as a test image. An average execution time about 6 min using Fortran 77 on PDP 11/45 over a 512 x 512 x 8 bit image was reported.

Fourier descriptors and curvature descriptions were also used in [65, 73, 150, 171].

Due to their dealing with line and curve fitting, such methods using best fit criteria are also suited for CG. As for CV, though finding new best fit criteria is still a research topic, we do not believe in a spreading of these techniques into applications in the near future.

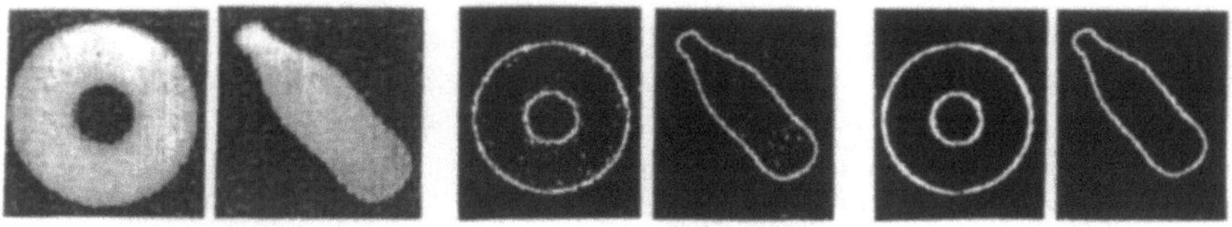

FIGURE 22. Context-free versus context-dependent ED: (a) noisy object images; detected edges using (b) zero-crossings and (c) a dynamic approach ([60], IEEE ©1988, reprinted with permission)

5 Context-Dependent ED

Two main subclasses making full use of pictorial context are discriminated: one looking for an overall best model of a boundary occurring in an image and the other itself adapting an initial contour hypothesis to a boundary occurring in an image. They are just briefly and not extensively dealt with in the following, due to their having been not consistently resorted to over the last decade.

5.1 Dynamic methods

As a pure mathematical tool, dynamic programming was used for solving optimization problems where not all the variables in the evaluation function featured simultaneous interdependence. Boundary detection formulation as a dynamic programming approach is owed to Montanari. In 1971 he stated the particular problem as detecting an optimal curve of a given length in given image sizes on a basis of some figure of merit function. Three main steps were involved in [112, 113]:

Algorithm 5.1 (Montanari's Dynamic ED)

1. *Find the cost of the optimal curve of a given length ending at each pixel, using a procedure as much times as the value of the given length.*

2. *Find the global optimal end point in the image.*

3. *. Locate by backward search the other points on the chosen curve.*

Though also contributed to in the next '70s [7, 10, 105, 106, 107], Montanari's algorithm was embodied in its original form in four VLSI designs [29].

In [60] the edge context was stated for each pixel as being the set of all row monotonically increasing paths through that pixel, which in turn was assigned an edge state having the highest edge probability among all paths. Two results of this approach are compared to those of a context-free zero-crossing detector in figure 22.

Shape constraints were also embodied within cost functions in [4, 9]. Using two different vision systems, 11 and 35 s were reported on 256 x 256 x 6 bit images [9].

Among lattest contributions: simulated annealing [153] and robust detection using image sequences [162].

Considering models of optimal curves seems to be a method suited rather for (biomedical) PR. But it might be also used within CG if one does not meet with limitations due to computational complexity involved in. As for CV, conceiving and using optimality criteria should not still be a trend of context-dependent ED research from our own point of view.

5.2 Relaxation techniques

Context-dependent ED by relaxation is an iterative discrimination making use of an initial probabilistic or fuzzy knowledge about a point's belonging or not to an edge. At each iteration, decisions concerning each point are taken in parallel. They are refined at successive iterations, taking into account decisions from previous iterations on neighbouring points, that is, on a local context [138].

Initial interest seemed to have been focussing rather into carrying relaxations through a few iterations than into process convergence. Therefore, a strange behaviour of an early relaxation algorithm (from 1976) was finally noticed. Henceforth, it was only seldom that relaxation techniques have been resorted to within ED over a decade. A theoretical explanation of that early algorithm's behaviour was provided in [92]. Furthermore, a new algorithm avoiding the previous drawbacks was proposed. Resemblance to intimate processes within human visual system was also featured. Ten iterations were performed over 256 x 256 x 8 bit images within about 3 min on a VAX 780 (figure 7). Only 3 ms were estimated on a fully parallel machine.

More contributions were: multiresolution relaxation [40] and parameterised relaxation labelling [42]. An application was in extracting edges from 3D scenes [76, 177].

Due to their conceptual nature, such approaches are not suited for CG, where edge pixels are rather clearly located and their assumming as belonging or not to an edge would be rather useless. In PR and CV we might witness a revival in ED relaxation techniques, owed to enlightments brought by Levy.

6 ED Perspectives

We finally try to summarize nowadays commonly used ED techniques and to anticipate trends of in-field future research.

6.1 Currently Used Methods

For the sake of computational simplicity, several applications still widely make use just of local operators to perform ED and do not attempt resorting to more sophisticated methods.

As for the field of application, we found some definite choices. When not simply using local operators, (biomedical) PR researchers mainly resort to dynamic techniques and sometimes to Hough approaches. Performing their tasks also requires some heuristic post-processing methods to be finally used. Whereas CV researchers seem to have already given up merely using either local operators or EF techniques. Context-free overall image smoothing is what they widely use instead.

Recently they reconsidered context-dependent methods too. Contributions to a modern theory of ED also emerge from their work. Meanwhile, IP both theoreticians and practitioners attempt finding new models for masks to occur from or lines and curves to be fitted to. Masks and maybe dynamic methods are also suited for CG. EF techniques, like generalized Hough algorithms, are already in use, mainly in CAD.

Whatever the field of (applicative) research interest, apart from CG, Sobel among local operators and LOG/DOG among overall smoothing techniques are most widely used nowadays.

6.2 Future developments

Which concept will be proved as more successful in the near future: context either -free or -dependent ED, or may be a new one to occur within few years? Newcomer's answer to this dilemma would be ...context free in itself. Whereas experienced one's answer were ...context-dependent in itself. Here comes just a novice researcher's own point of view.

May we perform first a comparison between some context-free and -dependent ED techniques. Overall ED techniques deal with context's optimal filtering, whereas dynamic methods consider context's optimal use instead. The former group has originally proposed optimal filters which detected either peaks or zero-crossings. These methods have been revealing not only edges (this was obviously desired) but also ambiguities and limitations (this was not desired at all). Such drawbacks were attempted in being removed by alternative approaches using dynamic programming. But even these approaches have also been originated on a basis of an optimality criterion. However, optimality within overall smoothing has been aiming to ED itself. Whereas optimality within dynamic techniques has been pursueing a curve model as its goal.

It seems natural to us that a context-free approach would seek for an optimal operator. Though such a way would lead to some failure after all. But it seems unnatural to us that a context-dependent approach would still be seeking for an optimal model of a curve within an image.

We conclude this apparent speculation by two assertions. First, it is likely that a huge research effort might be saved by finally giving up looking for optimality criteria within ED. Second, ED is rather a context-dependent problem. If both assertions were proved to be false in the near future, ED researchers would have to be alternatively looking for an answer to a serious question: is context-dependent ED necessarily be thought of in terms of optimality?

And so we have come to draw the line and make our survey. We have dared to be positive for just two among all reviewed techniques. Gradient masks and local filters, peaks' and zerocrossings' detection, EF by all means and finally dynamic techniques have been rather rejected. It was just for multiscale filtering and relaxation approaches that true perspectives have been noticed. Was it just at random that these conclusions were met? Here at last comes an answer for both this question and the still unanswered one from section 3.3.

As for our own point of view regarding trends in ED techniques, it is our belief that it were just from these two positively valuated approaches for a modern theory of ED to occur in the near future. We would even dare to anticipate it were a kind of a context-dependent multi-scale filtering. Our assumption is based on the following ideas:

- Stephen Grossberg's hypothesis about human visual system's using two types of scales within performing an ED process: structural (system resident) and functional (occurring just temporarily as a result of the interaction between system and pattern) [57].

- C. Enroth-Cugell and J. Robson's hypothesis on retinal ganglion cells' performing a LOG/DOG filtering, a basis to keep with into multi-scale filtering [104].

- Michel Levy's neurophysiological interpretation of his relaxation algorithm [92].

- Our belief that hypothesised resident, structural scales perform a context-free multi-scale filtering. It remains to be decided whether they reside as a continuum (as suggested by Witkin) or rather as a discrete set (as proposed by Marr and Hildreth), to find out how are scales selected under certain conditions and how are to be linked different scales for recovering edge data (as formulated in [98]).

- Our belief that hypothesised functional scales' occurrence as an interaction between system and pattern is similar to a relaxation process. It is up to the deep understanding of such intimate process to discard whatever among open questions from above and/or to raise new ones to be further on answered to.

- D. Lee's proposal of an edge detector consisting of a pattern/filter pair[89].

Maybe time will be a healer for the consequences of our possible proving to have been wrong with our assumption.

7 Conclusion

First, we were leafing through pages of ED philosophy to notice various acceptances of the edge concept, contour models, criteria for good detection, steps in edge extraction and features for edge detectors to be classified according to.

Second, we proposed another classification based on particular ED techniques' being dependent of pictorial context or not. Main techniques within each group were reviewed to... contour the state-of-the-art in ED.

Third and final, we estimated trends in ED techniques.

Acknowledgements:

I am grateful to Professor Roland T. Chin (University of Wisconsin at Madison), Professor Olivier D. Faugeras (INRIA-Sophia-Antipolis, France), Professor Ramesh C. Jain (University of Michigan at Ann Arbor), Professor Takeo Kanade (Carnegie-Mellon University, Pittsburgh, Pennsylvania), Professor Alberto Martelli (Università degli Studi di Torino, Italia), Professor Ugo Montanari (Università di Pisa, Italia), David Pycock, M. Sc. (University of Birmingham, UK) and Professor Azriel Rosenfeld (University of Maryland at College Park) for having provided me with the hereby referenced works of their own/staffs. *Two vision classics* [10, 104] were gifted to me by Professor Thomas C. Henderson (University of Utah at Salt Lake City) whom I am grateful too. I also feel morally indebted to Professor Stefano Levialdi (Università degli Studi *La Sapienza*, Roma, Italia) for his kind encouragement.

8 References

[1] J.F. Abramatic. Digital image restoration. In O.D. Faugeras, editor, *Fundamentals in Computer Vision*, pages 69–90. Cambridge University Press, Cambridge, UK, 1983.

[2] J.F. Abramatic. Two-dimensional signal processing. In O.D. Faugeras, editor, *Fundamentals in Computer Vision*, pages 27–56. Cambridge University Press, Cambridge, UK, 1983.

[3] M.G. Albanesi and M. Ferretti. A space saving approach to the Hough transform. In *Proceedings of the 10th International Conference on Pattern Recognition (ICPR) (II)*, pages 472–475, June 1990.

[4] A.A. Amini, T.E. Weymouth, and D.J. Anderson. A parallel algorithm for determining two-dimensional object positions using incomplete information about their boundaries. *Pattern Recognition*, 22(10):21–28, 1989.

[5] E. Antoniu. Detecting edges with DOGs. In preparation, 1991.

[6] M. Asada, Y. Fukui, and S. Tsuji. Representing a global map for a mobile robot with relational local maps from sensory data. In *Proceedings of the 9th ICPR, 14–17 November, Rome, Italy*, pages 520–524, 1988.

[7] G.P. Ashkar and J.W. Modestino. The contour extraction problem with biomedical applications. *Computer Graphics and Image Processing*, 7(3):331–355, 1978.

[8] K. Atsuta, M. Sangworasil, and S. Kondo. A new method of estimating shape from shading by using a constraint at zero-crossings of image brightness. In *Proceedings of the 9th ICPR, 14–17 November, Rome, Italy*, pages 666–668, 1988.

[9] P.J. Azzopardi, D. Pycock, C.J. Taylor, and A.C. Wareham. An experiment in model-based boundary detection. In *Proceedings of the Alvey Conference AVC'89, UK*, pages 31–36, 1989.

[10] D.H. Ballard and C.M. Brown. *Computer Vision*. Prentice Hall Inc., Englewood Cliffs, NJ, USA, 1982.

[11] E. Bartfeld, G. Zajicek, G. Kenet, and D. Schwartz-Arad. Measuring hepatocyte reaction to dymethylnitrosamine using computerised microscopy. In *Proceedings of the 9th ICPR, 14–17 November, Rome, Italy*, pages 465–467, 1988.

[12] M.O. Berger and R. Mohr. Towards autonomy in active contour models. In *Proceedings of the 10th ICPR (I)*, pages 847–851, 1990.

[13] R.B. Boppana and A. Rosenfeld. Some properties on Hueckel-type edge operators. Technical Report TR-1178, Computer Vision Laboratory, University of Maryland, College Park, MD, USA, 1982.

[14] P. Boulanger, F. Blais, and P. Cohen. Detection of depth and orientation discontinuities in range images using mathematical morphology. In *Proceedings of the 10th ICPR (I)*, pages 729–732, 1990.

[15] G. Brugal. Pattern recognition, image processing, related data analysis and expert systems integrated in medical microscopy. In *Proceedings of the 9th ICPR*, pages 286–293, 1988.

[16] P.J. Burt. The pyramid as a structure for efficient computation. In A Rosendfeld, editor, *Multiresolution Image Processing and Analysis*, pages 6–35. Springer, New York, 1984.

[17] P.J. Burt. Attention mechanisms for vision in a dynamic world. In *Proceedings of the 9th ICPR*, pages 977–987, 1988.

[18] J.F. Canny. Finding edges and lines in images. Technical Report TR-720, Artificial Intelligence Laboratory, MIT, MA, USA, 1983.

[19] J.F. Canny. A computational approach to edge detection. *IEEE Transactions on Pattern Analysis and Machine Intelligence*, 8(6):679–698, 1986.

[20] L. Carrioli, M. Diani, and L. Lombardi. Hierarchical Hough: advantages and automatic construction of the models. In *Proceedings of the 9th ICPR*, pages 791–794, 1988.

[21] S. Castan, J. Zhao, and J. Shen. New edge detection methods based on exponential filter. In *Proceedings of the 10th ICPR (I)*, pages 709–711, 1990.

[22] A. Chehikian, J. Hérault, and J.E. Mendez. Un processeur de detection de contours en temps réel dans une image de television. *Ann. Télécommunic*, 38(3–4):91–98, 1983.

[23] K. Chen, A. Åström, and P.E. Danielsson. PASIC. A smart sensor for computer vision. In *Proceedings of the 10th ICPR (II)*, pages 286–291, 1990.

[24] M.H. Chen, D. Lee, and Th. Pavlidis. Some results on feature detection using residual analysis. In *Proceedings of the 10th ICPR (I)*, pages 668–670, 1990.

[25] P.D. Chen and P. Sly. Forward/backward contour tracing with feedback. *IEEE Transactions PAMI*, 9(3):438–446, 1987.

[26] R.T. Chin, H.K. Wan, D.L. Stover, and R.D. Iverson. A one-pass thinning algorithm and its parallel implementation. *Computer Vision, Graphics and Image Processing*, 40:30–40, 1987.

[27] R.T. Chin and C.L. Yeh. Quantitative evaluation of some edge-preserving noise-smoothing techniques. *Computer Vision, Graphics and Image Processing*, 23:67–91, 1983.

[28] F Clara. *Realisation d'un filtre adaptif d'images couleur avec critère psychovisuel de qualité.* PhD thesis, Université Pierre et Marie Curie, Paris VI, 1980. Thèse de doctorat.

[29] M.J. Clarke and C.R. Dyer. Curve detection in VLSI. In K.S Fu, editor, *VLSI for Pattern Recognition and Image Processing*, pages 157–174, 1984.

[30] M.A. Cohen and S. Grossberg. Neural dynamics of brightness perception: features, boundaries, diffusion and resonance. In S. Grossberg, editor, *The Adaptive Brain II: Vision, Speech, Language and Motor Control*, pages 211–272. Elsevier North-Holland, Amsterdam, 1988.

[31] I.J. Cox, R.A. Boie, and D.A. Wallach. Line recognition. In *Proceedings of the 10th ICPR (I)*, pages 639–645, 1990.

[32] P.E. Danielsson and Q.Z. Ye. Rotation-invariant operators applied to enhancement of fingerprints. In *Proceedings of the 9th ICPR*, pages 329–333, 1988.

[33] K. Deguchi. Multi-scale curvatures for contour feature extraction. In *Proceedings of the 9th ICPR*, pages 1113–1115, 1988.

[34] R. Deriche. Optimal edge detection using recursive filtering. *International Journal of Computer Vision*, pages 501–505, 1987.

[35] R. Deriche. Separable recursive filtering for efficient multi-scale edge detection. In *Proceedings of the International Workshop on Industrial Applications of Machine Vision and Intelligence, 2–4 February Roppongi, Tokyo, Japan*, pages 18–23, 1987.

[36] R. Deriche. Fast algorithms for low-level vision. In *Proceedings of the 9th ICPR, 14–17 November, Rome, Italy*, pages 434–438, 1988.

[37] R. Deriche, J.P. Cocquerez, and G. Almouzny. An efficient method to build early image description. In *Proceedings of the 9th ICPR*, pages 588–590, 1988.

[38] R. Deriche and O. Faugeras. 2D curve matching using high curvature points: application to stereo vision. In *Proceedings of the 10th ICPR (I)*, pages 240–242, 1990.

[39] R. Deriche, H. Guiot, and G. Randall. A general recursive filtering structure for early vision and its hardware architecture. In *IAPR Workshop on CV, October 12-14, Tokyo, Japan*, pages 266–269, 1988.

[40] Z. Dingding, L. Jian, and W. Faguan. Multiresolution relaxation: experiments and evaluations. In *Proceedings of the 9th ICPR*, pages 712–714, 1988.

[41] G. Dudek and J.K. Tsotsos. Recognizing planar curves using curvature-tuned smoothing. In *Proceedings of the 10th ICPR (I)*, pages 130–135, 1990.

[42] J.S. Duncan and T. Birkhölzer. Edge reinforcement using parameterised relaxation labelling. In *Proceedings of the Conference on Computer Vision and Pattern Recognition, 4–8 June, San Diego, CA, USA*, pages 19–27, 1989.

[43] J. Dupraz. Probabilités, signaux, bruits. *Eyrolles, Paris*, 1983.

[44] U. Eckhardt and G. Maderlechner. A general approach for parameterising the Hough transform. In *Proceedings of the 10th ICPR (I)*, pages 626–630, 1990.

[45] K.B. Eom and J. Park. Recognition of shapes by statistical modelling of centroidal profile. In *Proceedings of the 10th ICPR (I)*, pages 860–864, 1990.

[46] N. Fan, C.C. Li, and F. Fuchs. Myofibril image processing for studying sarcomere dynamics. In *Proceedings of the 9th ICPR*, pages 468–471, 1988.

[47] O.D. Faugeras, R. Deriche, N. Ayache, F. Lustman, and E. Giuliano. Depth and motion analysis: the machine being developed within ESPRIT Project 940. In *IAPR Workshop on CV*, pages 35–45, 1988.

[48] P. Feng, G. Weikang, J. Renjie, and Y. Qindong. One-pass preprocessing algorithm for real-time image processing systems. In *Proceedings of the 9th ICPR*, pages 851–853, 1988.

[49] L.A. Ferrari, P.V. Sankar, S. Shinnaka, and J. Sklansky. Recursive algorithms for implementing digital filters. *IEEE Transactions PAMI*, 9(3):461–466, 1987.

[50] N.D. Francis, G.R. Nudd, T.J. Atherton, D.J. Kerbyson, R.A. Packwood, and J. Vaudin. Performance evaluation of the hierarchical Hough transform on an associative M-SIMD architecture. In *10th ICPR (II)*, pages 509–511, 1990.

[51] C.S. Fuh and P. Maragos. Region-based optical flow estimation. In *Proceedings of the conference CVPR*, pages 130–135, 1989.

[52] M. Gökmen and C.C. Li. Edge detection with iteratively refined regularization. In *Proceedings of the 10th ICPR (I)*, pages 690–693, 1990.

[53] R.C. Gonzalez and P. Wintz. *Digital Image Processing.* Addison-Wesley, 1977.

[54] K. Gould and M. Shah. The trajectory primal sketch: a multi-scale scheme for representing motion characteristics. In *Proceedings of the CVPR*, pages 79–85, 1989.

[55] G.H. Granlund, H. Knutsson, and R. Wilson. Image enhancement. In O. D. Faugeras, editor, *Fundamentals in Computer Vision*, pages 57–68. Cambridge University Press, Cambridge, UK, 1983.

[56] P. Grattoni, F. Pollastri, and A. Premoli. A contour detection algorithm based on the minimum radial inertia criterion. *CVGIP*, 43:22–36, 1988.

[57] S. Grossberg. The quantized geometry of visual space: the coherent computation of depth, form and lightness. In S. Grossberg, editor, *The Adaptive Brain II*, pages 1–79. Elsevier North-Holland, Amsterdam, 1988.

[58] S. Grossberg and E. Mingolla. Neural dynamics of form perception: boundary completion, illusory figures and neon colour spreading. In S. Grossberg, editor, *The Adaptive Brain II*, pages 80–142. Elsevier, Amsterdam, 1988.

[59] S. Grossberg and E. Mingolla. Neural dynamics of perceptual grouping: textures, boundaries and emergent segmentations. In S. Grossberg, editor, *The Adaptive Brain II*, pages 143–210. Elsevier, Amsterdam, 1988.

[60] R.M. Haralick and J.S.J. Lee. Context dependent edge detection. In *Proceedings of the 9th ICPR*, pages 203–207, 1988.

[61] K.H. Hedengren. Decomposition of edge operators. In *Proceedings of the 9th ICPR*, pages 963–965, 1988.

[62] F. Heitz and P. Bouthemy. Multimodal estimation and segmentation using Markov random fields. In *Proceedings of the 10th ICPR (I)*, pages 378–383, 1990.

[63] S.C. Hinds, J.L. Fisher, and D.P. D'Amato. A document skew detection method using run-length encoding and the Hough transform. In *Proceedings of the 10th ICPR (I)*, pages 464–468, 1990.

[64] K.H. Höhne, M. Bomans, A. Pommert, M. Riemer, and U. Tiede. 3D segmentation and display of tomographic imagery. In *Proceedings of the 9th ICPR*, pages 1271–1276, 1988.

[65] J. Hong and H.J. Wolfson. An improved model-based matching method using footprints. In *Proceedings of the 9th ICPR*, pages 72–78, 1988.

[66] S.L. Horowitz and Th. Pavlidis. A graph-theoretic approach to picture processing. *CGIP*, 7(2):282–291, 1978.

[67] A. Huertas and G. Medioni. Detection of intensity changes with sub-pixel accuracy using Laplacian-of-Gaussian masks. *IEEE Transactions PAMI*, 8(5):651–664, 1986.

[68] E. Hundt and M. Lang. Digital image processing in engineering applications. *Siemens Forschung und Entwicklung*, 13(3):90–94, 1984.

[69] T.L. Hwang and J.J. Clark. On local detection of moving edges. In *Proceedings of the 10th ICPR (I)*, pages 180–184, 1990.

[70] T.L. Hwang and J.J. Clark. A spatiotemporal generalization of Canny's edge detector. In *Proceedings of the 10th ICPR (I)*, pages 314–318, 1990.

[71] P.D. Hyde and L.S. Davis. Sub-pixel edge estimation. Technical Report TR-1164, Computer Science Center, University of Maryland, College Park, MD, USA, 1982.

[72] H. Jarosz and J.P. Crettez. Adaptive size for operators in line image processing. In *Proceedings of the 9th ICPR*, pages 814–817, 1988.

[73] T. Jiang and M.B. Merickel. Boundary estimation in complex imagery using Fourier descriptors. In *Proceedings of the 9th ICPR*, pages 187–190, 1988.

[74] K. Kamei, Y. Nakamura, and S. Abe. Fast shape detection using Hough transform by raster operation. In *Proceedings of the 9th ICPR*, pages 1109–1112, 1988.

[75] I. Kasantsev. Radon-space straight edge detection in digital images. *Computers and Artificial Intelligence*, 8(2):189–197, 1989.

[76] T. Kasvand. Extraction of edges in 3D range images to subpixel accuracy. In *Proceedings of the 9th ICPR*, pages 93–98, 1988.

[77] H. Katayose, T. Fukuoka, K. Takami, and S. Inokuchi. Expression extraction in virtuoso music performances. In *Proceedings of the ICPR10 (I)*, pages 780–784, 1990.

[78] J.J. Kim and A. Rosenfeld. Feature detection based on pairwise consistent labelling. Technical Report CAR-TR-272, Computer Vision Laboratory, Center for Automation Research, University of Maryland, College Park, MD, USA, 1987.

[79] Y. Kita and Y. Shirai. Extraction of accurate stomach contour from X-Ray images of barium filled stomachs. In *Proceedings of the 9th ICPR*, pages 917–919, 1988.

[80] R. Kories, N. Rehfeld, and G. Zimmermann. Towards autonomous convoy driving: recognizing the starting vehicle in front. In *Proceedings of the 9th ICPR*, pages 531–535, 1988.

[81] W.G. Kropatsch. Preserving contours in dual pyramids. In *Proceedings of the 9th ICPR*, pages 563–565, 1988.

[82] P. Kultanen, L. Xu, and E. Oja. Randomized Hough transform (RHT). In *Proceedings of the 10th ICPR (I)*, pages 631–635, 1990.

[83] A. Kundu. Robust edge detection. In *Proceedings of the conference CVPR*, pages 11–18, 1989.

[84] M. Kunt. Acquisition and visualization. In O. D. Faugeras, editor, *Fundamentals in Computer Vision*, pages 1–26. Cambridge University Press, UK, 1983.

[85] P.C.K. Kwok. Thinning in a distributed environment. In *Proceedings of the 10th ICPR (I)*, pages 694–699, 1990.

[86] V. Lacroix. The primary raster: a multiresolution image description. In *Proceedings of the 10th ICPR (I)*, pages 903–907, 1990.

[87] Y.G. Leclerc and S.W. Zucker. The local structure of image discontinuities in one dimension. *IEEE Transactions PAMI*, 9(3):341–355, 1987.

[88] C.H. Lee and G.P. Quek. Partial matching of two-dimensional shapes using random coding. In *Proceedings of the 9th ICPR*, pages 64–67, 1988.

[89] D. Lee. Edge detection, classification and measurement. In *Proceedings of the conference CVPR*, pages 2–10, 1989.

[90] M.K. Leung and T.S. Huang. Detecting wheels of vehicles in stereo images. In *Proceedings of the 10th ICPR (I)*, pages 263–267, 1990.

[91] S. Levialdi. Edge extraction techniques. In O. D. Faugeras, editor, *Fundamentals in Computer Vision*, pages 117–144. Cambridge University Press, UK, 1983.

[92] M. Levy. A new theoretical approach to relaxation, application to edge detection. In *Proceedings of the 9th ICPR*, pages 208–212, 1988.

[93] S.P. Liou and R.C. Jain. Road following using vanishing points. *CVGIP*, 39(4):337–356, 1987.

[94] S. C. Liu and J G Harris. Generalized smoothing networks in early vision. In *Proceedings Conference on CVPR*, pages 184–191, 1989.

[95] S. M. Liu, W. C. Lin, and C. C Liang. An interactive edge linking algorithm with noise removal capability. In *Proceedings 9th ICPR*, pages 1120–1122, 1988.

[96] T. Løonnestad. Connected filters for noise removal. In *Proceedings 9th ICPR*, pages 848–850, 1988.

[97] J Lopez-Krahe and P Pousset. The detection of parallel straight lines with the application of the Hough transform. In *Proceedings 9th ICPR*, pages 939–941, 1988.

[98] Y. Lu and R. C Jain. Behaviour of edges in scale space. *IEEE Transactions PAMI*, 11(4):337–356, 1989.

[99] S.D. Ma and X. Chen. Hough transform using slope and curvature as local properties to detect arbitrary shapes. In *Proceedings of the 9th ICPR*, pages 511–513, 1988.

[100] F. Macias-Garza, A.C. Bovik, K.R. Diller, and S.J. Aggarwal. Determining the 3D structure of serial sectioned microscopic objects: analysis and limitations. In *Proceedings of the 9th ICPR*, pages 974–976, 1988.

[101] M. Magnusson, R. Lenz, and P.E. Danielsson. Evaluation of methods for shaded surface display of CT-volumes. In *Proceedings of the 9th ICPR*, pages 1287–1294, 1988.

[102] H. Maître. Contributions to Prediction of Performances of the Hough Transform. *IEEE Transactions PAMI*, 8(5):669–674, 1986.

[103] S. Mallat and S. Zhong. Signal characterization from multi-scale edges. In *Proceedings of the 10th ICPR (I)*, pages 891–896, 1990.

[104] D. Marr. *Vision*. W.H. Freeman & Co., San Francisco, CA, USA, 1982.

[105] A. Martelli. Edge detection using heuristic search methods. *CGIP*, 1(2):169–182, 1972.

[106] A. Martelli. Contour detection in noisy pictures using heuristic search methods. In *Proceedings of the 1st International Joint Conference on Pattern Recognition, 30 October - 1 November, Washington D.C., USA*, pages 375–388, 1973.

[107] A. Martelli. An application of heuristic search methods to edge and contour detection. *Communications of the Association for Computing Machinery*, 19(2):73–83, 1976.

[108] A.M. McIvor. Edge recognition in dynamic vision. *CVPR*, pages 118–123, 1989.

[109] P. Meer, S. Wang, and H. Wechsler. Edge detection by associative mapping. Technical Report CAR-TR-281, Computer Vision Laboratory, Center for Automation Research, University of Maryland, College Park, MD, USA, 1987.

[110] F. Mokhtarian. Fingerprint theorems for curvature and torsion zero-crossings. In *Proceedings of the conference CVPR*, pages 269–275, 1989.

[111] O. Monga, R. Deriche, G. Malandain, and J.P. Cocquerez. 3D edge detection by separable recursive filtering and edge closing. In *Proceedings of the 10th ICPR (I)*, pages 652–654, 1990.

[112] U. Montanari. On the optimal detection of curves in noisy pictures. *CACM*, 14:335–345, 1971.

[113] U. Montanari. Optimization methods in image processing. In *Information Processing 74*, pages 727–732. North-Holland, 1974.

[114] D.G. Morgenthaler. Feature detectors based on higher order polynomials. Technical Report TR-896, Computer Vision Laboratory, University of Maryland, College Park, MD, USA, 1980.

[115] K. Murakami, H. Koshimizu, and K. Hasegawa. An algorithm to extract convex hull on Hough transform space. In *Proceedings of the 9th ICPR*, pages 500–503, 1988.

[116] Y. Nakamura and M. Nagao. Recognition of overlapping 2D objects by local feature construction method. In *Proceedings of the 9th ICPR*, pages 1046–1048, 1988.

[117] V.S. Nalwa. Edge detector resolution improvement by image interpolation. *IEEE Transactions PAMI*, 9(3):446–451, 1987.

[118] K.R. Namuduri, R. Mehrotra, and N. Ranganathan. Fast spatiotemporal filters. In *Proceedings of the 10th ICPR (II)*, pages 479–483, 1990.

[119] H. Nan, M.G. Abbott, and R.J. Beattie. Approaches to low-level image processing for vision guided seam tracking systems. In *Proceedings of the 9th ICPR*, pages 601–603, 1988.

[120] N.M. Nasrabadi and J.L. Chiang. A stereo vision technique using curve-segments and relaxation matching. In *Proceedings of the 9th ICPR*, pages 149–151, 1988.

[121] N.S. Netanyahu and A. Rosenfeld. Mask matching for linear feature edge detection. Technical Report CAR-TR-254, Computer Vision Laboratory, Center for Automation Research, University of Maryland, College Park, MD, USA, 1987.

[122] S.X. Ning, Y.P. Fan, and C. Tong. A new smoothing filter for directional detection and enhancement. In *Proceedings of the 9th ICPR*, pages 628–630, 1988.

[123] G. Odawara, T. Kurokawa, Y. Tamiya, and T. Fujii. An integrated visual inspection system for solder inspection. In *Proceedings of the 9th ICPR*, pages 663–665, 1988.

[124] L. O'Gorman. Curvilinear feature detection from curvature estimation. In *Proceedings of the 9th ICPR*, pages 1116–1119, 1988.

[125] W.G. Oh, M. Asada, and S. Tsuji. Model-based matching using skewed symmetry transformation. In *Proceedings of the 9th ICPR*, pages 1043–1045, 1988.

[126] D. Pao, H.F. Li, and R. Jayakumar. Detecting parametric curves using the straight line Hough transform. In *Proceedings of the 10th ICPR (I)*, pages 620–625, 1990.

[127] Th. Pavlidis. *Structural Pattern Recognition.* Springer, New York, 1977.

[128] Th. Pavlidis. *Algorithms for Graphics and Image Processing.* Computer Science Press, New York, 1982.

[129] S.L. Peng and G. Medioni. Spatiotemporal analysis for velocity estimation of contours in an image sequence with occlusion. In *Proceedings 9th ICPR*, pages 236–241, 1988.

[130] M. Pietikäinen, T. Seppänen, and P. Alapuranen. A hybrid computer architecture for machine vision. In *Proceedings of the 10th ICPR (II)*, pages 426–431, 1990.

[131] I. Pitas and A.N. Venetsanopoulos. Edge detectors based on nonlinear filters. *IEEE Transactions PAMI*, 8(4):538–550, 1986.

[132] W.K. Pratt. *Digital Image Processing.* John Wiley and Sons, New York, 1978.

[133] J. Princen, J. Illingworth, and J. Kittler. A hierarchical approach to line extraction. In *Proceedings of the conference CVPR*, pages 92–97, 1989.

[134] N. Ranganathan and M. Shah. A scale space chip. In *Proceedings 9th ICPR*, pages 420–424, 1988.

[135] A. Rattarangsi and R.T. Chin. Scale-based detection of corners of planar curves. In *Proceedings of the 10th ICPR (I)*, pages 923–930, 1990.

[136] S.E. Reichenbach, S.K. Park, and R. Alter-Gartenberg. Optimal, small kernels for edge detection. In *Proceedings of the 10th ICPR (II)*, pages 57–63, 1990.

[137] A. Rosenfeld. The simplest Hueckel edge detector is a Roberts operator. Technical Report TR-747, Computer Science Center, University of Maryland, College Park, MD, USA, 1979.

[138] A. Rosenfeld and A.C. Kak. *Digital Picture Processing.* Academic Press, New York, 1982.

[139] A. Rosenfeld and A.C. Sher. Direction weighted line fitting to edge data. Technical Report CAR-TR-189, Center for Automation Research, University of Maryland, College Park, MD, USA, 1986.

[140] P. Saint-Marc, J.S. Chen, and G. Medioni. Adaptive smoothing: a general tool for early vision. In *Proceedings of the conference CVPR*, pages 618–624, 1989.

[141] S. Sarkar and K.L. Boyer. Optimal, efficient, recursive edge detection filters. In *Proceedings of the 10th ICPR (I)*, pages 931–936, 1990.

[142] S. Sasaki, T. Gotoh, and M. Yoshida. IDATEN: A reconfigurable video-rate image processor. In J. L. C. Sanz, editor, *Advances in Machine Vision.* Springer, New York, 1989.

[143] M. Sato, T. Wada, and H. Kawarada. A morphological study on structure line. In *Proceedings of the 9th ICPR*, pages 559–562, 1988.

[144] E. Saund. Adding scale to primal sketch. In *Proceedings of the conference CVPR*, pages 70–78, 1989.

[145] I. Schreiber and M. Ben-Bassat. Polygonal object recognition. In *Proceedings of the 10th ICPR (I)*, pages 852–859, 1990.

[146] B.G. Schunck. Edge detection with Gaussian filters at multiple scales of resolution. Technical report, Computer Vision Research Laboratory, Department of Electrical Engineering and Computer Science, University of Michigan, Ann Arbor, MI, USA, 1987.

[147] B.G. Schunck. Generic vision algorithms for industrial inspection. In *Proceedings of the conference VISION'87, 8–11 June 8-11, Detroit, MI, USA*, 1987.

[148] J. Shen and S. Castan. Further results on DRF method for edge detection. In *Proceedings of the 9th ICPR*, pages 223–225, 1988.

[149] D.B. Shu, J.G. Nash, M.M. Eshaghian, and K. Kim. Straight line detection on a gated connection VLSI network. In *Proceedings of the 10th ICPR (II)*, pages 456–461, 1990.

[150] L.H. Staib and J.S. Duncan. Parametrically deformable contour models. In *Proceedings of the conference CVPR*, pages 98–103, 1989.

[151] M.H. Sunwoo and J.K. Aggarwal. A sliding memory plane array processor for low-level vision. In *Proceedings of the 10th ICPR (II)*, pages 312–317, 1990.

[152] R. Szeliski. *Bayesian Modelling of Uncertainty in Low-Level Vision.* Kluwer Academic Publishers, Boston, MA, USA, 1989.

[153] H.L. Tan, S.B. Gelfand, and G.J. Delp. A cost minimization approach to edge detection using simulated annealing. In *Proceedings of the conference CVPR*, pages 86–91, 1989.

[154] C.H. Teh and R.T. Chin. Two-dimensional CAD-based object recognition. In *Proceedings of the 9th ICPR*, pages 382–384, 1988.

[155] D. Terzopoulos. Multilevel reconstruction of visual surfaces: variational principles and finite element representations. In A Rosenfeld, editor, *Multiresolution Image Processing and Analysis*, pages 237–310. Springer, 1984.

[156] E.Z. Tihanyi and J.L. Barron. Spatiotemporal edge focussing. In *Proceedings of the 10th ICPR (I)*, pages 213–216, 1990.

[157] H. Tremblay and D. Poussart. MAR: An integrated system for focal plane edge tracking with parallel analog processing and built-in primitives for image acquisition and analysis. In *Proceedings of the 10th ICPR (II)*, pages 292–298, 1990.

[158] N. Ueda and S. Suzuki. Automatic shape model acquisition using multiscale segment matching. In *Proceedings of the 10th ICPR (I)*, pages 897–902, 1990.

[159] R. Vaillant, R. Deriche, and O.D. Faugeras. 3D vision on the parallel machine CAPITAN. In *International Workshop MVI89, Tokyo, Japan, 10–12 April*, pages 326–331, 1989.

[160] T. Wada and M. Sato. Scale-space tree and its hierarchy. In *Proceedings of the 10th ICPR (II)*, pages 103–108, 1990.

[161] F.M. Wahl. Analysing Hough nets for recognition of polyheder-like objects. In *Proceedings of the 9th ICPR*, pages 550–554, 1988.

[162] A. Waks and O.J. Tretiak. Robust detection of region boundaries in a sequence of images. In *Proceedings of the 10th ICPR (I)*, pages 947–952, 1990.

[163] R. Wang, A.R. Hanson, and E.M. Riseman. Fast extraction of ellipses. In *Proceedings of the 9th ICPR*, pages 508–510, 1988.

[164] X.J. Wang, J. Fu, and L.D. Wu. A matching algorithm based on hierarchical primitive structure. In *Proceedings of the 10th ICPR (I)*, pages 285–287, 1990.

[165] H. Wechsler and K.S. Fu. Image processing algorithms applied to rib boundary detection in chest radiographs. *CGIP*, 7:375–390, 1978.

[166] J.S. Weszka. Survey of threshold selection techniques. *CGIP*, 7:259–265, 1978.

[167] B Widrow and S.D. Stearns. *Adaptive Signal Processing*. Prentice Hall, Englewood Cliffs, NJ, USA, 1985.

[168] D.J. Williams and M. Shah. Normalized edge detector. In *Proceedings of the 10th ICPR (I)*, pages 942–946, 1990.

[169] W.J.C. Witts and G.P. Otto. Optimizing edge detection. In *Proceedings 9th ICPR*, pages 279–281, 1988.

[170] Z.M. Wojczik. Rozprawy detekcij i rozpoznawania konturow obrazu (Method of detecting and recognizing image contours). *Rozprawy elektrotechniczne*, 29:959–983, 1983. in Polish.

[171] C. Wu, X. Lu, D. Xiao, and Y. Jiang. An effective regional descriptor and its application to target recognition. In *Proc 10th ICPR (I)*, pages 671–673, 1990.

[172] L. Wu and Z. Xie. On fingerprint theorems. In *Proceedings of the 9th ICPR*, pages 1216–1220, 1988.

[173] Y. Wu and H. Maître. A new dynamic programming method for stereo vision ignoring epipolar geometry. In *Proceedings of the 9th ICPR*, pages 146–148, 1988.

[174] Y. Wu and H. Maître. Registration of a SPOT image and a SAR image using multiresolution representation of a coastline. In *Proceedings 10th ICPR*, pages 913–917, 1990.

[175] W. Xiang-Qi, L. Ji-Rong, and W. Qi-Qiu. The processing and recognition of X-Rays of spine tumor. In *Proceedings of the 9th ICPR*, pages 914–916, 1988.

[176] Z. Xie and L. Wu. The $\nabla^2 G$ performance in the presence of noise. In *Proceedings of the 9th ICPR*, pages 637–639, 1988.

[177] G. Xu and X. Wan. Description of 3D object in range image. In *Proceedings of the 9th ICPR*, pages 20–22, 1988.

[178] L. Xu. A method for recognizing configurations consisting of line sets and its application to discrimination of seismic face structures. In *Proceedings of the 9th ICPR*, pages 610–612, 1988.

[179] S. Xuanjing, W. Yao, L. Zhongrong, and H. Mingzeng. A dynamic target recognition system. In *Proceedings of the 9th ICPR*, pages 901–904, 1988.

[180] M. Yamada and K. Hasuike. Document image processing based on enhanced border following algorithm. In *Proceedings of the 10th ICPR (II)*, pages 231–236, 1990.

[181] J. Ylä-Jääski and O. Kübler. Segmentation and analysis of 3D volume images. In *Proceedings of the 9th ICPR*, pages 951–953, 1988.

[182] N. Yokoya and M.D. Levine. Volumetric description of revolution in a range image. In *Proceedings of the 10th ICPR (I)*, pages 303–308, 1990.

[183] A.L. Yuille, D.S. Cohen, and P.W. Hallinan. Feature extraction from faces using deformable templates. In *Proceedings of the conference CVPR*, pages 104–109, 1989.

[184] Y.T. Zhou. Fitting smooth curves. In *Proceedings of the 10th ICPR (I)*, pages 455–459, 1990.

[185] C. Zhuang. Scale-based hierarchical description and matching of waveforms. In *Proceedings of the 9th ICPR*, pages 1268–1270, 1988.

Font Rasterization: The State of the Art

Roger D. Hersch

1. Introduction

Outlines are becoming the standard way of storing character fonts. In the late seventies and early eighties, only fonts for photocomposers were stored by their outline description. Screen fonts and printer fonts were generally stored in bitmap form. The advent of resolution independent page description languages (Adobe 1985) and of outline grid fitting algorithms (Hersch 1987) provided the means to print a given document page with the same appearance on middle-resolution laser printers and on high-resolution photocomposers. This concept has recently been extended to display devices thanks to interactive resolution-independent window interfaces like NeWS (Gosling 1989) or DisplayPostScript (Holzgang 1990).

Due to competition on the marketplace, formats for the description of font outlines and hints have been published (Karow 1987), (Adobe 1990), (Apple 1990). The *TrueType* format, designed by Apple Computers, provides a complete langage for the description and processing of hinting commands. In this language, font manufacturers are responsible for specifying outline fonts and associated hints. Therefore, creating hints for outline characters is no longer restricted to a few specialists. Anyone willing to create a *TrueType* description for his outline font will need either an automatic tool (Hersch 1991) or will have to add the hints one by one to the outline description. This tutorial presents current outline character representation techniques, gives an overview of basic and advanced grid constaints and describes the philosophies behind the *Adobe Type 1* hinting system and the *TrueType* character hinting language defined by Apple Computers.

Rendering of typographic outline characters involves three main steps: outline grid fitting, outline scan-conversion and filling. Outline grid fitting is based on the piecewise deformation and grid adaptation of outline parts (Hersch 1989). Grid constraints or hints are rules which specify how a character outline should be modified in order to preserve features like symmetry, thickness and uniform appearance on the rasterized character. Basic grid constraints are responsible for keeping the characters aligned with the reference lines (Betrisey 1989), for keeping the symmetry of stems and for producing discrete arcs of acceptable quality (Hersch 1989).

Advanced grid constraints include *snapping* and *dropout control* for producing regular and continuous characters at low resolutions (figure 1).

Fig. 1 Character appearance with decreasing font size

2. Outline descriptions

Document description languages like PostScript (Adobe 1985) require font descriptions to be invariant under affine transformations. Therefore, most commercial font manipulation and rasterization systems describe character outlines using cubic splines. In the past however, straight line segments and circular arcs were considered to be sufficient (Coueignoux 1981). Several researchers advocate the use of conics (Pratt 1985) or conic splines (Pavlidis 1985).

Cubic splines are described by piecewise polynomial parametric curves. They may generate very smooth contour forms (Rogers 1976). Therefore, they are also used for character boundary descriptions. Cubic spline segments $P_i(t_i)$ have the following parametric equation

$$x_i(t_i) = a_{xi} + b_{xi} \cdot t_i + c_{xi} \cdot t_i^2 + d_{xi} \cdot t_i^3$$
$$y_i(t_i) = a_{yi} + b_{yi} \cdot t_i + c_{yi} \cdot t_i^2 + d_{yi} \cdot t_i^3 \quad (1)$$

Care must be taken when choosing parameter t_i. On an ideal curve, the parameter t should be proportional to the arc length (Farin 1988). To keep computations low, ideal parametrization is only applied on circular arc segments. In the case of cubic spline segments, the parameter range is generally chosen so that it is proportional to the chord length.

A character with outlines described by cubic splines and straight line segments, for example in the Ikarus IK format (Karow 1987), is completely defined. For ease of scan-conversion and filling, the simple cubic spline description (1) is generally converted into an equivalent form based on the Bézier-Bernstein basis.

A spline segment with parameter t varying from 0 to 1, given by its interpolation points V_0, V_3 and by its tangent vectors T_0 and T_3 in V_0 and V_3 can be described in the following way as a Bézier spline segment. Two new control points V_1 and V_2 are computed :

$$V_1 = V_0 + \frac{1}{3} T_0 \quad (2)$$

$$V_2 = V_3 - \frac{1}{3} T_1 \quad (3)$$

Points V_0, V_1, V_2 and V_3 are the control points of the Bézier control polygon (figure 2).

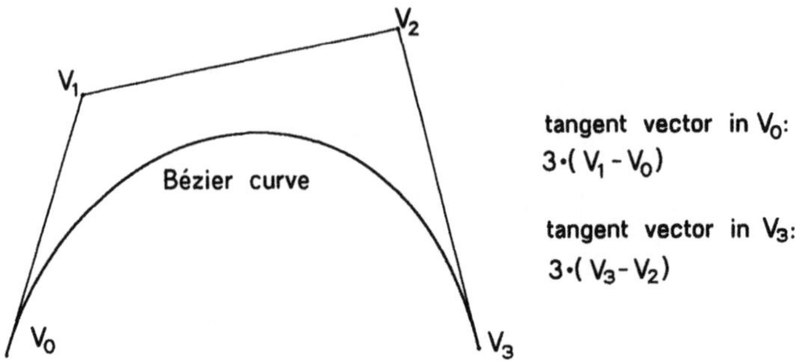

Fig. 2 Interpolation points V_0, V_3, tangents and corresponding Bézier control points V_1, V_2

The corresponding spline segment in Bézier form is given by the following parametric equation for $P(u) = (x(u), y(u))$:

$$P(u) = V_0\cdot(1-u)^3 + V_1\cdot 3\cdot u\ (1-u)^2 + V_2\cdot 3\cdot u^2\ (1-u) + V_3\cdot u^3 \quad (4)$$

with $u \in [0,1]$

One can easily verify, by derivating $\dot{P}(u)$, that the tangents at the departure point $\dot{P}(0)$ and at the arrival point $\dot{P}(1)$ correspond to equations (2) and (3).

In order to convert a spline segment from (1) to (4), it is necessary to convert first the original spline segment with arbitrary parametrization $(0..t_k)$ into an equivalent description with uniform parametrization. For this purpose we introduce the parameter transformation $u = \frac{t}{t_k}$. The intermediate spline equation will be

$$P(u) = P\left(\frac{t}{t_k}\right) \quad (5)$$

The tangent $\dot{P}(u)$ is :

$$\frac{dP}{du} = \frac{dP}{dt}\cdot\frac{dt}{du} = \frac{dP}{dt}\cdot t_k \quad (6)$$

Parameter normalization produces t_k times longer tangent vectors. This is natural, since by reducing the available time (parameter t) by a factor t_k, an object flying along the curve needs a t_k time greater velocity to go from departure point P_0 to arrival point P_1. Once spline segments with uniform parametrization have been obtained, it is easy to describe each of them in Bézier form by applying equations (2) and (3).

Quadratic Bézier splines are given by a Bézier triangular control polygon (figure 3).

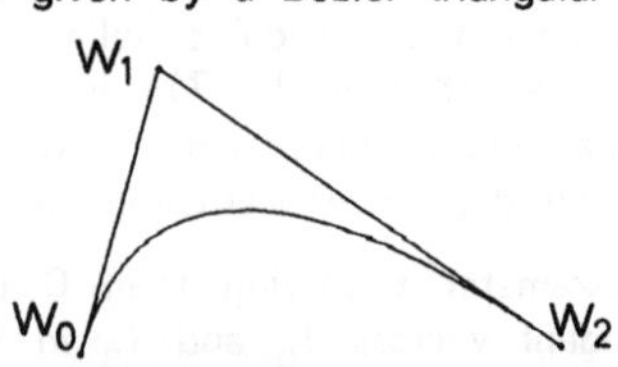

Fig. 3 A quadratic Bézier spline segment given by its control polygon

$$W(u) = W_0\cdot(1-u)^2 + 2\cdot W_1\cdot u\cdot(1-u) + W_2\cdot u^2$$

with $u \in [0,1]$

One can check that its tangents at the spline departure and arrival points are:

$$\dot{W}(0) = 2 \cdot (W_1 - W_0)$$
$$\dot{W}(1) = 2 \cdot (W_2 - W_1)$$

In the *TrueType* format, outlines are described by quadratic B-splines. Curve segment support points are either *off the curve* or *on the curve*. Off the curve points belong to the B-spline control polygon. On the curve points are tangential locations (TT_0, TT_3) where the quadratic B-spline curve touches its B-spline polygon given by its *phantom* vertices (B_0, B_3) at the extremities (Bartels 1987) and by its intermediate *off the spline* vertices B_1 and B_2 (figure 4).

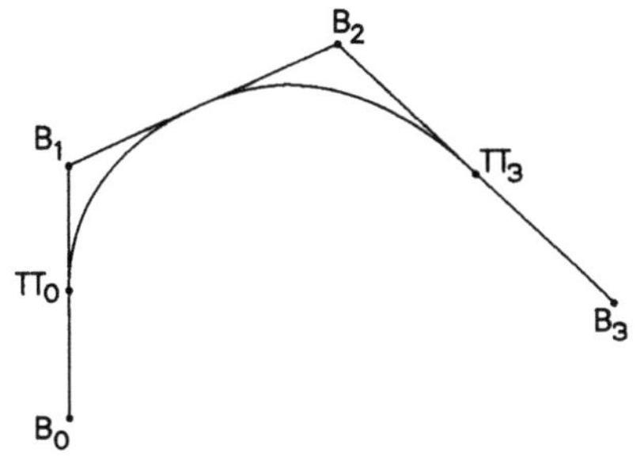

B_0, B_1, B_2, B_3 : Quadratic B-spline control polyogon

TT_0, B_1, B_2, TT_3 : TrueType control points

$$TT_0 = \frac{B_0 + B_1}{2}$$

$$TT_3 = \frac{B_2 + B_3}{2}$$

Fig. 4 TrueType curve given by its control points (TT_0, B_1, B_2, TT_3)

Quadratic B-splines with given parametrization (knot sequence) can easily be converted into series of quadratic Bézier splines having first derivative continuity (Farin 1988). For example, a quadratic B-spline with TrueType control points (TT_0, B_1, B_2, TT_3) having a uniform knot sequence produces the following two quadratic Bézier splines:

First quadratic Bézier spline:	Second quadratic Bézier spline
$S_0 = TT_0$	$T_0 = \frac{1}{2} \cdot (B_1 + B_2)$
$S_1 = B_1$	$T_1 = B_2$
$S_2 = \frac{1}{2} \cdot (B_1 + B_2)$	$T_2 = TT_3$ (7)

The following algorithm converts one cubic Bézier spline segment (V_0, V_1, V_2, V_3) into a quadratic B-spline with four control points. The resulting quadratic B-spline will have at its extremity a tangent (first derivative) which is very close to the tangent of the original cubic Bézier spline segment. Therefore, the proposed algorithm almost keeps first derivative continuity at extremity points.

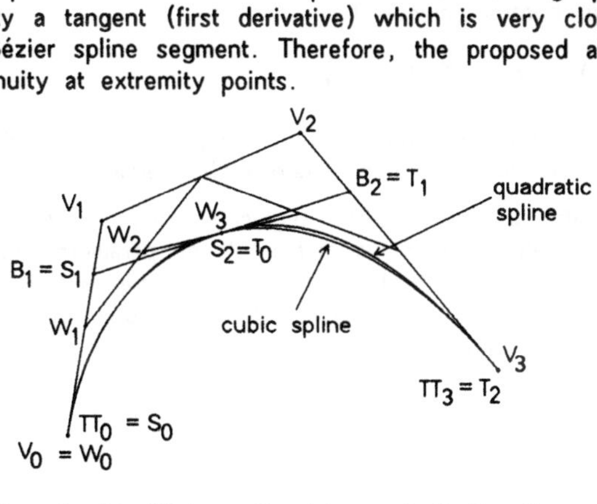

Fig. 5 Conversion of cubic Bézier spline into quadratic B-spline

The resulting quadratic B-spline (TT_0, B_1, B_2, TT_3) can be considered as two consecutive quadratic Bézier splines (S_0,S_1,S_2) and (T_0,T_1,T_2) having first-order continuity between them. Quadratic Bézier spline support points S_2 and T_0 are identical and they lie on the straight line segment $\overline{S_1T_1}$. Due to (7), the control points of the desired quadratic B-spline are:

$$TT_0=S_0$$
$$B_1=S_1$$
$$B_2=T_1 \tag{8}$$
$$TT_3=T_2$$

The unknown quadratic Bézier spline support points S_1 and T_1 are computed so that the tangents at the departure and arrival points of the cubic Bézier spline and of the quadratic Bézier spline become similar. When seeking the quadratic Bézier spline support point S_1, one should consider the first cubic Bézier polygon (W_0,W_1,W_2,W_3) obtained by the DeCasteljou subdivision (see section 4) of the original cubic Bézier polygon (V_0,V_1,V_2,V_3). From this cubic Bézier spline we know that :

$$W_0= V_0$$
$$W_1= \frac{1}{2} \cdot (V_0+V_1) \tag{9}$$

This cubic Bézier polygon obtained by subdivision describes a spline segment having approximatively the same length as the unknown quadratic Bézier spline (S_0,S_1,S_2). Therefore, their parametrization intervals can be considered as identical and their tangents made equal. The tangent at departure point W_0 is

$$\dot{W}(0) = 3 \cdot (W_1-W_0) = \frac{3}{2} \cdot (V_1-V_0)$$

The tangent of the unknown quadratic Bézier spline (S_0,S_1,S_2) at departure point S_0 is

$$\dot{S}(0) = 2 \cdot (S_1-S_0)$$

By making tangents $\dot{S}(0)$ and $\dot{W}(0)$ equal, S_1, the intermediate control point of the first quadratic Bézier control polygon becomes :

$$S_1 = \frac{3}{4} \cdot (V_1-V_0) + V_0 = \frac{3}{4} \cdot V_1 + \frac{1}{4} \cdot V_0 \tag{10}$$

By applying similar considerations, one obtains the intermediate control point of the second quadratic Bézier control polygon T_1:

$$T_1 = \frac{3}{4} \cdot (V_2-V_3) + V_3 = \frac{3}{4} \cdot V_2 + \frac{1}{4} \cdot V_3 \tag{11}$$

Support point B_1 of the resulting quadratic B-spline is identical to S_1 and support point B_2 is identical to T_1 for uniform parametrization intervals.

The deviation of the quadratic spline segments from the original subdivided cubic spline segments can be computed at the middle of the parametrization intervals. In order to lower this deviation, one can further subdivide the original cubic Bézier spline (see section 4) and convert separately each new subdivided cubic Bézier spline segment into one B-spline having four control points.

3. Scan-conversion and filling: the basics

The outline scan-conversion and filling algorithm developed for character generation is an extension of the well-known flag fill algorithm (Ackland 1981). It is based on the assumption that any pixel whose center lies within the continuous border of a shape is to be considered as an interior pixel. This assumption is derived from the fact that shape boundaries are relatively smooth. The shape boundary part which intersects a pixel can generally be approximated by a straight line segment. Therefore, pixels are selected as interior pixels if their surface coverage is more than 50% (figure 6).

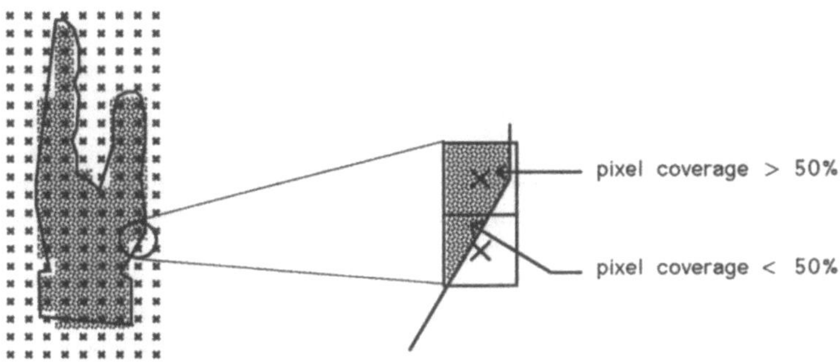

Fig. 6 Interior of filled shape

The bitmap which will be generated by the flag fill algorithm can be considered as a set of black horizontal spans for the inside of the outline and as white horizontal spans for the outside. The first pixel of each span is marked by a flag. Once all the flags corresponding to an outline have been set, the flag fill algorithm scans the flag image memory from left to right. Each flag encountered indicates the start of a new horizontal interior or exterior span.

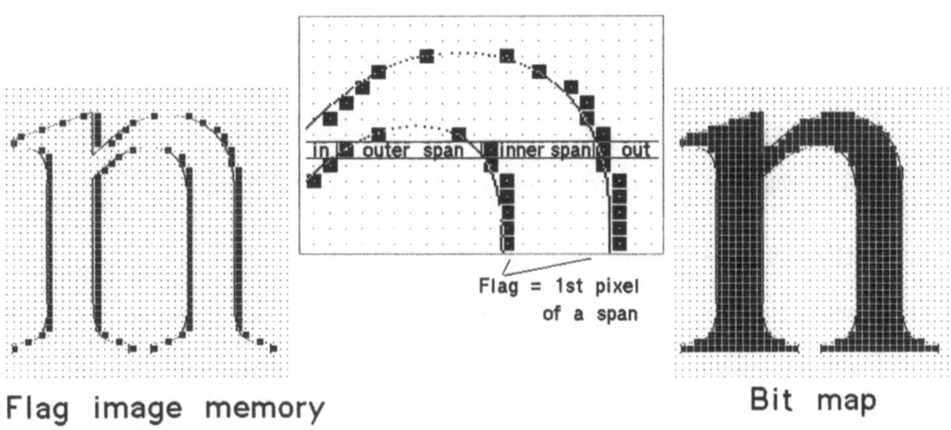

Fig. 7 Example of the flag fill algorithm applied to a character

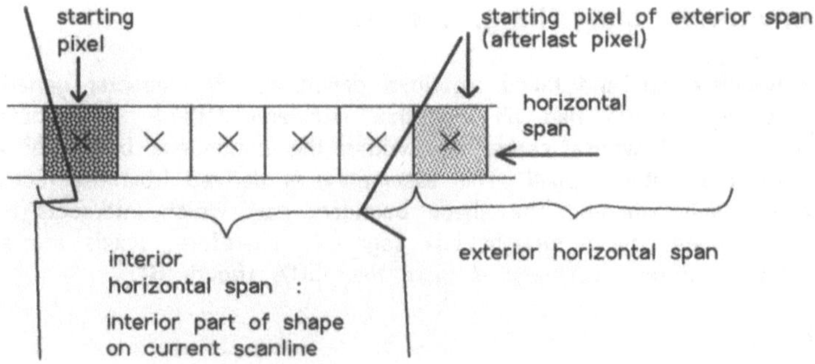

Fig. 8 Interior horizontal span defined by starting and afterlast pixels

Filling horizontal spans lying between starting pixels can be carried out very efficiently with the help of table accesses. Each word of image memory is checked for the existence of one or more starting pixels. Each starting pixel has the effect of reversing the colour of the following horizontal scanline part. Therefore, an image memory word containing a starting pixel will be put back into memory with the run from the starting pixel to the last pixel of the word written in a complementary colour. Each further starting pixel within the current word will have the effect of inverting the colour of the remaining horizontal pixel run (figure 9). The same rules apply to starting pixels lying in the next words of the same image memory scanline.

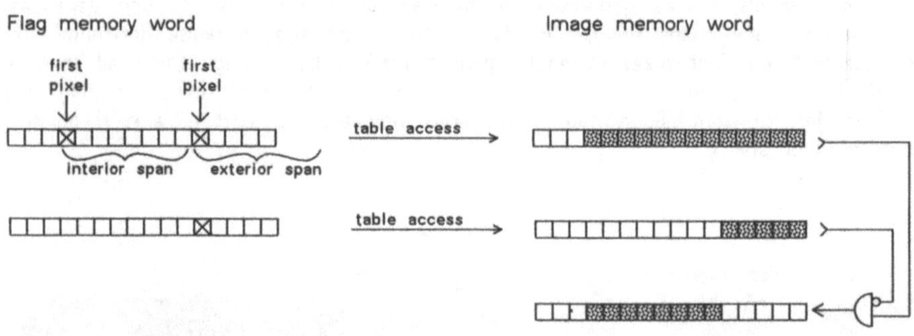

Fig. 9 Illustration of parity flag fill

4. Outline scan-conversion

Rasterization algorithms described in computer graphics books (Newman 1979) are inadequate for the rendering of raster characters. They suggest rounding segment coordinates to integer grid values before scan-conversion. Shapes can be rendered in such a way, but rasterization effects cannot be adequately controlled.

Intermediate approaches suggest overlaying a higher resolution grid over the basic pixel grid (Pratt 1985). High-resolution grid overlay may provide better rasterization control but it requires more scan-conversion steps to generate the same graphic primitive.

The last and in our eyes most successful approach is to scanconvert character contour segments with a digital differential analyzer (Rogers 1985) working with real fixed-point numbers (Hersch 1988).

Vertical Scan-Conversion:

The Bézier splines and line segments which make up an outline have to be converted into flags for the filling algorithm. Two strategies can be adopted to scan-convert a Bézier spline: recursive subdivision and forward differencing (Newman 1979). Both strategies have been developed in order to reduce the number of required operations without reducing the precision of the scan conversion.

Ordinary forward differencing had one main drawback: the incremental step of the parameter used to describe the curve was a constant. Adaptive forward differencing (AFD) corrected this problem (Lien et al. 1987). AFD ensures that most of the points which are generated will be used to trace the curve. Integer AFD further improved the algorithm by using fixed point or pseudo floating point arithmetic instead of floating point arithmetic (Lien et al. 1989) (Gonczarowski 1989). The resulting algorithm is even faster.

Recursive subdivision has also been optimized (Hersch 1990). It presents several advantages over forward differencing. First, computation errors aren´t amplified in the same way as in AFD In order to get the same quality result, recursive subdivision requires a significantly smaller amount of precision bits than AFD (Morgan et al. 1991). Secondly, recursive subdivision can be carried out with the control points of a Bézier curve rather than its polynomial equation. This allows for a better understanding and monitoring of the algorithm. On the other hand, the recursive aspect of subdivision has to be implemented with a stack. Stack access will slow down subdivision. This problem can be partially eliminated by working with an iterative version of the DeCasteljou subdivision algorithm, where the Bézier polygon control points obtained by subdivision (Hersch 1990) are explicitely stored on a dedicated data stack. If this data stack resides in cache memory, recurrent subdivision of Bézier control polygons will be as fast as adaptative forward differencing.

Scan-conversion subdivision of Bézier splines

Recursive subdivision of Bézier splines is based on DeCasteljou´s theorem (Farin 1988). As figure 10 shows, a Bézier spline represented by its control polygon (V_0,V_1,V_2,V_3) can be subdivided into two smaller Bézier splines, (V_0,S_1,S_2,S_3) and (S_3,T_1,T_2,V_3). The smaller splines will have their control polygons closer to the spline. Therefore, if a spline is subdivided enough times, the resulting control polygons can be assimilated to the spline. One of the delicate points of the algorithm is the criterion for stopping subdivision. It is based on the convex hull property of Bézier curves: a Bézier curve always lies within the convex hull formed by its control polygon.

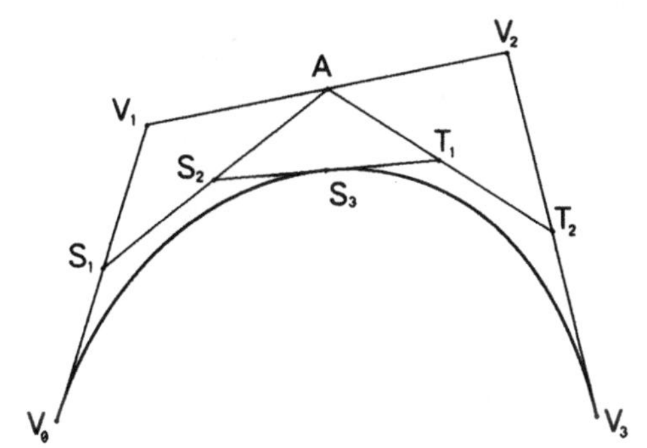

Subdivision of (V_0,V_1,V_2,V_3) into (V_0,S_1,S_2,S_3) and (S_3,T_1,T_2,T_3):

$S_1 = (V_0 + V_1) / 2$
$T_2 = (V_2 + V_3) / 2$
$A = (V_1 + V_2) / 2$
$S_2 = (S_1 + A) / 2$
$T_1 = (T_2 + A) / 2$
$S_3 = (S_2 + T_1) / 2$

Fig. 10 DeCasteljou's subdivision of Bézier splines

Repeated subdivision of Bézier splines can result in three types of Bézier splines:

- splines which don´t intersect any scan line, and which can be discarded since they won´t generate any flag,

- splines which don't intersect any vertical grid lines, and can be assimilated to vertical line segments,
- splines which still intersect a scan line and a vertical grid line.

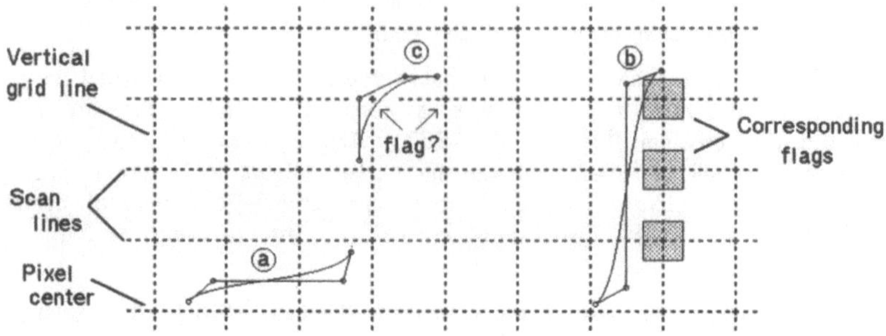

Fig. 11 The three possible final outcomes of a Bézier subdivision

The third case raises the problem of knowing when to stop subdividing a spline and how to choose the position of the corresponding flag. The choice of stopping a subdivision has to take into account the amount of errors which are tolerated and the precision used in the computations. The criterion we chose is to have the spline's bounding box smaller than the parameter *MinFracLength* along both the x and y axis. When this criterion is met, the small spline is assimilated to the three line segments which make up its control polygon. Experience shows that a good trade off for *MinFracLength* is 1/8 of a pixel. Such a precision is generally sufficient for outline character generation, since most hinting algorithms work with a grid precision lower then 1/16 of a pixel.

5. Basic grid constaints

Rasterization algorithms working with real fixed- or floating-point numbers allow us to predict the discrete outlook of the rasterized shape. Fractional displacements of the continuous shape in respect to the grid will produce different discrete shape boundaries (figure 12).

Fig. 12 Rasterized curved shapes having different phase at horizontal or vertical tangential points

On vertical bars, phase determines the discrete width of the bar. In order to be able to respect original relationships between different horizontal and vertical bars, it is necessary to fix their phase relative to the pixel grid. The phase is computed in order to minimize the difference between the width of the continuous bar and the width of the resulting discrete bar (figure 13).

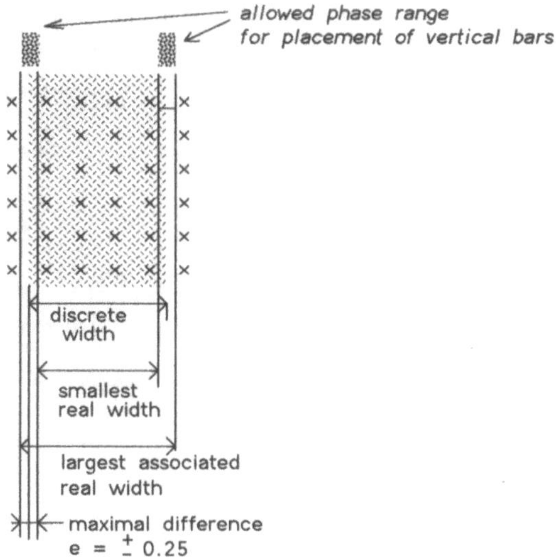

Fig. 13 Phase placement of bars generated with different scan-conversion algorithms

Basic grid constraints are sufficient to produce normal quality characters at 300 dpi. Each grid constraint contains a definition part and an application part. The definition part consists of a pair of points and of parameters specifying a given character part which will have to be fitted in the allowed phase range. Grid-fitting rules for fitting stems and bowls require two outline support points specifying the stem or bowl width.

The evaluation of a given hint produces a subpixel displacement which must be applied to certain parts of the outline. The application part specifies the character parts on which the computed displacement is applied by giving their starting and ending outline support points (figure 14).

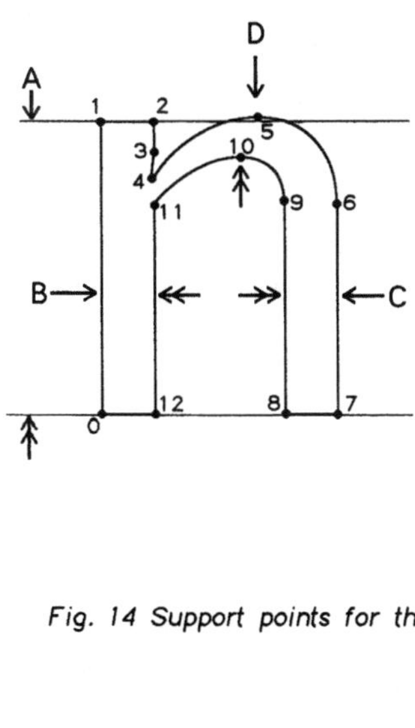

A: **hint specification:** vertical phase control of reference lines
hint application: complete character

B: **hint specification:** horizontal phase control of vertical stem
stem width given by Pt0, Pt12
hint application: complete character

C: **hint specification:** horizontal phase control of vertical stem
stem width given by Pt8, Pt7
hint application:
fixed displacement: Pt6 to Pt9
proportional displacement: Pt4 to Pt6
fixpoint: Pt4
max. displacement point: Pt6
proportional displacement: Pt9 to Pt11
fixpoint: Pt11
max. displacement point: Pt9

D: **hint specification:** vertical phase control of shoulder with respect to reference lines
shoulder thickness given by Pt10, Pt5
hint application:
proportional displacement: Pt4 to Pt6
fixpoint: Pt4, Pt6
max. displacement point: Pt5
proportional displacement: Pt9 to Pt11
fixpoint: Pt9, Pt11
max. displacement point: Pt10

Fig. 14 Support points for the specification of grid constraints

Proportional deformation of curved outline parts can be produced by specifying a fixed point and a point on which the full displacement is applied (figure 15).

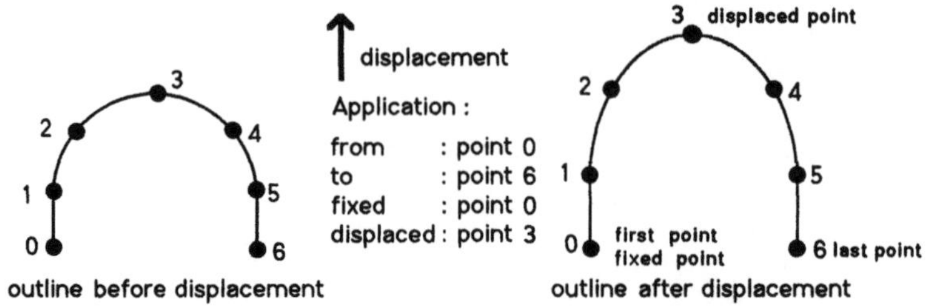

Fig. 15 Proportional application of a computed subpixel displacement

Basic constraints provide facilities to center pairs of horizontal reference lines (base line, x-height line, caps line) on the grid (figure 16).

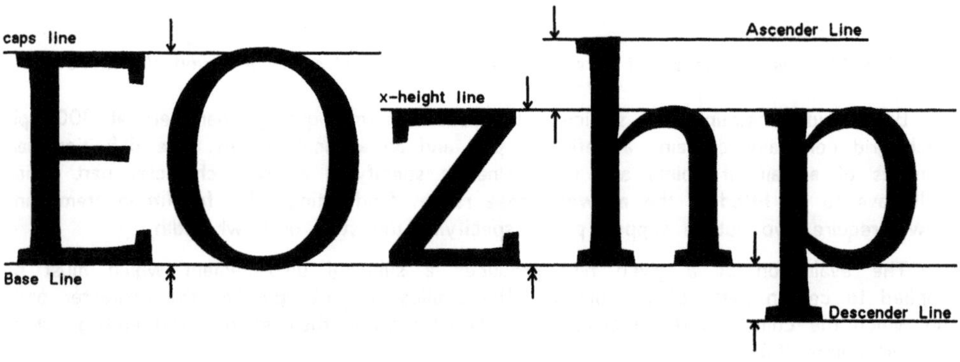

Fig. 16 Phase control of reference lines

These constraints produce a vertical displacement which is used to center the character between the base line and the given reference line. The character is slightly rescaled in order to place the horizontal reference lines halfway between pixel centers.

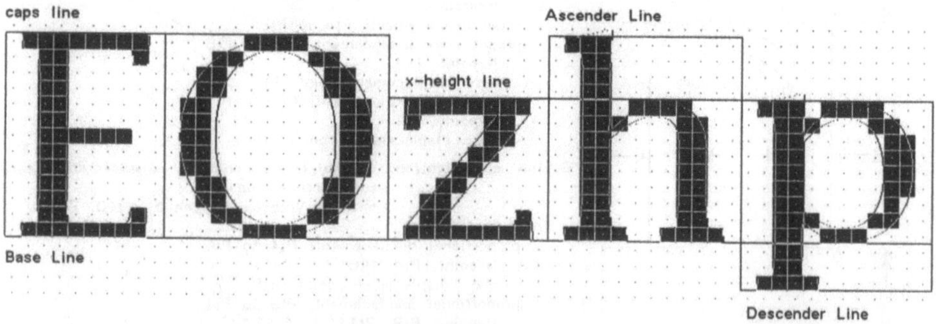

Fig. 17 Result of reference lines phase control application

The initial horizontal positioning of characters on the grid is also highly important. Completely different rasterizations will be obtained if the center of a symmetric character is placed on a pixel center or half-way between two pixels.

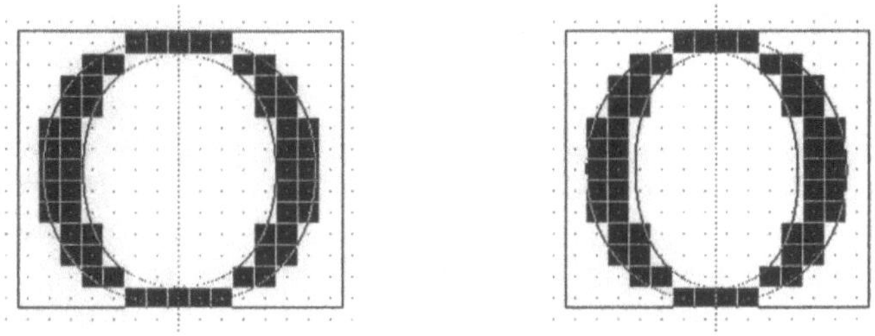

a) character center lying on a pixel center

b) character center lying half-way between pixel centers

Fig. 18 Different phase positioning for the center of symmetry of a character

Horizontally, curvilinear letters are centered between their two extremal points. For characters like "C" having a curve only on one side, the width of character "O" found in the standard width table is used in order to guess the position of the character center.

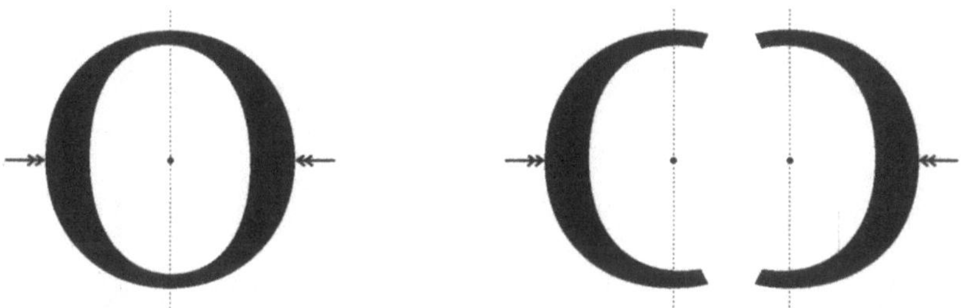

Fig. 19 Horizontal centering constraints

These constraints use the width of character "O" or "o" in order to center in the same way the curvilinear letters "o", "c", "p", "d", "b", "q". They should, at small sizes, provide a uniform appearance.

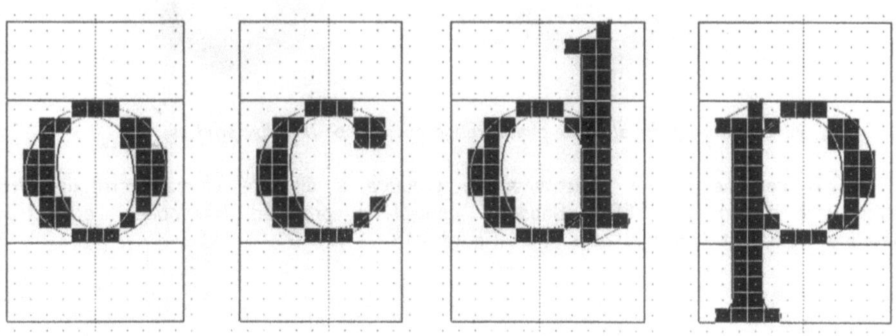

Fig. 20 Uniform appearance of similar characters at small sizes

Horizontal stems are controlled individually or in relation to a given reference line. Bowls and curved character parts are controlled by keeping the phase of the vertical or horizontal extremity of arcs within a given phase range. The phase range influences the flatness of the produced discrete arc (figure 22).

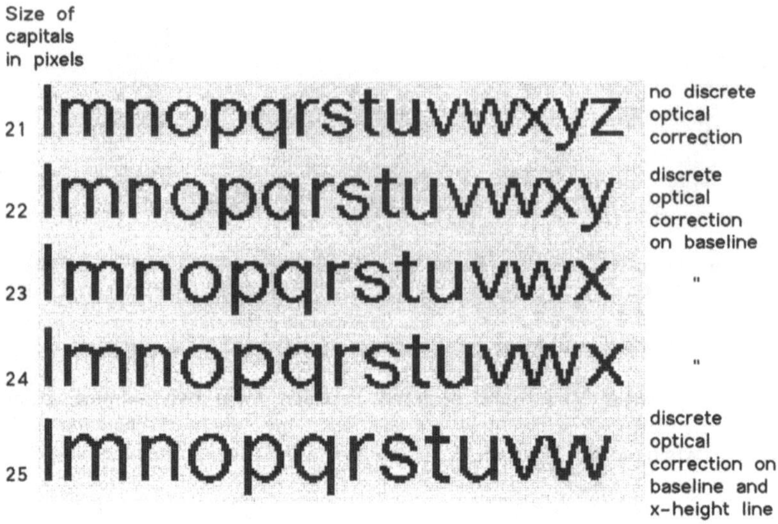

Fig. 21 Rasterized Haas Unica: optimal corrections at different sizes

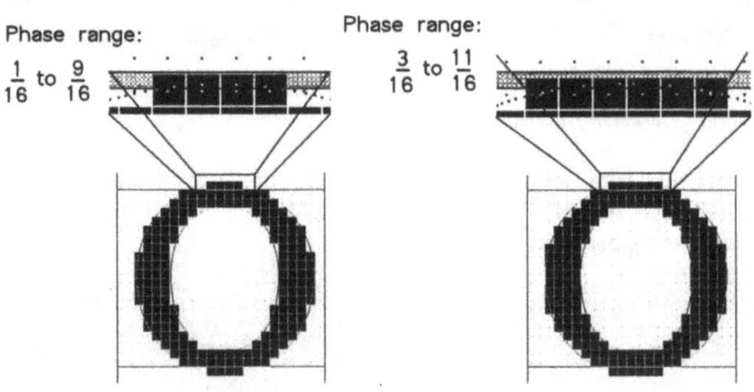

Fig. 22 Specifying an allowed phase range for the bowl's extremities

Bowls can be further constrained to produce a discrete optical correction from a given size (Betrisey 1989). Separate control is provided for optical correction on baseline, x-height line and caps line (figure 21).

6. Advanced grid constraints

The previously shown basic constraints are sufficient for generating raster characters at 300 to 800 dpi as long as highly regular character outlines are provided. Manual or automatic digitizing of master art work does not provide highly regular outlines. The width of stems may be subject to some variations. Curves at stem junctions may also be slightly different. At rasterization time, slight outline variations sometimes produce important variations on digitized raster characters (figure 23).

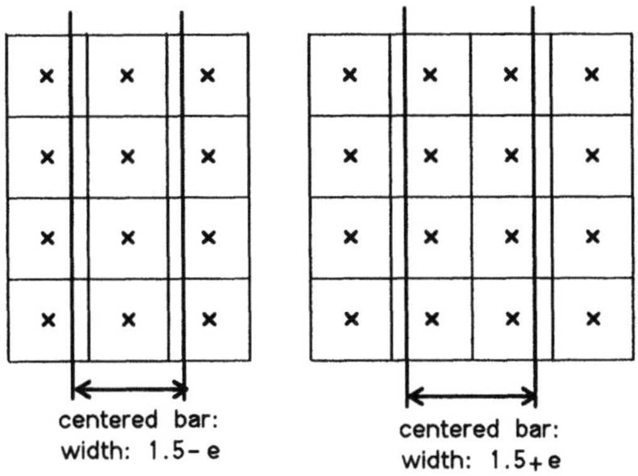

Fig. 23 Small stem width variation produces different rasterizations

Therefore, on systems incorporating only basic hints, a work-intensive interactive character regularization step is required in order to produce highly regular outlines.

The designers of *IKARUS* (Karow 1987) and of the *TRUETYPE* character hinting language (Apple 1990) provided a solution to the problem of slight shape differences: they introduced a set of reference values called ***snapping values*** for important character metrics like stem widths. When grid contraints applied on the original outline are liable to produce an ambiguous rasterization (see figure 23), instead of using the width specified by the constraint parameters, the reference values are consulted and the corresponding snapping value is taken. Centering stems having slightly different stem widths will therefore produce the same rasterization, since at each hint displacement computation, identical stem widths will be fetched from the reference value table (figure 24).

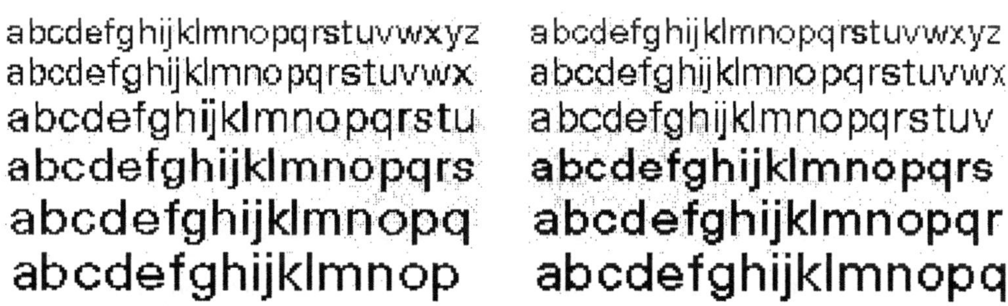

a) Without snapping b) With snapping

Fig. 24 Rasterization of unregularized Haas-Unica

Snapping can be generalized for controlling serif appearance and diagonal line width. At digitizing time, serifs should start to appear on characters larger than a given font size. At smaller sizes, all serifs should disappear. Control of serif appearance can be mastered by snapping half-serif widths (figure 25) to predefined values. At very small sizes, the half-serif width can snap to zero and the serif will disappear.

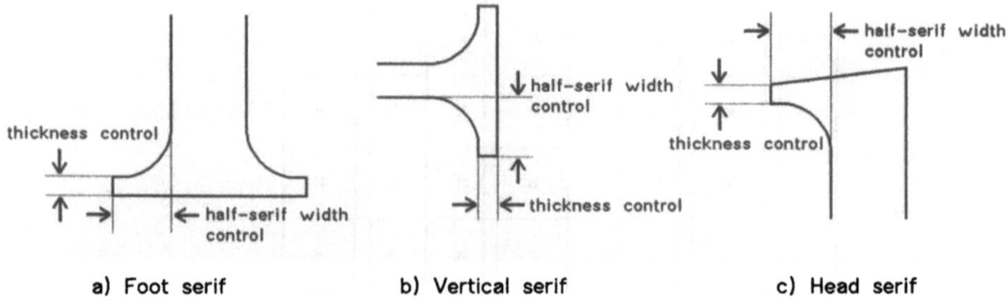

Fig. 25 Control of half-serifs

Phase control of diagonal bars is necessary in order to ensure a constant bar width. At small sizes, snapping will also help to maintain identical thicknesses of diagonal and vertical bars. In order to be effective, phase control of diagonal bars must also ensure that bars are given by a pair of strictly parallel lines.

Parallelizing diagonal bars given by their four extremities implies a slight rotation of one of the bar´s border lines (figure 26). At small character sizes, the bar width in the horizontal direction can be snapped with a predefined value taken from the reference values table. This bar width is used to apply a horizontal translation to one or to both borders in order to obtain an integer horizontal bar width. An integer horizontal bar width ensures that both border lines will have the same phase. This means that the produced discrete bar will be of constant width.

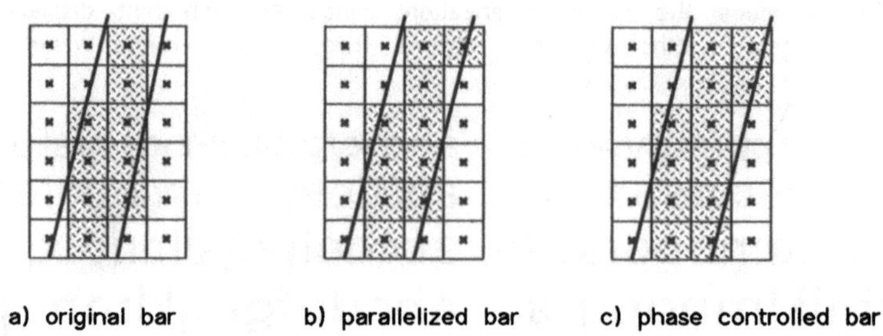

Fig. 26 Control of diagonal bars: parallelisation, snapping, phase control

Control of diagonal bars is only effective if the border lines are straight line segments. In many fonts, border lines are defined by flat curves. Since diagonal control is not effective on flat curves, either no control is applied at all, or flat curves must be replaced by staight line segments in an off-line process.

Italic characters can be hinted in the same way as normal characters. The rasterizer is informed by the font header whether the current font is italic. It will interpret standard hints found in italic characters in a slightly different, appropriate way.

For the vertical phase control of horizontal bars, hint specifications of italic characters remain essentially the same: the current displacement direction will follow the direction of the vertical stems (figure 27). Support points used for horizontal phase control of vertical or italized stems can be defined in such a way that the same hints produce acceptable rasterizations in both cases.

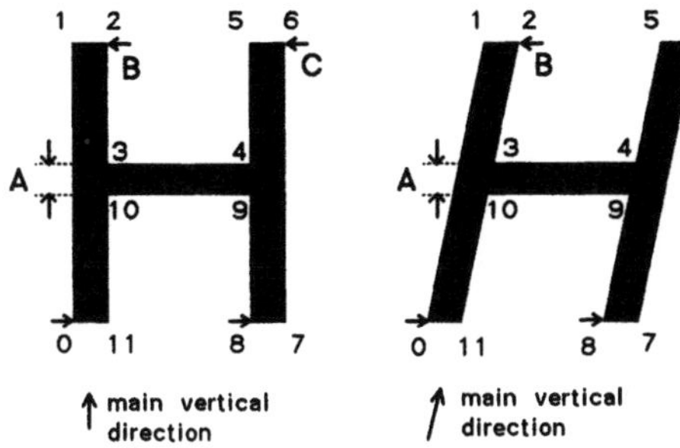

A: hint specification:
vertical phase control of horizontal bar;
bar width given by Pt10, Pt3
hint application:
vertical displacement along main direction of horizontal bar: Pt3, Pt4, Pt10, Pt9

B: hint specification:
horizontal phase control of vertical stem;
stem support points given by Pt0, Pt2
hint application:
displacement of stem borders $\overline{Pt0Pt1}$, $\overline{Pt3Pt2}$, $\overline{Pt10Pt11}$
if vertical stem: horizontal phase control only
if oblique stem: horizontal and diagonal phase control

Fig. 27 Common hints for upright and italic characters

Using the same hints for upright and italic typefaces, gives quite acceptable results (figure 28).

Fig. 28 Rasterization of automatically hinted italic outline characters

7. Dropout control

At screen resolution it is difficult to render outline characters. Thanks to snapping techniques, it is possible to ensure that the appearance of the characters throughout different font sizes remains quite regular. But since some stroke or bowl parts are thinner than one pixel, the produced raster character may have some holes (drops). Since holes disturb the perception of the character, an artifact called *dropout control* is used in order to detect the location of drops and to insert one dot at the place of the drop. Dropout control is executed at rasterization time. The rasterization algorithm mentioned in section three is able to detect dropouts: a dropout may occur if the scan-conversion of two contour lines leads to the selection of the same span starting pixel. Depending on the direction of the scan-converted contour lines and on their respective intersection location with the current scanline, the dropout is either an interior null-span or an exterior null-span segment (figure 29). An interior null-span will produce an active dot at its nearest pixel location.

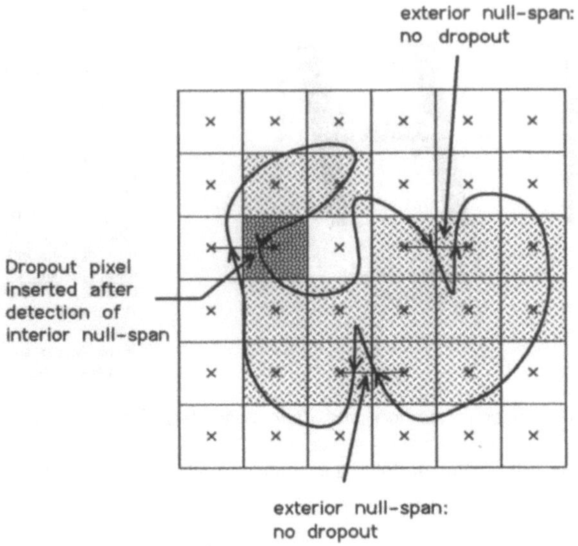

Fig. 29 Dropout control

Dropout control must be applied horizontally and vertically. For fast application of vertical dropout control, one can rotate the original outline by 90 degrees, rasterize it with horizontal dropout control and add the new set of dropout points to the original rasterized shape.

8. The "TrueType" hinting language

TrueType is a character description and hinting language (Apple 1990) which provides a general-purpose framework for the definition of outline fonts and grid-fitting rules. A *TrueType* interpreter has to apply the grid-fitting rules associated to the character description by deforming and adapting its outline to the grid. After grid-fitting, the *TrueType* interpreter carries out scan-conversion and filling as described in the previous sections.

In addition to normal filling, the interpreter is capable of detecting and correcting *dropouts* which occur when some stroke or bowl parts are thinner than one pixel width. Without dropout control, characters rasterized at screen resolution may have holes (figure 30).

Fonts described in the *TrueType* language provide information about metrics, reference and overhang lines as well as snapping values. The original outline description (current glyph) can be completed by adding some positional information about reference points (shadow glyph). At grid-fitting time, the current grid-fitted glyph and the original glyph remain available.

Outline descriptions are given by points defining quadratic B-splines and straight line segments. B-spline segment extremities lie on the outline. Intermediate control points define the spline behavior. Outline points are numbered according to their contour orientation (figure 31).

a) Without dropout control

b) With dropout control

Fig. 30 Characters at low resolution with and without dropout control

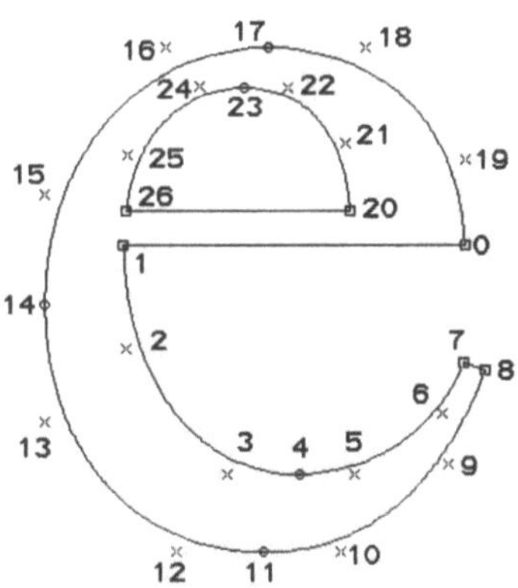

Fig. 31 Example of TrueType outline description

Glyph element pointers are used as pointers to given outline support points. The hint description language is a stack-based binary-encoded language incorporating instructions to initialize glyph element pointers, to compute distances between outline points pointed by glyph element pointers, to apply mathematical operations on values previously pushed onto the stack, and to displace individual or series of outline support points by values found on the stack. Outline support points can be displaced vertically, horizontally or in any given direction given by the current *freedom vector*. Furthermore, the language includes instructions for measuring values along a given projection vector, for adjusting the angle of diagonals, for snapping to values stored in the control value table and for defining character size ranges for certain special instructions.

TrueType is a relatively comprehensive hinting language. It does not provide any solution for the hinting of outline characters. Font makers must either develop their own hinting strategy and apply their hints manually on each font, or resort to an automatic tool for producing hints (Hersch 1991).

9. The "Adobe Type 1" hinting philosophy

The Adobe approach to hinting is quite different from the hinting strategies described in the previous sections. The previously described grid-fitting techniques are based on deforming and adaptating the outline to the grid. Adobe (Adobe 1990) and Bitstream (Appley 1987) apply techniques which are based on optimal distribution of grid rows and columns within the space of an outline character.

In *Type 1* terminology, hints are merely specifications of horizontal and vertical bands over the character space. Such bands (figure 32) are given for example by pairs of reference lines (*BlueValues*) such as *BaseLine* and *BaseLineOverhang*, *XHeightLine* and *XHeightLineOverhang*, *CapsLine* and *CapsLineOverhang*. Further parameters (*BlueScale, BlueShift*) define the limit in point size or arc depth from which optical correction affects the rasterized character.

Individual hints required to produce regular straight and curved stems (bowl parts) are specified by a pair of x-coordinates for horizontal stems (*hstem*) and a pair of y-coordinates for vertical stems (*vstem*). For a given set of hints, the bands defined by pairs of horizontal or vertical coordinates should not overlap.

Fig. 32 Bands defined by reference lines and individual stem hints

The *Type 1* rasterizer is capable of optimizing, for each separate character, the distribution of rows and columns of discrete pixels among the bands specified by font reference lines and individual hints.

If a given character requires overlapping hints, a first set of hints is described and applied to the character. Afterwards, a new set of hints with bands overlapping those described by the first set of hints can be used to produce further improvements of the rasterized discrete shape.

This hinting philosophy is not as flexible as the hinting philosophy offered by the Apple *TrueType* language. Hints contain only information about vertical and horizontal bands within the character glyph space. It is up to the rasterizer to use this information in an intelligent way and to optimize the distribution of pixel rows and columns along the glyph space. Distribution of pixel rows and columns is equivalent to stretching or compressing character outlines within given horizontal or vertical bands.

Due to its extended analyzing and decision capabilities, the *Type 1* rasterizer will perform more operations than a rasterizer which has to grid-fit outlines along predefined rules. But since *Type 1* hints are very simple, it is easy to develop an automatic hinting package capable of recognizing vertical and horizontal stems and bowl parts (Andler 1990).

10. Remaining problems

Basic and advanced grid constraints are nice tools for controlling the rasterization of simple shape parts like straight line and diagonal bars, bowls and serifs. However, they are inadequate for solving more complex shape rasterization problems, like the rasterization of slightly curved character parts (figure 33)

Fig. 33 Characters in Optima font, given by slightly curved shape parts

As already mentioned, many shapes incorporate straight line segments for vertical and horizontal bars, but slightly curved arc segments for diagonal lines. At small sizes and especially for bi-level screen characters, regularized straighted outlines are required. It doesn´t make sense to convert slightly curved shape parts into straight line segments at rasterization time. A preprocessing step is needed for generating regularized and straightened low-resolution outlines. This regularization program can make use of a priori information about location of nearly straight outline parts (Hersch 1991). These locations can be checked and low-curvature curves can be replaced by straight line segments.

At low resolution, much of the original font features are lost by grid-fitting and scan-conversion (figure 34). Essential features disappear and important geometric relationships are destroyed. Completely different fonts appear to be very similar.

Since most workstations have colour displays capable of displaying 256 colours or grey levels out of 24 million, current hardware provides the possibility to use grey levels for rendering outline fonts at low resolution.

Grey-level characters produced by filtering a large size character master (Naiman 1987) have not found wide acceptance in the computer industry: the characters look too fuzzy to be used for interactive work. They may however find applications for proofing purposes. Further research is needed in order to regularize the appearance of grey-scale fonts and to remove some of their fuzzy appearance.

Fig. 34 Nimbus Roman and Haas Unica rendered at low resolution

11. Conclusions

Basic and advanced grid constraints are needed for controlling the rasterization of outline characters at low resolution. Research efforts led by industry have brought solutions for the generation of outline characters on page printers and displays. At low resolution, grid-fitting introduces significant shape distortion. Features of the original font can hardly be recognized. Therefore, current research is directed towards an increased use of grey-scale fonts at screen resolution.

Further research efforts are required in order to produce more legible characters at small size (optical scaling) and to compensate certain printer effects like ink traps.

12. Acknowlegments

Claude Bétrisey made important contributions to the hinting techniques described in this tutorial. The author would also like to acknowledge the contributions made by André Gürtler and John Brillon, from The School of Design, Basel. They contributed to the esthetic evaluation of basic and advanced hints and to their improvements.

13. Bibliography

(Ackland 1981) B.D. Ackland, N.H. Weste, The Edge Flag Algorithm - A Fill Method for Raster Scan Displays, IEEE Trans. on Computers, Vol 30, No 1, January 1981, 41-48

(Adobe 1985) Adobe Systems Inc, Postscript Language Reference Manual, Addison-Wesley, 1985

(Adobe 1990) Adobe Systems Inc, The Type 1 Format Specification, Addison-Wesley, 1990

(Andler 1990) S. Andler, Automatic Generation of Gridfitting Hints for Rasterization of Outline Fonts or Graphics, Proceedings of the International Conference on Electronic Publishing, Document Manipulation & Typography, September 90, (R. Furuta, Ed.) Cambridge University Press, 221-234

(Apple 1990) Apple Computer, TrueType Spec - The TrueType Font Format, July 1990

(Appley 1987) Philip Apley, Automatic Generation of Digital Typographic Images From Outline Masters, ACM SIGGRAPH'88 Tutorial on Digital Typography

(Bartels 1987) R.H. Bartels, An introduction to splines for use in computer graphics and geometric modeling, Morgan Kaufmann Publishers, 1987

(Betrisey 1989) C. Bétrisey, R.D. Hersch, Flexible Application of Outline Grid Constraints, in André, Hersch (eds.),Proceedings International Workshop RIDT'89, Cambridge University Press, 1989, 242-250

(Coueignoux 1981) Philippe Coueignoux, Character Generation by Computer, Computer Graphics and Image Processing, Vol 16, 240-269

(Farin 1988) G. Farin, Curves and Surfaces for Computer Aided Geometric Design, Academic Press, 1988

(Gonczarowski 1989) J.Gonczarowski, Fast Generation of Unfilled and Filled Outline Characters, Raster Imaging and Digital Typography, Cambridge University Press, 97-110. (1989)

(Gosling 1989) J. Gosling, D.S.H. Rosenthal, M.J. Arden, The NeWS Book, Springer-Verlag, 1989

(Hersch 1987) R.D. Hersch, Character Generation under Grid Constraints, Proceedings SIGGRAPH'87, ACM Computer Graphics, Vol 21, No. 4, July 1987, 243-252

(Hersch 1988) R.D. Hersch, Vertical scan-conversion for filling purposes, Proceedings CGI'88, in Thalmann (ed.), New Trends in Computer Graphics, Springer-Verlag, 318-327

(Hersch 1989) R.D. Hersch, Introduction to font rasterization, in André, Hersch (eds.),Proceedings International Workshop RIDT'89, Cambridge University Press, 1989, 1-13

(Hersch 1990) R.D. Hersch, Efficient Rendering of Outline Characters, Proceedings SID Internation Symposium, Las Vegas, May 1990, SID Digest of technical papers, Vol XXI, 392-394

(Hersch 1991) R.D. Hersch, C. Bétrisey, Model-based matching and hinting of fonts, Proceedings SIGGRAPH'91, ACM Computer Graphics, Vol 25

(Hersch 1993) R.D. Hersch (Ed.), Visual and Technical Aspects of Type, Cambridge University Press, 1993

(Holzgang 1990) D.A. Holzgang, Display PostScript Programming, Addison-Wesley, 1990

(Karow 1987) Peter Karow, Digital Formats for Typefaces, URW Verlag, Hamburg, 1987

(Lien et al. 1987) S.L.Lien, M.Schantz, V.Pratt, Adaptive Forward Differencing for Rendering Curves and Surfaces, Proceedings SIGGRAPH'87, ACM Computer Graphics, Vol. 21, No. 4, 111-118

(Lien et al. 1989) S.L.Lien, M.Schantz, R.Rocchetti, Rendering Cubic Curves and Surfaces with Integer Adaptive Forward Differencing, Proceedings SIGGRAPH'89, ACM Computer Graphics, Vol. 23, No. 3, 157-166. (1989)

(Morgan et al.) M. Morgan, R.D. Hersch, An Asic for Outline Character Generation, Proceedings SID Symposium 1991, Anaheim, SID Digest Vol XXII

(Naiman 1987) A. Naiman, A. Fournier, Rectangular convolution for Fast Filtering of Characters, Proceedings SIGGRAPH'87, ACM Computer Graphics, Vol 21, No 4, 233-242

(Newman 1979) W.M. Newman, Principles of Interactive Computer Graphics, McGraw-Hill, 1979

(Pavlidis 1985) Theo Pavlidis, Scan-Conversion of Regions bounded by Parabolic Splines, IEEE Computer Graphics and Applications, Vol 5, No 6, June 1985, 47-53

(Pratt 1985) V. Pratt, Techniques for Conic Splines, Proceedings SIGGRAPH'85, ACM Computer Graphics, Vol 19, No 3, 151-159

(Rogers 1976) David F. Rogers, Mathematical Elements for Computer Graphics, Mc Graw Hill, 1976

(Rogers 1985) D.F. Rogers, Procedural Elements for Computer Graphics, McGraw-Hill, 1985

Media Technology: An Expanding Forum for Advanced Computer Graphics

Patrick Purcell

1 Introduction

The growth of digital techniques underpinning a range of applications in the media, has been the impetus for new programmes of computer graphic and videographic research. The resultant advances in graphic techniques, indicate the way in which the media industries will develop in the nineties. Current work is impacting on developments in HDTV, also is affecting the techniques by which, future movies will be shot, edited & finally viewed. New graphic research is providing fresh vistas for synthetic holography and is creating the technical basis for a new genre of visual information systems.

Apart from these individual technical developments, a further over arching issue stems from the fact that many of these discrete applications share a common digital base. The resultant convergence of advanced media applications promises to generate new forms of entertainment and information technology. This paper looks at both these issues, namely individual advance and media convergence in the following cases.

2 Visual Information System

"A picture is worth a thousand words", a maxim of long standing, is being progressively well served in a new area of information technology. Three erstwhile discrete technologies, optical storage media, computer networks and modern videographic workstations are combined to create a new application, the Visual Information System (VIS). VIS is doing for visual information what has already been accomplished in the world of alphanumerics by online catalogues, bibliographies and full-text search systems. As a referencing facility, VIS is rapidly finding application in those disciplines and professions, where the image has a special significance, for example in architecture and planning, in graphic & fine arts, in biology, in medicine and in photography.

The VIS case study presented here is the "Light Table", [15]. The electronic "Light Table" takes its name from the traditional back-lit, translucent light tables that are used to assemble and view collections of slides for lectures and seminars. An initial aim of the Light Table project, was to see if a VIS system, could make the visual collections of Massachusetts Institute of Technology available to a campus-wide student population. The Light Table project was conceived and designed to respond to a search command, of the type "locate and retrieve images of the work of architect Gropius between 1930 and 1940, but only the interiors of his residential buildings". A Parallax graphics 1280 board as a videographic subsystem is used to automatically digitize the video directly into the frame buffer, which then downloads them into the user's directory as digital files, for subsequent manipulation by the user, or for incorporation into an electronic publishing system.

The context for these developments has been MIT Project Athena, a comprehensive educational development program, [14, 12]. The core of the user interface in the Light Table system is "X Windows", [18], a powerful network-transparent windowing program with special videographic processing facilities which allows software applications to operate across a variety of machine architectures and networks.

As part of the Light Table project, a special package, Galatea, [1] was designed not only to provide remote access to centralized video devices, but also to handle a distributed arrangement of video resources. Shared devices need not all be located on a "master" server, but can be located at several locations. This distributed flexibility was essential in the Project Athena environment, since each videographic workstation usually had its own video resources, in addition to its access to the central server, located remotely. Galatea is an attempt to standardize access to video resources, so that various video client programs can work together on a single workstation, and so that client programs are portable from site to site. Currently there are about one dozen universities and corporations using Galatea as the video device control system for their research. Light Table demonstrated that a widespread cross-campus community of videographic work station users could effectively access a distributed visual information system.

Current development in visual information systems include two broad areas, namely conversion to a digital video infrastructure and the development of image banks, which visual information systems draw on, as a referencing facility. The rationale for conversion to digital imaging is both cogent and various. Lippman A, [11] reviewing the case for digital moving picture and still frame systems, comments "digital representation of moving pictures requires at least the degrees of freedom available in the optical video disc: random access, high quality still frame retrieval, and variable rate bi-directional sequencing. Lacking these, the only advantage of a digital representation would be features gained through coding: compactness and usability in networks and local storage media."

With increased availability of image banks, the VIS user may enjoy the prospect of accessing a catalog of image libraries, [17]. Many famous repositories of images have now produced electronic versions of their collections on optical media. For example, major museums such as the Louvre in Paris, the State Museum of the USSR, and the National Gallery in Washington DC have done so. The US Library of Congress and the National Geographic Magazine have indexed their 200,000 plus image collections on optical media. Progress towards nationally distributed digital image networks are indicated in a series of recent experiments to transfer digital image files between remote sites. For example, digital image files have been transmitted between Colombia University and the US Library of Congress. The Image Query system at the University of California at Berkeley has been extended to enable users in the Smithsonian Institution in Washington DC to query and retrieve collections of images from the Berkeley/Stanford University system over a high speed network. These developments point to a steadily growing facility for national and international image traffic on future visual information systems.

3 The New Television

Compared with the automotive design and certain areas of consumer electronics, the television receiver has not been much affected by electronic advance. However, the current trends in TV research & development promise to change this situation significantly. The initial proposals for HDTV indicated linear projections of technical advance. They were essentially based on the idea of merely increasing screen resolution and changing the aspect ratio of the screen. A concomitant of these developments has been the prospect of a plethora of incompatible TV broadcast standards technically and geographically isolated and restricting the scale of TV reception and inhibiting international program exchange.

Recently however, other more radical proposals have been entering the arena of future HDTV. The are essentially predicated on the idea that international televison should take account of the onset of digital techniques, that have begun to affect so many applications in the fields of media, communications and information technology. This alternative view of the future of television technology was evidenced during the recent submissions to the FCC appraisal and testing programme. For example, Netravali et al [13] reporting on the Zenith/AT&T system describes "a high performance HDTV Codec", whose compression scheme is optimized for an NTSC terrestial broadcast environments. The Zenith/AT&T scheme indicates the union of computers and telecommunications with new broadcasting technology that informs much current television research & development.

This union is responsible for the paradigm shift that views new television not as a tightly coupled programme origination, transmission & reception triad, but as a modular digital system architecture, whose three constituent elements have been decoupled. As the technology of television moves away from its analogue antecedents towards the digital, it finds a close alignment with those technologies whose digital infrastructure it shares. Given the view of future TV as an intensive digital technology, with much of that processing occurring in the TV receiver, Bender, Bove et al [2] predict that the future television will "introduce large scale computing into our homes and daily lives". Indeed, the modern work station with its high-definition videoprocressing capability, may be perceived as the TV receiver of the future.

At the MIT Media Lab, the underlying conceptual structure of the new digital TV system is the Open Architecture Receiver (OAR). Bove & Lippman [8] describe the OAR as "a set of image input converters, each designed to accept some distribution standard and translate it into a common Digital Input Format (DIF) for transport along an internal image bus. This high speed bus may also act as a communications pathway for the components of a work station as well as for television transmission". This specification of advanced TV provides it with a basis for convergence with other active research programmes such as digital movies, holographic video and visual information systems (each referred to in this paper). Versatility is claimed as the cardinal virtue of the OAR structure. The key features of digital TV and digital video generally are listed by Bove & Lippman [8] as being modularity, scalability, extensibility & amenability to data compression. Consequently, the OAR approach supports the representation of a television video signal having different resolutions, frame rates and aspect ratios.

The OAR project in the MIT Media Lab is configured to simulate television encoding, transport and decoding facilities using a variety of program sources, distribution systems and television receivers. The progressive intersection of the new TV transmission media with other media, including computer and telecommunication networks is linking television with new forms of electronic publishing, for example, electronic yellow pages, online cartographic information, visual information systems and "dial up" movies.

In future publishing, Bender et al [3] discuss customised electronic information delivery in the context of future mass media & the linking of this with personalised computing. The authors believe that that the future news system should not only be personalised, but "update continuously and and provide relevant feedback and have multi-media capabilities". One role for the computer is to act as a computational intermediary on behalf of the reader.

Amongst the technical adantages that we may expect from the new television include more efficient transmission, enhanced audio, ghost-free reception, & the incorporation of a variety of communications interfaces. Apart from the alignment of digital television with other new forms of entertainment and information technologies, we may expect progressive reduction in the need for live broadcast (this ultimately being reserved for sports and newscasts). Cumulatively, it seems clear, that the new television will play much more extensive and multivarious roles in the living room of the future, going far beyond entertainment to have a major impact on our work and life styles generally.

4 Digital Cinema

In certain respects the technology of of digital HDTV & digital cinema share many overlapping topics. In other respects they two areas are quite distinct. Lippman & Butera [11] commenting on the distinction, observe that the digital movie is an application "requiring comprehensive coding and a corresponding simpler decoder ..... unlike videotelephony where the delay between encoding and remote image presentation may be minimized, we assume that we may process the entire moving image sequence before any of it may be viewed" . For digital movie encoding the coding process may scan backward and forward in time, optimizing image quality and time. In the technology of digital movie processing, the issues of scale, bandwidth, frame rate resolution are all independent variables.

Bender & Mollitor [4], report on the development of "micro movies" in entertainment and professional contexts. One objective is to facilitate the incorporation of videographics into the work station environment in the form of "little movie windows that may be orchestrated to operate in parallel together with text windows". In a similar context Davenport & Brondmo [9] describe the development of MICONS (Movie ICONS), which take the form of low bandwidth digital motion picture icons. The prime role of these icons to act as navigational cues in complex multimedia systems. In effect, the Micon operates as four second loop of motion of a particular scene, which the user needs to recall and return to a later stage. Bove [7] describes the incorporation of range sensing cameras into movie making as a feature in the development of 3D movies and the consequent ability to manipulate real world scenes with the freedom usually associated with computer generated 3D models.

The impact of digital techniques will have a profound effect on all aspects of film making, scripting, shooting, editing, transmission, projection and most significantly, how we may experience movies both as an entertainment and as an educational medium in the future.

5 Virtual Presence

The art and technology of visualisation has been a longstanding and prime motivation for research in computer graphics. From its origin in monochromatic vector graphics, the impetus to depict both real and imagined objects and processes has been a major goal. Advances in colour, simulation of texture, complex digital modelling, specular reflection, translucency, transparency, sciagraphy and image resolution, has each made its distinct contribution to the realistic depiction of complex objects, scenes and processes. Now computer graphic rendering techniques and computer animation have been conjoined with the physics and chemistry of holography to generate a new range of visually refined and iridescent imagery. The distinctive optical character of these new images reflect both the ultra precise fabrication techniques of holography and the power of modern computer graphic processing engines.

The artifacts, resulting from this conjunction of technologies generally play a role as objects of aesthetic interest in the art gallery or as a powerful medium of visualisation in the laboratory. The extension of this composite technology to applications in medicine and in systems for industrial design, architecture and engineering is providing the impetus for further research and development in this interdisciplinary field.

Benton [6] describes the research program of the pioneering Spatial Imaging Group at MIT, detailing both design and technical advances that have been achieved in spatial imaging. This interdisciplinary research program includes full colour three dimensional portraits, medical visualisation of CAT and MRI scans, automotive design and architectural CAD data bases, large scale holograms, wide-angle holography & very recently the first holographic video. The ability to generate realistic full colour holographic images from CAD/CAM models represents a major advance in design communication, as a form of "design hardcopy", [16]. The development of the computer based hologram represents a distinct departure from the "true" hologram, which must be exposed in laser light to an object of nearly the same size as the desired image, size being no constriction for computer modelled objects.

In a computer generated synthetic hologram, the three dimensional object is represented as a set of discrete perspective views or slices, which are subsequently composited to create the holographic image. A very powerful visualisation feature of the resultant synthetic hologram is the sweep of the of the foreground images over the background images as the viewer's eyes moves from side-to-side, experiencing horizontal motion parallax. An angle of view of one hundred and eighty degrees is needed to produce the effect of a solid object suspended in space. This has been achieved by "wrapping" the hologram within a concave half-cylinder, so a three dimensional image of the object is projected into the alcove or niche. For example, an optical model of an automobile (generated from a CAD/CAM data base), "appears to float right at the viewers finger tips", [5].

While these holographic stereograms were generated as a series (between two hundred and fifty and one thousand) perspective images and synthesised as a form the "frozen" computer animation to achieve the "look around" effect, more recent work in the Spatial Imaging Group, is extending the role of computer animation to produce moving or animated holographic video in real time, [10]. The technical resources for this new holographic video combine a supercomputer, an acoustic-optical modulator and a custom built rotating display system. One may predict in the near future that the impact of digital modelling and computer graphics on the techniques of holography, will be such that computer generated 3D holography-type images will look to classical holography more as an inspiration, than as a source of operating techniques.

6 Conclusion

The previous sections evidenced the role of computer graphics research in such diverse applications as advanced television, digital cinema, spatial imaging, and visual information systems. The increasing involvement of graphics is providing a common linking infrastructure to these former discrete areas of study. While to the superficial eye, the operation of a digital movie is comparable with an analogue video sequence, the difference in underlying technology presages a marked difference in terms of future modes of entertainment offerred, and the provision of electronic information.

The progressive convergence of advanced digital television with videographic movies, electronic mail and visual information systems will generate many new forms of multifunctional display devices. Today's videographic workstation, as an embryonic advanced digital HDTV, is incipient evidence of such hybrid machines. The proliferation of choice (such as the "dial up" movie) and the personalised information service will drive the gradual reduction of mass live broadcast.

The shared digital infrastructure of many machines in the future will lead to an increased plurality in terms of delivery options, such as terrestrial broadcast, ground wire or satellite shared between television, videoconferencing services, electronic publishing or videophone systems. One of the side effects of this "trading places" delivery syndrome should be a markedly enhanced media portability and "location- independent" entertainment and information delivery. Taking a longer term look into the future one may also speculate that advances in computer graphic technology will provide us with the prospect of interactive holographic movies, with customised newscasts, or with 3D display of sportscasts, which will allow one to choose one's place in the grandstand. By that time may we expect future Eurographic Conferences to have special sessions entitled "Graphics and the new HDTV", "Graphics and Digital Cinema" and "Graphics and Holography". I hope so!

Finally, I would very much wish to pay tribute to the work of my erstwhile colleagues at the MIT Media Lab, whose work has been frequently referenced here, as examples of the leading edge of computer graphics research in all those new applications which will affect our modes of entertainment, our professional roles and our future life styles generally. They include Walter Bender, Stephen Benton, Michael Victor Bove Jr., Muriel Cooper, Glorianna Davenport, Andrew Lippman, Nicholas Negroponte and many others.

7 References

[1] D.I. Applebaum. The Galatea Network Video Device Control System. Technical report, MIT Media Laboratory Paper, Cambridge MA 02139, 1990.

[2] W. Bender, Jr V.M. Bove, A. Lippman, Lin Liu, and J. Watlington. HDTV in the 1990s: Open Architecture and Computational Video. In *HDTV World Review Summer '90*, CT USA, 1990.

[3] W. Bender, H. Lie, J. Orwant, L. Teodosio, and N. Abramson. Newspace: Mass Media and Personal Computing. In *Proc USENIX*, Nashville TN USA, 1990.

[4] W. Bender and R. Mollitor. Digital Movies for 'off-the-shelf' Displays. In *SPIE*, volume 1258, Bellingham WA USA, 1990.

[5] S.A. Benton. Alcove Holograms for Computer-Aided Design. In *SPIE*, volume 761, pages 53–61, Bellingham WA, 1987.

[6] S.A. Benton. Steps in Synthetic Spaces: The Dimensions of Holographic Process. In B. Conners and D. Friis-Hansen, editors, *Synthetic Spaces: Holography*. MIT. Massachusetts Institute of Technology, Cambridge MA, 1990.

[7] V.M. Bove. Pictorial Applications for Range Sensing Cameras. In *SPIE*, volume 901, Bellingham WA, 1989.

[8] V.M. Bove and A. Lippman. Open Architecture Television Receivers and Extensible/Intercompatible Digital Video Representation. In *IEEE ISCAS'90*, New Orleans LA, 1990.

[9] G. Davenport and H.P. Brondmo. Creating and Viewing the Elastic Charles - a Hypermedia Journal. In *York Multi Media Conference*, York England, 1989.

[10] P. St Hilaire, S.A. Benton, M.L. Jepson, J. Kollin, M. Lucente, J. Underkoffler, and H. Yoshikawa. Electronic Display System for Computational Holography. In *SPIE*, volume 1212, Bellingham WA, 1990.

[11] A. Lipmann and W. Butera. Coding Image Sequences for Interactive Retrieval. *Communications ACM*, 32(7), 1989.

[12] E.M. Murman. The Athena Project: Goals, Philosophy Status & Experiences. Technical report, MIT Athena Report, Cambridge MA 02139 USA, 1989.

[13] A. Netravali, E. Peterjan, S. Knaur, K. Matthews, B. Safranek, and P. Westerink. A High Performance Digital HDTV CODEC. In *NAB HDTV World Conference*, 1991.

[14] P.A. Purcell. Athena: A Context for the Incorporation of Computation into the Design Studio. In *ACSA Conference*, Charleston SC USA, 1984.

[15] P.A. Purcell and D.I. Applebaum. Light Table: Interface to Visual Information Systems. In W. McCullogh et al, editor, *Electronic Design Studio*. MIT Press, Cambridge MA USA, 1990.

[16] P.A. Purcell and W. Plesniak. Computer Imagery in Spatial Imaging. *BCS Computer Bulletin*, 4(2), 1988.

[17] P.A. Purcell and M.W. Smith. Imaging Technology for Arts Information. In *IFLA Conference*, Moscow USSR, 1991.

[18] R.W. Scheifler and J. Gettys. The X Window System. *ACM Transactions on Graphics*, 5(2):79–109, 1987.

List of Authors

Jarek R. Rossignac
Interactive Geometric Modeling
IBM, T.J. Watson Research Center
Yorktown Heights, NY 10598, USA

H. Ruder, T. Ertl, K. Gruber, M. Günther
F. Hospach, M. Ruder, J. Subke, K. Widmayer
Theoretische Astrophysik
Universität Tübingen, Auf der Morgenstelle 10
D-72076 Tübingen

Marie-Paule Gascuel, Claude Puech
LIENS, Ecole Normale Supérieure
CNRS URA 1327, 45, Rue d'Ulm
F-75230 Paris Cedex 05, France

Huw Jones
School of Mathematics, Statistics and Computing
Faculty of Engineering, Science and Mathematics
Middlesex Polytechnic
London N11 2NQ, England

Arie Kaufman
Department of Computer Science
State University of New York at Stony Brook
Stony Brook, NY 11794-4400, USA

Eric Hibbard, Michael Bauer, Margaret Bradshaw,
Glenn Deardorff, Ken Hu, David Whitney
NASA Ames Research Center, M/S 233-14
Moffett Field, CA 94035-1000, USA

Michel Beaudouin-Lafon
Laboratoire de Recherche en Informatique
URA 410 du CNRS, Bât. 490
Université de Paris-Sud
F-91405 Orsay Cedex

Eduard Antoniu
Research Institute for Theoretical Informatics
Subsidiary of the Romanian Academy
22 A Copou Avenue
RO-6600 Iasi, Romania

Roger D. Hersch
Laboratoire de Systèmes Périphériques, EPFL
CH-1015 Lausanne

Patrick Purcell
The Media Laboratory
Massachusetts Institute of Technology
Cambridge, MA 02139, USA

Focus on Computer Graphics

(Formerly EurographicSeminars)

Eurographics Tutorials '83. Edited by P. J. W. ten Hagen.
XI, 425 pages, 164 figs., 1984. Out of print

User Interface Management Systems. Edited by G. E. Pfaff.
XII, 224 pages, 65 figs., 1985. Out of print (see below, Duce et al. 1991)

Methodology of Window Management. Edited by F. R. A. Hopgood, D. A. Duce, E. V. C. Fielding, K. Robinson, A. S. Williams. XV, 250 pages, 41 figs., 1985. Out of print

Data Structures for Raster Graphics. Edited by L. R. A. Kessener, F. J. Peters, M. L. P. van Lierop. VII, 201 pages, 80 figs., 1986

Advances in Computer Graphics I. Edited by G. Enderle, M. Grave, F. Lillehagen. XII, 512 pages, 168 figs., 1986

Advances in Computer Graphics II. Edited by F. R. A. Hopgood, R. J. Hubbold, D. A. Duce. X, 186 pages, 96 figs., 1986

Advances in Computer Graphics Hardware I. Edited by W. Straßer.
X, 147 pages, 76 figs., 1987

GKS Theory and Practice. Edited by P. R. Bono, I. Herman.
X, 316 pages, 92 figs., 1987. Out of print

Intelligent CAD Systems I. Theoretical and Methodological Aspects.
Edited by P. J. W. ten Hagen, T. Tomiyama. XIV, 360 pages, 119 figs., 1987

Advances in Computer Graphics III. Edited by M. M. de Ruiter.
IX, 323 pages, 247 figs., 1988

Advances in Computer Graphics Hardware II. Edited by A. A. M. Kuijk, W. Straßer. VIII, 258 pages, 99 figs., 1988

CGM in the Real World. Edited by A. M. Mumford, M. W. Skall.
VIII, 288 pages, 23 figs., 1988. Out of print

Intelligent CAD Systems II. Implementational Issues. Edited by V. Akman, P. J. W. ten Hagen, P. J. Veerkamp. X, 324 pages, 114 figs., 1989

Advances in Computer Graphics IV. Edited by W. T. Hewitt, M. Grave, M. Roch. XVI, 248 pages, 138 figs., 1991

Advances in Computer Graphics V. Edited by W. Purgathofer, J. Schönhut.
VIII, 223 pages, 101 figs., 1989

User Interface Management and Design. Edited by D. A. Duce, M. R. Gomes, F. R. A. Hopgood, J. R. Lee. VIII, 324 pages, 117 figs., 1991

Advances in Computer Graphics Hardware III. Edited by A. A. M. Kuijk. VIII, 214 pages, 88 figs., 1991

Advances in Object-Oriented Graphics I. Edited by E. H. Blake, P. Wisskirchen. X, 218 pages, 74 figs., 1991

Advances in Computer Graphics Hardware IV. Edited by R. L. Grimsdale, W. Straßer. VIII, 276 pages, 124 figs., 1991

Advances in Computer Graphics VI. Images: Synthesis, Analysis, and Interaction. Edited by G. Garcia, I. Herman. IX, 449 pages, 186 figs., 1991

Intelligent CAD Systems III. Practical Experience and Evaluation. Edited by P. J. W. ten Hagen, P. J. Veerkamp. X, 270 pages, 116 figs., 1991

Graphics and Communications. Edited by D. B. Arnold, R. A. Day, D. A. Duce, C. Fuhrhop, J. R. Gallop, R. Maybury, D. C. Sutcliffe. VIII, 274 pages, 84 figs., 1991

Photorealism in Computer Graphics. Edited by K. Bouatouch, C. Bouville. XVI, 230 pages, 118 figs., 1992

Advances in Computer Graphics Hardware V. Rendering, Ray Tracing and Visualization Systems. Edited by R. L. Grimsdale, A. Kaufman. VIII, 174 pages, 97 figs., 1992

Multimedia. Systems, Interaction and Applications. Edited by L. Kjelldahl. VIII, 355 pages, 129 figs., 1992. Out of print

Advances in Scientific Visualization. Edited by F. H. Post, A. J. S. Hin. X, 212 pages, 141 figs., 47 in color, 1992

Computer Graphics and Mathematics. Edited by B. Falcidieno, I. Herman, C. Pienovi. VII, 318 pages, 159 figs., 8 in color, 1992

Rendering, Visualization and Rasterization Hardware. Edited by A. Kaufman. VIII, 196 pages, 100 figs., 1993

Visualization in Scientific Computing. Edited by M. Grave, Y. Le Lous, W. T. Hewitt. XI, 218 pages, 120 figs., 1994

Photorealistic Rendering in Computer Graphics. Edited by P. Brunet, F. W. Jansen. X, 286 pages, 175 figs., 1994

From Object Modelling to Advanced Visual Communication. Edited by S. Coquillart, W. Straßer, P. Stucki. VII, 305 pages, 128 figs., 38 in color, 1994

MIX
Papier aus verantwortungsvollen Quellen
Paper from responsible sources
FSC® C105338

If you have any concerns about our products,
you can contact us on
ProductSafety@springernature.com

In case Publisher is established outside the EU,
the EU authorized representative is:
Springer Nature Customer Service Center GmbH
Europaplatz 3, 69115 Heidelberg, Germany

Printed by Libri Plureos GmbH
in Hamburg, Germany